A STUDY OF HISTORY

Arnold Toynbee writes:

ENCOUNTERS between contemporary civilizations are not the only way in which one civilization meets with another. A living civilization has an encounter with an extinct one when it brings this back to life in a renaissance; and this is the first subject dealt with in Volume 9. In this volume, I also try to explore the extent of human freedom. Evidently Man is free to some extent, but not completely. The comparative study of the breakdowns and disintegrations of the civilizations that have risen and fallen in the past has brought to light what look like regularities or uniformities in the course of human affairs. How much of human life is subject to natural law and how much of it falls within the field in which Man is free to choose life and good instead of death and evil? This question, which is in everyone's mind today, is dealt with in a discussion of the prospects of one particular living civilization, namely the Western. Within the last few centuries, all the other living civilizations have been dominated by the Western Civilization to some extent; so today the Western Civilization holds in its hands the destiny of the whole human race.

Volume 10 takes up the question: What is it that excites our interest in mankind's future and past? The study of history is exciting because it is one approach to the mystery of the universe. This belief that history finds its ultimate explanation in religion has usually been taken for granted in the past. Today it is highly controversial; and so is the belief that a comparative study of civilizations brings to light patterns in the history of human affairs.

A STUDY OF HISTORY

10

The Inspirations of Historians

ARNOLD J. TOYNBEE

But at my back I always hear
Time's wingèd chariot hurrying near.

ANDREW MARVELL

ποιεῖν τι δεῖ ἇς γόνυ χλωρόν.

THEOCRITUS: *Κυνίσκας Ἔρως*, 1. 70

γηράσκω δ' αἰεὶ πολλὰ διδασκόμενος.

SOLON

My times are in Thy hand.

Ps. xxxi. 15, in the A.V.

But Thou art the same, and Thy
years shall have no end.

Ps. cii. 27, in the A.V.

A Galaxy Book

New York OXFORD UNIVERSITY PRESS 1963

A Study of History was first issued under the auspices of the Royal Institute of International Affairs, of which Arnold J. Toynbee was then Director of Studies.

First published, 1954
First published as a Galaxy Book, 1963

The illustration on the cover of this volume is a rendering by Charles Gottlieb of Moses (detail) by Michelangelo, A.D. 1513-1516 [Rome, San Pietro in Vincoli].

PRINTED IN THE UNITED STATES OF AMERICA

CONTENTS

XIII. THE INSPIRATIONS OF HISTORIANS

ANNEX

A NOTE ON CHRONOLOGY

ACKNOWLEDGEMENTS AND THANKS

INDEX TO VOLUMES VII–X, by V. M. TOYNBEE 242

XIII
THE INSPIRATIONS OF HISTORIANS

A. THE HISTORIAN'S ANGLE OF VISION

WHY do people study History? Why, to put the question *ad hominem*, had the writer of the present work been studying History since he was a child and been spending thirty years on this book which he was now finishing? Is an historian born or made? Every historian will have his own answer to this question, because he will be speaking from his own experience. *Quot homines, tot sententiae*:[1] each must speak for himself. The present writer's personal answer was that an historian, like anyone else who has had the happiness of having an aim in life, has found his vocation in a call from God to 'feel after Him and find Him'.[2]

If this personal answer finds any favour with the reader, it may help us also to answer a second question that is implicit in the one from which we have started. In beginning by asking ourselves why we study History we have begged the question: What do we mean by History? And the writer, continuing to speak simply for himself from his personal experience, would reply that he meant by History a vision—dim and partial, yet (he believed) true to reality as far as it went[3]—of God revealing Himself in action to souls that were sincerely seeking Him. Since 'no man hath seen God at any time'[4] and our clearest visions are but 'broken lights' of Him,[5] there are as many angles of vision as there are vocations, and the historian's angle is only one among a number of diverse angles from which souls with diverse gifts and diverse experiences obtain diverse partial visions of God seen through diverse fractions of His 'inconceivably mighty works'.[6] Besides the historian's angle there is the astronomer's, the physicist's, the mathematician's, the poet's, the mystic's, the prophet's, the priest's, the administrator's, the lawyer's,

[1] Terence: *Phormio*, Act II, scene iv, line 14 (= line 454 of the play).

[2] Acts xvii. 27.

[3] Man's vision of God has been aptly compared by Edwyn Bevan to a dog's vision of his human master. In the dog's association with his master there are some fields of action in which the master's activity comes within the range of the dog's understanding, while there are other fields in which the dog does not and cannot comprehend what his master is about. What the dog does come to feel and know, even with his limited intelligence, if he is a good dog and his master a good master, is that he is in the service of a being who is immeasurably superior to the dog himself; and from this intuition the dog—mere dog though he is—draws an intellectual and a moral conclusion. His intellectual conclusion is that his master's unintelligible acts and orders are likely to be as wise as those which the dog can understand have always proved to be. The dog's moral conclusion is that it is his own duty to take this superior being's acts and orders on trust—always obeying the orders with alacrity and acquiescing in the acts with resignation.

The present writer cannot find in Edwyn Bevan's published works any passage setting out this simile. He may perhaps have had it direct from this Christian historian's own mouth in conversation.

[4] John i. 18; I John iv. 12.

[5] Tennyson: *In Memoriam*, Invocation, stanza 5, line 3.

[6] 'Die unbegreiflich hohen Werke'—Goethe: *Faust*, l. 249, quoted in II. i. 276.

the soldier's, the sailor's, the fisherman's, the hunter's, the shepherd's, the husbandman's, the artisan's, the engineer's, the physician's—and this roll-call could be extended over many pages, since human vocations are as numerous and as various as the glimpse of God that each of them gives is narrow and feeble. Among these innumerable angles the historian's angle is only one; but, like the others, it makes a distinctive contribution of its own to Mankind's piecemeal vision of reality. History's contribution is to give us a vision of God's creative activity on the move in a frame which, in our human experience of it, displays six dimensions. The historical angle of vision shows us the physical cosmos moving centrifugally in a four-dimensional frame of Space-Time; it shows us Life on our own planet moving evolutionarily in a five-dimensional frame of Life-Time-Space; and it shows us human souls, raised to a sixth dimension by the gift of the Spirit, moving, through a fateful exercise of their spiritual freedom, either towards their Creator or away from Him.

B. THE ATTRACTIVENESS OF THE FACTS OF HISTORY

(I) RECEPTIVITY

IF we have been right in seeing in History a vision of God's creation on the move, from God its source towards God its goal,[1] we shall not be surprised to find, in the minds of creatures endowed with consciousness, an awareness of History being awakened by the mere experience of being alive; but, since we have observed that Time's 'ever rolling stream'[2] flows at a varying pace,[3] and that the surface of its waters is sometimes calmer and sometimes rougher, we shall also not be surprised to find that, in human minds whose innate receptivity to the impress of History is presumably always much the same on the average, the actual strength of the impression varies in accordance with the patient's historical circumstances.

For example, we have noticed in an earlier context[4] that the vividness of historical impressions is apt to be proportionate to their violence and their painfulness. In the Western World in the generation that was in its childhood at the time of the transition from a Modern to a post-Modern Age of Western history towards the end of the third quarter of the nineteenth century of the Christian Era, a child who had lived through the American Civil War in the territory of the Southern Confederacy would be likely to grow up more historical-minded than one who had lived through the same experience at the North, while for the same reason a French child who had lived through the Franco-Prussian War and the subsequent establishment and suppression of the Parisian Commune in A.D. 1870–1 would be likely to be more aware of History than any of this French child's Belgian, Swiss, or English contemporaries. Yet even the Englishman or New Englander of that generation, who had been lucky enough not to have been given the unsolicited and unpleasant grounding in History that had been inflicted by Fate upon his Parisian and South Carolinian class-mates, could not help becoming automatically aware of History in some degree, simply in virtue of having been born into a social milieu in which the process of Civilization happened at the time to be in full swing. Even in the pleasantly placid reach of the mighty river in which his lot had fallen to him, a thousand familiar experiences would be constantly making him aware of his goodly heritage.[5] History would be impressed on his receptive mind by the war memorials and other monuments in public places;[6] by the names of streets, piazzas, farmsteads, and fields; by the architecture of the old buildings that the child had found already in existence when he had first become conscious of the outer world and by the architecture of the new buildings

[1] 'Ilayhi marji'ukum jamī'an' ('To Him return ye every one')—*Qur'ān*, x. 4.
[2] Watts, Isaac: 'Our God, our help in ages past', quoted in I. i. 459.
[3] See XI. ix. 348–77. [4] In XII. xi. 421–3. [5] Psalm xvi. 6.
[6] The present writer's debt to the Albert Memorial in Kensington Gardens, London, for having given him a visual education in History (though not in Beauty) is mentioned among his acknowledgements on p. 214, below.

that he had since seen rising alongside of the older buildings, or in their place;[1] by the changes in fashions of dress;[2] by political events such as general elections to representative parliamentary bodies, the inaugurations of presidents and the coronations of kings and queens; by regularly recurrent festivals and ceremonies such as, in London, the Trooping of the Colour and the Lord Mayor's Show; and by the liturgy performed in church.

The conservatism of the bodies ecclesiastical that had come to encase the surviving higher religions had made these churches into incomparably potent radiators of impressions of historic events and historic characters; for the problem—which all the missionary religions had had to face—of converting illiterate populations *en masse* had been solved by them through the device of telling their story, conveying its moral, and inculcating its doctrine, in visual form.[3] Even in a mosque, in which the possibilities of an educational use of Visual Art were restricted by the Prophet Muhammad's faithfulness to the second of the Mosaic Com-

[1] The changes which the present writer had seen, since his childhood, in the architecture of Park Lane, London, had given him an education in current social history. In the eighteen-nineties, new palaces, built for South African millionaires, were thrusting their way in between the older palaces of the English nobility. Between the First and the Second World War, palaces of both kinds were being pulled down to make way for blocks of flats and for mammoth hotels.

[2] The present writer used to be told by his Mother that, as a child, he had once announced to her that he had discovered the difference between 'ladies' and 'women'. 'Ladies', he had explained, 'wear bonnets; women wear shawls'—and it was true that, in England in the eighteen-nineties, feminine headgear still displayed the sharp differentiation into two categories that had been characteristic of it since the dawn of Civilization. While a small minority was privileged to follow the vagaries of a fashion that was deliberately kept on the move in order to make profits for the producers and to advertise that their customers were rich enough not to have to wait to make a new purchase till their last purchase had worn out, a majority still draped their heads in the timeless scarf (*Turcicè* charshaf) that had been consecrated for Christian eyes through figuring in the conventional garb in which the Virgin Mary was portrayed in the traditional representations of her. Since then, the writer had lived long enough to see this differentiation between two categories of feminine headgear not only disappear in England but also first appear and then begin to disappear in Turkey.

At the time of his first visit to Turkey in A.D. 1921, all Turkish women of all classes were still wearing the timeless charshaf; at the time of his third visit in A.D. 1929, the situation in Turkey was what it had been in England in the eighteen-nineties: while Turkish 'women' were then still wearing scarves over their heads, Turkish 'ladies' were by this time already wearing hats. By the time, however, of the writer's fourth visit to Turkey in A.D. 1948, feminine costume was already reverting towards egalitarianism—though now not *alla Turca* but *alla Franca*—by conforming to a new rule of 'fashions for all', in place of the old rule of 'charshafs for all' which had still been in force only twenty-seven years back. On the morning of the 3rd November, 1948, the writer and his wife, on the summit of the *qal'eh* (the citadel) at Ankara, found themselves walking along the principal street just behind three women, parading in a row, who were inadvertently displaying a *tableau vivant* of the last quarter of a century of the history of female dress in their country. The two youngest of the three were dressed according to the standard oecumenical Western fashion of the year. If an old-fashioned jinn had picked either of them up, transported her on a carpet to London or New York, and deposited her on the pavement or the side-walk, she would have been indistinguishable from the other young women of her age walking along the Edgware Road or Broadway. The third member of this Ankaran trio, who might have been the girls' mother, was wearing a quaint mixture between the current fashion and the timeless feminine costume which reminded the writer of the eclectic dress that he had seen men—not women—wearing in A.D. 1929 in Japan. On the steps of one of the houses that we passed in procession on the main street of the citadel at Ankara on the 3rd November 1948, there was sitting a grandmother wearing the traditional Turkish female dress complete—including conspicuous shalwar (trousers). As the two girls paraded past her, we saw her eye them with an air in which self-assurance and disapproval were struggling comically with admiration and misgiving.

[3] See V. vi. 508–34.

mandments, the *qiblah*, towards which the lines of the architecture skilfully drew the worshipper's eye, pointed, through the eloquent symbolism of an impressively empty niche, not only inwards in the Space-dimension towards the Ka'bah at Mecca, but also backwards in the Time-dimension towards the Prophet of Allah who had been the human Founder of the Faith. In a Christian church—unless it were the tabernacle of a Protestant sect of Western Christians in which the Second Commandment was obeyed with an Islamic punctiliousness—the apostles, prophets, and martyrs cited collectively in the *Te Deum* could be seen portrayed individually with their traditional distinctive attributes—the cross, sword, wheel, or other means of death through which the martyr had attained his crown, or the evangelist's book and pen—and these pictures, bas-reliefs, or statues told the spectator, at a glance, what they stood for, while the meaning of the Mass sung in 'a dead language' was declared to the devout worshipper's eye by the church's counterpart of the mosque's *qiblah*, since, all the time, the tabernacle on the altar was speaking to the worshipper visually of Christ, His passion, His divinity and His incarnation.

It will be seen that, in the days when the surviving civilizations were all still living under the aegis of the surviving higher religions clad in their traditional forms, 'going to church' (or mosque or synagogue or Hindu or Buddhist temple) was an automatic education in History that was apt to carry the passive recipient of it far afield in Time as well as in Space; and this education was as effective as it was informal, since it reached broad strata of the population that had no chance of going to school, while it taught lessons that came nearer to the heart of its pupils' lives than any formal book-learning. Christ and His apostles, the saints and the martyrs, the patriarchs and the prophets, and the biblical vista of History from the Creation through the Fall and the Redemption to the Last Things, were in truth realities of far greater importance for Christian souls than the parochial secular histories and the national notables, military, civil, literary, and scientific, that were subsequently to be thrust down the throats of a *plebs Occidentalis nuper Christiana* by the well-meaning but myopic-eyed organizers of national systems of compulsory universal education in post-Modern Western states. To put the case, once again, *ad hominem*, the longer the writer of this Study lived, the more glad he was that he had been born early enough in the Western Civilization's day to have been taken to church as a child every Sunday as a matter of course and to have received his formal education at a school and a university in which the study of the Greek and Latin classics, by which the Medieval Western study of Scripture and Theology had been replaced as a result of a fifteenth-century Italian renaissance,[1] had not yet been ousted in its turn by a study of Western vernacular languages and literatures, Medieval and Modern Western history, and a latter-day Western physical science.[2]

This automatic stimulus from the social milieu in which a human being grows up, and in which he continues to live and work as an adult, is the earliest and most widely radiative of the inspirations of potential

[1] See X. ix. 68, n. 2. [2] See X. ix. 63–70.

historians; but this primal inspiration, while indispensable, is at the same time insufficient, and this in two ways.

In the first place, even in the civilizations of the third generation, which had all enjoyed the advantage of having had churches for their chrysalises,[1] the informal education in History through an ecclesiastical medium had never penetrated Society to its depths, since, throughout the Age of the Civilizations up to date, the vast majority of the population of every society in process of civilization had consisted of a Primitive Peasantry that, in A.D. 1952, still accounted for about three-quarters of the living generation of Mankind, and, for the Peasantry since the dawn of Civilization, History, as they had experienced it so far, had been a tale that had signified nothing, in spite of being 'full of sound and fury'.[2] This Peasantry, which had been rounded up into the fold of the civilizations and which had been fleeced there to provide a surplus for a privileged minority, had remained much like its less unfortunate brethren still at large in surviving primitive societies that the civilizations had not yet managed to devour; and, in the Peasantry's consciousness, the Government that was always impinging on their life so disagreeably was not the historical pageant, moving along an irreversible course through Time, that it looked like to a cultivated minority which had been trained to learn by heart the names and dates of the kings of England, Judah, Israel, Assyria, Babylon, and Ur, or alternatively those of the pharaohs of Egypt and the emperors of China and Japan; Government for the Peasantry was just an everlasting inevitable affliction of the same timeless presentness as the wars in which Government abused its power and as the pestilences and the famines that Government was powerless to avert.

One passage of History in which the Peasantry might have felt some interest, had they been aware of it, was the prehistoric mutation through which Sub-Man had once become Man in a Yang-movement in the evolution of Life that was a more prominent historical landmark than the subsequent rise of the civilizations;[3] but this historic event, which latter-day Western archaeologists, anthropologists, and psychologists had recently begun to bring to light, had faded, ages ago, out of the folk-memory of their contemporaries who in A.D. 1952 were still lying torpid in Primitive Man's Yin-state; and, for practical purposes, the primitive human substratum of the living civilizations was still thoroughly unhistorical-minded. The movement in the fabric of Creation that set the tune to which the Primitive Peasantry danced was the cyclic rhythm of Physical Nature: the cycle of the seasons, which governed their food-supply; the cycle of Day and Night, which dictated to them their time-table of alternating labour and rest; and the cycle of Birth and Death, which determined the life-span of every human being in his generation. The festivals that had a meaning and a value for the Peasantry were not the Fourth of July, Dingaan's Day, Guy Fawkes' Day, Armistice Day, and such like; they were the unhistorical red-and-black-letter days of the annually recurrent agricultural year. In fact, for at least three-

[1] See VII. vii. 392–409.

[2] Shakspeare: *Macbeth*, Act v, scene v, line 26.

[3] See II. i. 192–5.

quarters of the men and women alive on Earth in A.D. 1952, History was virtually non-existent—not because this majority were less receptive to the educative influence of their social milieu than were the minority that were at this time in process of Civilization, but because the majority were then still living in a social milieu that spoke to them, not of History, but of Nature.

Even, however, for the minority whose social milieu did speak to them of History, this exposure to the radiation of an historical social environment was not enough in itself to inspire a child to become an historian. A passive receptivity without which he would never get under way would also never avail to waft him into port unless it inspired him to travel under his own steam by awakening his mind to an active curiosity. A light glider will answer more readily than a heavy aeroplane to the fits and starts and twists and turns of a fitful veering breeze, but, for this very reason, its pilot will remain at the mercy of a capricious atmosphere unless his craft is converted from a glider into an aeroplane by being fitted with an engine; for, until he commands a driving-power of his own, he will never be able to choose a course and hold to it.

(II) CURIOSITY

The potential historian's mind is like an aeroplane driven by jet-propulsion. After it has received its first impulse to study History by being made aware of History through the impress of an historic social environment, the mind obtains its next impulse through a mutation of receptivity into curiosity. This transition from a passive to an active mood inspires the apprentice in History to take the initiative, go into action, and set off on aerial voyages of discovery into unknown skies.

Without this creative stirring of curiosity, the most familiar, impressive, and numerous monuments of History will perform their eloquent dumb-show to no effect, because the eyes to which they will be addressing themselves will be eyes that see not.[1] This truth that a creative spark cannot be struck without a response as well as a challenge was borne in upon the Modern Western philosopher-pilgrim Volney when he visited the Islamic World in the years A.D. 1783–5.[2] Volney had been born and brought up on one of the fringes of the *Oikoumenê*, in Transalpine Western Europe, in a region which had been drawn into the current of the histories of the civilizations only as recently as the time of the Hannibalic War (*gerebatur* 218–201 B.C.),[3] whereas the region that Volney was visiting had been a theatre of History for some three or four thousand years longer than Gaul, and was proportionately well stocked with those relics of the Past of which the France of Volney's day could show comparatively few. Yet, in the last quarter of the eighteenth century of the Christian Era, the living generation in the Middle East were squatting among the amazing ruins of extinct civilizations, piled stratum upon

[1] Isaiah xlii. 20; Jeremiah v. 21; Ezekiel xii. 2; Matt. xiii. 14; Mark iv. 12; Luke viii. 10; John xii. 40; Acts xxviii. 26; Romans xi. 8.

[2] See Volney, C. F.: *Voyage en Syrie et en Égypte pendant les Années 1783, 1784, et 1785*, 2nd ed. (Paris 1787, Desenne et Volland).

[3] See I. i. 40.

stratum, without being moved to inquire what these monuments were; when, how, or why they had been first erected and then overthrown or allowed to decay; or what light these historic tragedies might throw upon the meaning of Human Life.[1] The curiosity to ask these questions had been stirred, not on the spot, in the cradle of Civilization, where the stimulus was at its maximum, but in a corner of the Old World where the stimulus was relatively weak. Yet, in Western Europe in the Modern Age of Western history, the faint impress of History which this weak stimulus had made on receptive minds had aroused in them a curiosity that was keen enough to draw Volney from his native France to Egypt in A.D. 1783[2] and, in his wake, the goodly company of French *savants* who seized the opportunity offered to them in A.D. 1798 by Buonaparte of

[1] See Volney, C. F.: *Les Ruines, ou Méditation sur les Révolutions des Empires*, chaps. 1 and 2, in *Œuvres Complètes de Volney* (Paris 1876, Firmin-Didot), pp. 9–12.

The indifference to the monuments of a pre-Islamic past which the Muslim population of Egypt and Syria showed in the ninth decade of the eighteenth century of the Christian Era, at the time of Volney's visit to those countries, was not peculiar to that generation of Muslims and was not confined to the field of archaeology. It was one facet of a catholic indifference 'to anything that is not directly of moment for his life in This World or the next' which is enjoined upon every pious Muslim by the precepts of orthodox Islamic theology (see MacDonald, D. B.: *The Religious Attitude and Life in Islam* (Chicago 1909, University Press), p. 120). 'And this is not simply theological; it is in the very texture of the Muslim mind. We can say: "This is an interesting book"; in Arabic you cannot express that idea. . . . Even curiosity, in the highest and finest sense, we cannot render. . . . The free, self-determining, self-developing soul may not walk its own path, however innocently, but must fit itself to the scheme and pattern of schools' (ibid., pp. 120–1).

MacDonald goes on to quote 'Odysseus' [Sir C. Eliot]: *Turkey in Europe* (London 1900, Edward Arnold), p. 98, as a witness that there is the same lacuna in the Turkish vocabulary as there is in the Arabic. 'The Turkish language, copious as it is, contains no equivalent for "interesting". . . . The ordinary Turk does not take an interest in anything. . . . A natural want of curiosity, and a conviction that their own religion contains all that Man knows or needs to know, keep the provincial population in a state of ignorance which seems incredible and fantastic.' As far as Turkey, at least, was concerned, an intellectual indictment which had perhaps still been warranted by the facts as they had been in A.D. 1900 had become an anachronism by A.D. 1948 as a result of the Westernizing revolution through which Turkey had put herself in the meanwhile (see p. 10, n. 2, below).

[2] Volney has informed his readers—in prose in the preface to his *Voyage en Syrie et en Égypte* and in poetry in *Les Ruines*—of the considerations which led him to choose Asia—and, in particular, Syria and Egypt—in preference to America or Europe as the theatre for a bout of foreign travel on which he had decided to spend a legacy.

'C'est en ces contrées, me dis-je, que sont nées la plupart des opinions qui nous gouvernent; c'est de là que sont sorties ces idées religieuses qui ont influé si puissamment sur notre morale publique et particulière, sur nos lois, sur tout notre état social. Il est donc intéressant de connaître les lieux où ces idées prirent naissance, les usages et les moeurs dont elles se composèrent, l'esprit et le caractère des nations qui les ont consacrées. Il est intéressant d'examiner jusqu'à quel point cet esprit, ces moeurs, ces usages, se sont altérés ou conservés; de rechercher quelles ont pu être les influences du climat, les effets du gouvernement, les causes des habitudes; en un mot, de juger, par l'état présent, quel fut l'état des temps passés'.—Volney, C. F.: *Voyage en Syrie et en Égypte pendant les Années 1783, 1784 et 1785*, preface.

'Ah! si tu lis dans mon cœur, tu sais combien il désire la vérité, tu sais qu'il la recherche avec passion. Et n'est ce pas à sa poursuite que tu me vois en ces lieux écartés? . . . J'ai dit: . . . "J'irai dans la solitude vivre parmi les ruines; j'interrogerai les monuments anciens sur la sagesse des temps passés; j'évoquerai du sein des tombeaux l'esprit qui jadis, dans l'Asie, fit la splendeur des états et la gloire des peuples. Je demanderai à la cendre des législateurs par quels mobiles s'élèvent et s'abaissent les empires; de quelles causes naissent la prospérité et les malheurs des nations; sur quels principes enfin doivent s'établir la paix des sociétés et le bonheur des hommes." '—Volney, *Les Ruines*, in *Œuvres Complètes*, pp. 13–14.

Read also the invocation at the beginning of this work of Volney's, ibid., p. 9. The double title of the work—*Les Ruines, ou Méditation sur les Révolutions des Empires*——tells, in itself, the tale of the author's successive passages, in his intellectual voyage of exploration, from receptivity to curiosity and from curiosity to investigation.

accompanying his expeditionary force. Unlike these intrepid men of science, neither Napoleon himself nor his officers and men were drawn to Egypt primarily by History's call; the mainsprings of their action were the barbarian's restlessness and ambition; yet Napoleon knew that he was striking a note to which even the uneducated rank-and-file of an eighteenth-century Western army would respond when he reminded them, before going into action on the decisive battlefield of Imbābah,[1] that forty centuries of History were looking down on them[2] from the Pyramids which their audacious march on Cairo had now brought within their view. We may be sure that Murād Bey, the commander of the opposing Mamlūk force, never thought of wasting his breath by addressing any similar exhortation to his own incurious comrades.

The French *savants* who visited Egypt in Napoleon's train distinguished themselves by finding a new dimension of History for a Modern Western Society's insatiable curiosity to conquer. This curiosity's first objective, at the dawn of the Modern Age, had been the classical languages and literatures of an Hellenic Civilization to which the Western Civilization was affiliated;[3] and by A.D. 1798 it had followed up this feat of recovering possession of its own cultural heritage by taking possession of the cultural heritages of its contemporaries. After remastering their own Greek and Latin classics, Western scholars had proceeded to master the Islamic Society's Arabic and Persian classics, the Far Eastern Society's Sinic classics, and the Hindu Society's Sanskrit classics; and, not content with mastering the Hebrew original of the scriptures which a Christian Church shared with a Jewish diasporà, Western scholarship had also mastered by this time the Iranian language of the Zoroastrian scriptures of a Parsee diasporà which, like Jewry, was a fossil of an extinct Syriac Society that had been the Hellenic Society's sister. After having thus gone far towards appropriating all the treasures of the Past that had been preserved in the cultural heritages of the surviving civilizations, Western scholarship now went on to disinter other treasures that had been lying buried underground, wrapped in the napkin of oblivion,[4] for hundreds and even thousands of years.

This was a much more formidable intellectual enterprise, for here the chain of tradition had long since been broken, and there were therefore no living interpreters to induct Western scholar-catechumens into these mysteries. By their own unaided efforts they had to decipher forgotten scripts and discover the structure, vocabulary and meaning of dead languages which were dead in the exact sense of being no longer in living use for any purpose whatsoever, in contrast to such so-called 'dead languages' as Latin or Sanskrit, which had merely passed out of current vernacular employment without ever having ceased to be spoken in liturgies and read in classical works of literature. The disinterment of the Egyptiac Civilization by the enterprise of Western scholars in and after A.D. 1798 was thus a more remarkable achievement of Modern Western historical curiosity than the Italian renaissance of Latin and

[1] See IV. iv. 459–60.
[2] 'Soldats, quarante siècles vous regardent.'
[3] This Late Medieval Italian renaissance of Hellenic letters has been discussed in X. ix. 62–73.
[4] Luke xix. 20.

Greek letters in the fourteenth and fifteenth centuries of the Christian Era; and by the present writer's day no fewer than eleven once dead civilizations—the Egyptiac, the Babylonic, the Sumeric, the Minoan, and the Hittite, together with the Indus Culture and the Shang Culture, in the Old World, and the Mayan, Yucatec, Mexic, and Andean civilizations in the New World—had thus been brought to life again in Western minds whose curiosity had led them to make these arduous voyages of intellectual exploration. The present writer's own lifetime (*vivebat* A.D. 1889–) had already, by the year A.D. 1952, seen the discovery of the most recently discovered four out of the eleven—namely the Shang Culture, the Indus Culture, and the Hittite and Minoan civilizations—and it had also seen vast progress made in the increase of Western knowledge and understanding of the rest.

Nor was this either the limit or the summit of these Western intellectual pioneers' achievement. Their *chef-d'œuvre* had been to infect with their own curiosity those non-Western peoples who, only a century and a half back, in Volney's and Napoleon's day, had been living and working under the shadow of the visible monuments of the Past without being moved by them.[1] In A.D. 1952, Japanese, Chinese, Indian, Egyptian, and Turkish philologists, historians and archaeologists[2] were labouring side

[1] 'Je pris l'hospitalité chez de pauvres paysans arabes, qui ont établi leurs chaumières sur le parvis même du temple [dédié au soleil à Palmyre] . . . Ah! comment s'est éclipsée tant de gloire? Comment se sont anéantis tant de travaux?'—Volney: *Les Ruines*, chaps. 1 and 2.

[2] In Turkish minds the present writer had seen, at first hand, this mental revolution in their attitude towards Turkey's pre-Turkish and pre-Islamic past accomplished since his first visit to the country in A.D. 1921.

In A.D. 1921, when the Ottoman Turkish people was engaged in a life-and-death struggle to retain possession of its homeland in Anatolia, the local monuments of a pre-Turkish and pre-Islamic past were still regarded by all but a tiny sophisticated minority as so many *pièces justicatives* which the Turks' Orthodox Christian *ra'iyeh* and their Frankish patrons could and would place on exhibition in support of their contention that the Turks were recent interlopers who had never acquired a prescriptive right to the territories on which they had squatted, and who therefore ought to be evicted in order to reinstate lawful proprietors who had been ousted by the Turkish intruders without ever having lost their title. Even in April 1923, when the writer paid his first visit to Ankara, this attitude still prevailed, though by that date the Turks had already succeeded in saving themselves by their own exertions. The Greek invaders' attempt to reach Ankara had been foiled; the fortunes of war had been dramatically reversed by a débâcle of the Greek army in Anatolia; and fresh negotiations for a peace-settlement between Turkey and the West European Powers were being conducted—this time on a footing of equality—at Lausanne. Yet in April 1923 the impression made on the writer by the spectacle of the temple of Augustus—occupied by a garden, annexed to a mosque, and crowned with storks' nests—was the same as that made on Volney 138 years earlier by the spectacle of the ruins of the temple of the Sun at Palmyra.

When the writer paid his next visit to Ankara in the summer of 1929, some six years after the Peace Treaty of Lausanne had been duly signed on the 24th July, 1923, he found the temple of Augustus cleared of its incrustations, converted into a museum, and filled with Hittite monuments collected from all parts of the country. By this time the Turks had begun to acquire confidence in their own future, and President Mustafā Kemāl Atatürk had launched a counter-offensive on the battlefield of political archaeology by ruling that the Hittites had been proto-Turks. This ruling may not have been good history, but it was a good thing for History nevertheless, since its practical corollary was the revolutionary idea that Hittite monuments were Turkish national assets which it was the Turkish people's patriotic duty to preserve.

By the time of the writer's fourth visit to Turkey in the autumn of 1948 the change of attitude was complete. A public directorate of museums in the capital was matched by a local museum in every seat of a provincial administration, and this Turkish public archaeological service was working enthusiastically—undaunted by the inadequacy of its means for coping with the immensity of its task—to preserve and study all monuments

by side with the Western pioneers in intellectual fields that were 'white already to harvest';[1] and the progressive achievements of an intellectual pursuit that was exacting an ever increasing degree of specialization from scholars who set themselves to acquire its technique was at the same time arousing an ever increasing interest in an ever widening circle of laymen.

The popularity of Archaeology in the writer's day was attested by the alacrity with which the weekly illustrated papers and magazines found space for publishing pictures of archaeological excavations and finds. The discovery, on and after the 4th November, 1922, of the tomb of the Pharaoh Tutankhamen (*imperabat circa* 1362–1352 B.C.) created almost as great a furore in England as the birth of a polar bear cub in the Zoological Gardens in Regent's Park in A.D. 1950. The publication, in and after A.D. 1924, of the earlier volumes of *The Cambridge Ancient History*, dealing with once forgotten chapters of history which the archaeologists had recently brought to light, likewise caught the imagination of a cultivated lay public; and the contemporary interest in the history and literature of the Hellenic Civilization did not appear to have been diminished either in volume or in intensity as a result of the change in its character resulting from the breaking, in the writer's lifetime, of the virtual monopoly which, in England for some four hundred years past, the Greek and Latin Classics had shared with Mathematics alone in furnishing the staple pabulum of formal higher education. In a generation in which Hellenic studies were being pushed out of the centre into a corner of the field of education in the formal sense of the word, the absolute number of boys and girls learning Latin and Greek in at least this one Western country was apparently rising—and this without a catastrophic decline in the relative number—as a result of the great increase in the number of the recipients of a secondary education in some intellectual discipline or other,[2] while the growth of a popular interest in the life and letters of the Hellenic World among a wider public which had not mastered the Greek and Latin Classics in the original languages was attested by the

of the Past in every stratum without discrimination. At Ankara on the 3rd November, 1948, the writer and his wife met a pair of young Turkish archaeologists—man and wife—who had just found a trove of business archives accumulated, in the second millennium B.C., by a colony of Assyrian business men in their suburb outside the proto-Hittite city of Kanesh (on the 9th November, 1948, we visited this site, now known as Kültepe, near Qaysari). At Bursa on the 21st November, 1948, the writer was asked by the professor of history in the local secondary school to give a lecture at the Club on the pre-Turkish and pre-Islamic history of the region to a group of Bursans with antiquarian interests. The lecturer found an audience of several hundred people waiting for him, though the lecture had been arranged at not more than eight hours' notice, and, in conversation after the lecture was over, several of those present asked him to give them references to editions of the Greek texts of the works of Dio of Prusa and Arrian of Nicomedia with French or English translations in parallel columns, with the intention of acquainting themselves at first hand with the literary remains of a citizen of Bursa and a citizen of Ismid who were such eminent figures in the past history of this section of the country. This experience at Bursa made it clear to the writer that the Turkish people's change of attitude towards History was now an accomplished fact.

[1] John iv. 35. Cp. Matt. ix. 37–38; Luke x. 2.

[2] The vicissitudes of Greek and Latin studies in schools in England were indicated by the figures, given in the annual reports of H.B.M. Ministry of Education (published by H.B.M. Stationery Office) showing the numbers of those taking the School Certificate and the Higher Certificate in the various subjects. The following selection—which Mr. F. J. Kinchin Smith of the University of London Institute of Education had kindly

mounting sales of an increasing number of translations attaining ever higher levels of literary excellence. The distinguishing feature of these latter-day translations—and this was no doubt what commended them to their readers—was their success in making the Greek and Latin originals come alive in the vernacular. Instead of deliberately putting distance between the Classics and their readers by rendering the Classics into a 'translationese' unknown to real life, they exerted themselves to bring home to their readers the 'philosophical contemporaneity' and 'philosophical equivalence'[1] of the Hellenic and the Western Civilization by reproducing the originals in the living language of the corresponding literary genres of the day.

This Faustian insatiability of inquiring Western minds had come to be a theme of Western poetry. The impetus of a curiosity that had pressed on from an exploration of a physical ocean in the fifteenth century of the Christian Era to the sounding of the psychic abyss of the Subconscious in the twentieth century is deftly conveyed by Martyn Skinner in his *Letters to Malaya*.[2] Yet this cumulative collective achievement of curiosity, impressive though it be, is not the heart of a passion and a drama that can have no other theatre than a soul; and this individual experience had found its immortal expression in the English language in Keats' sonnet *On First Looking into Chapman's Homer*.

> Then felt I like some watcher of the skies
> When a new planet swims into his ken,
> Or like stout Cortez when, with eagle eyes,
> He stared at the Pacific, and all his men
> Look'd at each other with a wild surmise,
> Silent, upon a peak in Darien.

In the present writer's mind, the heroic exemplar of an invincible curiosity's response to the challenge of heart-breaking circumstances had always been Heinrich Schliemann (*vivebat* A.D. 1822–90), ever since a memorable day at Winchester when the writer as a boy had listened spell-bound to his master M. J. Rendall retailing, with zest, the salient episodes of this romantic life in a parenthesis during a session officially allocated to the construing of the Iliad.

'If I begin this book with my autobiography [Schliemann himself has

communicated to the writer—would give an idea of the tendency during the thirty years ending in A.D. 1949.

SCHOOL CERTIFICATE

Absolute Figures			*Relative Figures*		
Year	*Latin*	*Greek*	*Year*	*Latin*	*Greek*
1919	10,102	1,215	1919	35·1%	4·2%
1929	25,456	2,327	1929	42·7%	3·9%
1939	28,508	1,989	1939	35·3%	2·4%
1949	36,916	2,411	1949	32·1%	2·1%

HIGHER CERTIFICATE

Absolute Figures			*Relative Figures*		
Year	*Latin*	*Greek*	*Year*	*Latin*	*Greek*
1929	1,980	818	1929	21%	9%
1949	4,159	915	1949	12%	2%

[1] See I. i. 172–7.

[2] Skinner, Martyn: *Letters to Malaya III and IV* (London 1943, Putnam), pp. 40–47, quoted in VII. vii. 496–7.

written in the introduction to his *Ilios*],[1] it is not from any feeling of vanity, but from a desire to show how the work of my later life has been the natural consequence of the impressions I received in my earliest childhood, and that, so to say, the pickaxe and spade for the excavation of Troy and the royal tombs of Mycenae were both forged and sharpened in the little German village in which I passed eight years of my earliest childhood.'[2]

In the village of Ankershagen, between Waren[3] and Penzlin in the Duchy of Mecklenburg-Schwerin, of which Heinrich's father, Ernst Schliemann, was the Protestant pastor, and where Heinrich lived from his second to his fifteenth year (A.D. 1823–36), there were two elements in the social milieu—the local folk-lore and the pastor's personal interest in Hellenic history—that made their impress on Heinrich's receptive mind; and 'the persistence with which, throughout his life, he recalled the scenes of his youth and wrote to the people there—a family-feeling which no love of country had helped to nourish in this cosmopolitan —indicates the depth of those first experiences and discoveries'.[4]

'Just behind our garden was a pond called "das Silberschälchen", out of which a maiden was believed to rise each midnight, holding a silver bowl. There was also in the village a small hill surrounded by a ditch, probably a prehistoric burial-place (or so-called *Hünengrab*), in which, as the legend ran, a robber knight in times of old had buried his beloved child in a golden cradle. Vast treasures were also said to be buried close to the ruins of a round tower in the garden of the proprietor of the village. My faith in the existence of these treasures was so great that, whenever I heard my father complain of his poverty, I always expressed my astonishment that he did not dig up the silver bowl or the golden cradle, and so become rich.'[5]

The curiosity of the future excavator of the treasures buried in the Second City at Troy and in the royal tombs at Mycenae was diverted from Mecklenburg to the Mediterranean by his father's talk of the excavations at Pompeii and Herculaneum and his recital of the tale of the Trojan War; and here, twelve days before Heinrich's eighth birthday, the decisive impact was made by an engraving,[6] representing the flight

[1] This account of Schliemann's career by the hero himself is as thrilling as it is brief (Schliemann takes no more than eighteen pages to bring himself from the cradle to the Troad in his forty-seventh year, A.D. 1868); but it was not written till Schliemann was nearly sixty years old, and it does not tally at all points with Schliemann's current records, which run to 150 manuscript volumes and 20,000 papers (see Ludwig, Emil: *Schliemann of Troy* (London 1931, Putnam), p. 24) and which have also been used by Schliemann's biographer. In op. cit., p. 27 n., and pp. 47 and 52, Ludwig hints that the retrospective autobiography must be taken *cum grano salis* in the light of the contemporary documents. (One specimen of these (see Ludwig, op. cit., p. 48) is an autobiographical letter, written by Schliemann in his twenty-first year to his sisters, which would fill eight printed pages.) The ampler contemporary information which Ludwig has had at his command has not, however, led him to impugn the authority of any of the passages from Schliemann's autobiography that are quoted in this Study.

[2] Schliemann, H.: *Ilios* (London 1880, John Murray), p. 1.

[3] The Waren from whom this village had received its name were presumably representatives of a Teutonic-speaking North European barbarian people—the Warings *alias* Warni *alias* Varini—who in the post-Hellenic Völkerwanderung (*aestuabat* A.D. 375–675) had anticipated Heinrich Schliemann's nineteenth-century descent from the Baltic upon the Aegean (see Chadwick, H.M.: *The Origin of the English Nation* (Cambridge 1907, University Press), pp. 102–10).

[4] Ludwig, E.: *Schliemann of Troy* (London 1931, Putnam), p. 135.

[5] Schliemann, ibid., pp. 1–2.

[6] Reproduced by Emil Ludwig in his *Schliemann of Troy* (London 1931, Putnam), facing p. 106.

of Aeneas from the burning city of Ilium, in a *Universal History*[1] which was the father's present to his son on Christmas Day, 1829. The boy had long been grieved to hear from his father that Troy had vanished without leaving a trace, and this picture—depicting massive city-walls—was naïvely taken by little Heinrich as evidence that his father had, after all, happily been mistaken, since the author of the book must have seen Troy as it was here represented. When his father replied that the picture was merely a fanciful one, Heinrich drew from him the admission of his belief that Troy must, in fact, have had walls as massive as those which the imaginary picture displayed.

'"Father", retorted I, "If such walls once existed, they cannot possibly have been completely destroyed: vast ruins of them must still remain, but they are hidden away beneath the dust of ages." He maintained the contrary, whilst I remained firm in my opinion, and at last we both agreed that I should one day excavate Troy. . . . Thanks to God, my firm belief in the existence of that Troy has never forsaken me amid all the vicissitudes of my eventful career; but it was not destined for me to realise, till in the autumn of my life . . . , our[2] sweet dreams of fifty years ago'.[3]

[1] Written by Dr. Georg Ludwig Jerrer, and published at Nuremburg in 1828. Some forty years after Schliemann's death, this volume was found among his books and papers in his house at Athens by his biographer (see Ludwig, Emil: *Schliemann of Troy* (London 1931, Putnam), p. 24).

[2] The second person in this 'our' is not Heinrich Schliemann's father, whose character and conduct were not such as to inspire in his son's heart an admiration or a love to match the stimulus that the father's archaeological interests gave to his son's intellect; the second person was Minna Meineke, a girl of Heinrich's own age who was the daughter of a neighbouring farmer; and the words omitted in the passage quoted above are 'and then without Minna—nay, far from her'.

Schliemann, like Dante, had projected his anima on to a feminine figure of flesh and blood. In 1829, just after he had found his aim in life, 'Minna . . . showed me the greatest sympathy and entered into all my vast plans for the future. Thus a warm attachment sprang up between us, and in our childish sympathy we exchanged vows of eternal love' (Schliemann, ibid., p. 4). But, like Dante, Schliemann lost his love in the flesh to recapture her in the spirit by redirecting his tragically thwarted passion into a mighty piece of creative work on to which he projected her image.

'Εργάσομαι μεγάλ' ἔργα· δι' ἔργων σοῦ πελάσαιμ' ἄν·
ἂν δ' ἄρα λείψωμαι, μείζον' ἔτ' ἐργάσομαι.

The mighty works are eventually accomplished; but who is this 'thou' for whose sake they are undertaken? Is it really the lost living woman, or is it the hero's own indomitable and inescapable anima ('quam scilicet, ut fit, effugere haud potis est') in search of an alternative object?

Heinrich Schliemann inherited the destiny of the Trojan hero who, in Jerrer's picture, was displayed in flight from the City of Destruction to a new world. He, too, had to lose his Creusa in order to be free to espouse his Lavinia in the fullness of time; and Heinrich Schliemann relived Aeneas' legendary experience in real life in seeing Minna Meineke slip three times from his clasp—the first two times as a vicarious punishment for his father's misdemeanours (see ibid., pp. 5 and 6) and the third time by a cruel mistiming (pp. 11–12). His account of his unexpected meeting with Minna on Good Friday, 1836 (p. 6), is not unworthy to be compared with the fourteenth chapter of Dante's *La Vita Nuova*.

Ter conatus ibi collo dare bracchia circum,
Ter frustra comprensa manus effugit imago
Par levibus ventis volucrique simillima somno.

'It had indeed happened to Minna and me as it often happens to us in our sleep, when we dream that we are pursuing somebody and can never catch him, because as often as we reach him he escapes us again. I thought I could never get over the misfortune of losing Minna as the partner of my life; but Time, which heals all wounds, at last healed mine, so that, although I remained for years mourning for her, I could at least continue my mercantile pursuits without further interruption' (Schliemann, ibid., p. 12).

[3] Schliemann, ibid., pp. 3 and 5.

These dreams, once formed, remained the constant inspiration of Heinrich Schliemann's life.

'As long as I live, I shall never forget the evening when a drunken miller came into the shop. . . . He was the son of a Protestant clergyman in Roebel, Mecklenburg, and had almost completed his studies at the gymnasium of Neu Ruppin when he was expelled on account of his bad conduct. . . . Dissatisfied with his lot, the young man gave himself up to drink, which, however, had not made him forget his Homer; for, on the evening that he entered the shop, he recited to us about a hundred lines of the poet, observing the rhythmic cadence of the verses. Although I did not understand a syllable, the melodious sound of the words made a deep impression upon me, and I wept bitter tears over my unhappy fate. Three times over did I get him to repeat to me those divine verses, rewarding his trouble with three glasses of whisky, which I bought with the few pence that made up my whole fortune. From that moment I never ceased to pray God that by His grace I might yet have the happiness of learning Greek.'[1]

The shop was Theodore Hückstädt's grocer's shop at Fürstenberg, and the year—A.D. 1837—was the second year of Heinrich Schliemann's employment there and the sixteenth of his age. Some five years later, when he had already risen from being an assistant in a North German village grocer's shop to being a clerk in a Dutch financial house at Amsterdam, he once more proved his faithfulness to his dreams by paying a high price for another step towards making them come true.

'My annual salary amounted only to 800 francs (£32), half of which I spent on my studies; on the other half I lived—miserably enough, to be sure.'[2]

And the rest of the acts of Heinrich Schliemann, and all that he did between his arrival in Amsterdam in A.D. 1842 as a ship-wrecked cabin-boy and his winding up of his business in St. Petersburg in A.D. 1863 as a millionaire—how he made his fortune by importing indigo into Russia and by trading in gold dust in California (automatically becoming, in the process, a citizen of the United States), and how, in the meantime, he taught himself to read and write English, French, Dutch, Spanish, Italian, Portuguese, Russian, Swedish, Polish, Modern Greek, Ancient Greek, Latin, and Arabic—is it not written in the Trojan hero's autobiography and in the book of Emil Ludwig?[3]

'Heaven continued to bless all my mercantile undertakings in a wonderful manner, so that at the end of 1863 I found myself in possession of a fortune such as my ambition had never ventured to aspire to. But in the midst of the bustle of business I never forgot Troy, or the agreement I had made with my father and Minna in 1830 to excavate it. I loved money indeed, but solely as the means of realising this great idea of my life.'[4]

The idea was indeed realized beyond all expectation; for the hero, who had spent his fifteenth to his forty-second year (A.D. 1836–63) in

[1] Schliemann, ibid., p. 7.
[2] Ibid., p. 9.
[3] Ludwig, E.: *Schliemann of Troy, The Story of a Gold-Seeker* (London 1931, Putnam).
[4] Schliemann, ibid., p. 17.

accumulating the means, spent his forty-seventh to his sixty-ninth year (A.D. 1868–90)[1] in disinterring from the ground, and retrieving from oblivion, not only Troy, but Ithaca, Mycenae, Orchomenos, and Tiryns as well. The first of these two chapters in the story of Heinrich Schliemann's life might have come straight out of Smiles' *Self-Help*, and the second straight out of *The Arabian Nights*; but, of the two, it is the first that is, not only the more illuminating, but also the more romantic.

The writer of this Study, who was born only twenty months before the date of Schliemann's death, was compensated for having thus missed the chance of meeting this hero of History alive by coming to know two younger contemporaries of his own who had been inspired by the same indomitable spirit of curiosity to win victories over hardly less fearful odds.

Professor H. W. Bailey (*natus* A.D. 1899), a philologist of world-wide renown who in A.D. 1952 was the Professor of Sanskrit in the University of Cambridge, had awoken to consciousness as a child on a farm in Western Australia; and it would be hard to think of a more unpromising environment than this for producing a *savant* in the field of Oriental languages. The virgin soil of a recently colonized *terra nullius* exhaled no folk-lore to play the part of those local legends that had put Heinrich Schliemann, in his Varangian village, on the track of buried treasure; but the local human environment in Western Australia in the first decade of the twentieth century of the Christian Era did provide Harold Walter Bailey with the equivalent of the *Universal History* that had given the decisive turn to Heinrich Schliemann's life when it had come into Schliemann's hands on Christmas Day, 1829. The books that descended from Heaven upon the boy on the West Australian farm were 'a set of seven volumes of an encyclopaedia (eagerly devoured) and four other volumes with lessons in French, Latin, German, Greek, Italian, and Spanish. Later came Arabic and Persian, out of which Persian took the lead (joined later to Sanskrit)'.[2]

This was the trove that set Bailey's curiosity on fire; and in A.D. 1943 the present writer induced the modest scholar to describe to him how his family used to watch him, with a benign but whimsical gaze, while, during the noonday rest from their common labours in the field, he would be conning his Avestan grammar in the shade of an Antipodean haystack. By the time when he was approaching the age to matriculate at a university, the young student of Oriental languages had become aware that he had reached the limit of what he could teach himself, unaided, out of the books on which he could lay hands. What was the next step? At the University of Western Australia at this date there was no

[1] In this symmetrically rhythmic life, the caesura between the strophe and the antistrophe was marked by a voyage round the World in A.D. 1864–5 and a study of Archaeology in Paris in and after A.D. 1866.

[2] Note communicated, on the 7th April, 1952, by Professor Bailey to the writer of this Study with his letter granting the writer's request for his permission to allow his intellectual history to be cited here. The writer is most grateful to Professor Bailey for his kind consent. 'I am most flattered', this eminent scholar modestly and humorously remarks, 'to find I have left at least a faint streak on the surface of this tossing world of Samsāra!'

provision for Oriental studies; for help in these, the would-be student would have to go on to Western Europe or to North America. So Bailey taught himself Latin and Greek; took these as his subjects at his own university; won a scholarship at the University of Western Australia to take him to the University of Oxford; and found at Oxford the help that he needed in order to complete his mastery of Oriental languages.

Yet even Cambridge, England, could not provide this Australian philologist with a chair specifically allocated to the Khotanese language, akin to Persian and to Sanskrit, which had been introduced into the Tarim Basin by the Sakas[1] and which, while H. W. Bailey was studying Avestan under his haystack in Western Australia, had been recovered from oblivion by the labours of a series of Western pioneers in the Tarim Basin, culminating in the Hungarian-British archaeologist-explorer Sir Aurel Stein's trove of religious and secular literature in known and still all but unknown languages, on which this path-finder had lighted in May 1907 in a Taoist shrine at Ch'ien Fo-tung ('the Caves of the Thousand Buddhas'), near Tun-huang in the Su-lo-ho Basin, 'a natural corridor' leading from North-Western China into Central Asia, at the Western terminus of the former *limes* of a Sinic universal state;[2] and Khotanese and Tokharian were the fields in which Bailey, in the next stage of his intellectual career, was to give the most impressive demonstrations of his prowess in advancing the frontiers of philological knowledge.[3]

Schliemann's and Bailey's experience of being kindled into an undying glow of curiosity by the casual impact of one or two books was shared by another contemporary and colleague of the writer's, F. C. Jones, who in A.D. 1952 was a lecturer in Modern History at the University of Bristol with a special commission in the field of Far Eastern studies. At the same university, some thirty years earlier, Jones, as an undergraduate, had happened, while exploring the stacks of the university library, to stumble upon a cache of old books concerning the Far East that had been bequeathed to the university by F. V. Dickins, an Englishman who had

[1] For this Indo-European-speaking wave of Eurasian Nomads, see VI. vii. 580–689 *passim*: 'The Administrative Geography of the Achaemenian Empire.'

[2] See Stein, Sir Aurel: *On Ancient Central Asian Tracks* (London 1933, Macmillan), pp. 203–16 = chap. 13: 'Discoveries in a Hidden Chapel', with fig. 86, facing p. 204.

'The priest summoned up courage that morning to open before me the rough door closing the entrance to the rock-carved recess where the great trove had lain hidden. . . . The sight disclosed in the dim light of the priest's little oil-lamp made my eyes open wide. Heaped up in layers, but without any order, there appeared a solid mass of manuscript bundles rising to ten feet from the floor and filling, as subsequent measurement showed, close on 500 cubic feet. Within the small room measuring about nine feet square there was left barely space for two people to stand on' (ibid., pp. 203–4).

[3] See, for example, Bailey, H. W.: 'Hvatanica', in the *Bulletin of the London School of Oriental Studies*, vol. viii, Part 4 (London 1937, Luzac), pp. 923–36; 'Ttaugara', ibid., pp. 883–921; *Zoroastrian Problems* (Oxford 1943, Clarendon Press); 'Recent work in "Tokharian",' in the Philological Society's *Transactions* (London 1947, David Nutt), pp. 126–53; *Khotanese Texts*, vol. i (Cambridge 1945, University Press); *Khotanese Buddhist Texts* (London 1951, Taylor's Foreign Press).

In his letter of the 7th April, 1952, to the writer of this Study, Professor Bailey tells him: 'Only this morning I sent off to Sven Hedin a volume explaining his documents in the Khotanese language of the Sakas (four years' work). The Cambridge University Press is at this moment printing vol. ii, and I still plan two or three more volumes of this material. Persian and Sanskrit have come together for me in Khotanese studies—the Iranian speech with the Buddhist culture. My "curiosity" is as great as ever for this Central Asian miscellany!'

served as a medical officer in China and Japan in A.D. 1866–70 and had eventually become the university's Reader in Japanese. The dust with which the youthful explorer found these books covered told him that he was the first member of his university ever to have taken any interest in them; but this hitherto neglected batch of books now had a decisive effect on one student's mental life. From that moment onwards, Jones persistently pursued Far Eastern studies as a personal interest in addition to his regular academic work. He continued this pursuit as a lecturer in history, first at Dalhousie and King's University at Halifax, Nova Scotia, and then at Harvard. After that, with the aid of the Rockefeller Foundation, he made his way to China and spent nearly two years there—from the autumn of A.D. 1935 to the summer of A.D. 1937—partly studying Chinese at the College of Chinese Studies in Peking and partly travelling about the country; and, though China was in turmoil at the time, he managed to make his way far and wide into the interior. At the end of the year 1937 he joined the staff of the Far Eastern department of the Royal Institute of International Affairs in London, and eventually returned from there to his *alma mater* at Bristol. The present writer, who, by A.D. 1952, had had the pleasure of knowing, and of working with, this devoted student of Far Eastern history for more than fourteen years, had never seen a sign that his friend's curiosity was abating. Throughout he had continued to show the same steadily burning zeal to widen and deepen his knowledge and understanding of his beloved subject.

An experience that had meant so much to F. C. Jones, H. W. Bailey, and Heinrich Schliemann had also come the way of the present writer.[1] He will never forget a memorable morning in one of the early months of the year A.D. 1898 when a row of four books in a uniform binding made its first appearance[2] on a bookshelf in the dining-room of his parents' house in London, No. 12 Upper Westbourne Terrace. The series was Fisher Unwin's *The Story of the Nations*, and the subjects of the four volumes were *Ancient Egypt; Assyria; Media, Babylon, and Persia*; and *The Saracens*.[3] The writer, who on that day was either approaching the end of his ninth year or just entering on his tenth, had awoken to consciousness in the most favourable human environment imaginable for the making of an historian, since, in his Mother, he had had an historian to bring him up. In A.D. 1898 he could already remember his Mother's having written *True Stories from Scottish History*,[4] and could recall the

[1] In the present Part of this Study the writer has drawn, among other sources, upon his personal experience—not, of course, in any delusory belief that this is particularly interesting or important in virtue of being his own, but because, in the nature of the case, it is the only first-hand information about the subject of this Part that has been at his disposal.

[2] The date is approximately fixed by the fact that the books had been given to the writer's Mother, because she was an historian, when her mother-in-law's personal possessions were being distributed among the members of the family; for the date of the writer's grandmother's death was the 19th December, 1897.

[3] For the authorship and dates of publication of these four volumes, see the acknowledgements in the present volume, on p. 219.

[4] Toynbee, Edith: *True Stories from Scottish History* (London N. D., Griffith Farren Browne). There is no imprint of the date; but, in the copy which the writer took down just now from the bookcase, given him by his Mother, which stands behind his shoulder in his study at No. 45 Pembroke Square, London, the book is dated by the inscription, in his Mother's handwriting: 'Arnold Joseph Toynbee, October 1896, with Mother's love'.

excitement of seeing the proofs of the illustrations arrive and of finally holding the first bound copy in his hands. His Mother had written the book in order to pay for keeping his nurse till he was five years old instead of four; and, though, when the additional year ran out, he had been desolated to see his nurse leave, he had quickly been reconciled to the change by the intimate companionship that his Mother had given him during the years that had followed. Night by night, while she was putting him to bed, she had told him, in brief instalments, the history of Britain from Caesar's landing to the Battle of Waterloo, and the child had been readily receptive to this gracious impact of the parochial history of the Western country in which he had happened to be born. Yet that morning in A.D. 1898 on which those mighty suns the Egyptiac, Babylonic, and Syriac civilizations swam into his ken in all their overwhelming grandeur was the decisive moment in the intellectual experience of this young watcher of the skies of History; for the advent of these hitherto unknown heavenly bodies shook him out of the Yin-state of receptivity into a Yang-movement of curiosity which, happily for him, was still a flowing tide on the 15th September, 1952, more than fifty-four years later.

Omnes
Restinxit stellas, exortus ut aetherius sol.[1]

The epiphany of those civilizations of the first and the second generation took the light out of such commonplace planets as the parochial histories of ephemeral nations spawned in a parvenu Western World. The shallow landlocked waters of Lake Tenochtitlan could no longer satisfy the soul of a seeker after new worlds when once he had stared at the Pacific.

The child flung himself upon the Ocean,[2] and from that time onwards its expanse continued to open out in front of him faster than his ship's prow could cleave the ever widening waters. His inquiries whether Mexico was part of the United States and whether the Persians were Muhammadans were referred by his Mother to his Father. At school his awakened curiosity led him to relive Herodotus's experience of breaking his way into the new world of the Achaemenian Empire, and to explore two marooned enclaves of Christendom, Georgia and Abyssinia. At the university it led him to break into the new world of the Far East, via the Great Eurasian Steppe, in the footsteps of his fellow Franks John of Piano Carpini, William of Rubruck, Marco Polo of Venice, and their living successors Sven Hedin the Swede and Aurel Stein the Hungarian,[3] and to acquaint himself with the career of the renegade Ottoman

[1] Lucretius: *De Rerum Naturâ*, Book III, ll. 1043–4.

[2] In A.D. 1952 the writer's earliest surviving memory was a recollection of having taken and carried out, at the age of two, on the beach at Abersoch in Wales, a decision to run into the sea in order to find out what would happen. What did happen was that his nurse ran in after him, pulled him out, and, in the act, sprained her ankle. There was no benevolently officious nurse to pull him back from the intellectual plunge that he made, six years after that, into the ocean of History.

[3] The writer could still recapture the excitement to which he had been moved at the time by a lantern-lecture that Sir Aurel Stein had given at Oxford, in the great hall of the Examination Schools, at some date while the writer was an undergraduate (*studia exercebat* A.D. 1907–11). The panoramas of huge snow-covered mountain ranges would

qul, Scanderbeg. As soon as he was quit of his final examinations, it led him to spend a year surveying the theatre of Hellenic history on foot, as a student of the British archaeological schools at Rome and Athens, and to make the discovery of a living Ottoman World which eventually found him a place in the Turkish section of the Foreign Office division of the British Delegation to the Peace Conference of Paris in A.D. 1919. Between the First and the Second World War it led him to widen his range by taking into his cognizance the general course of current international affairs, and to add a new dimension to this mental universe by transhipping, with C. G. Jung as his navigator-psychopompus, from a surface-craft to a submarine in order to sound the Psyche's subconscious abyss. After the Second World War the same still irresistibly beckoning curiosity led him into making an excursion on the economic plane into a science of business cycles which promised to throw light on the larger and more momentous subject of the relation between Law and Freedom in History; and on the 15th September, 1952, when he was midway through his sixty-fourth year, the peremptorily rising note in the roar of Time's wingèd chariot's[1] accelerating engine was urging him to press forward, ἆς γόνυ χλωρόν,[2] into new worlds which this curiosity had marked down long since for future conquest.

At that age he was being spurred on by the example of the historian-banker-statesman George Grote (*vivebat* A.D. 1794–1871), who, more than two years before he had returned to the printer, on the 23rd December, 1855,[3] the last corrected proof-sheets of the twelfth and concluding volume of his history of Greece, had begun to knap off two sister works on the philosophies of Plato and Aristotle.[4] The work on Plato had straightway been written and published in three volumes;[5] and, 'no sooner had the *Plato* been completed, and the printing begun,[6] than the author "set the loom" afresh for his *Aristotle*—scarcely permitting himself breath' before applying himself 'to the preparation of the third part of what he used to call "my trilogy."'[7] Yet, notwithstanding the diligence of Grote's response to the challenge of Time's hurrying chariot's clatter, Death had overtaken him with his *Aristotle* still incomplete.

In taking to heart this example set by George Grote, the present writer was following in the footsteps of Lord Bryce (*vivebat* A.D. 1838–1922), who, whenever he was writing a book, used to have on his agenda not only the next book but also a perpetual next book but one. This permanent lure on the intellectual athlete's literary horizon was a projected

flash up in his visual memory, and he could recall how, when the lecturer had mentioned, in passing, that he had lost some toes there through frost-bite, the eager listener had recognized that he was in the presence of a discoverer who was indeed in earnest about his intellectual mission.

1 Marvell, Andrew: *To His Coy Mistress*, l. 22.

2 Theocritus: *Κυνίσκας Ἔρως*, l. 70.

3 See Grote, Harriet: *The Personal Life of George Grote* (London 1873, John Murray), p. 224.

4 See Grote, George: *A History of Greece*, vol. xi (London 1853, John Murray), preface dated the 15th April, 1853, pp. iii–iv.

5 London 1865, John Murray. On the 23rd April, 1951, the present writer took down from the shelf in the Athenaeum Club in London the set of these volumes that had been given to the Club by their author, with an inscription in vol. i in George Grote's handwriting.

6 In September 1864.

7 Grote, Harriet, op. cit., p. 277.

work on the lives and time of the Roman Emperor Justinian I and his consort Theodora; and, though this most lovingly cherished of all the historian-jurist-statesman's literary projects eventually had the same fate as the historian-banker-statesman's work on Aristotle, this ever receding and never captured intellectual quarry performed for Bryce the invaluable service that 'the electric hare' performs for the greyhound on the racing track. It kept the runner's energies at full stretch; and his never flagging eagerness to catch his *Justinian* was, no doubt, not the least potent of the stimuli that prompted him to achieve the heroic feat of producing his *Modern Democracies* (*conscriptum* A.D. 1918–21)[1] after he had turned eighty.

[1] The present writer had had the good fortune to become personally acquainted with Lord Bryce in his seventy-seventh year, when the writer, as a young man, had been commissioned to compile, under Lord Bryce's direction, a blue book on *The Treatment of the Armenians in the Ottoman Empire*, published as Miscellaneous No. 31 (1916) [Cmd. 8325] (London 1916, H.M. Stationery Office); and, thanks to the friendliness which Lord and Lady Bryce never ceased to show to people of younger generations, he had had the happiness thereafter of continuing to see something of the historian during the last eight years of his life.

At this age, Bryce still displayed an astonishing youthfulness which showed itself physically in his persistence in the habit of running upstairs two stairs at each step. This apparently inexhaustible fount of physical energy was replenished (so it seemed to the writer) from spiritual sources, and one of these was an unfailing curiosity. Γηράσκω δ' αἰεὶ πολλὰ διδασκόμενος (Solon, fragment 17, in Bergkh-Hiller-Crusius's edition). At a time when Bryce was clearing his decks from war-work in order to go into action on *Modern Democracies*, the writer happened to mention in conversation with him that he knew G. D. H. Cole, who at that time was active in expounding the idea of Guild Socialism. Lord Bryce instantly began to ask the writer whether he could direct him to any literature that had been published on the subject, as he had already made a mental note that he must not fail to take account of Guild Socialism in his own forthcoming work. This was evidence indeed of Bryce's freshness of mind at the age of eighty. When, at this age, he was girding himself for the huge task of writing a comprehensive work on the political phenomena of the Modern Western World, he might have been expected to feel, not exhilaration, but repugnance, at the prospect of having to take account of yet another mushroom ideology; and an intellectual inhibition might well have been reinforced by a political prejudice, considering that Bryce himself was, not a socialist, but a life-long liberal. Yet his vaulting curiosity cleared both these psychic fences at one bound. On the 23rd April, 1951, the present writer's own curiosity moved him to take Bryce's *Modern Democracies* (London 1921, Macmillan, 2 vols.) down from the shelf in a library to look up 'Guild Socialism' in the index. Sure enough, it is described in vol. ii, on p. 645.

The writer never ceased to be struck by the contrast, in their respective responses to the challenge of chronological age, between Lord Bryce and another historian, James Leigh Strachan-Davidson, the Master of Balliol, who was Bryce's junior by five years (*vivebat* A.D. 1843–1916). In A.D. 1913–15, at meetings on academic business in the Master's study, the writer, scanning the books on his shelves, discovered, to his surprise and concern, that there had been hardly any fresh acquisitions since the early eighteen-eighties—hardly any, that is to say, since the historian had passed his fortieth year (see Mackail, J. W.: *James Leigh Strachan-Davidson* (Oxford 1925, Clarendon Press), p. 53). Down to about that date the principal English, American, French, and German publications in the fields of Hellenic history, Hellenic and Western philosophy, Western political economy, and contemporary Western *belles lettres* were well represented, but, after that, the flow of new acquisitions had suddenly ceased, and this could only mean that, in his early forties, the fire of this scholar's curiosity had gone out. The writer could never discover any outward event in this period of Strachan-Davidson's life that would account for this intellectual mishap, but a clue to the whole of the Master's intellectual history had come into his hands on the 22nd October, 1913; for that day had been the Master's seventieth birthday; the fellows of the College had given a dinner in the Master's honour that evening; and the keypoint in the speech in which the Senior Fellow had proposed his health had been the remarkable fact that the Master had never been away from the College for as long as twelve months running at any time since his first arrival there as an undergraduate at the age of eighteen. As the writer listened, he was struck with dismay; for he himself, being at that time in his twenty-fifth year, had just returned to the College after a sixteen months' absence and had been inducted as a fellow on terms which

Encouraged and admonished by the examples of Bryce and Grote, the present writer took his arrival in December 1950 at the threshold of the twelfth part out of the planned thirteen parts of this Study as a signal for him to cast his mind forward, in anticipation of the now imminent date at which this current work would be over, to plan the writing of a *Religio Historici* and the completion of a history of the Hellenic World—begun in A.D. 1914 on an invitation from the editors of *The Home University Library*—of which he had written the first forty-two sheets[1] when his progress had been interrupted by the outbreak of the First World War.

In A.D. 1952 the present writer's curiosity was also agog to finish learning the Arabic and Ottoman Turkish languages and to begin learning Classical New Persian. He had found himself compelled to suspend work on acquiring these three languages when, after having started in A.D. 1924 to produce an annual *Survey of International Affairs* under the auspices of Chatham House, he had started in A.D. 1927 to make systematic notes for the present Study, which he began to write, *pari passu* with the *Survey*, in A.D. 1930. Ever since the time, towards the close of his five years at Winchester (A.D. 1902–7), when he had gained a sufficient mastery over the Greek and Latin languages to make him at home in the Hellenic classics, it had been his ambition to make himself equally at home in the Islamic classics, and he had taken the first step towards this end between A.D. 1915 and A.D. 1924 at the London School of Oriental Studies—starting to learn there the rudiments of Turkish during the First World War from 'Alī Rizā Bey,[2] and the rudiments of

were tantamount to a life tenure so long as he did not marry, go bankrupt, or commit any other immoral act. That night he dreamed that the corresponding toast was being proposed in his own honour as a veteran fellow of the College on the 14th April, 1959, after another forty-five years, five months, and twenty-three days had passed as swiftly as he knew that they would pass for him if he were to adopt the Master's regimen. Next morning he woke up firmly resolved not to allow this doom to overtake him.

[1] As he wrote these words, he took these sheets out of a drawer in a bookcase, given him by his Mother, in his study at No. 45 Pembroke Square, Kensington, London.

[2] The experience that had brought the writer to the point of starting his long since projected attack on the Turkish language at this date had been his horror at the events which he had been recording in the blue book on *The Treatment of the Armenians in the Ottoman Empire* that he had been compiling under the direction of Lord Bryce. How had any human beings come to perpetrate those inhuman acts? The 'Osmanlis, being human, must be men of like passions with his and his fellow-countrymen's English selves. What was the explanation of this appalling mystery? The first step towards arriving at it would be to understand the Turks, and the key to that woul d be to learn the Turkish language.

When the writer enrolled at the London School of Oriental Languages in A.D. 1916 in order to begin learning Turkish, the lecturer in Turkish, 'Alī Rizā Bey, demurred to being asked to take as a pupil a man who, as he saw it, had just shown himself, in a published work, to be an enemy of 'Alī Rizā Bey's country. When he submitted this objection to the Director of the School, Sir Denison Ross, the Director pointed out to him that, if his patriotism was founded—as it was—on a sincere belief in the sterling qualities of the Turkish national character, he was now being presented with an opportunity—which, as a patriot, he ought not to let slip—of making an English convert. The Turkish lecturer was convinced by the Director's shrewd argument, and happily he did not afterwards have to regret that he had taken Sir Denison Ross's advice; for the knowledge of the Turkish language—rudimentary thought it still was—which the writer had acquired from 'Alī Rizā Bey by A.D. 1920 enabled he writer in A.D. 1921 to make an exposure of the treatment of the Turks in that year in the Ottoman territories then under Greek military occupation.

By that time the writer had made an empirical discovery of the truth that Human Nature is nowhere and never proof—not even in the communities that have travelled the

Arabic after the Peace Conference of A.D. 1919 from Professor Sir Thomas Arnold and Professor H. A. R. Gibb. By A.D. 1952 a craving that had been dammed back since A.D. 1924 had accumulated a powerful pressure of urgency. The writer was stung by shame whenever he recollected that his hero Heinrich Schliemann had taught himself no less than thirteen languages during the twenty-seven years (A.D. 1836–63) that he had had to spend on making his fortune; but he could then recruit his courage by recalling that his heroine Jane Ellen Harrison had taught herself both Persian and Russian after she had passed her sixty-fifth year; for this example carried with it the admonition 'Go and do thou likewise'.[1]

In A.D. 1952 the writer's curiosity was also still being stimulated through still being tormented by longings to make his pilgrimage to historic points on the face of the *Oikoumenê* on which he had never yet set eyes or which had once tantalized him with a Pisgah sight. He had seen Assisi from Spello on the 30th October, 1911, without ever having succeeded in reaching Assisi at any time during the next forty years. He had been shunted in and out of Venice on the Orient Express three times without ever having come nearer to Saint Mark's than into the presence of the pair of Roman emperors in porphyry who stood clasped in a mutual embrace outside a door that was barred and bolted at 5.30 a.m. He had twice passed Qāramān by train without having had time, either on the 31st August, 1929, or on the 13th November, 1948, to break his journey in order to view the interior of those romantic city-walls and press on, beyond, across Cilicia Tracheia to Selefkeh. On the 14th September, 1929, he had gazed longingly up the River Kārūn into Persia while his ship bore him on inexorably, past the confluence of the Kārūn with the Shatt-al-'Arab, *en route* from Basrah to Karachi. On the Great Wall of China, at the Nankow Pass, he had had to turn back without being able to pursue the Wall on its snakelike westward course towards a terminus thirteen hundred miles and more away. And he had never yet come near to setting eyes on Trier, Ravenna, Monte Vulture,[2] Yannina, Rhodes, Diyārbekīr, Qars, Ani, Van, Ispahan, Yazdikhwast, Persepolis, Shīrāz, Khotan, Turfan, the Najd, the Yaman, Abyssinia, Qayrawān, the High Atlas, Cholula, Mayaland,[3] Easter Island, or the hyper-cyclopean masonry of the Andean highlands.

Whenever the writer was racked by this unfulfilled Herodotean

farthest along the road towards Civilization—against the temptation to commit inhuman atrocities. There will always and everywhere be a point at which the mounting pressure of this temptation will burst the precarious dam within which social habit imprisons the floodwaters of Original Sin. An education in the psychology of atrocities which the writer began as an eye-witness on the Qaramursal Peninsula in the Sea of Marmara in A.D. 1921 was completed when he came back to England to hear of what the English 'Black and Tans' had been doing meanwhile in Ireland.

By this time, 'Alī Rizā Bey and the writer had become fast friends; but it was not till long afterwards that the writer was told about 'Alī Rizā Bey's conversation with Sir Denison Ross in A.D. 1916.

[1] Luke x. 37.

[2] Climbed on the 7th October, 1953, while this page was in the press.

[3] Thanks to a grant from the Rockefeller Foundation for travelling with an eye to producing a revised edition of the present work, the writer and his wife had now visited Cholula on the 20th April, 1953, and Palenque, Chichén Itzá, Uxmál, and Kabah between the 7th and the 14th May of the same year, and were planning to visit the Andean World in the autumn of A.D. 1956.

ambition to complete his oecumenical pilgrimage, he used to revive his drooping hopes by recalling an anecdote which he had once heard from the mouth of that triumphantly world-wide traveller Lord Bryce. After having explored half the surface of the globe in the course of a long life, Lord Bryce had felt one day a slight misgiving lest his advance in chronological age might hinder him from carrying out the rest of his peregrinational agenda; so he had decided, in consultation with Lady Bryce, that they would choose for the field of their next journey some region that would serve to test their physical stamina. Their choice had fallen upon Siberia; and, when they had ascertained that they could stand this physical ordeal without feeling any strain, they had been able to put their anxiety behind them and to proceed with their exploration of the remainder of the Inhabited World.[1] Lord Bryce's example became the more encouraging to the writer the nearer he approached to the end of *A Study of History*; and, midway through his sixty-fourth year, he was thanking God that a curiosity which had set sail fifty-four years ago had, so far, never found itself becalmed. Rather than be condemned to the Ancient Mariner's life-in-death, he would pray to be carried on by the divine wind of curiosity's unflagging inspiration at the risk of meeting *Kon-Tiki's* end among deadly breakers on a Raroia Reef[2] at the Ocean of History's unimaginable limit.

(III) THE WILL-O'-THE-WISP OF OMNISCIENCE

Without the inspiration of curiosity, no one can be an historian, since, without it, no one can break out of a Yin-state of infantine receptivity by setting the mind on the move and taking bearings in the Universe. No one can either become an historian till he has acquired curiosity or remain an historian if ever he loses it. Yet an inspiration which is indispensable is at the same time insufficient; for curiosity is a faculty which is valuable only as a driving force for generating higher activities. If it is allowed to spin round in a vacuum, turning nothing but its own wheels, it stultifies itself and also sterilizes the soul in which it has thus been allowed to run amok. Curiosity by itself is of no more avail than is receptivity by itself for bringing a budding mind to flower. The mind that is to blossom into an historian's mind must rise to a higher flight; and, if it allows its curiosity to set its spiritual ceiling for it, it will be guilty of a grave moral error that will prove also to have been a serious

[1] Looking up this episode, on the 23rd April, 1951, in H. A. L. Fisher's *James Bryce* (London 1927, Macmillan, 2 vols.), the writer found it duly recorded there in vol. ii, on pp. 104–6. On his retirement in A.D. 1913, when he had turned seventy-five, from being British Ambassador at Washington, Lord Bryce seized the opportunity of returning home to England via the Pacific, Japan, Manchuria, and Siberia; and, travelling via the Transsiberian Railway, he was unwilling to let slip the further opportunity of catching a glimpse of the Altai Mountains, as these lay not more than a mere four hundred miles or so off his course. Accordingly the Bryces detrained from the Transsiberian Express at Taiga, embarked on a river-boat at Tomsk, and proceeded by water down the Tom and up the Tobol via Novonikolayevsk (afterwards renamed Novosibirsk) and Barnaul to Biisk. Transferring here from boat to tarantas, they then experienced 'eight of the hardest days of travelling we have ever gone through'. Their reward was a sight of the Altai Range from the summit of the Semenski Pass on the 22nd August, 1913. The 'round-trip' had mounted up to some 1,200 miles before they re-entrained for Moscow.

[2] Read Thor Heyerdahl: *Kon-Tiki, Across the Pacific by Raft* (Chicago 1950, Rand McNally).

intellectual mistake; for, if curiosity is a Pegasus from which the historian must never dismount, this winged steed is also one which he must never allow himself to ride without a curb.

The scholar who permits his curiosity to run away with him is courting the danger of condemning his creativity to be blighted; and this was a danger to which Western scholars were peculiarly exposed by a Western educational tradition in which the goal of education that was set before the pupil's eyes by his masters was, not adult active life, but an examination. This institution, which had worked such havoc with Western intellects during the last eight centuries of Western history, had presumably been introduced by the Early Medieval fathers of the Western universities into the educational field from the theological; for the myth of a Last Judgement had been part of the Christian Church's heritage from the Osirian Church through the Zoroastrian,[1] and, while the Egyptiac fathers of the worship of Osiris had conceived of the Last Judgement as an ethical test symbolized in a weighing of the departed soul's good and bad deeds against one another in the scales of Osiris' balances, a Christian Church which had taken on board a top-heavy freight of Hellenic philosophy[2] had overlaid an Osirian ethical questionnaire in which the query was 'Good or bad?' with an Aristotelian intellectual questionnaire in which the query was 'True or false?'

When this abomination of intellectualism, standing in the place where it ought not,[3] had thus been given dominion over Western secular education as well as over Western Christian theology, the anxiety not to be found wrong by a human examiner on matters of mundane fact had come to weigh as heavily on the souls of apprentices in Western schools of higher education as if the penalty for being caught out in an intellectual mistake had been, not the mere refusal of a degree which was the severest censure that a university could inflict in reality, but the awful condemnation to eternal torment in Hell which, in Medieval and Early Modern Western Christian belief, was the inexorable retribution for the holding of unorthodox tenets in the sphere of theology.

In Western educational circles a fear of intellectual damnation that had thus originally been inspired by an analogy taken from current religious ideas had survived when, in a Late Modern chapter of Western history, the belief that eternal damnation after death was the penalty for theological error had gradually ceased to haunt Western minds and oppress Western spirits. As, in the course of this age, the quantity of mundane information at the disposal of Western examiners for use as ammunition in their intellectual warfare with Western examinees came to increase by geometrical progression, Western educational examinations came to be the nightmare that Western theological inquisitions had once been; and the worst of their effects was the posthumous one; for even an alumnus who had passed with honours all the ordeals that his *alma mater* had known how to inflict upon him was apt to emerge from his education haunted by an abiding subconscious fear of being weighed in an imaginary future examiner's

[1] See V. vi. 34.
[2] See VII. vii. 465–506.
[3] Dan. xi. 31 and xii. 11; Matt. xxiv. 15; Mark xiii. 14; Luke xxi. 20.

balances and found wanting,[1] and such victims of an intimidating Western examinational system of education would need the intervention of God's grace to save them from spending the rest of their lives, not in living and acting and making practical use of what they had learned, but in still anxiously preparing for an unseen final examination lying in wait to confound their disembodied souls after they had carried their life-long accumulation of learning with them into the grave.

This pursuit of the will-o'-the-wisp of omniscience convicts its addicts of a moral error in two degrees. In ignoring the truth that the only legitimate purpose of learning is to make something of it, within the learner's lifetime, that can become part of Mankind's common stock of useful knowledge, the scholar-sinner betrays a lack of sociality; in ignoring the further truth—which is just as true on the intellectual plane of human activity as on any other—that completeness and perfection are unattainable by human souls in This World, he betrays a lack of humility; and the second of these two sins, which is the graver, is also the more insidious; for the scholar's intellectual hybris masquerades as humility itself. A scholar is proving himself guilty of a subconscious hypocrisy to which he is wilfully shutting his mind's eye when he pleads guilty of ignorance and protests that his conscience will not permit him to publish, write, or even say anything on his subject until he has mastered the last jot and tittle of the information available up to date. This profession of humility is a camouflage for the three deadly sins of Satanic pride, undutiful negligence, and culpable sloth.

The professedly humble-minded scholar stands convicted of pride because the intellectual standard which he is confessing his failure to attain so far is the omniscience of Almighty God and not the partial and relative knowledge which is the most that can actually be compassed in human life by any mind which, like the scholar's mind, is a mortal human being's; and this apology of his for being a little lower intellectually than his Creator therefore betrays a mood that is the antithesis of modesty. The scholar-hypocrite also stands convicted of negligence, because a scholar's proper study is the modest but useful task of producing, within the brief span of time that is the inexorable limit of the longest human life, some provisional addition to human understanding which this intellectual worker bee's contemporaries and successors can use, criticize, improve, and eventually discard in favour of other slightly closer provisional approximations to an ineffable divine truth. The transient scholar of the day would have done his intellectual duty and have won his spiritual crown if, in passing through This World, he had made it his business, following the example of the first two servants in the parable of the talents,[2] to contribute one fresh thimbleful of water to the great and growing stream of collective human knowledge.[3]

In hiding the talent entrusted to him in the earth,[4] or keeping it laid

[1] Dan. v. 27.
[2] Matt. xxv. 14–30; Luke xix. 12–26.
[3] 'The thought once worked out to the point of written record is complete, its work done. It is a fragment, a grain, added to the thought of the Universe, a grain of sand added to the ever-growing edifice of God.'—Walter Leaf, quoted by Charlotte M. Leaf in *Walter Leaf* (London 1932, John Murray), p. 167.
[4] Matt. xxv. 25.

up in a napkin,[1] he has shown himself to be an unprofitable servant.[2] He has left open merely the question whether the motive of his misdemeanour was disaffection or sloth;[3] and the charge of slothfulness is one from which he cannot clear himself by filing evidence to prove that he has sat at work for six and a half days out of every week and for ten and a half hours out of every day; for the unprofitable scholar's dreaded post-mortem examiner will not fail to parry this plea by asking the prisoner at the bar what kind of work his has been; and every scholar knows that he is under constant temptation to postpone or evade the ordeal of doing creative work on any plausible excuse, because this kind of intellectual work, which is the only kind that has any intrinsic and ultimate value, is also the kind that exacts the most excruciating and most repugnant intellectual travail. The inborn spiritual frailty which tempts every human being at all times to renounce his birthright of sharing in the bliss of creation for the sake of escaping its pangs tempts the scholar at his desk to go on reading, so long as he can find any excuse for this, instead of taking up his pen to write, and then, when that excuse fails him, to write, not those painfully-begotten wingèd words that are required in order to convey one mind's thoughts to another mind, but a string of facilely pedestrian entries on the cards of a bibliographical index. This perpetual human proneness to take the easier option is as natural, but also as culpable, in the scholar as it is in other men.

The intellectual mistake inherent in the pursuit of omniscience is, like the moral error, a multiple one; and the beginning of evils here is a mistaken identification of innumerability with infinity. It is true that human souls have an inborn need to put themselves in tune with the Infinite on the intellectual plane as on every other; but, on this plane, as on the rest, the only way in which a communion with the Creator is ever attainable by the creature is, 'like a light caught from a leaping flame',[4] through a personal encounter. Omniscience, as Faust's insatiable mind discovered to its discomfiture, cannot be attained by adding item to item, art to art, and science to science in an infinite regress.

> Habe nun, ach! Philosophie,
> Juristerei und Medizin,
> Und leider auch Theologie!
> Durchaus studiert, mit heissem Bemühn.
> Da steh' ich nun, ich armer Tor!
> Und bin so klug als wie zuvor . . .
> Und sehe dass wir nichts wissen können!
> Das will mir schier das Herz verbrennen.[5]

Faust has, in fact, as we have noticed in an earlier context,[6] merely succeeded in imprisoning himself in the immobility of a Yin-state. Yet in Goethe's tragedy the hero is deemed to have succeeded in his misguided intellectual endeavour at least to the extent of acquiring all the information accessible to any scholar in his ephemeral time and transient place. Here, however, Goethe has allowed himself a poetic licence; for,

[1] Luke xix. 20. [2] Matt. xxv. 30. [3] Matt. xxv. 26.
[4] Plato's Letters, No. 7, 341 B–E, quoted in III. iii. 245.
[5] Goethe: *Faust*, ll. 354–9 and 364–5. [6] In II. i. 276.

as the present writer learnt at an early age from his Mother, Dante had been the last man in Western history who had actually mastered all the Western lore of his day; and even the sixteenth-century historical prototype of Goethe's Faustian projection of his own eighteenth-century self had been born too late to emulate Dante's achievement in real sixteenth-century life.[1]

Since Dante's time, Western scholars had been seeking to solve a self-imposed insoluble problem by electing to 'know more and more about less and less'; but this procedure had been merely more perverse than a Goethean Faust's without having been, in truth, more practical; for, as fast as each Western scholar was reducing the diameter of his boring in the hope of being able still to drill deep enough to strike oil, an advancing Western science was demonstrating that infinitesimal quanta were as infinitely complex as quanta of an infinite positive immensity; and, even if the pursuit of infinitesimals had proved to be less chimerical than the pursuit of infinite magnitudes, the academic huntsmen could have made nothing of their captured intellectual quarry; since, as we ascertained in the opening chapter of this Study,[2] it is impossible for human minds to emulate an eternal-instantaneous divine comprehension of an infinite-infinitesimal Here-Now by piecing together scraps of information, produced by a division of intellectual labour, in an intellectual assembly plant constructed on the analogy of a post-industrial Western factory. To an historian's eye the last judgement on the mania for encyclopaedism of both the microscopic and the telescopic variety had been pronounced by History herself; for this mistaken intellectual ideal had been apt to be the last intellectual folly to be abandoned by a senile civilization *in extremis* and the first to be abandoned by an infantile civilization[3] as soon as the time had come for it to put away childish things.[4]

The present writer—to illustrate this point, too, *ad hominem*—had once gone through the stultifying experience of taking this wrong intellectual turning.

The writer had first been made aware of the choice in his eighteenth year, when, in December 1906, he had been staying with a pair of distinguished scholars in the persons of his uncle Paget Toynbee (*vivebat* A.D. 1855–1932), the author of *A Dictionary of Proper names and Notable Matters in the Works of Dante*,[5] and his aunt Helen Toynbee (*vivebat* A.D. 1868–1910),[6] the editor of Horace Walpole's letters. At the close of an agreeable and stimulating visit, in which the boy had unselfconsciously disclosed historical interests embracing the Assyrians, the Fourth Crusade, and whatnot, he was chilled by a piece of parting advice which his uncle gave him out of the kindness of his heart. 'Your Aunt Nellie and I',

[1] The historical Dr. Faust is believed to have lived *circa* A.D. 1480–1540.

[2] In I. i. 1–8.

[3] Encyclopaedism was, as we have noticed in X. ix. 53–57, a weakness of the Sinic, as well as the Hellenic, Civilization in its last phase; and, like the Hellenic again, the Sinic Civilization bequeathed this weakness to its successors. This heritage of encyclopaedism perhaps partly accounts for the subsequent emergence of a system of education by examination in the Far Eastern and in the Western World alike; but the latter-day Far Eastern examinees were at least less unfortunate than their Western fellow-victims in being exempt from the terror imported into an intellectual ordeal by the Zoroastro-Osirian myth of a Last Judgement.

[4] 1 Cor. xiii. 11.

[5] Oxford 1898, Clarendon Press.

[6] *Née* Helen Wrigley, of Bury, Lancs.

the Dante scholar had announced, 'have come to the conclusion that you have been dispersing your interests too widely, and our advice to you is to make your choice of some single subject and to concentrate hereafter on that.' In A.D. 1952 the writer had a still freshly vivid recollection of his own instantaneous conviction that this advice was bad, and of his likewise instantaneous decision not to follow it; and his uncle subsequently gave him reason in retrospect by amiably sacrificing his own pernicious intellectual principles on the altar of personal affection when his wife's literary work was cut short by her premature death. From that day onwards, her loving survivor took her Walpole, as well as his Alighieri, under his wing in order to complete her edition of the letters as a labour of love.[1] Meanwhile, his nephew was heading, in spite of his good resolution at the end of the year A.D. 1906, towards the intellectual blind alley from which the Dante scholar was to be harshly extricated in A.D. 1910 by a tragic event in his personal life.

During eleven years of adolescence, from the autumn of A.D. 1900 to the summer of A.D. 1911, the present writer was continuously at the stretch in the intellectual hurdle-race of alternately preparing for and sitting for examinations; and the cumulative demoralizing effect of this ordeal slowly but surely undermined his resolve never to allow himself to be corralled in a specialist's pound. As late as his last undergraduate academic year A.D. 1910–11, he was still wholesomely shocked to find the dismal orthodox cult of specialization capturing an older contemporary of his, G. L. Cheesman, who at school had gone out of his way to stimulate his junior's interest in the Late Roman Empire after having noticed that the younger boy was reading Hodgkin's *Italy and Her Invaders*.[2]

With these exhilarating memories of the catholicity of his older friend's intellectual interests still fresh in his mind, the writer, one day at Oxford, had come straight to Cheesman's rooms in New College (where Cheesman was then a tutorial fellow, teaching Roman history) from a meeting in Dr. F. W. Bussell's rooms at Brasenose which this mature scholar had convened in the hope of generating in Oxford a wave of interest in Byzantine studies. On separating, we had agreed to widen our circle by recruiting brother enthusiasts, and the writer had taken it for granted that his schoolfellow at New College would be as enthusiastic

[1] Paget Toynbee was handsomely rewarded for an unprofessional human piety that had taken for its counsellor an unerring heart instead of a fallible head. For one thing, he became almost as highly distinguished in the field of scholarship bequeathed to him by his wife as he had long since been in his own field. But his most gratifying reward was that, when he had made room in his quiver for Horace Walpole's works beside Dante's, he found himself armed with an unfailing store of apt quotations. It was hardly possible for there to be any event in the news which a scholar who had thus made himself a double *hāfiz* could not illustrate by a passage from one or other of the two authors whose works this intellectual archer now knew by heart. On the slightest provocation he would shoot a letter, containing a quotation from either Walpole or Dante, at the editor of *The Times*; and, as the quotation was always attractively felicitous and the covering letter always discreetly short, the literary arrow usually went home and, in the course of years, the deft archer scored a prodigious tale of hits. Thus, thanks to his unprofessional addition of a second string to his academic bow, Paget Toynbee succeeded in lodging in the columns of *The Times* a quantity of letters that can hardly have been equalled by any of his contemporaries.

[2] Hodgkin, Thomas: *Italy and Her Invaders* (Oxford 1892–9, Clarendon Press, 8 vols. in 9 parts).

over Dr. Bussell's project as he was himself. To his surprise and discomfiture, his confident approach was met by his friend with a vehement refusal that would have been becoming in a conscientious novice, bent on qualifying for admission to a rigorous monastic order, if Mephistopheles had approached him with some tempting alternative proposition. The apprentice tutor hastily explained that his manifest duty, now that he had obtained his appointment as a don, was to concentrate on the task of mastering the particular subject for the teaching of which he had made himself responsible to his college. Now that he had found the confines of his intellectual province, 'pastures new'[1] were henceforward out of bounds for him. His refusal to indulge his personal interest in Byzantium any further was decisive,[2] and his baffled tempter went away crestfallen yet unshaken in his own intellectual convictions by his admired friend's distressing lapse from intellectual grace.

After having been appointed in his turn, in the summer term of A.D. 1911, to a tutorial fellowship in Greek and Roman history at Balliol, and having subsequently taken his final academic examination in the School of *Litterae Humaniores*, the writer still saw light enough to lead him to make a resolve never to sit for any further academic examination in his life, and this was a vow which he had faithfully kept at any rate till his sixty-second birthday, on which he was writing these words. Yet the morrow of his final examination was the moment of his own fall; for the shades of the examinational prison house in which he had been doing hard labour for eleven years past now closed on him with the swift downrush of a tropical night. It was an idle gesture to foreswear further examinations in real life at a moment when he was capitulating to the intimidating spectral presence of an imaginary examiner post mortem.

After having spent two and a half years in preparing himself for being examined by fellow mortals in the summer term of A.D. 1911 in the history of the Hellenic World between 776 and 404 B.C., the writer proceeded to spend the ensuing long vacation on reading all the extant sources for the period following, and he had ploughed his way on through these from the end of the Great Atheno-Peloponnesian War to the death of Alexander the Great when he was mercifully interrupted by the advent of the day on which he was to start on a grand tour of Paris, Rome, and Athens as a prelude to returning to Oxford as a don in the autumn of A.D. 1912. From the moment when he found himself *en voyage*, an inborn passion for making a countryside his own by walking over it happily diverted him from spending more than a minimum of his travelling time in museums and libraries, reading books that would be accessible to him in England and poring over *objets d'art* which he could continue to study elsewhere in casts and photographs. He had the wit to realize that

[1] Milton: *Lycidas*, l. 193.

[2] How much longer G. L. Cheesman would have persisted in exploring his blind alley could never be known, since, some four years later, in A.D. 1915, he was killed on landing on the Gallipoli Peninsula. The present writer's personal belief is that, had he lived, he would have become the greatest Roman historian in his generation; and this belief is founded on the further belief that, possessing the magnificently inquisitive mind that he did possess, this potentially great scholar would soon have repented of his unfortunate resolution to try to make himself a Roman historian by the *via negativa* of refusing ever to be anything more than that.

the landscape of the Hellenic World was the spectacle which he must make sure of seeing with his own eyes because this was the field in which there was no substitute for autopsy; but, even then, he perversely strove at first to exclude from his contracting field of vision every scene that was not either Hellenic or Minoan.

It was through the grace of God, and not thanks to any native common sense, that other worlds did impinge upon the academic pilgrim's consciousness. In Paris during the week running from the 22nd to the 28th September, 1911, the reverberations of the Agadir Crisis did just patter, like spent bullets, against his ear-drums through the archaic iron lattice-work of the Eiffel Tower. *En retour* to Rome on the evening of the 8th November, 1911, from an expedition to visit the Etruscan tombs at Cerveteri and Corneto, the young antiquarian did ascertain that his fellow-passengers in the train were Neapolitan conscripts, and did notice, as the train passed through Civitâ Vecchia, droves of other young Italian soldiers, with a look of unenthusiastic resignation on their faces, in the act of embarking for the theatre of war in Tripolitania and Cyrenaica. At Brindisi on the 18th November, 1911, he had to transfer to a Greek steamer from the Italian one on which his passage to Patras had been booked, because the Italian boat was shy of running the gauntlet of an enemy Turkish coast between Acroceraunus and Préveza; and during the next eight months, passing his evenings in cafés in Greek villages, he heard, for the first time in his life, 'the foreign policy of Sir Edward Grey' being discussed, and the question whether 'the war' would break out this spring or next being canvassed by peasants and shepherds in zestful conversation with brothers and cousins just back home, with gold five-dollar pieces and napoleons in their wallets, from following the gainful occupations of shining shoes in Kansas City or selling fruit in Omaha. Meanwhile, in the landscapes of Continental Greece and Crete, Medieval French castles and Early Modern Venetian fortresses were competing for his attention with Hellenic temples and with Minoan palaces.

Twice, on that antiquarian tour, the Oxford don-elect was arrested as a Turkish spy, first on the evening of the 16th November, 1911, on the last lap of a day's march from Terracina to Formia, by an Italian carabiniere,[1] and then again, on the 21st July, 1912, by a Greek military patrol.[2] At Cattaro and Ragusa in August 1912 he found the streets thronged with Austro-Hungarian troops in a picturesque variety of old-fashioned uniforms reminiscent of the revolutionary year A.D. 1848. At

[1] On this occasion, the suspect was able to clear himself by showing a card with 'Balliol College, Oxford' engraved on it. 'Ah! Collegio! Dunque non siete Turco', reasoned the intelligent Italian security officer, and straightway left the suspicious-looking traveller in peace. Forty years later, in A.D. 1952, the carabiniere would, of course, no longer have been justified in acting on an *a priori* assumption that 'Turk' and 'college' were incompatible ideas.

[2] On this second occasion, he was arrested on the reasonable charge that he had walked across the perilously vulnerable railway viaduct over the gorge of the River Asopus at Elefterokhóri, where the sole railway running from Athens to the Graeco-Turkish frontier leaped across a chasm to come to earth again along the eastern flank of the Hellenic citadel of Trachis. This charge was supported by the less convincing argument that the trespasser must be a foreign military spy because he was wearing insignia in the shape of a military water-bottle that was not of the pattern affected by the Greek Army.

Trieste he gazed at the red fezes of a Bosniak regiment in garrison in the castello, and listened to an old Triestino explaining in Italian to a little boy that these were now loyal soldiers of the Emperor-King, though their fathers had made it hot for the old man and his comrades in A.D. 1878, when they had been serving in the expeditionary force that had been sent by the Imperial-Royal Government to occupy Bosnia in that year. Next day, in his through-carriage from Trieste to Flushing, he noticed quantities of German soldiers drilling in green fields sandwiched between greener hop-gardens in Bavaria, without registering any sharper impression from this ominous sight than he had received, eleven months earlier, from the headlines displaying the latest news from Agadir in special editions of the Parisian Press. He had no sooner reached his journey's end at Southwold than, finding himself in hospital with dysentery contracted through drinking treacherously clear running water from a stream between the mouth of the River Eurotas and the town of Yýthion, he plunged back into the reading that he had had to interrupt in the previous September. Before he was convalescent he had finished reading Strabo's *Geographica* and had started reading Pausanias' *A Personally Conducted Tour of Hellas*; and, before he had finished with Pausanias during his first term at Oxford as a don, he had begun to suffer acutely from the nemesis that is the penalty for the quest of omniscience within however narrowly restricted an intellectual allotment.

A scholar in quest of intellectual omniscience is, indeed, courting the same nemesis as a soul in quest of spiritual perfection. Each successive advance that he makes towards achieving his ideal sends his standard soaring higher in a geometrical progression that leaves his arithmetically progressing attainments ever farther behind. Just as the aspirant to sainthood is the more crushingly self-convicted of sin each time that he attains a yet loftier spiritual altitude above the ceiling of ordinary mortals, so the aspirant to omniscience is the more crushingly convicted of ignorance each time that he makes a fresh addition to an already superhuman stock of knowledge. In both careers the gap between aim and achievement thus grows only the wider the greater the achievement comes to be; and the nemesis of this inevitable progressive defeat, in a race which a finite Human Nature has condemned itself in advance to lose by impiously pitting itself against God's infinity, is a moral regress from frustration through disillusionment into cynicism.

After having tasted for himself the pains of this unprofitable pursuit of an hallucination, the present writer was liberated from the spell of an imaginary implacable post-mortem examiner by an intellectual event in his own *for intérieur* that had nothing to do with the wars and rumours of wars[1] which, from the outbreak of the First Balkan War on the 17th October, 1912, to the outbreak of the First World War on the 1st August, 1914,[2] were bearing down upon the Western World with a roar that was growing louder as fast as the thunder of an approaching express train.

In the summer of A.D. 1911, during his intensive course of reading

[1] Matt. xxiv. 6; Mark xiii. 7; Luke xxi. 9.

[2] Germany was at war with Russia by that date. Great Britain did not find herself at war with Germany till the 4th.

the original Greek sources for the history of the Hellenic World in the fourth century B.C., the writer's conscience had been troubled at intervals by finding himself occasionally falling short of his daily stint of reading because his mind had been insisting upon breaking with its habit of acquiring additional information in order to allow itself to begin putting two and two together. Pieces of information about the organization and numbers of the Lacedaemonian Army, at divers dates in the fourth century, which were presented by Xenophon incidentally in the course of his narrative, confirmed a dissatisfaction that had been implanted in the writer's mind, during his previous reading for the School of *Litterae Humaniores*, by Thucydides' presentation of the Lacedaemonian order of battle at Mantinea in 418 B.C.[1] What was more, the data supplied by Xenophon seemed to provide clues for tracing Thucydides' mistake—if he had indeed made a mistake—to its source and for penetrating, behind this error, to the truth. The question at issue was the ratio, at divers dates, between the respective strengths of the Spartiate contingent in the Lacedaemonian Army and the Perioecic contingents; this question turned, in the last analysis, upon the ratio between the respective areas of the arable land in the home territory of Sparta herself and in the aggregate of the territories of the Perioecic city-states in the Lacedaemonian dominions within their frontiers at the time; and this was a question, raised by reading, which could be settled only by autopsy.

In consequence, when, a few months later, the writer found himself in Greece, the historical inquiry which had already come into action in his mind conspired with the alluring beauty of the landscape in Messenia and Laconia to lead him into an inquisitive reconnaissance of the Perioecic states and their domains;[2] and this deliberate autopsy in A.D. 1912 reinforced the undesigned effect of his reading in A.D. 1911. The field work and the book work, between them, activated his mind to a degree at which a salutary impulse to take action gained the upper hand in A.D. 1913 over an insatiable craving to add still further to a hoard of inert knowledge. In that year he wrote and published an article on 'The Growth of Sparta';[3] and he had not had time to relapse into another debauch of aimless reading before the outbreak of the First World War compelled him to cease work on a history of the Hellenic World,

[1] See Thucydides: *A History of the Great Atheno-Peloponnesian War*, Book V, chaps. 64–74.

[2] In *ci-devant* Lacedaemonian territory the writer's itineraries in A.D. 1912 were as follows (the dates being those of nights passed at the places with which the dates are here coupled):

Kalamáta (by train from Athens) 20th February, Koron 21st, Navarino (via Módhon) 22nd, Philiatrá 23rd, Olympia (via Arkadhiá, *alias* 'Kyparissía') 24th.

Astros (by boat from Ermióni, via Pétses and Lenídhi) 15th April, Arákhova 16th, Sparta (via Sellasía) 17th–19th; Yeráki 20th, Moláous 21st, Neápolis-on-Malea 22nd, Monemvasía 23rd, Hiéraka (via the fjord) 24th, Káto Vezáni 25th, Ýýthion 26th–27th, Pýrghos-in-Máni 28th, Páliros-on-Taenarum 29th, Kótronas-in-Máni 30th, Tsímova-in-Máni ('Areópolis') 1st May, Liméni-in-Máni 2nd, Kalamáta 3rd, from Kalamáta by train to Athens 4th.

The kháni of Khelmós (from Sinán, *alias* 'Meghalópolis') 19th May, Sparta 20th–22nd, Trýpi (via Mistrá) 23rd, Kalamáta 24th, Mavrommáti (via Ithômê) 25th, Pávlitsa (Phigaleia) (via Sulimá) 26th.

[3] See *The Journal of Hellenic Studies*, vol. xxxiii (London 1913, Macmillan), pp. 246–75.

which he had just started to write for the *Home University Library*,[1] and impelled him to write and publish a book on the redrawing of the political map of the World in a forthcoming peace-settlement.[2] After that, the financial pressure of rising prices on the budget for a growing family completed his education in intellectual action by driving him into journalism as fuel for 'pot-boiling'. He had been saved so as by fire,[3] and he had found this salvation by making the simple discovery that his curiosity had been given to him, not in order to be turned loose to eat its head off on the pastures of a boundless prairie, but in order to be harnessed and put to work. When once he had embarked on a literary enterprise with a plan that determined its shape and with a shape that delimited its contents, he had found an intellectual talisman that had power to ban the demonic subconscious psychic force which had been tormenting him so long as he had been allowing himself to remain its slave instead of insisting upon making himself its master. In Hellenic language, he had succeeded in setting a limit (πέρας) to a previously unlimited chaos (τὸ ἄπειρον) which Hellenic minds had rightly abominated because they had correctly discerned that, at any moment, it might flood in upon them and overwhelm them.

By A.D. 1952, thirty-seven years and more after this decisive turn in the course of his intellectual life in A.D. 1913–15, the writer had long since worked out for himself an intellectual regimen that was the inverse of the course that he had followed in A.D. 1909–13. He had accustomed himself since then to making writing, not reading, the first charge on his time and energy. The reading and travelling that were requisite preparations for this writing had been left to fend for themselves; but at the same time the writer had learnt not to be so improvident as ever to give himself an excuse for suspending the hard labour of intellectual creation in order to indulge in the softer options of travelling and reading through having permitted himself to neglect to make the necessary intellectual preparations betimes. He had formed a habit of prompting himself to gather the required information a sufficient number of months or years ahead of the date at which he expected to reach the corresponding points in his agenda to ensure that the continuous flow of writing should never have to be checked.

In thus giving his intellectual energy an ever-open vent in action, this adult regimen had liberated him from the painful tyranny of a curiosity which, before it had been thus bitted and bridled, had been apt to be the more insatiable in its demands the more lavishly he had indulged it. Since A.D. 1916 he had been practising the trick of blunting the edge of any residual craving by keeping an amateur bibliographical card index of published works in the field of History interpreted in the broadest sense; but he had always taken care to confine this side-line of his intellectual activity within limits very far short of any professional pretension to exhaustiveness; for the appalling spectacle of the debauchery of potentially creative minds had soon taught him that a collector's mania to inscribe *ad libitum* dates, titles, and names of authors and publishers on

[1] See p. 22, above.
[2] *Nationality and the War* (London 1915, Dent).
[3] 1 Cor. iii. 15.

cards might be no less sterilizing than the bookworm's hunger to devour *ad libitum* the pages between the covers. While thus holding himself on the alert to keep his curiosity in order, the writer took care, however, not to put it to death, for that would have been as fatal a step in real life as the killing, in the fairy story, of the goose that laid the golden eggs. The proper course with curiosity is, not to kill the precious bird, but to clip its wings in order to make sure that it shall not fly away with its possessor. Curiosity is given to the mind to serve it as a bow serves a bow-string. The bow acquires the power to shoot only if and when the string bends it; and the mind must handle its curiosity as imperiously as the bow is handled by the string. It must insist on being the possessor, not the possessed, if its potentialities for creative work are to be realized; for the price of continuous creation is a perpetual tension.

The writer owed his narrow escape from intellectual perdition on the morrow of his completion of a standard Western course of education-by-examination to the happy accident of stumbling ingenuously upon a truth that might have been dismissed as a truism if so many once intellectually promising Western minds had not notoriously overlooked it to their undoing. This truth which is so obvious yet is so frequently ignored by scholars is the truth that Life is Action. A life which does not go into action is a failure; and this is just as true of a prophet's, a poet's, or a scholar's life as it is true of the life of 'a man of action' in the conventionally limited popular usage of the term. When Faust revolted against his servitude to the cult of a barren omniscience, the rebel scholar's thirst for action was salutary (though he need not consequently have fallen into the crude error of fancying that the only effective remedy for his academic complaint was to let Mephistopheles inoculate him with a *rabies Teutonica*).

> Geschrieben steht: 'Im Anfang war das Wort!'
> Hier stock' ich schon! Wer hilft mir weiter fort? . . .
> Mir hilft der Geist! Auf einmal seh' ich Rat
> Und schreibe getrost: 'Im Anfang war die Tat!'[1]

On a scholar's tombstone the epitaph *obiit rê infectâ* is just as damning as it is on a business man's, a statesman's, or a soldier's.

Why is it, then, that scholars are apt to be so much less alive to this fundamental common law of Man's calling than the general run of 'men of action' in the conventionally limited sense? The conventional limitation of the meaning of the phrase gives us a clue. Why has a phobia against taking action become the scholar's distinctive occupational disease? Perhaps the answer is to be found in the fact that action is a genus of divers species which have different terms and ranges because they operate in different media.

This was the discovery of the Hellenic philosopher who first drew a distinction between the life of longer-range activity (ὁ θεωρητικὸς βίος) and the life of shorter-range activity (ὁ πρακτικὸς βίος); but Plato, at any rate, never intended to convey the false suggestion—subsequently crystallized in a latter-day Western usage of the derivative words 'theory'

[1] Goethe: *Faust*, ll. 1224–5 and 1236–7.

and 'practice'—that the antithesis between two different kinds of action was really an antithesis between action and inactivity. Plato was alert to warn insouciant candidates for initiation into his philosophy that 'the sole way of acquiring it' was 'by strenuous intellectual communion';[1] and Elijah, when he heard the still small voice after the fire and the earthquake and the wind, was instantaneously and indubitably aware that he was now in the immediate presence of the spiritual Power that was the source of all the action in the Universe.[2] The 'great and strong wind' that 'rent the mountains and brake in pieces the rocks before the Lord' had come and gone, in advance of its Maker and Master, in order to put Elijah's prophetic intuition to the test. Elijah had to show, by waiting on the Lord, his recognition that the blustering physical force was merely one of God's mighty works, not Almighty God Himself, before he could hear God's voice and receive His commands. Elijah knew, as Lao-tse knew,[3] that the stillness of the Fount of Life, Wu Wei, is in truth a plenitude of activity which looks inert to uninitiated human eyes only because, being human, they are not born to see the Absolute as it really is.

Prophets, poets, and scholars are chosen vessels who have been called by their Creator to take human action of an etherial kind that is perhaps less unlike God's own action than any other kind that Human Nature can compass; and in this, as in every other, form of encounter between God and one of His creatures an ordeal is the price of a privilege; for the truth that Life is Action is as hard a saying for the tender-minded follower of a higher spiritual calling as it is an obvious platitude for the man of action who has been called to act on spiritually lower levels. Elijah himself had to be called to order by the Word of the Lord from a culpable truancy prompted by a despair that had been the nemesis of a loss of faith.[4] But this sin of omission, which is the besetting sin of prophets, poets, and scholars, does not beset business men or fighting men. When Hector and Ajax, striving with one another in physical combat on the Plain of Troy,[5] had each hurled his spear at his adversary without putting him out of action, neither warrior was tempted to stand at ease, since neither needed to be warned that if he did so he would instantly lose his life through having his throat cut by his adversary's sword. These warriors' sense of action was so keen that, without pausing to lose time in drawing their swords, they picked up the boulders at their feet and hurled these at one another; and, when these bolts, too, had been shot without producing a military decision, the liaison officers did not find themselves required to push the champions into continuing the struggle; on the contrary, all their tact had to be brought into play in order to induce Ajax and Hector to keep their swords in their scabbards and break off the action for that night at least.

Hector and Ajax did not need to be told that Life is either action or failure; but these were warriors equipped for hand-to-hand fighting with weapons that had no sooner been discharged than they registered

[1] Plato's letters, No. 7, 341 B–E, quoted in III. iii. 245.
[2] 1 Kings xix. 11–13.
[3] See III, iii. 187.
[4] 1 Kings xix. 1–18.
[5] *Iliad*: Book VII, ll. 244–312.

their hit or miss at a point-blank range at which their objective was in full view. By contrast, the prophet's, poet's, and scholar's spiritual armament resembles an archer's who is aiming at a target which is too far distant to be visible.

> I shot an arrow into the air,
> It fell to earth, I knew not where;
> For, so swiftly it flew, the sight
> Could not follow it in its flight.
>
> I breathed a song into the air,
> It fell to earth, I knew not where;
> For who has sight so keen and strong,
> That it can follow the flight of song?
>
> Long, long afterward, in an oak
> I found the arrow, still unbroke;
> And the song, from beginning to end,
> I found again in the heart of a friend.[1]

'Cast thy bread upon the waters, for thou shalt find it after many days.'[2] Ajax or Hector could not delude himself into imagining that his target, standing there before his eyes within a stone's throw, could ever be hit by his stone if he himself were to forbear to take the necessary action of picking the stone up and hurling it. The ineptitude of expecting inaction to produce an unperformed action's effect is the occupational folly of the archer whose target is out of sight or of the speculator whose return on his outlay lies hidden in a future beyond his mental horizon.

In thus outranging 'practical' action in the dimensions of both Space and Time, spiritual action shows itself to be the more godlike of the two kinds. An Agamemnon who has lived his brief physical life in the lime-light owes his literary immortality to a poet who has died in obscurity. The Homeric poems continue to move men's hearts and kindle their imaginations for ages after the ephemeral empire of Mycenae has ceased to have any perceptible effect on the political surface of life; and the long file of strong men armed who, before Agamemnon, must have stalked across the stage of History has passed into oblivion because these predecessors of Homer's hero failed to find a poet to make them famous.[3] Yet, just because Human Nature's spiritual activities have this divine power of producing effects at distances thousands of miles and years away from the human agent's own birthplace and lifetime, souls that have been called to these spiritual vocations are prone to stultify themselves, and to make failures of their lives, by overlooking the crucial difference between long-range action and inactivity—as if, just because the archer's target happens to be out of sight, it were any more feasible for him to hit it without ever shooting an arrow than it would be

[1] Longfellow: *The Arrow and the Song.*

[2] Eccl. xi. 1.

[3] Horace: *Carmina*, Book IV, Ode ix, ll. 25–28. Homer's continuing dominion over the imagination of Posterity was still so potent in a nineteenth-century Western World that, when Heinrich Schliemann was at last ruefully convinced by the arguments of his expert advisers that the royal bones which he had disinterred at Mycenae were those of *fortes ante Agamemnona*, not those of the Homeric heretoga and his contemporaries, he was disgusted. ' "What?" he exclaimed on one occasion. "So this is not Agamemnon's body, these are not his ornaments? All right, let's call him Schulze".'—Ludwig, E.: *Schliemann of Troy* (London 1931, Putnam), pp. 296–7.

for the swordsman to smite his adversary in hand-to-hand combat without ever striking a blow.

If Acton's calling,[1] no less than Ajax's, is thus in truth subject to an inexorable law that Human Life is either action or failure, then we must write off the scholar's cherished boasts as vapourings of an intellectual *miles gloriosus* who, in uttering them, is convicting himself of incompetence in the profession that he has chosen. When the devout disciples of Robert Browning's dead grammarian[2] sing of their master that he 'sucked at the flagon', we shall agree with them that he was 'soul-hydroptic', but we shall dispute their claim that his thirst was 'sacred'. When they ask 'How should Spring take note Winter would follow?' we shall reply that human souls are distinguished from 'the beasts that perish'[3] precisely by a God-given power to 'look before and after'.[4] When they quote his exclamation 'Let me know all! Prate not of most or least', we shall interpret this as either a childish petition to God or an impious emulation of His Almightiness. When they comment

> Others mistrust and say 'But Time escapes:
> Live now or never!'
> He said 'What's Time? Leave now for dogs and apes!
> 'Man has Forever',

we shall reply that Time is the medium in which God has ordained that Man shall live and work in This World, *vitaque mancipio nulli datur, omnibus usu.*[5] 'Eschew a line of study in which the work done dies together with the worker.'[6]

Man does not have 'Forever'—God's Eternal Now—in mortal human life. The grammarian's desperate assertion is not even true of the Collective Mankind that accumulates, in the course of successive generations, an increasing corporate heritage of Science and Technology; for even this human coral reef would never have come into existence if each of the innumerable animalculae that have co-operated to build it up had not performed the positive individual act, within its own brief lifetime and narrow field of operations, of mixing and carrying a minute contribution of mortar in its tiny hod. The collective achievements of Science and Technology do not accomplish themselves automatically any more than the unique achievements of Poetry and Prophecy. Like these, they owe their existence to creative acts of individual souls who have had the sense and grace to take action under the conditions laid down for human beings in This Life by their Creator. We therefore shall refuse to call a homunculus who has kept his talent laid up in a napkin[7] a 'high man' for missing a unit through aiming at a million; for, if it is the truth that he has 'a great thing to pursue', he has no business to die ere

[1] Acton's incapacity for taking intellectual action, and the sterilizing effect of this psychic inhibition upon that great Modern Western historian's intellectual career, have been noticed in I. i. 46–47.

[2] Browning, R.: *A Grammarian's Funeral shortly after the Revival of Learning in Europe.*

[3] Psalm xlix. 12 and 20.

[4] Shelley: *To a Skylark,* stanza 18.

[5] Lucretius: *De Rerum Naturâ,* Book III, l. 971.

[6] 'Fuggi quello studio del quale la resultante opera more insieme coll' operante d'essa'—Leonardo da Vinci, in *The Literary Works of Leonardo da Vinci,* compiled and edited from the original MSS. by J. P. Richter, 2nd ed. (Oxford 1939, University Press, 2 vols.), vol. ii, p. 244, No. 1169.

[7] Luke xix. 20.

he knows it. Even if we were to concede (as we do not) that the grammarian's conduct is *magnifique*, we should be bound, none the less, to damn it by pronouncing that *ce n'est pas la guerre*;[1] for it is not

> God's task [*sic*] to make the Heavenly period
> Perfect the Earthen.

It is Man's task to execute, within the time that God allots to him on Earth, a human mission to do God's will by working for the coming of God's Kingdom in Earth as it is in Heaven; and, when a man irresponsibly throws back on God the task that God has set him in This Life, we cannot agree with the grammarian's disciples in their confident assumption that God 'loves the burthen'. Say, rather, God loves to see His will done by 'that low man' who, in the strength of a sincerely God-fearing humility,

> seeks a little thing to do,
> Sees it and does it.

The doing of it is what matters in God's sight; for Acton, no less than Ajax, has been created by God to take action[2] under the divinely appointed conditions of Man's Earthly Life.

If scholarship is indeed subject, like every other human vocation, to the necessity of having to choose between going into action and being a failure, a scholar is being untrue to his calling if he retorts to God's special challenge to scholars—*Ars longa, vita brevis*[3]—by throwing in God's face the defiant falsehood 'Man has Forever' instead of eschewing rhodomontades in order to concentrate on the prosaically workmanlike job of cutting his coat according to his cloth. A scholar is no more justified than any other man of action in shirking the workman's duty of making an inventory of the materials and tools, and an estimate of the time and energy, that are at his disposal for executing the commission which has been entrusted to him. To leave his talent hidden in the Earth till his corpse is lowered into the grave to rot beside it is a sin of omission in which criminal negligence swells to the dimensions of high treason. The intellectual, like the manual, worker has, at the longest, one

1 Comment by the French Maréchal Bosquet on the charge of the British Light Brigade at the Battle of Balaclava in the Crimea on the 25th October, 1854.

2 The poet himself, of course, testified to this truth by producing his works; for Robert Browning was a happily uninhibited man of action on the plane of his own imaginative art. His own detestation of 'the unlit lamp and the ungirt loin'— 'the sin I impute to each frustrate ghost'— is declared in *The Statue and the Bust*. The poem that we have been dissecting in the present chapter is a particularly brilliant example of Browning's gift for entering imaginatively into the experience, feelings, and thoughts of souls whose temperaments differ widely from his own, but there is one passage in *A Grammarian's Funeral* where the author of *Dramatic Romances* can be caught napping.

> He settled *Hoti's* business—let it be!—
> Properly based *Oun*,
> Gave us the doctrine of the enclitic *De*,
> Dead from the waist down.

'Settled'! 'Let it be'! 'Properly based'! 'Gave us the doctrine'! Save the mark! Who but the incorrigible man of action that Robert Browning was would ever have credited an orthodoxly inhibited scholar with such unprofessionally conclusive conduct as this? If the dead grammarian really had taken action, he would hardly have thanked his disciples for these damagingly indiscreet revelations, and the disciples themselves might have hesitated to honour him, as they did, in their obsequies.

3 Ὁ βίος βραχύς, ἡ δὲ τέχνη μακρή—Hippocrates: *Aphorismata*, I. 1.

full working life to use to best advantage, and his own tenure of this life may, for all he knows, be shorter than the average; at every moment he has to reckon with the possibility that death, or the deadly living death of incapacitation, may pounce upon him next year, next month, next week, tomorrow, or today. With these pertinent hard facts of human life ever present in mind, he must take the brevity of life, and not the *longueurs* of intellectual dissipation, as the measure for his intellectual enterprises; he must keep his plans within human compass and must put these feasible plans into execution here and now; for, in real life, no miracle will intervene to enable Psyche to acquit herself of an impracticable task imposed upon her by an overweening Intellect, since it is one of the fundamental laws of Human Nature that an undertaking which is manifestly beyond the compass of a mortal man's or woman's maximum expectation of working time and energy is *ipso facto* convicted of being an undertaking that is inherently unsound. Indeed, an intellectual worker who is able and willing to learn by experience will discover that even the largest work of art that a human soul has the capacity to create will not necessarily occupy the whole length of the average span of a human working life.

In the creation of a work of art the actual length of the particular workman's working life is, of course, one of the limiting conditions; for, if his reasonable expectation of life is falsified in the event by the crash of Death's cruel coulter,[1] 'the best laid schemes' may 'gang a-gley'.[2] But the unpredictable limitations set upon human beings' opportunities for creation by the chances and changes of this mortal life are only external and negative; and the positive factor that determines the Time-span of an act of creation is one that is internal and intrinsic to the act itself. The artist's working tempo is set for him by a psychic chronometer, and the two hands of this human clock are the Intellect and its partner the subconscious well-spring of Spiritual Creativity. Human acts of creation are governed by a law of spiritual dynamics which can be conveyed in a mathematical simile. Each act has its own proper curve to describe at its own proper pace; and, in so far as it diverges from its inherent course, or takes this course slower or faster than its inherent speed, the action will be falling short, to that extent, of the optimum performance of which it is capable. In the incubation of each particular work of art, a human creator's soul has a corresponding particular period of profitable gestation which it will shorten or lengthen at its peril; and an egg that is allowed to go addled under the suffocating breast of a broody hen [3] will be just as sterile as the still-born fruit of a premature birth.

[1] Burns, Robert: *To a Mouse*, stanza 5. [2] Ibid., stanza 7.

[3] The error, to which scholars are notoriously prone, of spoiling their work by continuing to revise it after it has reached and passed its optimum state can often be traced to an infantile ignorance of one of the fundamental rules of art. The occasion on which the present writer had learnt this rule had made an indelible mark on his memory. On the 17th April, 1951, when he was writing this note, he could recall, as vividly as if it had been yesterday, a day in July, 1894, on which he was intently watching his Mother painting a water-colour sketch of a ruined church that then seemed to be on the verge of toppling over the edge of the cliff at Dunwich on the coast of Suffolk. When his Mother had finished the sketch and they were looking at it together, he pointed out to her that it was incomplete because she had put in only the ruined church wall and the seascape visible through its glassless windows, and had left out the luxuriant dock leaves and nettlebeds sprouting through the church's dislocated pavement (as sordid witnesses

The human creator, if he truly and earnestly intends to respond to God's call to co-operate with Him in His creative work, must speak to his anima in the poet-member-of-parliament Andrew Marvell's masterful words:[1]

> Had we but world enough, and time,
> This coyness, Lady, were no crime. . . .
> My vegetable love should grow
> Vaster than empires, and more slow, . . .
> An age at least to every part,
> And the last age should show your heart. . . .
> But at my back I always hear
> Time's wingèd chariot hurrying near. . . .
> Now therefore. . . .

and, with the sanction of Time's inexorable onset to enforce his demand, the man of action delivers Mortality's imperious ultimatum.

> Now . . . while thy willing soul transpires
> At every pore with instant fires, . . .
> Let us roll all our strength and all
> Our sweetness up into one ball
> And tear our pleasures with rough strife
> Thorough the iron gates of Life:
> Thus, though we cannot make our sun
> Stand still, yet we will make him run.[2]

of Man's ephemeral occupation of the site). His Mother answered quietly, but without hesitation, that the secret of sketching was to know what to leave out, and, fifty-seven years later, her son could still distinctly remember (though he could no longer reproduce in the unsophisticated language of a five-year-old child) the succession of thoughts that this notable answer sent chasing one another through his mind. His first thought was that, in leaving out the dock leaves, his Mother had shown something less than an absolute faithfulness to the truth, even though, for the moment, he could not put his finger on the weak spot in her defence. His second thought was that she had lifted a veil from his eyes and shown him the truth behind it.

This second thought was the one that had remained with him to illuminate him for the next fifty-seven years; and, indeed, within five years he had enjoyed the pleasant surprise of earning good marks at school for having acted in accordance with his Mother's invaluable precept. His class had been given the task of writing a brief account of the reign of Queen Elizabeth from their memory of the section dealing with it in a textbook of English history which they had been set to read the day before. The passage in the textbook had opened with the anecdote of the princess's exclaiming 'This is the Lord's doing, and it is marvellous in our eyes' (Psalm cxviii. 23; Matt. xxi. 42; Mark xii. 11) when, sitting under an oak-tree in Hatfield Park, she had received the news that she was to ascend the throne and not the scaffold. When the essays were read and compared by the form master, it was found that several boys who were endowed with a better verbal memory than the writer's had reproduced this anecdote *verbatim* and had then been forced to break off, before they had been able to mention any of the events of Queen Elizabeth's reign, by the expiry of the time that had been allotted for the task. The writer had employed this Time-allotment in setting down what he had judged, from the textbook, to have been the principal events of the reign without mentioning the inaugural anecdote. To his astonishment the master not only commented on the difference between these two ways of handling the task, but told the class that the writer's way (i.e. his Mother's way) was the right one.

[1] Marvell, Andrew: *To His Coy Mistress*, ll. 1–2, 11–12, 17–18, 21–22, 33.

[2] Ibid., ll. 33, 35–36, 41–46.

C. THE IMPULSE TO INVESTIGATE THE RELATIONS BETWEEN THE FACTS

(I) CRITICAL REACTIONS

IN our inquiry, up to this point, into the inspirations of historians, we have found that, if a child is to become an historian, its passive receptivity to the suggestions of its environment must pass over into an active curiosity to know the facts of History. While we have found that a child cannot become an historian, and an adult cannot remain one, if the mind's mill is not set and kept in motion by a perpetual flow of curiosity over the mill-wheel, we have also found that, if, instead of putting away childish things[1] after passing the threshold of manhood, the would-be historian then allows his curiosity to run amok, it is likely to lead him off in pursuit of the will-o'-the-wisp of omniscience, and that this is a wrong turning which leads nowhere.

What, then, is the right turning? 'Thinking means asking questions';[2] and, if the child is to become an historian in very truth and deed, it must learn to harness its curiosity about the facts to the service of something more purposeful and more creative than curiosity itself. It must come to be inspired with a desire, not just to know the facts, but also to divine their meaning;[3] and this is a quest in which there are several successive stages; for the meaning of the facts may be found either in their relations with one another or in their relations with something that is embodied in them or in their relations with something that lies behind them. This quest is, indeed, ultimately a quest for a vision of God at work in History; and the first blind step along this pilgrims' way is a desire to understand how the facts of History hang together. In this investigation into the relations between the facts, the first mental movement is a critical reaction to apparent discrepancies, and the second a creative response to challenging phenomena.

In an inquiry into the awakening of the critical faculty in a would-be historian's mind, the writer was reduced once again to drawing upon his personal experience because no other first-hand evidence was accessible to him.

He could remember, for instance, how in March 1897, on a visit to some friends of his family's towards the end of his eighth year, he had broken out into exclamations of dissentient surprise when one of the grown-up people present had begun to expatiate on the goodness, abundance, and variety of the fare on a Transatlantic voyage from which he had just landed. The listening child could not accept a statement that was irreconcilable with what he had heard, time and again, straight from the mouth of his own great-uncle Harry, who was then still alive and who surely must be regarded as a greater authority, considering that he had

[1] 1 Cor. xiii. 11.

[2] Collingwood, R. G.: *The Idea of History* (Oxford 1946, Clarendon Press), p. 281. An illuminating presentation of this truth that questioning is the method of History will be found ibid., on pp. 269–74 and 278–82.

[3] Cp. Collingwood in op. cit., p. 275.

been, not just a passenger on his own ship, but her captain. The child was never tired of hearing the old man telling how the mouldy taste of ship's biscuit was welcomely relieved by the sharp taste of a weevil when the eater's teeth happened to bite through one of the biscuit's living occupants, and how, when captain and crew from time to time lost patience with their fellow-travellers the rats, they would entertain themselves by organizing a rat hunt which would bring them in tasty rat-pie to supplement for the next few days their dull normal fare of salt beef and plum duff. These, the child knew for certain, were the facts, so this talk of high feeding on board ship could be nothing but a mendaciously spun traveller's yarn; and it was a revelation to him when the present traveller, just ashore from one of the Cunard or White Star liners of the day, explained good-humouredly, to the child who had been calling his veracity in question, that there had been a good deal of change in the conditions of sea-travel during the thirty-one years that had gone by since Captain Henry Toynbee's retirement from the sea in A.D. 1866. Thanks to this convincing explanation of the discrepancy which had startled the child's mind, it dawned upon it for the first time that human affairs were on the move, and that this movement might run so fast as to produce sensational changes within the span of a single lifetime.

The next discrepancy that exercised the writer's mind in childhood was one on which he stumbled in the first step that he took to enlarge a new vista of History that had opened up before his eyes at some date either just before or soon after the end of his ninth year. Having at that stage encountered and read, among four volumes in *The Story of the Nations* series, Z. A. Ragozin's *Media, Babylon, and Persia*,[1] which told the story of the Iranian-speaking peoples' entry on to the stage of Oecumenical History between the time of the decline and fall of the Assyrian Empire and the time of the Achaemenian Empire's collision with the Hellenes, he had become inquisitive to 'look before and after' into the antecedent and subsequent chapters of Iranian history, and had therefore chosen S. G. W. Benjamin's volume in the same series, entitled *Persia*,[2] for a present from his Aunt Elsie Marshall on his tenth birthday. Plunging into his new book excitedly, in the expectation of here beholding the entire Iranian historical landscape of which one tantalizing patch had been revealed to his eyes in *Media, Babylon, and Persia*, he found himself being led down unknown paths and began to race along these impatiently in the expectation of reaching an already familiar patch of Iranian history that would give him his bearings. Fifty-three years later he could still recall vividly his growing surprise and dismay as he gradually found himself forced to face the fact that Benjamin's and Ragozin's accounts of Iranian history were irreconcilable.

It was true that, at the beginning of Benjamin's seventh chapter,[3] a familiar Cyrus was at last introduced as a synonym for an outlandish Kay Khusraw; but the young reader's mind was not satisfied by this apparently arbitrary and certainly abrupt transformation scene; and no impression was made upon it, at the time, by the author's unsatisfactorily

[1] See p. 18, above. [2] Third edition: London 1891, Fisher Unwin.
[3] See Benjamin, op. cit., pp. 82–86.

evasive plea[1] that it was not 'expedient in a volume of this size to go into a discussion concerning the discrepancies or historic difficulties that exist between the records of the Persian and the Greek or classic historians'.

The sorely perplexed reader did not, of course, get to the bottom of these discrepancies until many years later. He had first to take the point that the versions of the story given in the Achaemenian emperors' own inscriptions and by the Hellenic historian Herodotus were authenticated by the remarkable closeness of the approximation to agreement between a contemporary and an all but contemporary source, and he had then to read Theodor Nöldeke's *Das Iranische Nationalepos*[2] in order fully to realize just how little his reading of the pre-Sasanian chapters of Benjamin's *Persia* had added to the knowledge of historical facts that he had previously gained from reading Ragozin's *Media, Babylon, and Persia*. He eventually came to see that Benjamin—down to the point where he had drawn abreast of Herodotus and had there clumsily swapped horses in mid-stream of Persian history—had been riding the latter-day Muslim New Persian poets Daqīqī (*obiit* A.D. 952) and Firdawsī (*vivebat circa* A.D. 932–1020/1), and that the written sources on which Firdawsī had drawn exclusively[3] had been translations, made into New Persian in Khurāsān in the tenth century of the Christian Era, of Pahlawī prose versions of a corpus of Iranian epic poetry[4] in which the true facts of Iranian history had been transmuted out of all recognition[5] as the result of the operation of a law of literary evolution which constrains an artistically promising story to develop on lines, not of maximum fidelity to historical truth, but of maximum accommodation to literary expediency.[6]

The Rustem cycle of legends, which looms so large in Firdawsī's legendary history of Iran because the richness of this lode of literary ore attracted the genius of a great poet, proves, under Nöldeke's scientific assay, to have been a piece of local colour from Seistan and Zābulistān which may have been deposited in those two East Iranian provinces by Saka invaders in the second century B.C.[7] In the miscellaneous assemblage of garbled history and rationalized myth from which the Iranian national epic had been concocted in the Sasanian Age, the ingredient that was most conspicuous by its absence was the Achaemenian episode of authentic Iranian history; for, after the overthrow of the Achaemenian Empire by Alexander the Great, almost all recollection of the Achaemenidae had dropped out of the Iranian peoples' folk-memory, and, of the few stray references to these Iranian empire-builders that are to be found in the Iranian national epic,[8] some, at least,[9] prove to

[1] See Benjamin, op. cit., p. 83.
[2] Second edition: Berlin and Leipzig 1920, de Gruyter.
[3] See Nöldeke, ibid., p. 41.
[4] See ibid., pp. 15–17.
[5] See V. v. 599–602.
[6] See ibid., 607–14.
[7] See Nöldeke, op. cit., pp. 9–11. Nöldeke rejects the hypothesis that this cycle may be of Saka origin, but his scepticism is based on the inadequate ground that the personal names in this cycle are Iranian, and he fails to reckon with the fact that the Sakas, like the previous occupants of these countries, were Iranian-speaking.
[8] See ibid., p. 13.
[9] See ibid., loc. cit.

have found their way into it through translations of the Alexander Romance.[1]

In April 1899, more than fifty-three years before the date at which this chapter was sent to press, these considerations were, of course, far above the head of a child trying to understand History; but, under the intellectual shock that he had suffered from stumbling upon a discrepancy which he had not found himself able to reconcile, the child had taken the point that 'authorities' could discredit themselves by disagreeing with one another, and this disconcerting discovery had been for him the painful beginning of historical wisdom,[2] inasmuch as it had taught him that 'authorities' were not to be taken at their word as if they were infallible oracles of gospel truth.

A year or so later the same boy was to suffer another shock of the kind from the detection of a tell-tale loose end in a chronological chart of Oecumenical History that was pinned up one day along two walls of the largest class-room in the preparatory boarding school—Wootton Court, near Canterbury—to which he had been sent in his eleventh year. At his previous day-school—Warwick House, adjoining the Regent's Canal, in London—a reading of the tenth chapter of the Book of Genesis had opened his mind to the fascinating and inspiriting truth that Mankind was all one family, and History all one story; and, when he had begun to play his subsequent game of locating the descendants of Shem, Ham, and Japhet on the map and identifying them with extant or extinct divisions and subdivisions of the Human Race, he had found, in the maps included in 'the Queen's Printers' Aids to the Student of the Holy Bible', data that had enabled him to people the *Oikoumenê* with the descendants of Noah as far afield from their centre of dispersion in the South-West Asian 'fertile crescent' as the western basin of the Mediterranean in one direction and Central Iran in another. For the moment, he had not looked farther; but the posting of the chart in the schoolroom suddenly confronted him with a problem that had hitherto escaped him.

Looking first at the beginning of the chart, he had been struck by the preciseness of the date 4004 B.C. that was here assigned to the year of the Creation.[3] Walking across from there to the far corner of the room, where the chart broke off at some date within the nineteenth century of the Christian Era, he noticed here, among the bands of various colours, representing the histories of divers peoples and states, one conspicuously broad band labelled 'China'. Were the Chinese descended from Shem, from Ham, or from Japhet? It had not occurred to him to ask the question before, but now it was going to be answered for him out of hand; for he had just ascertained that the chart began, at the opposite end, with the creation of the two parents of the Human Race, and he had now only to follow 'China' back in order to discover which of Noah's three

1 The Alexander Romance went through an evolution that is a romance in itself (see V. vi. 440–4.)

2 Prov. ix. 10.

3 This dating of the Creation was, of course, (see XI. ix. 178), the sign manual of Archbishop Ussher; and it therefore seems likely that his *Annales Veteris et Novi Testamenti* (London 1650–4, Flesher, 2 vols.) was the original source from which this chart had been derived.

sons it was through whom the Chinese went back to Adam and Eve. Verification should be easy, since the snakelike band labelled China was of a python's girth; and, sure enough, the young investigator's finger traced this continuous ribbon of colour back into the second millennium B.C. But his hair stood on end when, at this point in his moving finger's backward journey, the three-thousand-years-long Chinese dragon's solid body suddenly broke off without linking up with either Japhet, Ham, or Shem—as if, more than a thousand years after the date of disembarkation from Noah's ark, four hundred million Chinese had been conjured up out of nowhere by an act of spontaneous generation. The workmanship of the draftsman of this at first glance imposing chart had, in fact, proved, on inspection, to be as shoddy as the performance of a plumber who, later on, was to instal a bath for a grown-up historian-householder without taking the trouble to connect the overflow-outlet with the waste-pipe.

This damning analogy did not occur to a child who, in A.D. 1899, was still living in an age of English history in which middle-class households were not yet encumbered with bathrooms; but he did realize at once that the Ussherite cartographers stood convicted of a culpable neglect —or perhaps, worse still, of a sheer inability—to trace back to the fruitfulness and multiplication of Noah and his sons[1] the latter-day diversity-in-unity of a Mankind that had duly replenished the Earth; and this shocking discovery raised in a would-be historian's mind his first doubt as to whether a genealogical tree was a vehicle that could effectively convey the history of the progressive differentiation of the Human Family.

As this doubt persisted and grew stronger, the writer experimented with alternative systems of classification which might perhaps comprehend all the living and extinct branches of Mankind and might at the same time account for all the gradations of diversity and affinity between them. Could the key to this historical puzzle be found in Physical Race if a mythical criterion of racial relations in the shape of a Biblical genealogy were discarded in favour of a 'scientific' criterion compounded of such objective and measurable data as the colour of the skin, the texture of the hair, 'the cephalic index', and the facial angle? Or, alternatively, could the key be found in language if a myth of the confusion of tongues at the abortive building of a Tower of Babel[2] were discarded in favour of the findings of the Late Modern Western science of Comparative Philology? After the writer's critical faculty had thus been set to work upon the problem of Mankind's diversity-in-unity thanks to the shock administered to his mind by an Ussherian chart of Oecumenical History in A.D. 1899, it took him some ten or twelve years to arrive at the conclusion that the linguistic and the racial approach to the problem were each as unsatisfactory[3] as the genealogical approach had previously proved to be. It was only after this thrice-repeated preliminary negative process of drawing blank that the writer was able to clear the ground in his own mind for the positive solution proposed in the present Study, in which he has argued that, in human affairs, the significant differences

[1] Gen. ix. 1 and 7. [2] Gen. xi. 1–9.
[3] A critique of the racial approach will be found in II. i. 207–49.

and likenesses are not those of Race or Language, but are those of religious and secular Culture.

Another illuminating discrepancy impinged on the writer's mind one afternoon during the First World War when, as he was wandering through the Victoria and Albert Museum in South Kensington, his eye was caught by the bust of a girl in majolica in the naturalistic Modern Western style, and his curiosity was moved to ascertain the provenance and date of this attractive work of art. He was not surprised to find that a work as beautiful as this had been made in Italy, but he was astonished to discover that a work as modern as this had been made in the fourteenth century of the Christian Era. This bust was a piece of material evidence that, in the fourteenth century, Italy had already been living in the Modern Age of Western history; but in the rest of Western Christendom, with the possible exception of Flanders, the Modern Age had not dawned before the close of the fifteenth century or even the opening of the sixteenth. So Italy had been 'modern' already for perhaps as long as two hundred years before the rest of Western Christendom had followed suit to her; and this example proved that, within the bosom of one and the same society, it was possible for different 'sections' (in the 'geo-cultural' sense in which this word was used in the United States) to be historically out of step with one another. People who were chronological contemporaries might, in fact, be living side by side in two different cultural epochs.

This inference from the modernity of a fourteenth-century Italian bust was confirmed in the writer's mind when, some thirty years later, at the end of the Second World War, he paid another visit to the same museum in order to see on exhibition there the statues and other decorations from the English King Henry VII's chapel at Westminster Abbey. On this occasion he was able to appraise at close quarters the extent of the cultural gulf between the still inviolate Medieval Western style of the English work and the resurgent Hellenic style of the contemporary work of the imported Italian master Torrigiani.[1] This visual evidence of the temporary cultural precocity of Northern and Central Italy in a Late Medieval Age of Western history was one of the signals that drew the writer's attention to the historical role of creative minorities.

Light can also be thrown on History by critical reactions to discrepancies that have merely been suspected without having been verified. In September 1952 the writer could remember a day in March 1899 when his Mother was reading aloud to him Z. A. Ragozin's *Chaldea*[2] in *The Story of the Nations* series. Nineteenth-century Western Assyriologists and Egyptologists had been impressed by the length of their new vista of past history, by comparison with the relative shortness of the Biblical vista, much more forcibly than they had been impressed by the shortness of the Biblical and archaeological vistas alike by comparison

[1] This contrast has been noticed already in X. ix. 83.

[2] Fifth edition: London 1896, Fisher Unwin. This volume was the prolegomena to the same author's *Assyria*, which had already come into the present writer's hands (see p. 18, above). A curiosity to explore the antecedents of Assyrian history had moved him for the first time to spend his pocket-money on buying a learned work in preference to a box of lead soldiers.

with the relative length of the geological and astronomical vistas that were being opened up simultaneously by contemporary Western physical scientists; and consequently the antiquity of the 'Chaldean' (i.e. the Sumeric) Civilization was one of the principal themes of Ragozin's stimulating *œuvre de vulgarisation*. In expounding her thesis, the gifted authoress cited two by then already rediscovered chronological assertions that had been made by the Assyrian King Asshurbanipal (*regnabat* 669–626 B.C.) and by the Neo-Babylonian Emperor Nabonidus (*imperabat* 556–539 B.C.) without questioning whether these latter-day sovereigns' historical advisers had really possessed authentic information warranting their confidently presented figures. On Asshurbanipal's figure of 1,635 years for the length of the time that had elapsed since a statue of the goddess 'Nana',[1] which Asshurbanipal had brought back to Uruk (Erech) from Susa in 645 B.C., had been carried away into an Elamite captivity, her comment[2] was that '1,635 added to 645 make 2,280, a date not to be disputed'; and, though she boggled[3] at the antiquity of the date—3750 B.C.—which was assigned to the *floruit* of the Akkadian war-lord Naramsin by Nabonidus's statement that Naramsin had reigned 3,200 years before Nabonidus's own day, she took refuge here in 'the possibility of an error of the engraver' of the inscription, without considering the alternative possibility that the latter-day emperor-archaeologist himself might have been drawing the long bow in the dark and might therefore perhaps not deserve to be taken *au pied de la lettre*.

Ragozin's unquestioning assumption that Nabonidus and Asshurbanipal had known what they were talking about was, of course, accepted by the listening child uncritically, but it suddenly occurred to him to wonder how the authoress knew that these Assyrian and Babylonian 'years' were periods of the same length as the familiar years in which time was reckoned in a nineteenth-century England, and he interrupted his Mother's reading by putting this question to her. Perhaps the question had been evoked in his mind by some echo of a nineteenth-century 'fundamentalist' Western Christian attempt to salvage the veracity of the Book of Genesis by suggesting that the 'years' of life attributed there, in generous hundreds, to the Patriarchs were in reality periods that would read, not as 'years', but possibly as 'months', if the chronological terminology of the Bible were to be translated into current parlance with a pedantic precision. Probably, if he had been country-bred, he would never have entertained the idea that there could be any such arbitrary variations in the length of the year, considering that its span was settled for the farmer, not by human fiat, but by a cycle of the seasons that invariably came round in the same course within the same period, whatever the human calendar-makers might choose to say. As, however, the child happened to be town-bred, he was blind to Nature's visual clock on whose face the fixed spans of the revolving and recurring seasons were registered by the regular alternation of the spring of the blossom and the fall of the leaf. In his cockney *Weltanschauung* in his tenth year,

[1] i.e. Inanna, the original Sumerian name of the goddess whose Akkadian name was Ishtar. The Sumerian 'Nanna' was not a goddess but a god—the moon-god whose Akkadian name was Sin.

[2] In op. cit., on p. 195.

[3] Ibid., pp. 211–15.

'years' presented themselves as artificial spans of Time which human beings could expand or contract at will because human wills were presumed to have created them arbitrarily *ex nihilo*.

The naïve questioner lived to laugh at his childish ignorance, and then lived on to discover that his question had been shrewder than his wit. He had no sooner been sent to school in the country than he became aware of Nature's solar year, and he had no sooner followed up Arthur Gilman's *The Saracens*[1] in *The Story of the Nations* series by getting hold of Stanley Lane-Poole's *Mohammadan Dynasties*[2] than he discovered that Nature's clock displayed more than one dial, and that, where, as in this instance, Nature was at variance with herself, human wills were consequently invested with at least the limited freedom of choosing which dial to follow. The calendar of Babylonic origin that was current in an English boy's world at the turn of the nineteenth and twentieth centuries of the Christian Era was based on the solar cycle of the seasons, and, in the course of centuries, it had been readjusted several times over to coincide with this cycle with an ever closer approximation to exactitude—leaving the lunar cycle of the months to take care of itself, as best it could, by submitting perforce to a Procrustean process of arbitrarily stretching or docking the lengths of the months in order to fit them into a paramount solar framework. The English boy now made the discovery that the method of calendrical reckoning that happened to be current in Christendom was not the universal way of the World; for here, in current use in the Muslim quarter of the *Oikoumenê*, was a calendar—based, not on the solar, but on the lunar cycle—whose nominal 'year' of literally lunar months, ignoring the recurrent procession of the seasons, allowed itself to fall short of the true solar year's full measure, with the result that, as the tale of Islamic 'years' had mounted up from the initial date of the Era of the *Hijrah*, these *soi-disant* 'years' had been travelling time and again round the face of Christendom's Babylonic solar clock.

It was not, however, until A.D. 1950, when he was making his preparations for writing the note on Chronology printed in this Study in the present volume,[3] that the writer realized the full bearing of an Islamic lunar calendar upon the question regarding the length of the Sumeric year which he had put to his Mother more than fifty solar years back. At Princeton, New Jersey, in the fall of the solar year A.D. 1950, he first read Poebel's articles[4] on the recently rediscovered Assyrian King-List from Khorsabad and marvelled at the ingenuity of this accomplished contemporary Assyriologist's ways and means of harmonizing with this list the chronological assertions of two latter-day sovereigns—in this case, not Nabonidus and Asshurbanipal, but Esarhaddon (*regnabat* 680–669 B.C.) and Shalmaneser I (*regnabat* 1272–1243 B.C. according to Poebel's dating).[5] He then went on to read Sidney Smith's critique[6] of

[1] London 1887, Fisher Unwin.
[2] London 1894, Constable.
[3] On pp. 167–212, below.
[4] In the *Journal of Near Eastern Studies*, vol. i, pp. 247–306; ibid., pp. 460–91; and vol. ii, pp. 56–90 (Chicago 1942–3, University of Chicago Press).
[5] See *J.N.E.S.*, vol. i, pp. 290–5.
[6] Smith, Sidney: 'Middle Minoan I–II and Babylonian Chronology', in the *American Journal of Archaeology*, vol. xlix, No. 1 (Concord, N.H. 1945, Rumford Press), pp. 1–24.

Poebel's reconstruction of Assyrian chronology and was astonished to find one eminent contemporary professional archaeologist here putting to a confrère the very question that the writer himself, as a child, had once put to his Mother: How could one be sure that the 'years' in which the Assyrian chronologists reckoned were solar years or, indeed, even would-be approximations to them?

This hypothetical correspondence, which Poebel had tacitly taken for granted throughout his own reconstruction of Assyrian chronology from the recently discovered Khorsabad King-List in combination with the rest of the evidence, was roundly challenged by his distinguished adversary. In Assyria, Sidney Smith submitted,[1] the Babylonian solar calendar, which had arrived at a close approximation to the true solar year, did not appear to have been adopted for official use before the reign of Tiglath-Pileser I (*regnabat* 1114–1076 B.C.). 'Over a long period of years that calendar remains equivalent to Julian years in reckoning. . . . But the Assyrian calendar previously in use shows considerable variations from the Babylonian, and no precision in converting Assyrian years into Julian reckoning is possible.' In the non-Babylonian calendar current in Assyria before Tiglath-Pileser I's day there may have been a different and inferior system of intercalation; 'but the known facts at present favour the view that there was no intercalation at all'; and 'this is an important factor in calculating early dates'.[2] Sidney Smith suggests[3] that the calendar which, in his belief, had been discarded in Assyria in 1114 B.C. in favour of the Babylonian solar calendar of the day, had been a lunar one—i.e. one constructed on the same basis as the calendar which, 1,736 years after the date at which it may have been abandoned in an Assyria that lay next to the heart of the Babylonic World, was still in use in the remote and backward Arabian oasis of Mecca, and which then, through the accident of its survival in this insulated desert-girt fastness, was to have its fortune made for it by automatically becoming the official calendar of a new oecumenical church founded by a Meccan prophet.

This controversy between Sidney Smith and Poebel, in which these two champion Assyriologists were hurling lunar and solar calendars at one another as Hector and Ajax had once hurled boulders, demonstrated that a critical reaction even to a disputable discrepancy might play an important role in a debate involving an entire scheme of chronology for the history of the Sumeric Civilization.

(II) CREATIVE RESPONSES

(*a*) MINUSCULA

If the observation, or even the unverified suspicion, of discrepancies between historical facts may inspire human minds to take intellectual action by arousing a negative critical faculty, we may expect, *a fortiori*, to see minds moved to act by the observation, or even by the unverified in-

[1] Smith, Sidney, ibid., p. 19. [2] Ibid., p. 19.

[3] See ibid., pp. 22–23. This suggestion was rejected by some contemporary scholars (see the Note on Chronology, p. 177, below).

tuition, of connexions between historical facts which call for some positive explanation.

Rudimentary historical puzzles of this positive kind are set by the observation of the currency, at widely different points in Space and in Time, of identical elements of culture—identical clothes, for example, or identical words; for, however far apart from one another on the stage of History these identical elements may have made their successive separate epiphanies, a resemblance that approximates to identity is less likely to be a coincidence than to be due to some continuous chain of historical tradition and geographical diffusion which it may be possible to retrace.

How comes it, for example, that, on a bronze medal made in A.D. 1439 by the Italian master Vittore Pisano (Pisanello) for the East Roman Emperor John VII Palaiológhos (*imperabat* A.D. 1425–48), and in a fresco—painted on the west wall of the Church of San Francesco at Arezzo, at some date between A.D. 1452 and A.D. 1466,[1] by Piero della Francesca—in which the same John VII Palaiológhos is depicted in the role of Constantine the Great at the Battle of the Milvian Bridge,[2] this last but one of the occupants of a Byzantine imperial throne should be portrayed by two contemporary Italian witnesses[3] as wearing a head-dress which looks uncommonly like the Egyptiac Double Crown[4]—a

1 For the date, see Clark, Kenneth: *Piero della Francesca* (London 1951, Phaidon Press), pp. 35–36.

2 See the plates, in op. cit., of the whole fresco (Plate 57), of the left-hand half of it depicting Constantine and his army (Plate 58), and of the head of Constantine (represented by John VII Palaiológhos) himself (Plate 62).

3 'Warburg and others have supposed that Piero took the likeness of Palaeologus from Pisanello's medal of 1439, but this is not entirely true. The characteristic shapes and rhythms of the two heads are different ... Piero', who had been living in Florence in A.D. 1439 when the Emperor John VII had come to Florence to attend the Church Council that had sat at Florence in that year, 'almost certainly saw Palaeologus with his own eyes' (Clark, op. cit., p. 26, n. 1). In Piero della Francesca's picture of the Flagellation, at Urbino, which was probably painted in the fourteen-fifties, both John VII's countenance and his head-dress reappear, but here no longer in association with one another (see Clark, op. cit., p. 19 and Plates 27–28).

4 The resemblance is particularly striking in Piero della Francesca's fresco, which brings out two points that are not apparent on Pisanello's medal (though, in the light of the fresco, the first point of the two can perhaps be detected on the finer of the two exemplars of the medal in the British Museum). The fresco shows that the two components of the head-dress were separate: the bottom edge of the conical inner component is just visible below the lower edge of the front portion of the outer component, which resembles the looped-up brim of an eighteenth-century Western three-cornered hat; and this detail is visible because the two components are of sharply different colours.

Since the plates of this fresco in Sir Kenneth Clark's book are not among those in which the original colours are reproduced, they reveal merely that the conical inner component of the imperial head-dress is relatively light in colour and that the looped-up outer component is relatively dark. In the original fresco, is the inner component white, as the conical crown of Upper Egypt was, and the outer component red—the colour of the looped-up crown of Lower Egypt? The answer to this question is given in the following sentence in a letter of the 6th October, 1952, from the Reverend Father P. Benedetto Renzi, Rector of the Church of San Francesco at Arezzo, in answer to an inquiry from the writer of this Study: 'I colori della corona di Costantino risultano bianco con sfumature rosse nella parte superiore, verde cupo nella parte inferiore.' The colouring here described by an eye-witness is faithfully reproduced in d'Ancona, Paolo: *Piero della Francesca: Il Ciclo Affrescato della Santa Croce nella Chiesa di S. Francesco in Arezzo* (Milan 1951, Pizzi), Plate XVI. The streaks of red do not come out in Longhi, Roberto: *Piero della Francesca: La Légende de la Croix* (*Fresques d'Arezzo*) (Milan 1952, Sidera; Paris 1952, Amiot-Dumont), Plates xxxi, xxxiv and xxxv.

It will be seen that, in the Emperor John VII Palaiológhos's head-dress as painted by Piero della Francesca, the Crown of Upper Egypt (if such it is) preserves its pristine

head-dress that had become part of the insignia of the Pharaohs after the political unification of Upper and Lower Egypt by Narmer *circa* 3100 B.C.?[1] How could this complicated and outlandish headgear—which would look bizarre to anyone not acquainted with the crucial episode of Egyptiac history that it commemorated—have survived (if in truth it did survive) over a Time-span of more than four and a half millennia in order to make its eventual reappearance, not on the banks of the Nile where it had been invented, but on the alien shores of the Bosphorus at least a thousand years after the last remnants of a living Egyptiac tradition had become extinct in what had once been an Egyptiac World? An historian's mind in search of an answer to this question would recollect that the pre-Christian Roman Emperors had acted on their pretension to be the Pharaohs' legitimate successors by having themselves portrayed, on the monuments of the latest age of Egyptiac history, as wearing the Pharaohs' traditional insignia. Would it be too fanciful to imagine that these Roman impersonators of Egyptiac Pharaohs may have provided themselves with actual sets of the Pharaonic insignia, including the symbolic Double Crown, and that, in spite of the subsequent extinction of the Egyptiac culture and the eventual loss of Egypt itself by the Christian Roman Empire to its Primitive Muslim Arab invaders, these long-since obsolete Egyptiac regalia may first have been transferred from the Old Rome to the New Rome and afterwards been preserved there in the office of the Protovestiarios of an extinct Roman Empire's East Roman ghost till the last of the Palaiológhi came across them in some imperial lumber room and took the fancy to wear them—probably without being aware of either their origin or their significance.

How comes it, too (to pursue this fascinating subject of the diffusion of headgear),[2] that the brimless 'stove-pipe' hat (*Persicè* 'taka'), curving outwards towards its flat crown, in which the Persian guardsmen are portrayed on Achaemenian bas-reliefs, and in which Baluchi shepherds were still to be seen stalking over the highlands of South-Eastern Iran at the time of writing,[3] should have been in academic use in twentieth-

white with a taint of Lower Egypt's red, but that the Crown of Lower Egypt (if such it is) has changed its hue from red to bottle-green.

The same head-dress, in the same colours, has been placed by the same painter on Pilate's head in his picture of the Flagellation in the Ducal Palace at Urbino. In a letter of the 30th October, 1952, in answer to an inquiry from the writer of this Study, Signor Pietro Zampetti, Soprintendente alle Gallerie delle Marche, notes that this head-dress 'comes close, in its shape, to the beret of the "Clerici Vagantes", but might also be reminiscent of the ancient crown of Egypt—though it is distinguished from this by the cut of its peak, which is strongly pronounced.' 'Per quanto riguarda i colori, essi sono il rosato per la parte interna del copricapo ed il verde scuro per quella esterna. La striscia bianca dovrebbe essere cosa a sè, specie di fascia che si nota anche in altra figura dello stesso dipinto.'

The resemblance of Pilate's head-dress, in this picture, to the Egyptiac Double Crown is noticed by Longhi in his *Piero della Francesca* (Rome 1927, Valori Plastici), p. 41: 'Pilato si effigia faraonico.'

[1] See II. ii. 112 and 114–15, and IV. iv. 502–4.

[2] Two illustrations of it have already been noticed in this Study in other contexts: the derivation of the nineteenth-century Western 'top hat' from the sixteenth-century Western steeple-crowned hat in III. iii. 136, with n. 2, and the derivation of 'the cardinal's hat' from the shield-shaped or mushroom-shaped headgear of the Achaemenian Empire's subjects in the Aegean Archipelago in VI. vii. 681–2.

[3] See VI. vii. 681.

century English-speaking countries in the recognizably derivative shape of the 'college cap' or 'mortar-board'? The last link but one in the lost chain of transmission could readily be detected in the 'toque' worn by members of the legal profession in France; but from whom had this headgear been borrowed by these French representatives of one of the liberal professions of Western Christendom? From the Ottoman grandees who, before the revolutionary substitution of an egalitarian fez by Sultan Mahmūd II (*imperabat* A.D. 1808–39), had worn the Achaemenian 'taka' wrapped in a voluminous turban? Or from the priests of the Eastern Orthodox Christian Church *in partibus Ottomanicis*, on whom a plain black variant of this Persian headgear had been imposed by their Muslim masters? Or from the uhlans[1] whose Turkish appellation testifies that their accoutrements must have been introduced into Poland from Turkey on their way to becoming acclimatized in Prussia?

What, again, was the line of descent by which the hood that was associated with cap and gown in the academic costume of twentieth-century English-speaking countries had been derived from the 'hood' that, in the Achaemenian Emperor Darius I's bas-relief carved on the face of the cliff at Behistan before the close of the sixth century B.C., draws the eye to the last of the figures in the file of vanquished rebel leaders who are being brought to judgement before the face of their puissant subjugator? It is true that the enormously high pointed cap that the Massagetan Saka chieftain Skunkha is here portrayed as wearing bears slightly more resemblance to Little Red Ridinghood's headgear than it bears to the glorified scarf that twentieth-century Anglo-Saxon doctors and bachelors of Theology, Law, Arts, and Science wore slung over their shoulders; yet the identity of the name attests the historical connexion; for, in virtue of their distinctively peculiar headgear, the Massagetae were nicknamed by their Persian conquerors 'the Pointed-Hood Saka' (Sakā Tigrakhaudā). What were the successive stages in the subsequent metamorphosis of Skunkha's headgear?

Anyone contemplating Skunkha's 'pointed hood' in a photograph of Darius's bas-relief could predict that sooner or later its point would sag either forwards or backwards; and there was evidence to show that both these alternative possible variations in the fashion of wearing this preposterous Massagetan headgear were subsequently tried. At the time of writing, the forward-curving variant was to be seen in the Panjab in the horn-shaped cap of stiff dark blue felt round which the Sikh akalis wore their ring-shaped war-quoits, and in the flabbier headgear of the same shape that was part of the insignia of a Neapolitan Pulcinello, while the backward-curving variant was the Medieval Western *liripipium*—still familiar to Modern Western eyes in busts and portraits of Dante—whose point, transformed from a stiff felt steeple into a soft cloth pigtail hanging down between the shoulder-blades, had once captivated the male half of the population of the whole of a fourteenth-century Western Christendom, from Florence to Greenland.[2]

[1] *Turcicè* 'oghlanlar', meaning 'the boys'.

[2] The Norse settlers in Greenland, whose losing struggle for survival ended in their extinction round about the turn of the fifteenth and sixteenth centuries, continued (see Nørlund, P.: *Viking Settlers in Greenland and their Descendants during Five Hundred*

The survival of the forward-pointing variant of the Massagetan 'hood' in the Panjab was, of course, easily explained. It had been carried from the Oxus-Jaxartes Basin into the Indus Basin by the Massagetae themselves, together with their tribal name (the Jāts), in their Völkerwanderung in the second century B.C. It was not so easy to account for the epiphany of the self-same variant of the pointed hood on Pulcinello's head at Naples; yet an historian might hazard the guess that its carriers from Central Asia to Southern Italy might have been Alzeco's war-band of Bulgar Hun Turkish-speaking Eurasian Nomads who were passed on by Grimwald King of the Lombards (*regnabat* A.D. 662–671) to his son Romwald Duke of Benevento, and were then planted by Romwald in the depopulated territories of Bovianum, Saepinum, Aesernia, and other decayed city-states[1] in the district of Northern Samnium that afterwards came to be known as the Molise.[2] 'It seems probable that this settlement of the Bulgarians was partly a measure of precaution against attack from Rome or Naples';[3] and, if so, it might also seem not improbable that the Roman united empire loyalists who had continued, after the irruption of the Lombards, to hold bridgeheads at Naples and Gaeta and in the Ducatus Romanus for an Imperial Government at Constantinople should have given visual expression to their scorn and detestation of the Eurasian Nomad horde which the Lombard usurpers had now planted next door to them by clapping these ex-Nomads' distinctively outlandish 'pointed hood' upon the head of a puppet representing the arch-villain Pontius Pilate in a perfunctorily Christianized *Fabula Atellana*.

Though there is no evidence that the Bulgars' Hun ancestors had, in fact, picked up the Massagetan 'pointed hood' *en route* from Mongolia to the Great Western Bay of the Eurasian Steppe, it seems just possible that our Parthian shot in the dark may have hit the mark; but whence did Dante acquire his *liripipium*? What was the missing link here between the backward-trailing hood worn by a Florentine poet born in A.D. 1265 and a tendency towards a backward-curving fashion of wearing the Massagetan 'pointed hood' that was revealed in the extant works of art of an Achaemenian Empire that had been overthrown in 334–330 B.C.?

Years (London 1936, Cambridge University Press), pp. 110–11 and 126), to the last, to follow the latest fashions of a Western Christendom into which an abortive pagan Scandinavian Society had been absorbed at the turn of the tenth and eleventh centuries (see II. ii. 340–60). Among other articles of Medieval Western Christian dress the Greenlanders adopted the fourteenth-century *liripipium* (see Nørlund, op. cit., pp. 118–25); and the seventeen specimens (see ibid., p. 118) that had been recovered by Modern Western archaeologists among the clothing excavated from the graves in the churchyard at Herjolfsnes were probably (see ibid., pp. 123–4) the only representatives of the *liripipium* that were extant at the time of writing.

[1] See Paulus Diaconus: *Historia Langobardorum*, Book V, chap. 29. The historian, writing, as far as can be ascertained, at some date between A.D. 786 and 795, records of Alzeco's Bulgars that, 'usque hodie in his, ut diximus, locis habitantes, quamquam et Latinè loquantur, linguae tamen propriae usum minimè amiserunt'.

[2] This district was found desolate by Strabo (see his *Geographica*, Book V, chap. iv, § 11 (C 249–50), cited in IV. iv. 391, n. 2, and in V. v. 37, n. 2), not much less than a hundred years after its devastation in 81–80 B.C. by Sulla. The writer is not aware of any evidence that it had ever been resettled before Alzeco's Bulgars were planted there three-quarters of a millennium after the commission of Sulla's atrocity.

[3] Hodgkin, T.: *Italy and Her Invaders*, vol. vi (Oxford 1895, Clarendon Press), p. 284, n. 1.

Here again, a clue might be found by the historian in one of the periodic eruptions of the Nomads out of the Eurasian Steppe. In A.D. 1241 the unprecedentedly violent eruption of the Mongols out of the heart of the Steppe had sent the Cuman Turkish Nomads flying out of the Steppe's Great Western Bay into the detached enclave of steppe-land in the Hungarian Alföld, with the Mongols themselves following at the Cumans' heels. The Cumans had burst into Hungary as pagan barbarians, and such they might have remained if their Mongol pursuers had stayed there with them. But the wave of Mongol invasion had receded from Hungary as rapidly as it had swept over it, and, when once the Mongols were out of the way, the Magyars, who knew how to handle Nomads in virtue of being *ci-devant* Nomads themselves, had managed to convert the manageably small intrusive horde of Cuman strangers in their midst to the Western Christian religion and culture to which the Cumans' Magyar hosts had been converted a quarter of a millennium earlier.[1] Through the agency of Western Christendom's Magyar marchmen over against the Eurasian Steppe, the Cuman refugees in the Alföld had thus been brought into the fold of Western Christendom in the course of the second half of the thirteenth century of the Christian Era;[2] and it does not seem unduly fanciful to conjecture that they left a monument of their conversion in the subsequent captivation of the Western Christian World, into which these Eurasian Nomad immigrants had thus made their entry, by the backward-curving variant of the Massagetan 'pointed hood' in the *outré* form of the *liripipium*.[3]

We cannot take our eyes off Skunkha's steeple-shaped 'hood' without being moved to ask the further question whether this extraordinary headgear was an invention of the Massagetae's own, or whether it is not more likely that they had borrowed it from Anatolia, where the antiquity of its vogue is attested by its appearance on the heads of the warriors on the frieze in the Hittite sanctum at Yazyly Qaya, over against the Hittite capital city on Boghazqal'eh, while the persistence of its vogue there—latterly in the service, not of War, but of Religion—is attested by its retention as part of the insignia of the Islamic religious orders in Anatolia down to their dissolution on the 2nd September, 1925, by the fiat of the government of a Westernizing Turkish Republic. These orgiastic worshippers of the One True God are convicted by their headgear of having been the spiritual heirs of those orgiastic worshippers of the goddess Cybele who were nicknamed Corybantes ('High-Hats') by Hellenic observers. Was Anatolia the original centre of dispersion of 'the pointed hood' in the pristine form in which it appears on the head of the Massagetan chief Skunkha in the sixth century B.C. and on the heads of witches, astrologers, heretics, and dunces in Western Christendom?

Whatever its original provenance may have been, the Massagetan pointed hood' was in any case not the Eurasian Nomads' normal headgear. The common run of Eurasian Nomad peoples wore 'the Phrygian cap' in which the Scyths are portrayed in Hellenic and Helleno-Scythian works of art made in the fifth and fourth centuries B.C., and which is likewise

[1] See III. iii. 426. [2] See III. iii. 461.

[3] Was the Ottoman Janissaries' headgear a variant of the *liripipium* which had been slung into Anatolia by the same Mongol eruption in Eurasia?

the headgear in which Dacians, colliding with the Romans four or five hundred years after the Scythians' *floruit*, are depicted on Trajan's Column. In bringing this standard Eurasian Nomad headgear on to our stage, we have anticipated the answer to another question: How comes it that the official head-dress of the Doge of Venice, familiar to frequenters of the National Gallery in London in Giovanni Bellini's portrait of the Doge Leonardo Loredano (*ducebat* A.D. 1501–21), is identical with that displayed in clay figurines representing officials in the service of the T'ang Dynasty (*imperabant* A.D. 618–907) in a Far Eastern World that lay on the other side of the Eurasian Steppe from Western Christendom? The link becomes manifest when we realize that this Veneto-Chinese official headgear is the Eurasian Nomad's standard soft 'Phrygian cap' frozen stiff; and it is not difficult to understand how this came to be part of the insignia of public office in Northern China, considering that the Nomads had been politically dominant there for more than three hundred years before the T'ang régime was established with its headquarters within this domain that the Nomads had carved out for themselves *in partibus Sinarum*.[1] Presumably the same official headgear was picked up by the Venetians from one or other of the successive hordes of Nomads—Sarmatians, Huns, Bulgars, Pseudo-Avars, and Magyars—who repeatedly raided the plains of Northern Italy in the courses of the post-Theodosian and the post-Carolingian Völkerwanderungen.[2]

Nor was it only the headgear of the Eurasian Nomads that found its way into Western Christendom; for the historic accoutrements of the Scyths and the Dacians, as these are portrayed in Hellenic works of art, reappear, *cap-à-pie*, in the garb in which a mythical race of Dwarfs was subsequently clothed in a Western folk-lore. These Dwarfs were, of course, *numina*—projected by the Subconscious Psyche in response to the mind's challenging experience of extracting metallic treasure from the bowels of the Earth—who never had any existence in what the Conscious Psyche calls 'real life'; but the costume in which the Dwarfs made their epiphany in Fairyland must have been the authentic dress of some living people of flesh and blood who were encountered by the pioneers of a Medieval Western Christendom's eastward expansion overland. If we

[1] See X. ix. 651–2.

[2] See, however, Zanetti, G., in his dissertation *Della Berretta Ducale, Volgarmente Chiamata Corno, che portasi da' Serenissimi Dogi di Venezia* (1779), to which the writer's attention was drawn by Mr. James Laver, the Keeper of the Departments of Engraving, Illustration, and Design, and of Paintings at the Victoria and Albert Museum in London. Zanetti argues that the modern form of the Doge's official head-dress was not the original form, but was the recent result of a six or seven hundred years long process of evolution, of which he claims to have identified nine stages (illustrated at the end of the booklet). The current name *corno*—alluding to the point to which the Doge's cap, in its modern shape, rose at the back—could not be traced back earlier than the sixteenth century, in Zanetti's belief (ibid., pp. xviii–xix). Zanetti finds the origin of the modern *corno* in a conical cap worn by dogi in representations of them in the oldest mosaics in St. Mark's (ibid., p. v). He suggests (ibid., pp. xix–xxi) that this conical cap was a Teutonic barbarian Transalpine headgear which was adopted by the Venetian dogi and was then progressively modified at Venice until it eventually arrived at its modern style. After following Zanetti's arguments and examining his illustrations, the writer of this Study did not find himself convinced that the T'ang-like *corno* and the Carolingian-like conical *berretta* were in truth successive stages in the evolution of one and the same cap.

may also hazard a guess at the provenance of this lost tribe whose dress was thus immortalized by being taken as the model for the clothing of imaginary Dwarfs, we may picture to ourselves a band of Nomad herdsmen straying beyond the limits of their cattle ranges in the Great Western Bay of the Eurasian Steppe as they push their way up the valley of the Dniestr into the Galician forests; and we may go on to picture these stray stock-breeders finding themselves constrained, in a strange physical environment, to change their economic occupation by taking to mining. The historic prototypes of the mythical Dwarfs would then be a mining community in some secluded valley of the Carpathians or the Riesengebirge whose Nomad origin was still advertised in their ancestral dress at the time when the first aggressive Medieval German mineral prospectors arrived on the scene to put these *ci-devant* Nomad miners out of business.

The itch to find explanations for connexions between historical facts is, of course, excited by facts of other kinds besides identities in fashions of clothes. In the field of Language, for example, how had it come to pass that the vocabulary of a late-nineteenth-century middle-class English nursery included the name of the Sumeric goddess Inanna? The history of the translation of Inanna to an English nursery from a Sumerian temple was illuminated by her epiphany under her original name—none the worse for its long journey through Time and Space, save for the weathering away of its initial vowel—as the Nanna who, in the pagan pantheon of a post-Carolingian Scandinavian heroic age, was still being honoured as the consort of Balder, 'the Lord' who dies and rises from the dead. Though, in Scandinavia in the tenth century after Christ, the Norse version of the dying and rising god's traditional epithet has eclipsed this Sumeric god's proper name, Balder's identity with Tammuz, which is proclaimed in Balder's passion, is established by the tell-tale survival of the Sumerian proper name of a great Mother who is Tammuz-Balder's wife.[1] In a Victorian nursery, where the child's nurse meant more than its mother meant to the child, it was natural enough that the child should apply the name of this unforgettable Mother Goddess to the most puissant female figure within its miniature horizon.[2]

What, again, was the etymology of βασιλεύς, the Greek word for 'king', which was as enigmatic as it was familiar? *Kral*, the Slavonic word for 'king', was familiar without being enigmatic. The word *kral* was known to have originated in the coining of a common noun out of the proper name of an historical King Karl whose fame had made so wide and so deep and so lasting an impression on the imaginations of the Slavonic-speaking barbarians beyond the eastern borders of Charlemagne's empire that in all Slavonic dialects, from those of the adjacent Wends and Sṛbs to those of the distant Russians and Bulgarians, the Great Karl's

[1] See V. v. 150.

[2] The writer could remember how once in his nursery, when his nurse and his mother seemed to him to be annoyingly preoccupied by talking business with one another, he sought in vain to distract their attention to himself by repeatedly crawling under the bed, exclaiming, each time: 'Mother and Nanny are good; Mother and Nanny are God; I am hiding from God.' Without knowing it, he was playing at one of the principal cults of a Sumeric religion which, on the adult surface of life, had been extinct for some two thousand years in its native land of Shinar.

non-Slavonic personal name came, *par excellence*, to denote any holder of the royal office of which Karolus Magnus had been such a preeminent incumbent. On this analogy, might an inquirer hazard the guess that the Greek, like the Slavonic, word for 'king' had been derived from the foreign proper name of an historical king who had made a comparable impression on the imagination of the Achaean barbarians at the moment of their entry on to the stage of History? The Hittite counterpart of an Austrasian Karl was forthcoming in the person of Biyassiliš the son of Suppiluliuma, who was installed by his father as the Hittite sub-king of Carchemish,[1] commanding the right bank of the Euphrates at its western elbow, mid-way through the fourteenth century B.C., at just about the time when the Achaean pirates were making their first lodgements on the coasts of Pamphylia and Cyprus. Though Biyassiliš's reign at Carchemish was short, he won swift renown by invading Mitanni on his imperial father's behalf and reinstating there, as a Hittite puppet, Mattiwaza, a refugee claimant to the Mitannian throne.[2] It would be the less surprising to find that Biyassiliš had made his way into the Greek vocabulary, considering that Biyassiliš's brother, and Suppiluliuma's second successor on the Hittite imperial throne, Muršiliš II, who is known to have crossed the Achaeans' path in Millawanda, certainly did make his way into Greek legend as Myrtilus, the tool and victim of the Anatolian adventurer Pelops, while a later Hittite emperor, Tutkhaliya IV, who likewise had dealings with the Achaeans in Western Anatolia, figures in Greek legend as Deucalion, the survivor of the Flood.

The itch to find a link between two widely sundered yet patently identical historical terms—linguistic, sartorial, or whatnot—might still set a would-be historian's mind in motion when not only the connecting link but also one of the two terminals was missing. Who had been the ancestors of the Etruscans? Who were the descendants of the Lost Ten Tribes of Israel? There could have been few obscure peoples that had not been cast by some Hellenic or Modern Western antiquarian for the role of having been the Etruscans' progenitors; and there could have been still fewer ambitious and conceited peoples in the broad domains of Christendom and Islam that had not claimed to be the heirs of the Lost Tribes.

The fantastic history of these spurious claims was a warning that the potentially creative intellectual impulse to investigate the relations between historical facts might lose itself in a sandbed of folly; and a prudent adult historian would sternly restrict the ration of time and energy that he allowed his mind to devote to such unsolved, and perhaps insoluble, questions concerning the connexions between things that had fascinated him since childhood. Yet there were at least two grounds for seeing in these alluring curiosities of History something more than unprofitable trivialities. In the first place they might throw light on general historical questions of manifest importance. Our string of Plutarchan questions about the history of divers articles of dress brings out, for

[1] See Contenau, G.: *La Civilisation des Hittites* (Paris 1934, Payot), p. 95; Delaporte, L.: *Les Hittites* (Paris 1936, La Renaissance du Livre), p. 98; Cavaignac, E.: *Le Problème Hittite* (Paris 1936, Leroux), pp. 35 and 37.

[2] See Delaporte, op. cit., p. 108.

example, the interesting truth that the conductivity of the social fabric of human life is exceptionally high in two particular social milieux: in a 'universal state', such as the Achaemenian Empire or the Roman Empire, and in a Nomad pastoral society cruising on the waterless ocean of the Steppe. Our speculations about the provenance of a word in a Victorian English nursery vocabulary similarly bring out the truth that the radiational energy of elements of culture is exceptionally high when these elements are divinities. Such lights on the landscape of Oecumenical History, fitful though they might be, were nevertheless sufficiently illuminating in themselves to justify the exercise of the Intellect in investigating the connexions between facts that at first sight might appear trivial; but the main justification for this childish-looking intellectual pursuit was that it was pregnant with a question—'How did this come out of that? And how did that turn into this?'—which was at the heart of every adult historian's serious business on the intellectual plane.

In endeavouring to trace forwards and backwards the history of Skunkha's arresting 'pointed hood', a child's mind would be setting out on the Intellect's ultimate quest 'rerum cognoscere causas';[1] and, in putting itself through a childish trial practice of this sovereign intellectual activity, the mind of a potential historian would be unconsciously preparing itself against the historic day when it might rise to the height of some great occasion for wresting from the Sphynx an answer to one of her more significant riddles.

(*b*) PAULLO MAIORA

I. *Inspirations from Social Milieux*

Clarendon, Procopius, Josephus, Thucydides, Rhodes

'How has this come out of that?' If we set ourselves now to trace the genesis of some of the classic achievements of great historians, we shall find that this simple question has presented the challenge to which their mighty works have been the response. In making a survey of instances that are particularly instructive or particularly celebrated or both, we may find it convenient to examine first those cases in which the intellectual challenge has been presented by some public event, and then those in which it has been presented by some personal experience.

Since, in the histories of the civilizations down to the time of writing, wars had been the most frequent and most conspicuous agencies of social change at a pace fast enough to make the change perceptibly revolutionary even within the span of a single lifetime, it is not surprising to find that the intellectually inspiring elemental question 'How has this come out of that?' had often clothed itself in the form: 'How has this post-war state of affairs come out of that pre-war state?'

This question had suggested the subject for a classic historical work to Clarendon, Procopius, Josephus, Thucydides, and James Ford Rhodes; and, of these five great historians, the last-mentioned was perhaps the most remarkable witness to the strength of the inspiration that might be breathed into a potential historian's mind by the question how

[1] Virgil: *Georgics* II, l. 490.

the transit has come to be made from an ante-bellum dispensation to a post-bellum one that is strikingly unlike its predecessor, though it is separated from this previous dispensation chronologically by just a few alchemic war years.

Clarendon, after all, might have been expected to become the historian of the English Civil War of A.D. 1642–7; for, by the date of the outbreak of that war, Clarendon was already active and prominent in English parliamentary politics; as soon as war broke out, he became King Charles' principal adviser on legal and constitutional questions; and, before the war was over, he had risen to be one of the foremost statesmen in the Royalist camp. In short, the Civil War had been as great an event in its historian's personal life as in the public life of the nation that had been rent in twain by it. Procopius, the historian of the wars of Justinian, served in Belisarius's campaigns as the commander-in-chief's private secretary.[1] As for Josephus and Thucydides, the outbreak of the wars of which they eventually wrote histories found both of them of an age and social rank that qualified them for military service in commands of considerable responsibility, while Josephus's dramatic personal fortunes in the Great Romano-Jewish War of A.D. 66–70 gave him the advantage—inestimably valuable for a future historian—of seeing the military conflict that was to be his subject first from the side of his Jewish compatriots and afterwards from the side of his Roman captors, thanks to the open-mindedness and perspicacity shown by Vespasian in employing his gifted Jewish prisoner-of-war as a confidential adviser on Jewish affairs.[2] It is not surprising that Thucydides, as he tells us in the first sentence of his history, should have foreseen, at the outbreak of the Atheno-Peloponnesian War of 431–404 B.C., that this was going to be, not merely a great war, but perhaps actually the most important of all wars that had yet been waged within Hellenic memory,[3] or that Josephus,

[1] See Procopius's preface to *A History of the Wars of Justinian* (Book I, chap. 1).

[2] 'My own record of the war as a whole and of the incidental details is correct, since I was a first-hand witness of all the events. I was in command of our Galilaeans so long as resistance was possible, while after my capture I was a prisoner with the Romans. Vespasian and Titus compelled me to remain in constant attendance upon them under guard, at first in chains, though afterwards I was released and was sent from Alexandria, on Titus's staff, to the siege of Jerusalem. During this period there was no transaction that escaped my observation. The events in the Roman camp I sedulously recorded at first hand, while I was the only person present who could understand the reports of the deserters from the Jewish side. When all my material was in the proper state of preparation, I took advantage of a period of leisure at Rome to employ the services of collaborators to help me with the Greek language, and I thus wrote out my narrative.'—Josephus: Preface to *Contra Apionem* (Book I, chaps. 47–50).

[3] 'Thucydides of Athens has written the history of the war between the Peloponnesians and the Athenians. He began to write as soon as war broke out, in the belief that this war would eclipse all its predecessors in importance. He drew this inference from the fact that both belligerents, when they started hostilities, had reached the highest degree of preparedness in every arm, while the rest of the Hellenic World was already taking sides—some countries intervening at once and others intending to follow their example. This war was, indeed, the greatest upheaval ever experienced by Hellas and by a part of the non-Hellenic World (it would hardly be an exaggeration to say: by the Human Race). It is true that the passage of time has rendered accurate research into the recent as well as the remote past impossible; but, in the light of the earliest evidence that I consider trustworthy, I do not imagine that the past has produced either wars or other events on an important scale.'—Thucydides: *A History of the Great Atheno-Peloponnesian War*, Book I, chap. 1.

At Princeton, New Jersey, on the 22nd February, 1947, the writer of this Study had the interesting experience of hearing Thucydides' high estimate of the importance of the

in the first sentence of his history likewise, should have claimed for the Romano-Jewish War of A.D. 66–70 in retrospect that it was 'the greatest war of our own times' and that it would hardly be an exaggeration to add that it was 'the greatest of any wars on record between either city-states or nations.'[1] By contrast, James Ford Rhodes was not merely remote from public life but was also still only a boy at the time of the war[2] that inspired him to carry out his intellectual life-work. The only direct personal connexion, known to the present writer, that Rhodes had with the great public events in the United States either during or immediately before or after the Civil War was his father's participation, as one of the Douglasite Democratic delegates from Ohio, in the Democratic Party's Convention at Charleston, South Carolina, on the 23rd April–1st May, 1860.[3] Yet Rhodes' responsiveness to the intellectual challenge of the revolution in his country's life during his boyhood was apparently so vigorous that even in his schooldays, it is said, 'he had conceived the purpose of writing American history',[4] while in his adult life he demonstrated the steadfastness of an already settled purpose by the patience with which he waited until A.D. 1887 before starting work on his grand historical design[5] and by the persistence with which he then spent the next nineteen years (A.D. 1887–1906) in bringing *A History of the United States from the Compromise of 1850* down *to the Final Restoration of Home Rule at the South in 1877*,[6] and another sixteen years (A.D. 1906–22) after that in carrying the story on from A.D. 1877 to A.D. 1909.[7]

war of which he became the historian endorsed by a great living American soldier who had just taken on his shoulders the burden of the Secretaryship of State. In an address at Princeton on that date, in which he was impressing upon his audience the importance for the country of an enlightened public opinion that could co-operate intelligently with the Administration in the choice and execution of a national foreign policy, General Marshall suggested to them that one way of equipping themselves mentally for this contemporary political task would be to study the history of the Hellenic World during the generation ending in the outbreak of the War of 431–404 B.C.

[1] The intellectual advantageousness of a position in which he had a foot in both the contending camps and an insight into both the conflicting cultures inspired Josephus not merely to write a history of the war in which he had participated personally, in two successive different capacities, but also to publish an edition of his work in Greek as well as one in Aramaic. In his preface to *The Romano-Jewish War* (Book I, chaps. 1–16) he has recorded that his dissatisfaction with the histories of this war previously published [in Greek] 'has induced me to offer to the public of the Roman Empire, in a Greek translation, a work of my own, originally composed in my native [Aramaic] language and published in the non-Hellenic Orient. . . . I felt it a paradox that the truth concerning events of such importance should be allowed to remain unsettled and that the Parthians, the Babylonians, the most remote populations of Arabia, my own compatriots beyond the Euphrates, and the inhabitants of Adiabênê should be accurately informed, through my labours, of the origin, vicissitudes, and issue of the war, while the Hellenes and all Romans who did not serve in the campaign should have nothing better at their disposal than flattering or fictitious accounts which conceal the truth.'

The wideness of the range of the currency of Aramaic as a *lingua franca* in the Syriac World of Josephus's day has been noticed in V. v. 487–91.

[2] Rhodes was born on the 1st May, 1848, so he was not yet thirteen years old on the 12th April, 1861, when fire was opened on Fort Sumter, and not yet seventeen years old on the 26th April, 1865, when Johnson signed with Sherman the definitive convention for the surrender of all Confederate forces still under arms.

[3] See Nevins, Allen: *The Emergence of Lincoln* (New York 1950, Scribner, 2 vols.), vol. ii, p. 206.

[4] Morse Jr., John Torrey: 'Memoir of James Ford Rhodes', in the *Proceedings of the Massachusetts Historical Society*, October, 1926–June, 1927 (Boston 1927), p. 178.

[5] The pattern of Rhodes' working life is examined on pp. 147 and 154, below.

[6] See Morse, ibid., p. 180; A. L. Lowell, ibid., p. 124.

[7] See ibid., p. 190.

The experience of living through a war—whether as a prominent participant in the catastrophe or as a sensitive spectator of it—was thus the inspiration of all these five historians, but it is also evident that the theme with which a war presented each of them was a revolution in human affairs which was of greater magnitude and significance than the military conflict by which it was signalized.

Clarendon's underlying theme is the decision, in the English Civil War, of a momentous controversy over the evolution of the traditional constitution of the kingdom;[1] and, though Clarendon may hold that this decision was the wrong one, and may hope that its ostensible reversal at the Restoration may prove to have been genuine and permanent, his belief in the importance of his constitutional theme is attested by his act of writing his history.

Rhodes' underlying theme is the discomfiture, registered in the defeat of the Confederacy in the American Civil War, of one section of the United States and province of the Western World of the day which had been alienated from the rest of an American Commonwealth and a Western Society by the fateful heritage of 'the peculiar institution' of Negro Slavery. In the American Civil War the slave-holding South failed to preserve by the *ultima ratio* of political secession a traditional social evil that, by this date, had been decisively condemned by the conscience of the Western World as a whole. In recording the political failure of eleven of the slave states included in the United States in 1861 to emulate the thirteen colonies that had revolted against the British Crown in A.D. 1775 by establishing a new sovereign independent confederation to house a nation struggling to be born, the historian is at the same time recording the social failure of a slave-holding branch of a Late Modern Western Society to emulate a city-state cosmos which had differentiated itself from the main body of Western Christendom in the Medieval chapter of Western history.

Thucydides' underlying subject is the larger one of the tragic breakdown of a promising civilization;[2] and an intuition of this theme, and recognition of its importance, were no doubt the considerations that led an American soldier-statesman, on the 22nd February, 1947, to exhort an audience composed of the faculty, students, and alumni of a great American university to study the antecedents of the war that Thucydides had immortalized.[3]

Josephus's underlying theme was an episode in the long-drawn-out encounter between the Syriac and the Hellenic Society in which a Palestinian Jewry, posted in the perilous front line of the Syriac order of battle, had been partly inflamed and partly intimidated by a Zealot minority into embarking on the forlorn hope of taking up arms against an Hellenic universal state.[4]

'The revolutionary element among the Jews, which was at its zenith both in funds and in forces, timed its rebellion to take advantage of the prevailing disorders. The consequent convulsions were so violent that the

[1] See III. iii. 318.
[2] See III. iii., 291.
[3] See p. 60, n. 3, above.
[4] See II. ii. 285–6; III. iii. 294–6; and V. v. 68 and 125–6.

fate of the East hung in the balance between the two belligerents, who had everything respectively to hope and to fear from the issue. The Jews hoped that the entire body of their compatriots beyond the Euphrates would join in their rising, while the Romans were harassed by attacks from their German neighbours, unrest among their Celtic subjects, and the world-wide convulsions that followed the death of Nero.'[1]

As for Procopius, his underlying subject is the rally, registered in Justinian's wars, of an Hellenic Society, embodied politically in a Roman Empire, after both the empire and the society had appeared to be moribund. The questions raised in Procopius's mind by this series of Roman military counter-offensives against the barbarian intruders on Roman territory are: 'How have the Romans managed to regain the upper hand? What have been the new military equipment and tactics through which they have won their victory?[2] How has the Imperial Government acquired the resources for building churches as well as fortresses? And what is this revolutionary style of architecture in which Anthemius, in building the church of the Ayía Sophía,[3] has vindicated the Justinianean rally of the Hellenic Civilization as signally as Belisarius has vindicated it by overthrowing the Vandals and the Ostrogoths? How, in short, has the Romania of Arcadius and Theodosius II (*imperabant* A.D. 395–450) become the Romania of Justinian (*imperabat* A.D. 527–65)?' These were the questions that moved Procopius to write *The Wars of Justinian* and *Justinian's Public Works*;[4] but the sixth-century Caesarean historian-barrister had not reached the end of his tether before the unhappy outcome of a reign that, on the surface, had looked so magnificent had raised a further question in Procopius's mind: 'Has not this apparent rally really been a delusion? Has not Justinian's policy of action and outlay on the grand scale been a megalomaniac's irreparable blunder? Has not he proved, *en fin de compte*, to have achieved nothing more than barren and ephemeral triumphs purchased at the cost of dissipating irreplaceable resources which Arcadius and Theodosius II had conserved and which Leo the Great, Zeno, and Anastasius had augmented?'[5] This was the question that moved Procopius to think his second thoughts and to put these on record in *A Secret History of the Reign of Justinian and Theodora*.

Polybius

It will be seen that, while all five of the historians whom we have been considering were inspired to write their works by their experience of a war, the elemental question 'How has this come out of that?' came, in all five minds, to embrace a much wider gamut of historical change than just those events that could be construed as direct effects of the war which had originally precipitated the spate of intellectually fruitful questions. There are other historians to whom the elemental question presented itself from the outset in this broader form. For example, Polybius of Megalopolis (*vivebat circa* 206–128 B.C.) lived to see the number of

1 Josephus: Preface to *The Romano-Jewish War* (Book I, chaps. 4–5).
2 See the passage quoted in III. iii. 163.
3 See IV. iv. 54–55.
4 The *De Aedificiis*.
5 See IV. iv. 324–6.

Great Powers in a post-Alexandrine Hellenic World reduced from the five that had still been in existence at the time of the historian's birth to a single victorious survivor.

'The events which he has chosen as his subject are sufficiently extraordinary in themselves to arouse and stimulate the interest of every reader, young or old. What mind, however commonplace or indifferent, could feel no curiosity to learn the process by which almost the whole World fell under the undisputed ascendancy of Rome within a period of less than fifty-three years,[1] or to acquaint itself with the political organisation that was the secret of a triumph without precedent in the annals of Mankind? What mind, however much infatuated with other spectacles and other studies, could find a field of knowledge more profitable than this?'[2]

The experience of this political revolution in the Hellenic World of his day, which thus moved Polybius to ask the question 'How has this revolution come about?' also moved him to go on to ask two supplementary questions: 'Who are these Romans who have conquered the World within my lifetime?' and 'What is the intelligible field of historical study?'[3]

'If the two commonwealths which contended for world-power in this war had been objects of common knowledge [to the cultivated minority of the general public in the Hellenic World], it would perhaps have been superfluous to insert an introductory section in order to explain the policies and resources that inspired them to embark upon enterprises of such magnitude. Actually, however, the previous resources and transactions of the Roman and Carthaginian commonwealths are so unfamiliar to the majority of the Hellenic public that it has seemed essential to preface this history with two introductory volumes. This will ensure that no reader will find himself at the commencement of my main narrative without an answer to the question: "What policy was in the Romans' minds and what resources, military and economic, were in their hands at the time when they embarked upon these projects, which resulted in their becoming masters of the entire Mediterranean and its littoral?" These two introductory volumes will make it clear that the means at the Romans' disposal were admirably adapted to the end of world-power and world-empire, as conceived and attained by them.'[4]

The intellectual task, undertaken by Polybius, of putting these marchmen-conquerors of the Hellenic World on the Hellenic public's mental map was one for which the Megalopolitan statesman-historian had been singularly well equipped by the vicissitudes of his own life.[5] Like Josephus after him, Polybius was deported from his native land by the Roman authorities—not, indeed, as the prisoner-of-war in chains that Josephus was when he was taken to Alexandria, but as a political hostage sentenced to internment. Like Josephus, again, Polybius, in the next chapter

[1] i.e. from the spring of 219 B.C., when Hannibal laid siege to Saguntum, to the 22nd June, 168 B.C., when Lucius Aemilius Paullus won his decisive victory over the Macedonians at Pydna.—A.J.T.

[2] Polybius: Preface to *Oecumenical History since the* [*initial year of the*] *One Hundred and Fortieth Olympiad* [220–219 B.C.] (Book I, chap. 1), quoted already in III. iii. 312–13.

[3] This second of Polybius's two supplementary questions was the key which opened the door into a study of History in the mind of the present writer (see the present work, I. i. 1–50).

[4] Polybius, op. cit., Book I, chap. 3.

[5] See III. iii. 310–18.

of his personal story, succeeded in winning his Roman captors' confidence and esteem, and in Polybius's case this esteem flowered into a warm personal friendship between the Megalopolitan internee and his younger Roman contemporary, Publius Cornelius Scipio Aemilianus,[1] the son of the victor at Pydna who came to the front in Roman public life, both as a military commander and as a statesman, during the period of Polybius's internment in Italy (166–150 B.C.), and who subsequently took Polybius with him on his staff to the African front for the two Roman campaigns (*gerebantur* 147–146 B.C.) under Scipio's command that ended in the destruction of Carthage. When Polybius's fellow deportees from the city-states of the Achaean Confederacy had been relegated to Italian country towns, Scipio had obtained for Polybius the special privilege of being allowed to continue to reside in the capital. It will be seen that Polybius's portrait of Rome for the instruction of Hellenic eyes had been drawn from the life under exceptionally favourable conditions for the achievement of a faithful likeness.

Polybius's second supplementary question—'What is the intelligible field of historical study?'—opened up wider mental horizons.

'The coincidence by which all the transactions of the World have been oriented in a single direction and guided towards a single goal is the extraordinary characteristic of the present age, to which the special feature of the present work is a corollary. The unity of events imposes upon the historian a similar unity of composition in depicting for his readers the operation of the laws of Fortune on the grand scale, and this has been my own principal inducement and stimulus in the work which I have undertaken.'[2]

The virtual unification of the Hellenic World, within the historian's own lifetime, on the political plane opened his eyes to the continuity,[3] the universality,[4] and the unity[5] of History.

'Writers and readers of History ought to concentrate attention less upon the bald narrative of transactions than upon the antecedents, concomitants, and consequences of any given action. If you eliminate from History the "Why" and the "How" and the "Wherefore" of the particular transaction and the rationality—or the reverse—of its result, what is left of her ceases to be a science and becomes a *tour de force*, which may give momentary pleasure, but which is of no assistance whatever for dealing with the Future.'[6]

'It is impossible to obtain from the monographs of historical specialists a comprehensive view of the morphology of Universal History. By reading a bald and isolated narrative of the transactions in Sicily and Spain, it is obviously impossible to realise and understand either the magnitude or the unity of the events in question, by which I mean the methods and institutions of which Fortune has availed herself in order to accomplish what has been her most extraordinary achievement in our generation. This achievement is nothing less than the reduction of the entire known world under the dominion of a single empire—a phenomenon of which there is

1 See Polybius, op. cit., Book XXXI, chaps. 22–30.
2 Ibid., Book I, chap. 4, already quoted in III. iii. 317, n. 5.
3 See ibid., Book III, chaps. 31–32.
4 See ibid., Book V, chaps. 31[6]–33.
5 See ibid., Book VIII, chap. 2.
6 Ibid., Book III, chap. 31.

no previous example in recorded history. A limited knowledge of the processes by which Rome captured Syracuse and conquered Spain is, no doubt, obtainable from the specialists' monographs; but without the study of Universal History it is difficult to comprehend how she attained to universal supremacy. . . . It is only when we consider the fact that the same government and commonwealth was producing results in a variety of other spheres simultaneously with the conduct of these operations, and when we include in the same survey the internal crises and struggles which hampered those responsible for all the above-mentioned activities abroad, that the remarkable character of the events comes out clearly and obtains the attention which it deserves. This is my reply to those who imagine that the work of specialists will initiate them into Universal and General History.'[1]

A post-Modern Western historian, re-reading these passages from Polybius's work on the 18th September, 1952, was moved to wonder whether he might live to see 'the reduction of the entire known world under the dominion of a single empire'—a phenomenon of which there had in truth been as many previous examples in recorded history as there had been 'universal states'—inspire another Polybius to write the history of the political unification of another society. At the time of writing, it was impossible to foretell whether 'Fortune' would present this challenging theme to some responsive historian in the rising generation; it was not even possible yet to foretell whether, if a twentieth-century *Oikoumenê* did crystallize into unity, it would crystallize round the United States or round the Soviet Union. It might be guessed, however, that, if Rome's role were to be played in a post-Modern Western World by the United States, the historian of her involuntary assumption of dominion would be a West European, and it could be prophesied with greater confidence that, if the latter-day West European Polybius did leave his native land to do this piece of creative intellectual work, he would visit the United States neither as a prisoner-of-war nor as a political hostage but as the hospitably invited guest of some politically disinterested non-governmental American institution dedicated single-mindedly to the promotion of knowledge.

Josephus and Ibn al-Tiqtaqā

The opportunity, which Polybius found and seized, of making his conquered fellow-countrymen acquainted with their Roman conquerors was equally open to Josephus, who repaired to Rome some 236 years after Polybius had been deported thither; but the account of Roman institutions and policy which Josephus was so well qualified to write for the instruction of an Aramaic-reading Jewish public might not have found a market among the remnants of a shattered yet still Zealot-minded Jewry, in whose eyes the victorious Romans were still the same uninterestingly abominable Gentiles that they had always been, and in whose judgement the victory of Roman over Jewish arms was due, not to any notable human strength or virtue in the Roman Commonwealth, but to the inscrutable will of an omnipotent Yahweh. Josephus did emu-

[1] Polybius, op. cit., Book VIII, chap. 2.

late Polybius in turning to good account his intellectually advantageous footing in two culturally diverse camps, but the use that Josephus made of his opportunity was to address himself, as Polybius had done, to an Hellenic public whose curiosity was still insatiable. The supplementary question that Josephus took up after he had responded to the question raised by the Great Romano-Jewish War of A.D. 66–70 was, not 'Who are these Romans who have crushed an insurgent Palestinian Jewry?', but 'Who are these Jews who have brought this fate upon themselves by daring to challenge the might of an oecumenical empire commanding all the resources of a politically united Hellenic World?' This was the question that Josephus answered by writing, for an Hellenic public, *The Ancient History of the Jews*.

In this work Josephus commemorated, for the instruction of their conquerors, the history and êthos of a Jewish advance-guard of the Syriac Society which had gone down to disaster in a forlorn hope in one of the many engagements in the course of a one-thousand-years-long struggle between a post-Cyran Syriac and a post-Alexandrine Hellenic Civilization; and what Josephus had thus done for a Palestinian Jewry was done for the Syriac Society as a whole, in the last phase of its history, by the Shī'ī Muslim historian Ibn al-Tiqtaqā of Hillah[1] (*natus circa* A.D. 1262).

Ibn al-Tiqtaqā had been born in the metropolitan province of a re-integrated Syriac universal state on the morrow of the extirpation of the 'Abbasid Caliphate and incidental devastation of 'Irāq[2] by the Mongol war-lord Hūlāgū in A.D. 1258. The question presented to him by his social milieu was: 'How has this world in which I have grown up—a world in which 'Irāq is economically derelict and politically subject to the rule of a Eurasian Nomad barbarian war-band—come out of the world in which my forefathers lived from one generation to another over a Time-span of more than five hundred years: a world in which 'Irāq was the garden and granary of the *Oikoumenê*, and in which an 'Abbasid oecumenical government ruled from Baghdad a universal state extending north-eastward to the Jaxartes, northward to the Caucasus, westward to the Atlantic, and southward to the Arabian and Sindī shores of the Indian Ocean?' The supplementary question that arose for Ibn al-Tiqtaqā, as it had arisen for Josephus, was: 'What have been the history and the êthos of this society that has met with this disaster?' And, in Ibn al-Tiqtaqā's generation, as in Josephus's, this was a question that was of some interest to the alien conquerors by whose hands the disaster had been inflicted; for Ibn al-Tiqtaqā lived to see a militarily subjugated Dār-al-Islām begin to take its savage Eurasian Nomad conquerors captive.[3]

[1] 'Ibn al-Tiqtaqā', 'the son of a chatterbox', was an onomatopoeic nickname for Jalāl-ad-Dīn Abu Ja'far Muhammad b. Tāji'd-Dīn Abi'l-Hasan 'Alī, the spokesman of the Shī'ī community in the Shī'ī holy cities—Hillah, Najaf, and Karbalā—in an 'Irāq that was to remain the stronghold of Shī'ism (see the note by Professor H. A. R. Gibb, printed in the present Study, I. i. 400–2) until the forcible conversion of Iran by Shah Ismā'īl Safawī. See the notice of Ibn al-Tiqtaqā by Clément Huart in the *Encyclopaedia of Islam*, vol. ii (Leiden 1927, Brill), pp. 423–4. According to E. G. Browne's English version of Mīrzā Muhammad b. 'Abdi'l-Wahhāb-i-Qazwīnī's edition of 'Alā-ad-Dīn 'Atā Malik-i-Juwaynī's *Ta'rīkh-i-Jahān Gushā* (London 1912, Luzac), p. lx, Ibn al-Tiqtaqā's name was Safīyu'd-Dīn Muhammad b. 'Alī b. Muhammad b. Tabātabā.

[2] See IV. iv. 42–45.

[3] See Horace: *Epistulae*, Book II, Ep. i, l. 156.

After the Mongol conqueror Hūlāgū's son and second successor Ahmad Takūdar (*dominabatur* A.D. 1252–4) had paid for his conversion to Islam by losing both his throne and his life at the hands of his outraged pagan Mongol *comitatus*,[1] Hūlāgū's sixth successor Ghāzān Khān embraced Islam in the year of his accession, A.D. 1295, without suffering his great-uncle Takūdar's fate;[2] and this definitive conversion of the House of Hūlāgū inaugurated a change of attitude on the converts' part towards a religion and culture that had now become theirs as well as their subjects'.[3] The question 'What have been the history and êthos of this society that is now captivating its conquerors?' was answered by Ibn al-Tiqtaqā in a history of Islam from the epiphany of the Prophet Muhammad down to the sack of Baghdad by the Mongols in A.D. 1258, and a work that has become celebrated as *Al-Fakhrī* obtained its title from the name of Ghāzān Khān's governor of Mawsil, Fakhr-ad-Dīn 'Īsā, to whom the book was dedicated by the author. In this answer to the supplementary question that the historian's social milieu had presented to him, Ibn al-Tiqtaqā has succeeded in recapturing and reproducing something of the freshness and radiance of a dawn in which the Primitive Muslims Arab, as they went 'from strength to strength',[4] had found it 'bliss to be alive'[5] under a new dispensation in which the long despised and rejected[6] Children of Ishmael were fortified by the conviction that they had been chosen by God to become the instruments of His will and purpose in place of the Jewish and Christian People of the Book.

'The same stone which the builders refused is become the headstone in the corner. This is the Lord's doing, and it is marvellous in our eyes.'[7]

[1] See Browne, E. G.: *A Literary History of Persia*, vol. iii (Cambridge 1928, University Press), pp. 25–26.

[2] See I. i. 363.

[3] On the 4th Sha'bān, 694 (the 19th June, 1295), Ghāzān 'and ten thousand Mongols made their profession of faith in the presence of Shaykh Sadr-ad-Dīn Ibrāhīm, the son of the eminent doctor Sa'd-ad-Dīn al-Hamawī. Nor did Ghāzān lack zeal for his new convictions; for, four months after his conversion, he permitted [the Mongol amir] Nawrūz [, a previous convert who had been instrumental in converting Ghāzān,] to destroy the churches, synagogues, and idol-temples at Tabrīz. He also caused a new coinage bearing Muhammadan inscriptions to be struck, and by an edict issued in May 1299 prohibited usury, as contrary to the Muhammadan religion. In November 1297 the Mongol amīrs adopted the turban in place of their national head-dress' (Browne, E. G.: *A Literary History of Persia*, vol. iii (Cambridge 1928, University Press), pp. 40–41).

Ghāzān Khān's conversion secured for Islam not merely its survival but the recovery of its supremacy in the Il-Khāns' dominions, which included Iran, Armenia, and Eastern Anatolia, as well as 'Irāq. On this occasion the anti-Islamic reactions in the converted Il-Khān's pagan Mongol *comitatus* were successfully repressed (see Browne, op. cit., p. 41); and Ghāzān's brother and successor Khudābandah, *alias* Ūljaytū (*accessit* A.D. 1305), who had been converted to Islam by his wife, promptly confirmed his predecessor's re-establishment of Islam as the official religion of this Mongol successor-state of the 'Abbasid Caliphate (see Browne, op. cit., p. 48), though his Christian mother had had him baptized as a child under the name of Nicholas (op. cit., p. 46).

The tragic losing battle fought by the Nestorian Christian Church in the Il-Khāns' dominions against a refluent tide of Muslim fanaticism, which the triumphant conversion of Ghāzān Khān had let loose, is graphically described in 'The History of the Life and Travels of Rabban Sāwmā, Envoy and Plenipotentiary of the Mongol Khāns to the Kings of Europe, and Markōs who, as Mār Yahbhallāhā III, became Patriarch of the Nestorian Church in Asia', translated from the Syriac by Sir E. A. Wallis Budge under the title *The Monks of Kūblāi Khan, Emperor of China* (London 1928, The Religious Tract Society).

[4] Psalm lxxxiv. 7.

[5] Wordsworth, W.: *The French Revolution, as it appeared to Enthusiasts = The Prelude*, Book XI, l. 108.

[6] Isaiah liii. 3.

[7] Psalm cxviii. 22–23.

In this portrait of Primitive Islam, painted by a scion of the House of 'Alī, on the morrow of the death of a pre-Mongol Islamic commonwealth, to satisfy the slayers' posthumous curiosity about their victim, there is a touch of the serenity that comes over a human countenance when the hand of Death smoothes away the lines drawn there by the struggles of life.

'Alā-ad-Dīn Juwaynī and Rashīd-ad-Dīn Hamadānī

The 'Irāqī historian Ibn al-Tiqtaqā's attractive history of the pre-Mongol Muslim Commonwealth in his own Arabic tongue was not the only notable historical work that was written under a Eurasian Nomad domination in the eastern half of Dār-al-Islām, on the morrow of the catastrophe of A.D. 1258, in response to questions raised by this harrowing experience; nor was this the only historical *motif* that was suggested by the spectacle of the 'Abbasid Caliphate's fatal collision with an erupting Mongol Eurasian Nomad Power.

One of the incidental and undesigned effects of the overthrow of the 'Abbasids and devastation of 'Irāq was, as we have noticed already in an earlier context,[1] the birth, in a *ci-devant* Syriac World's now derelict north-eastern provinces, of an Iranic Muslim Civilization, affiliated to the Syriac, in which, for most purposes other than the exposition of Islamic theology, a New Persian language and literature were to supplant the Arabic language and literature that had been dominant in all provinces of Dār-al-Islām during the six centuries intervening between the overthrow of the Sasanids by the Primitive Muslim Arab ghāzis and the overthrow of the 'Abbasids by the pagan Mongols. When a previously oecumenical Arabic culture retreated westwards before the face of the oncoming Mongols into a fastness in Egypt with a glacis in Syria and an eastern frontier at the western elbow of the River Euphrates, a New Persian literature that, by this time, had been on the rise for some three hundred years now at last came fully into its own; and this was perhaps the only creative cultural activity in the conquered and devastated half of Dār-al-Islām that benefited from the disaster on the very morrow of it. During the lifetime of the survivors of a generation in Dār-al-Islām that was old enough to have completed its education in a classical Arabic language and literature before the catastrophe of A.D. 1258, the cultivation of the New Persian language and literature was already relieved of the incubus of the cultural ascendancy of Arabic without being yet impoverished by being cut off from the living sources of Arabic literary inspiration. The period of Mongol domination in Iran and 'Irāq (*currebat* A.D. 1258–1337) was an age in which the leading Persian men of letters were still bilingual in the full sense of still being able not merely to read Arabic but also to write in it, as well as in their native Persian tongue;[2] and it was also an age which produced

[1] See I. i. 71, with n. 3.

[2] This point is made by Browne in op. cit., vol. iii, pp. 62–65. The historian Rashīd-ad-Dīn (*vivebat circa* A.D. 1247–1318), for example, made it his practice to arrange for the translation of his Persian works into Arabic and the translation of his Arabic works into Persian. Rashīd-ad-Dīn's own account of these arrangements of his is quoted

incomparably eminent Persian historians,[1] in contrast to both the previous and the subsequent age, in which the brightest stars in the firmament of a New Persian literature were, not historians, but poets.[2]

The ascendancy of the historians in the intervening Il-Khānī Age is significant; and it is no less significant that the two greatest members of this pleiad—'Alā-ad-Dīn 'Atā Malik-i-Juwaynī (*vivebat* A.D. 1226–83) and Rashīd-ad-Dīn Fadlallāh Tabīb al-Hamadānī (*vivebat circa* A.D. 1247–1318)—were also eminent civil servants in the Mongol Il-Khāns' service, and that two of the lesser lights, Wassāf-i-Hadrat 'Abdallāh b. Fadlallāh of Shīrāz and Hamdallāh Mustawfī of Qazwīn, both of whom were protégés of Rashīd-ad-Dīn's, were officials of the Il-Khānī Government's Internal Revenue Department.[3]

The pagan barbarian conquerors of Iran and 'Irāq, who held out for thirty-seven years (A.D. 1258–95) after their conquest of Baghdad before succumbing to Islam themselves, had found themselves from the outset unable to dispense with the services of their newly acquired Muslim subjects; for the conquerors' purpose in invading Dār-al-Islām and overthrowing the Caliphate had been to step into the Caliph's shoes; and the only means by which these interloping barbarians could ensure that, after they had extinguished the Caliphate, the Caliph's government should be carried on for their benefit was by drawing upon an existing panel of native Persian Muslim professional administrators. The historian 'Alā-ad-Dīn 'Atā Malik-i-Juwaynī's brother, Shams-ad-Dīn Muhammad Juwaynī, managed the administration of Hūlāgū's appanage for the conqueror and for his first two successors during twenty-one years (A.D. 1263–84) of the Il-Khānī régime as their *sāhib-dīwān*,[4] and the two brothers were the sons of a *mustawfi'l-mamālik* (minister of finance) and the grandsons of a prime minister of a by then already *fainéant* 'Abbasid Caliphate's Khwārizmian successor-state in the northeastern marches of Dār-al-Islām, over against the Eurasian Steppe, on which the Mongol storm had broken in its full fury in A.D. 1220[5] at the fiat of a world-conquering Chingis.

The grandfather had accompanied the last of the Khwārizm Shahs, Sultan Muhammad, and his indomitable son and successor Jalāl-ad-Dīn Mankubirnī, when they had 'gone on the run', fighting rear-guard actions as they went.[6] The father, who had lingered in Khurāsān, had

verbatim, from *man. arabe* No. 356, foll. 1 et seqq. in the Bibliothèque Nationale [*ci-devant* Royale] in Paris, by E. M. Quatremère in his life of Rashīd-ad-Dīn prefixed to his edition of part of Rashīd-ad-Dīn's *Jāmi'-al-Tawārīkh* ('A Comprehensive Collection of Histories'), *Histoire des Mongols de la Perse*, vol. i (Paris 1836, Imprimerie Royale), pp. cxxxiv–cxxxvi. A student of History will be reminded of the cultural situation in Italy under an Ostrogoth domination (*durabat* A.D. 493–535), when the leading Italian men of letters were still conversant with Greek as well as with their native Latin.

[1] See Browne, op. cit., vol. iii, pp. 62 and 65.

[2] The pre-Mongol age of New Persian literary history had been made illustrious by Firdawsī (*vivebat circa* A.D. 932–1020/1) and by Sa'di (*vivebat circa* A.D. 1184–1292); the post-Mongol age was to be made illustrious by Hāfiz (*obiit* A.D. 1389) and by Jāmī (*vivebat* A.D. 1414–92). See I. i. 360, n. 1, and II. ii. 77, n. 1.

[3] See Browne, op. cit., pp. 67 and 87.

[4] For the dates, see Browne, *apud* Juwaynī, ed. cit., pp. xxix and xlvii–xlviii.

[5] See II. ii. 142, with n. 2.

[6] See Browne, E. G., in Mirzā Muhammad Qazwīnī's edition of 'Alā-ad-Dīn Juwaynī's *Ta'rīkh-i-Jahān Gushā* (London 1912, Luzac), p. xxi.

been rounded up at Tūs by the Mongol governor Jintimūr and taken, willy nilly, into the Mongols' service in A.D. 1232–3,[1] and his two sons, Shams-ad-Dīn and 'Alā-ad-Dīn, had followed in his footsteps. Shams-ad-Dīn had been in the service of Chingis' grandson and Qūbilāy's brother Hūlāgū, the commander of the Mongol forces on an anti-Islamic front in the Khwārizm Shāhs' already conquered domain to the north-east of the Caspian Gates, two years before his Mongol master's extirpation of the Ismā'īlī Shī'ī Assassins at Alamūt in A.D. 1257, and three years before his sack of Baghdad in A.D. 1258.[2] Shams-ad-Dīn's brother 'Alā-ad-Dīn, the historian (*natus* A.D. 1226), had entered the Mongol public service before he was twenty years old[3] as the protégé of his father's Mongol patron Arghūn, who had been the governor of the Mongol Empire's anti-Islamic march before Hūlāgū Khān's arrival on this front in A.D. 1256,[4] and he was one of three commissioners to whom Arghūn had entrusted the administration of Khurāsān when he had handed over his own command to Hūlāgū.[5] 'Alā-ad-Dīn Juwaynī had then accompanied Hūlāgū Khān on his campaigns (*gesta* A.D. 1256–8) against the Ismā'īlī Power in Central and Western Iran and against the remnant of the 'Abbasid Power in 'Irāq;[6] he was appointed governor of Baghdad by Hūlāgū in A.D. 1259, within a year of the conquest;[7] and he continued—save for a few months in A.D. 1281–2, when he was under a cloud[8]—to hold this responsible administrative post till his death in A.D. 1283.[9]

The historian Rashīd-ad-Dīn, who gained his first access to the Il-Khānī Court as a professional physician during the reign of Hūlāgū's first successor Abāqā Khān (*dominabatur* A.D. 1265–82),[10] was taken by Abāqā into the public administration, was appointed Grand Vizier by Ghāzān Khān (*dominabatur* A.D. 1295–1304),[11] and was retained in this post throughout the rest of Ghāzān's reign and the whole of his successor Khudābandah Ūljāytū's (*dominabatur* A.D. 1305–16). Both Shams-ad-Dīn Juwaynī and Rashīd-ad-Dīn Hamadānī obtained important posts in the public service for their sons and other relatives. One of Shams-ad-Dīn's sons, Bahā-ad-Dīn, had made his mark as governor of 'Irāq-i-'Ajam (the Jabal) and Fars before his death at the age of thirty;[12] and Rashīd-ad-Dīn's son Ghiyāth-ad-Dīn was appointed to his father's post of Grand Vizier[13] by Abu Sa'īd (*dominabatur* A.D. 1317–34), the last effective ruler of the Il-Khānī line.

Public service proved to be as dangerous a trade for Persian men of

[1] See Browne, ibid., pp. xxi–xxii.
[2] See Browne, *A Literary History of Persia*, vol. iii, p. 20.
[3] See Browne, *apud* Juwaynī, ed. cit., p. xxiii.
[4] See Browne, ibid., p. xxv.
[5] See Browne, ibid., p. xxvi.
[6] See Browne, ibid., pp. xxvii–xxviii.
[7] See Browne, ibid., pp. xxviii–xxix; eundem: *A Literary History of Persia*, vol. iii, p. 20, n. 1.
[8] See Browne, *apud* Juwaynī, ed. cit., pp. xxxix–xliv.
[9] Browne, *A Literary History of Persia*, vol. iii., p. 66.
[10] See Quatremère, E. M., in his life of Rashīd-ad-Dīn prefixed to his edition of part of Rashīd-ad-Dīn's *Jāmi'-al-Tawārīkh* ('A Comprehensive Collection of Histories'), *Histoire des Mongols de la Perse*, vol. i (Paris 1836, Imprimerie Royale), p. viii.
[11] See Quatremère, ibid.
[12] See Browne, *A Literary History of Persia*, vol. iii, p. 21. Another of his sons Sharaf-ad-Dīn Hārūn, was a poet.
[13] See Quatremère, op. cit., p. xlvii.

letters under a Mongol régime in Iran and ʿIrāq as it had been for Roman men of letters under an Ostrogoth régime in Italy. The historian-governor ʿAlā-ad-Dīn ʿAtā Malik-i-Juwaynī, after his fall in A.D. 1281 and reinstatement in A.D. 1282, was so fortunate as to die, as Cassiodorus had died, in his bed; but Boethius's fate overtook first the historian's brother, the *sāhib-dīwān*, and then Rashīd-ad-Dīn and Rashīd-ad-Dīn's son, Ghiyāth-ad-Dīn, in turn. Shams-ad-Dīn Muhammad Juwaynī and his surviving sons were Ahmad Takūdar Khān's fellow-victims in the anti-Islamic *émeute* among the Il-Khān's pagan Mongol *comitatus* that was provoked by Takūdar's rashly premature conversion to Islam.[1] Rashīd-ad-Dīn, after having been dismissed from office by Ūljaytū Khān's successor Abu Saʿīd Khān in October 1317, was put to death, with his young son Ibrāhīm, on the 18th July, 1318, at the age of seventy-three, as the penalty for his having incautiously allowed himself to be persuaded to resume office.[2] Ghiyāth-ad-Dīn and a surviving brother of his met their deaths by violence in A.D. 1336, in the anarchy in which the Mongol régime in Iran and ʿIrāq foundered after the death of Abu Saʿīd.[3] In a Mongol Iran, as in an Ostrogoth Italy, the civil service was thus a hazardous occupation[4] for a man of letters, but it was also a stimulating one.

The Persian civil servant historians of the Il-Khānī Age were stimulated by their social milieu to ask Polybius's questions as well as Josephus's and their own Josephan-minded Arab contemporary Ibn al-Tiqtaqā's.

Like Josephus, ʿAlā-ad-Dīn ʿAtā Malik-i-Juwaynī has commemorated, in the history of the Khwārizm Shāhs that constitutes the second part of his tripartite *Ta'rīkh-i-Jahān-Gushā* ('A History of the World-Conqueror' Chingis Khan),[5] the forlorn hope of an advance-guard of his society that had put up a valiant resistance to the onslaught of an overwhelming alien power, while Rashīd-ad-Dīn in his *Jāmiʿ-al-Tawārīkh*

[1] See Browne, *A Literary History of Persia*, vol. iii, pp. 27–29.

[2] See Quatremère, op. cit., pp. xxxix–xliv.

[3] See ibid., p. lii.

[4] In both situations the danger arose from the interaction of two untoward factors. One of these was the barbarian rulers' proneness to suspect disloyalty in alien subjects whose professional services were indispensable to them because the intricacies of a civilized administration were beyond their own comprehension. The second untoward factor was the mutual rivalry and jealousy of the native professional civil servants themselves, who found it difficult to resist the temptation to further their own careers by denigrating their colleagues in the eyes of their ignorant and therefore credulous barbarian masters. Under the Il-Khānī régime the principal Persian officers of state were almost driven into falling foul of one another by the practice—introduced, no doubt, by the Mongol rulers deliberately, as a safeguard against possible abuses of power on the part of their Persian employees—of appointing a pair of Grand Viziers, equal with one another in status, without any demarcation, either territorial or functional, between their respective competences (see Quatremère, op. cit., pp. xxxii–xxxiii).

[5] An edition by Mīrzā Muhammad b. ʿAbd-al-Wahhāb of Qaswīn has been published in the E. J. W. Gibb Memorial Series, No. xvi, in three volumes (London 1912, Luzac). See also Browne, *A Literary History of Persia*, vol. iii, pp. 65–66. This work, which was completed in A.D. 1260, stops short of the fall of Baghdad in A.D. 1258, but tells, in the third of its three parts, the story of the fall of Alamūt in 1256. The whole of this Part III is devoted to the history of the Ismāʿīlīs down to Hūlāgū's overthrow of their last Grand Master, Rukn-ad-Dīn Khurshāh, in Kuhistan and the Elburz. Juwaynī's work has been continued in Wassāf's, who has carried the regional history of Mongol rule in Iran and ʿIrāq on from A.D. 1257, where Juwaynī's history stops, down to A.D. 1328 in his *Tajzīyat-al-Amsār wa Tazjīyat-al-Aʿsār* (see Browne, op. cit., vol. iii, pp. 67–68).

('A Comprehensive Collection of Histories') has commemorated the history and êthos of the whole of the Syriac Society to which the Mongol invaders had given the *coup de grâce* that the Western Christian Crusaders had previously tried and failed to deliver. Moreover, in this part of his work, Rashīd-ad-Dīn has taken a broader view of the Syriac Civilization than has been taken by Ibn al-Tiqtaqā in *Al-Fakhīr*. The 'Irāqī Sayyid's historical vision is limited to the history of a pre-Mongol Islamic Commonwealth, whereas Rashīd-ad-Dīn treats the history of the Caliphate, from Abu Bakr to Musta'sim, merely as the second of three chapters of an essentially Iranian story in which the first chapter runs from a mythical dawn down to the fall of the Sasanian Dynasty, while the third chapter is occupied with the histories of the 'Abbasid Caliphate's Persian and Turkish successor-states down to the bursting of the Mongol Nomad tornado that has swept them all away.[1] The history of the same Syriac Civilization, seen from the same Iranian angle of vision, and presented within the same framework on the same lines, is the subject of the whole of Mustawfī's *Ta'rīkh-i-Guzīdah* ('A Select History'),[2] in which the author thus shows himself to be, on this point, Rashīd-ad-Dīn's disciple as well as his protégé.

Moreover, for Rashīd-ad-Dīn, the history of a Syriac Civilization that has fallen a victim to the Mongols is not, even on the broader lines on which the Persian historian approaches it, either a whole in itself or an end in itself, as it is for the contemporary Arab historian Ibn al-Tiqtaqā. In Rashīd-ad-Dīn's work the history of his own civilization is introduced as an integral part of Universal History, and he has included Universal History in his 'Comprehensive Collection' because he has undertaken to answer the three questions that have likewise been the inspirations of Polybius's *Oecumenical History*:[3] 'How has this revolution in human affairs come about?' 'Who are these previously obscure barbarians who have suddenly made their mark by conquering the World in our time?' 'What is the intelligible field of historical study?' According to Rashīd-ad-Dīn's own account of his intellectual history, he had begun to study the history of the Mongols on his own initiative;[4] but he had not thought of writing history[5] till he was commanded by his master Ghāzān Khān to write the history of the Eurasian Nomads[6] (the part of his work corresponding to Polybius's account of the institutions and policy of the Romans), and thereafter, by Ghāzān's successor Khudābandah Ūljaytū, to write a Universal History and Geography[7] (corresponding to the remainder of Polybius's work). Rashīd-ad-Dīn implies

[1] See Browne's arrangement of the component parts of Rashīd-ad-Dīn's 'Comprehensive Collection' in op. cit., vol. iii, p. 74. In this Iranocentric presentation of Syriac history the Arab Caliphate is treated, as will be observed, as the successor of the Iranian Empire of the Sasanidae, and not of the Arabian principality established by the Prophet Muhammad. Since Muhammad's career was contemporary with the last days of the Sasanian régime, his biography finds its place in this part of Rashīd-ad-Dīn's 'Comprehensive Collection', as a postscript to the volume devoted to the Sasanidae.

[2] See the table of contents of Mustawfī's 'A Select History', as reproduced by Browne in op. cit., vol. iii, pp. 90–94.

[3] See pp. 64–66, above.

[4] Rashīd-ad-Dīn: *Jāmi'-al-Tawārīkh*, preface, pp. 80–81 in Quatremère's edition and French translation of the Persian text.

[5] See Rashīd-ad-Dīn, preface to the *Jāmi'*, Quatremère's translation, p. 47.

[6] See ibid., pp. 7–9, 47, 51, 75, and 81.

[7] See ibid., pp. 37–39 and 59.

that he might have shrunk from embarking on this vast scholarly and literary enterprise in the narrow margin of leisure left to him by his exacting official duties if he had not felt it to be part of these duties to obey, as best he could, these royal commands in a field outside the normal range of a civil servant's activities.[1] The credit due to the two Mongol princes for having thus set Rashīd-ad-Dīn to work is proclaimed in the titles given by the author to the two parts of his 'Comprehensive Collection'. His special history of the Mongols and Turks is called the *Ta'rīkh-i-Ghāzānī*,[2] while his General History of Mankind is dedicated to Ūljaytū.

The historian's elemental intellectual question 'How has this come out of that?' presented itself in Rashīd-ad-Dīn's social milieu in the same terms as in Polybius's. 'What', this social milieu inspired the Persian historian to ask himself, 'has been the process by which almost the whole World has fallen under the undisputed ascendancy of the Mongols within a period of less than fifty-five years?'[3] And this question has been put by Rashīd-ad-Dīn in the preface to his *A Comprehensive Collection of Histories* in terms reminiscent of the corresponding passage[4] in Polybius's preface to his *Oecumenical History*.

'The beginning of every new religion or new empire constitutes a distinctive new era (*Ibtidā'-i-har milleti wa har dawlati ta'rīkh*[5]*-i-mu'ayyan bāshad*). Now what fact or event has ever been more memorable than the beginning of the dynasty of Chingis Khān, or has better deserved to be taken as marking a new era? The fact is that, within the span of a small number of years, this monarch . . . subjugated a great number of the kingdoms of the World and conquered and exterminated a host of unruly people. . . . When world-wide dominion devolved upon Chingis Khān and his noble kinsmen and illustrious descendants, all the kingdoms of the *Oikoumenê*—Chīn and Māchīn (South China), Khitāy (North China), Hind and Sind (India), Transoxania, Turkistan, Syria, Rūm, the Ās (Alans), the Russians, the Circassians, Qipchāq, Kalār (?),[6] the Bashkirs—or, to put it in one word, all the countries within the four quarters of the compass—submitted to these princes and became subject to their ordinances . . . [Chingis Khān] gave the whole Universe one and the same physiognomy and instilled identical feelings into all hearts. He purified the domains of the empires by delivering them from the domination of perverse usurpers and from the oppression of audacious enemies. He handed his empire on to his illustrious kinsmen and noble descendants.'[7]

[1] See Rashīd-ad-Dīn, preface to the *Jāmi'*, Quatremère's translation, pp. 47–51.

[2] The second volume of the *Ta'rīkh-i-Ghāzānī*, covering the history of the Mongol Khāqāns from the accession of Chingis' son Ogotāy to the death of Qūbilāy's grandson Timūr, has been edited by E. Blochet in the E. J. W. Gibb Memorial Series, vol. xviii (London 1911, Luzac). The chapters on the career of Hūlāgū Khān in the third volume, which covers the history of the Il-Khāns of Iran and 'Irāq down to the death of Ghāzān, have been edited, together with the preface to the whole of the *Jamī'-al-Tawārīkh*, by E. M. Quatremère in *Histoire des Mongols de la Perse*, vol. i (Paris 1836, Imprimerie Royale).

[3] i.e. from the overthrow of Wang Khān the Karāyit by Chingis Khān the Mongol in A.D. 1203 (see II. ii. 237–8) to the overthrow of the 'Abbasid Caliph Musta'sim by Chingis' grandson Hūlāgū in A.D. 1258.

[4] Quoted on p. 64, above.

[5] In the two preceding sentences the author has pointed out that 'new era' is one of two meanings of the word *ta'rīkh*, the other meaning being 'chronicle'.—A.J.T.

[6] See Quatremère's learnèd but inconclusive note 88, in op. cit., p. 72, on this enigmatic name.

[7] Rashīd-ad-Dīn, ibid., pp. 60–63 and 70–73.

This epoch-making revolution in the World's affairs raised, in minds that had grown up on the morrow of it, the two Polybian supplementary questions 'Who are these conquerors of the World?' and 'What is this World that they have conquered?' Rashīd-ad-Dīn addressed himself to the first supplementary question at Ghāzān's instance, and to the second at Ūljaytū's. In taking up the first of the two, Rashīd-ad-Dīn had been anticipated by 'Alā-ad-Din 'Atā Malik-i-Juwaynī; for the *Ta'rīkh-i-Jahān-Gushā* was finished in A.D. 1260,[1] forty-six years before the *Ta'rīkh-i-Ghāzānī* was presented by Rashīd-ad-Dīn to Ghāzān's successor Ūljaytū on the 14th April, 1306,[2] and the first of the three parts of Juwaynī's work deals with the history of Chingis Khān, his predecessors, and his successors down to his son Chaghatāy, whose appanage lay in Transoxania and the Zungarian Gap ('Mughalistan').[3] It was, indeed, only to be expected that a Persian Muslim historian whose father and grandfather had been in the public service of the Khwārizm Shāhs should have written his answer to the question 'Who are these irresistible Mongol invaders?' forty-six years before the same question was answered by a Persian Muslim historian whose birthplace was Hamadān; for the Mongol storm had broken upon the Kwārizmian march of Dār-al-Islām as early as A.D. 1220, while Western Iran had not been exposed to it till A.D. 1256, when the Mongols forced the passage of the Caspian Gates in their campaign of that year against the Ismā'īlīs.

The purpose of the special history of the Mongols and Turks which Rashīd-ad-Dīn wrote in accordance with Ghāzān Khān's instructions was, in the author's own Herodotean words, 'to make sure that the memory of the extraordinary events and important facts that have signalized the epiphany of the dynasty of the Mongols should not be obliterated and annihilated by lapse of Time . . . nor suffer the fate of remaining concealed under an impenetrably thick veil [of ignorance]';[4] and the civil servant historian proceeds to explain the grounds of his royal master's anxiety on this score. The history of the Mongols before and during their conquest of the World was by this time already unfamiliar to all but a few of Ghāzān Khān's subjects; it could be foreseen that the rising generation in the Il-Khān's Mongol *comitatus* would cease to feel any interest in their own family histories and in their ancestors' achievements; and it would be particularly disgraceful to allow oblivion thus to overtake the deeds of Chingis Khān and his Mongol companions, who had achieved, in their day, the unique feat of conquering the World. Reading between Rashīd-ad-Dīn's lines, we can surmise that Ghāzān had instructed his Persian Muslim civil servant to put on record the history of the pagan Nomads of the Eurasian Steppe because he had realized that his own *ci-devant* Nomad retainers—who had

[1] See p. 72, n. 5, above.

[2] See E. Berthels' article on Rashīd-ad-Dīn in the *Encyclopaedia of Islam*, vol. iii (Leiden 1936, Brill), pp. 1124–5.

[3] See II. ii. 145.

[4] Rashīd-ad-Dīn, ibid., pp. 78–79. Compare the opening words of Herodotus's preface: 'Herodotus of Halicarnassus presents the results of his researches in the following work, with the twofold object of saving the past of Mankind from oblivion and ensuring that the extraordinary achievements of the Hellenic and Oriental worlds shall enjoy their just renown—particularly the transactions which brought them into conflict with one another'.

migrated from 'the Desert' to 'the Sown' forty years before the date of his own accession in A.D. 1395,[1] and who, in the act, had changed their trade by becoming herdsmen of human cattle in place of their former ungulate livestock[2]—would have been bound in any case soon to become assimilated to their more highly cultivated sedentary subjects and were destined to lose their Eurasian Nomad social heritage all the more quickly now that Ghāzān himself had accelerated their assimilation by his policy of conversion to Islam. Ghāzān Khān had become a devout Muslim without having ceased to be a patriotic Mongol and a proud Chingisid; and, in commissioning Rashīd-ad-Dīn to write in the New Persian language a history of the Mongols and Turks, Ghāzān was seeking to reconcile his new loyalty with his old one.

Rashīd-ad-Dīn—in constant attendance, as he had to be, upon his Il-Khānī masters in North-Western Iran in an age in which the Central Government of the Mongol Empire no longer had the power to summon the administrators of such outlying appanages to the Khāqān's Court to account to him there for their stewardship—had not enjoyed the opportunities, that had been thrust upon Juwaynī,[3] of visiting Mongolia and

[1] The expeditionary force with which Hūlāgū made his conquests west of the Caspian Gates had left Qāraqorum in July 1252 and had left the Steppe behind for ever upon entering Transoxania in A.D. 1255, one season before the campaign of A.D. 1256 against the Ismā'īlīs (see Browne, E. G.: *A Literary History of Persia*, vol. ii (London 1906, Fisher Unwin, pp. 452–3)). Thus, by the date of Ghāzān's accession, they had been vegetating for forty years in a demoralizing Land of Milk and Honey.

[2] The social unhealthiness of this change in a Nomad horde's way of life has been noticed in III. iii. 22–25.

[3] Both 'Alā-ad-Dīn Juwaynī and his father Bahā-ad-Dīn Juwaynī before him had travelled more than once from Khurāsān to Mongolia and back in the course of their official duties in the Mongol public service. Bahā-ad-Dīn had been sent in A.D. 1235–6 by his captor and patron Jintimūr to the court of the Khāqān Ogotāy, who had confirmed the appointment to the post of *sāhib-dīwān* which Jintimūr had conferred upon him (Browne, *apud* Juwaynī, ed. cit., p. xxii); and he had been taken to Qāraqorum again by Arghūn, Jintimūr's second successor in the government of Khurāsān (see Browne, ibid). 'Alā-ad-Dīn 'spent some ten years of his life in these journeyings to and fro' (Browne, ibid., p. xxiv); and his third journey in Arghūn's company (*peregrinabantur* A.D. 1251–4, during the reign of the Khāqān Mangū) gave him the inspiration to write his history. On this occasion, he arrived at Qāraqorum on the 2nd May, 1252, and did not set out on his journey back to Khurāsān till September 1253.

'It was during this stay of a year and five months at the Mongol capital that it was suggested to our author by some of his friends . . . that he should compose this history to immortalize the great deeds and conquests of the Mongol sovereigns. A certain diffidence as to his capacity for this task at first prompted him to refuse, but he was ultimately convinced that he possessed certain almost unique qualifications for it, to wit his extensive acquaintance with the Mongol Empire and its most notable administrators, the free access to the most authentic sources of information permitted to him by the high official position which he held, and his first-hand knowledge of many important political events. He therefore finally agreed to undertake the task, which he began in A.H. 650 and concluded in A.H. 658 (A.D. 1252–60).'—Browne, *apud* Juwaynī, ed. cit., p. xxv.

A similar journey to the ordu of the Mongol Khāqān Mangū, in the heart of the Eurasian Steppe, inspired a notable work of Medieval Western Christian literature, the *Itinerarium Fratris Willielmi de Rubruquis, de Ordine Fratrum Minorum, Galli, Anno Gratie 1253, ad Partes Orientales*. Friar William of Rubruck arrived at Mangū's court some three months after the date of 'Alā-ad-Dīn Juwaynī's departure, and he attended on the Khāqān from January to June, inclusive, A.D. 1254.

Such journeys right across the breadth of the Old World were made possible by the Mongols' organization of what was certainly the farthest-flung—though it was perhaps also the shortest-lived—of all the imperial postal-services known to History (see VI. vii. 99). See Marco Polo's account of it in *The Description of the World*, ed. by Moule, A. C., and Pelliot, Paul, vol. i (London 1938, Routledge), pp. 242–7. The experience of travelling post-haste from the Great Western Bay of the Eurasian Steppe to the high plateau of Outer Mongolia was as fatiguing as it was inspiring. See William of Rubruck, op. cit.,

collecting information about the Mongols at the fountain-head; yet in many respects the sources made accessible to Rashīd-ad-Dīn within the bounds of the Il-Khāns' dominions could bear comparison with those to which Juwaynī had had access at Qāraqorum.

'An authentic chronicle, written in the Mongol language and script,[1] had been written and been brought up to date at intervals, and this was deposited in the [Il-Khānī] archives; but in this form it had no order or method in it; it was an assemblage of isolated and incomplete fragments; it remained inaccessible and unknown to any students who would have been capable of extracting from it some notion of the facts and events recorded in it; and no one had ever received authorisation or permission to make use of it....

'Ghāzān Khān ... conceived the idea of having these state papers brought together and put in order ... and the author ... was instructed to collect the facts concerning the origins and genealogies of all the Turkish peoples in contact with the Mongols and to put into writing [in the Persian language], article by article, the historical records relating to these peoples, part of which is in the Imperial Archives, while the remainder is to be found in the hands of the [Mongol] amīrs and [other] members of the [Il-Khānī] Court.

'Down to that time, no one had been in a position to collect these records or been so fortunate as to have it in his power to put them in order and make a systematic history out of them; and those authors who had [previously] made the attempt to write the history of part of these events had had to do their work without possessing an exact knowledge of the facts.[2] They had been reduced to collecting oral narratives from the mouths of plebeians, along lines dictated by their own preconceived ideas; and no one could count on these traditions being true or exact.

'The present writer was commissioned to put these fragments of historical materials in order after having made a scrupulous examination of them; he was to digest them in plain language; and he was [thus] to bring ... these hitherto completely inaccessible records to the light of day. If there were any events that were treated too summarily, or in too little detail, in these historical documents, he was instructed to fill the lacunae by collecting information on these subjects from the *savants* and doctors (*dānīyān wa hukamā*) of Khitāy [North China], India, Uighurland, Qipchāq and other countries—considering that representatives of all the peoples in the World are to be found at His Il-Khanian Majesty's Court.

chaps. 23, 24, and 55: 'In the space of two months and ten days, we did not rest except one single day, when we could not get any horses' (chap. 55). Friar William's predecessor, Friar John of Piano Carpini, ... who had made the journey in A.D. 1245–47, paints the same picture: 'Passing through Comania we rode most earnestly, having change of horses five times or oftener in a day.'—*Libellus Historicus Joannis de Plano Carpini, qui missus est Legatus ad Tartaros A.D. 1246*, chap. 21.

[1] As Quatremère points out in op. cit., p. lix, Rashīd-ad-Dīn must have been able to speak Mongol in order to transact official business with the Il-Khān and his *comitatus*. He had also written several works in Mongol, according to a statement of his own which his French editor cites from *man. arabe* 356, fol. 213 *r.*—A.J.T.

[2] Is this an allusion to Juwaynī's *Ta'rīkh-i-Jahān Gushā*? If so, its depreciatory innuendo recoils on Rashīd-ad-Dīn's own head; for Rashīd-ad-Dīn 'included in his great history ... practically the whole contents of the three volumes of the *Jahān-Gushāy*, condensing some portions (such as the history of the Mongol governors of Khurāsān and other provinces of Persia, and the history of the Khwārazm Shāhs), expanding others (such as the history of Chingīz Khān's youth and of his sons and grandsons, and the history of the Assassins), and leaving others (such as the history of Chingiz Khān's conquests in the domains of the Khwārazm Shāhs and in Persia, and the anecdotes of Ogotāy Khān's doings) almost unchanged' (Browne, *apud* Juwaynī, ed. cit., pp. lix–lx).—A.J.T.

'First and foremost, he was to consult . . . Pūlād Chingsang,[1] who has a unique . . . knowledge of the genealogies of the Turkish peoples and the events of their history—particularly the history of the Mongols.'[2]

These were the oral and documentary sources that Rashīd-ad-Dīn had at his disposal for carrying out Ghāzān Khān's instructions to write a Persian history of the Mongols; but, as the Persian historian tells us, Ghāzān's successor Khudābandah Ūljaytū Khān, when he read Rashīd-ad-Dīn's *Ta'rīkh-i-Ghāzānī*, found the historian's answer to Ghāzān's question 'Who were these Mongol conquerors of the World?' raising in his mind the further question 'What is this World that the Mongols have conquered?' And Rashīd-ad-Dīn's new employer also had the acumen to perceive that at least one of the sources of information on which the historian had drawn in answering Ghāzān's question could also be turned to account for answering Ūljaytū's own. After having read the *Ta'rīkh-i-Ghāzānī*, Ūljaytū pointed out to the author, so Rashīd-ad-Dīn tells us, that, hitherto, no one had ever written a comprehensive history of the whole *Oikoumenê* and all the peoples in it, but that an unprecedented opportunity for producing a work of this scope had arisen

'now that the *Oikoumenê*, from end to end, is subject either to us or to [other] Chingisids, with the result that doctors, astronomers, *savants* and historians (*hukamā wa munajjimān, wa arbāb-i-dānish wa ashāb-i-tawārīkh*), representing all religions and sects (*adyān wa milel*)—natives of Khitāy, Māchīn, Hind, Kashmir, Tibet, Uighurland and other nations, Turk, Arab, and Frank—are assembled in large numbers under Our eyes, and considering that each of them possesses books which set out his country's history, chronology, and religious beliefs, and has at least a partial acquaintance with these different subjects.'[3]

With these considerations in mind, Ūljaytū Khān, who had piously refused to have the dedication of Rashīd-ad-Dīn's *Ta'rīkh-i-Ghāzānī*, covering the history of the Eurasian Nomads, transferred from his dead brother's name to his own,[4] now commanded the dynasty's Persian civil servant historian to enlarge the *Ta'rīkh-i-Ghāzānī* into a *Jāmi'-al-Tawārīkh* by adding two new parts—a universal history and a universal geography[5]—which were to bear Ūljaytū's name. In this supplementary

[1] See Quatremère's note 95 ibid., pp. 77–78. Pūlād was a Mongol of the Durban tribe His father had been Chingis Khān's 'cook' (i.e. a confidential officer in his household). Pūlād himself had entered the service of Chingis' grandson and Hūlāgū's brother Qūbilāy, and had been invested by him with the Chinese title *chingsang* in addition to his hereditary Mongol title *baurji*, the Mongol word for 'cook'. He was the permanent diplomatic representative of the House of Qūbilāy at the Il-Khānī Court. In the Il-Khāns' own Mongol *comitatus* there was also a wealth of historical tradition to be harvested; for, as Rashīd-ad-Dīn records in his history of Hūlāgū Khān (see Quatremère's edition, pp. 130–3), Hūlāgū's brother the Khāqān Mangū, when he sent Hūlāgū to enlarge the bounds of the Mongol Empire south-westwards, reinforced Hūlāgū's existing *comitatus* by making for him a special levy of two men out of every ten in the war-bands of all the other Chingisid princes. 'This is why in our countries [i.e. in the Il-Khān's dominions] there always have been, and still are, [Mongol] amīrs who are descendants and relations of each of the amīrs of Chingis Khān, and each of these still holds his hereditary office.'

[2] Rashīd-ad-Dīn: Preface to the *Jāmi'-al-Tawārīkh*, Quatremère's edition: Persian text on pp. 74–78; Quatremère's translation on pp. 75–79.

[3] Rashīd-ad-Dīn, ibid., pp. 38–39.

[4] See ibid., pp. 36–37.

[5] No manuscript of Rashīd-ad-Dīn's universal geography was extant as far as was known at the time of writing.

work, which was duly completed in A.D. 1310–11,[1] the universal history fills four volumes. The first three are those presenting the history of the Syriac Civilization in terms of Iranian history which have already been mentioned.[2] The fourth breaks new ground[3] by bringing Turkish, Chinese, Israelite, Frankish, and Indian history into the picture.

Rashīd-ad-Dīn was exceptional among his co-religionists in the Il-Khānī dominions in his day in being psychologically as well as intellectually well qualified for carrying out his second and major historical task. The majority of his fellow Muslims had been exasperated by the temporary favour which a local Christian and Jewish minority had been enjoying during the first phase of a revolutionary régime in which the barbarian conquerors had remained, not merely pagan in their practice, but also positively anti-Muslim in their feelings. The fanatical mood consequently prevalent in the Persian Muslim community is in sharp contrast with Rashīd-ad-Dīn's respect and sympathy for non-Muslim scholarship.

'Although [he ventures to write in his preface][4] the tradition of the Muslims is greatly superior to that of the other peoples, all the same we cannot take it as our guide in dealing with the history of the non-Muslim peoples. It goes without saying that the facts which, in the traditions of any people, have been transmitted through a continuous chain of authorities have to be accepted as authentic,'

and he informs us that, in compiling his geographical gazetteer, he has lived up to his own principles.

'In his endeavour to draw on all available sources and to verify his results, the author, in this volume, has not been content merely to assemble everything that has hitherto been known in this country and has been described or delineated in [our] books; he has supplemented this existing information with the facts which, in this fortunate age, the doctors and *savants* (*hukamā wa dānīyān*) of Hind, Chīn and Māchīn, Frankland and other foreign parts have found in their books and have certified as being authentic after having scrupulously verified them.'[5]

A Persian Muslim theologian-historian, Nāsir-ad-Dīn al-Baydāwī, who was Rashīd-ad-Dīn's contemporary, records[6] that, when Rashīd-ad-Dīn was setting out to write his section on the history of Khitāy (North China), he consulted two Chinese scholars at Ūljaytū's Court—Li Tachi and Mak Sun—who were authorities on Far Eastern medicine, astronomy, and history and who had brought with them, from China, books dealing with these subjects. On the strength of their recommendation, Baydāwī tells us, Rashīd-ad-Dīn based his account of Chinese history on a compendium, written by three Chinese Buddhist monks, which,

1 See Browne, op. cit., vol. iii, p. 72.
2 On p. 73, above.
3 Rashīd-ad-Dīn had, however, had at least one predecessor in this exotic field. Abū Rayhān al-Bīrūnī (*natus* A.D. 973) had not only published, *circa* A.D. 1000, *A Chronology of Ancient Nations*; he had also taken the opportunity, opened up for Persian Muslim scholars by Mahmūd of Ghaznah's conquests in India, to publish, soon after A.D .1030, his *Indica* (see Browne, *A Literary History of Persia*, vol. ii, p. 101).
4 In Quatremère's edition, pp. 44–45.
5 Rashīd-ad-Dīn, ibid., pp. 58–61.
6 See Quatremère in his life of Rashīd-ad-Dīn, p. lxxviii. Baydāwī's historical work was still unpublished at the time of writing.

his two Chinese consultants assured him, had been verified, approved, and passed for the press by a consensus of Chinese litterati.

The oecumenical outlook with which Rashīd-ad-Dīn was thus inspired by the social milieu of the Il-Khānī Court was transmitted by him to at least one disciple, Abū Sulaymān Dā'ūd of Banākat in Transoxania, who enjoyed the same intellectual advantages in virtue of being Ghāzān Khān's poet laureate.

'His information about the Jews, Christians, Indians, Chinese, and Mongols, though largely directly borrowed, often in the same words, from the pages of Rashīd-ad-Dīn, was nevertheless undoubtedly supplemented by what the author learned orally from representatives of the peoples in question. In no Persian history before the Mongol period, and in few after it, do we find so many references to places, people, and historical events beyond the ken of most Muslim writers: places like Portugal, Poland, Bohemia, England, Scotland, Ireland, Catalonia, Lombardy, Paris, and Cologne; people like the Roman Emperors, from Romulus downwards, and the Popes from Saint Peter to the Pope contemporary with the author, who is said to be the two hundred and second in succession; and events like the different church councils, the conversion of Britain to Christianity in the time of Pope Eleutherius, the Nestorian heresy, and the like.'[1]

Herodotus

The element in their social milieu that thus inspired a Rashidian school of post-Mongol Persian Muslim historians to rise to an oecumenical view of History was evidently the abrupt encounter, at the Il-Khānī Court, between the representatives of diverse religions and cultures. This cultural effect of the temporarily high conductivity of the Mongol Empire, within an area extending to the Euphrates from Korea and to the Volga from Burma, was the feature that also made the strongest impression on the imaginations of Western Christian observers.[2] The lists, in Rashīd-ad-Dīn's pages, of subject countries and peoples—as alien from one another in their habits and êthos as they are physically far apart—are reminiscent of the similar lists in the inscriptions of the Achaemenidae and on the pages of Herodotus. The similarity is not fortuitous, for in both cases we are in the presence of a universal state that has been established, suddenly and unexpectedly, through sweeping conquests achieved by a hitherto obscure semi-barbarian people from the back of beyond, and it is not surprising that an identical social milieu should have inspired Herodotus, as well as Rashīd-ad-Dīn, first to ask the question 'What is this World that has just been united politically by conquest?' and then, in seeking for the answer, to arrive at the conclusion that no field smaller than the entire *Oikoumenê* since the dawn of Civilization is an intelligible field of historical study.

Like Clarendon, Procopius, Josephus, Thucydides, and Rhodes,

[1] Browne, op. cit., vol. iii, pp. 101–2.

[2] See, for example, the passage, illustrating this point, that has been quoted, in V. v. 113–14, from the narrative of the Flemish Franciscan friar William of Rubruck, who made the 'round trip' from the Crimea to the Khāqān Mangū's ordu at Qāraqorum and back, via Bātū Khān's ordu in the Great Western Bay of the Eurasian Steppe, in A.D. 1253–5.

Herodotus found his immediate inspiration in a great war that had been waged within his own lifetime. Native, as he was, of a Hellenized Carian city on the south-west coast of the Asiatic mainland, he had been born a subject of the Achaemenian Empire and had lived to see his birthplace exchange a Persian for an Athenian suzerainty. 'How has this revolutionary change in the political fortunes of the Asian Hellenes come about within my own lifetime?' was the first form in which the historian's elemental question 'How has this come out of that?' presented itself to Herodotus's mind, and in three books he duly wrote a history of the two decisive first campaigns in the Great Helleno-Persian War of 480–450/449 B.C.[1] But Herodotus, like Rashīd-ad-Dīn and Polybius, found himself unable to answer his original question without being moved to ask himself a supplementary one which eventually came to overshadow it; for the war whose history he had undertaken to write was a war in which the belligerents were representatives, not merely of different political Powers, but also of different civilizations. The Hellenic Society had collided with a Syriac Society which, through the agency of the Achaemenidae, had united the domains of a Babylonic, an Egyptiac, and a submerged Hittite Society with its own domain within the framework of a single universal state.[2] Thus, in writing the history of an Helleno-Persian War, Herodotus was led on to study a cultural encounter involving no fewer than five distinct civilizations and in fact six, considering that the Eurasian Nomads were also a party to the transaction; and from this contemporary scene he was led backwards in Time into a study of the separate history and origin of each of his dramatis personae and into an inquiry into previous encounters between them in a concatenation in which the Helleno-Persian War that had broken out in 480 B.C. came to look like the latest link in a long chain of episodes of the kind.[3]

Thus Herodotus's work, like Rashīd-ad-Dīn's, grew in its author's hands. Ūljaytū Khān's demand on Rashīd-ad-Dīn for a universal history led him to append five additional volumes (reckoning in the geographical gazetteer) to the three volumes of his *Ta'rīkh-i-Ghāzānī.* Herodotus's discovery of a concatenation of encounters between East and West led him to prefix six additional books to his three books recording the history of the two campaigns of 480–479 B.C. in the Great Helleno-Persian War.

In savouring the diversity in habits and êthos between the various civilizations whose encounters he was recording, Herodotus was on the brink of another supplementary question which might have carried him a long step nearer to the heart of the mystery of Human Nature and Destiny.

'When Darius was on the throne [Herodotus reports][4] he summoned

[1] 450/449 B.C., rather than 449/448, is the probable date of the Peace of Callias according to H. T. Wade-Gery in *Harvard Studies in Classical Philology*, special supplement volume, pp. 149–52 (Cambridge, Mass. 1940, Harvard University Press).

[2] See I. i. 78–81; II. ii. 137–8; IV. iv. 471; V. v. 122–3; and VI. vii. 64.

[3] See IX. viii. 454–63.

[4] Herodotus: Book III, chap. 38 (see this Study, VI. vii. 617, n. 5). The story might have been impugned as being merely *ben trovato* if its veracity were not vindicated by first-hand accounts of similar confrontations between irreconcilable practices and beliefs

into his presence the Hellenes at his court and asked them for what price they would consent to make a meal of their fathers when they died. The Hellenes replied that all the money in the World would not induce them to do such a thing, whereupon Darius summoned the Callatian Indians, who do eat their parents,[1] and asked them (in the presence of the Hellenes, who were kept informed, through an interpreter, of the tenour of the conversation) for what price they would be willing to burn their fathers when they died. The Indians shrieked aloud and begged him not to pursue such an unmentionable subject—a story which illustrates the habitual attitude of Mankind towards this question, and which, in my opinion, justifies Pindar's poetic aphorism that "Custom is king of all".'

Turgot

The confrontation of sharply diverse cultures with one another through the political union of their habitués under an oecumenical Achaemenian régime caught the imagination, not only of the contemporary Hellenic observer Herodotus, but of the Modern Western philosopher civil servant Turgot (*vivebat* A.D. 1727–81). 'Effet singulier', Turgot remarks in his *Esquisse d'un Plan de Géographie Politique*,[2] 'de la conquête de la Lydie par Cyrus, qui dévoila l'un à l'autre comme deux mondes politiques'; and the spectacle of a cultural phenomenon in which Herodotus had seen nothing more than one of those minuscula that could provide him with a piquant story opened up in Turgot's mind a new approach to the study of human affairs. This many-sided Modern Western man of genius was so sensitive to hints offered to him by his cultural heritage, and so perceptive in his intuition of the implications, that he succeeded in divining the historical significance of a universal state at second-hand; and he achieved this with a minimum of intellectual illumination from his own social milieu; for, though the eighteenth-century Western Society into which Turgot had been born was in contact with a number of alien civilizations and primitive societies as the result of a Modern Western conquest of the Ocean, Turgot's generation of Westerners was as remote in spirit as it was in time from any direct experience of the creative agony out of which a universal state is born.

The lesson that Turgot found in an Herodotean historical panorama was the idea that the observable diversity between different contingents in the living generation of Mankind might provide a key to the understanding of History.

'Je vois tous les jours inventer des arts;[3] je vois dans quelques parties

at the Courts of the Northumbrian King Oswiu (see II. ii. 335), the Khān of the Khazars (see VI. vii. 106, n. 3), the Russian war-lord Vladímir (see ibid.), the Mongol Khāqān Mangū (see William of Rubruck's narrative, chap. 51), and the Timurid Mughal Emperor Akbar (see V. v. 700–1).—A.J.T.

[1] This practice is ascribed to the Tibetans in William of Rubruck's narrative, chap. 28.—A.J.T.

[2] *Œuvres de Turgot* (Paris 1844, Guillaumin, 2 vols.), vol. ii. p. 618.

[3] This passage appears to have been written in or about the year A.D. 1750, when the Western Industrial Revolution, though imminent, had not yet broken out. Another illustration of Turgot's prescience is his prediction, on the 11th December, 1750, of a Declaration of Independence that was to be made a quarter of a century later. 'Les colonies sont comme les fruits qui ne tiennent à l'arbre que jusqu'à leur maturité: devenues suffisantes à elles-mêmes, elles firent ce que fit depuis Carthage, ce que fera un jour l'Améri-

du monde des peuples polis, éclairés, et dans d'autres des peuples errants au sein des forêts. Cette inégalité de progrès dans une durée éternelle aurait dû disparaître. Le monde n'est donc pas éternel; mais je dois conclure en même temps qu'il est fort ancien. Jusqu'à quel point? Je l'ignore.[1]

'Si je veux savoir quelque chose de précis, je suis entouré de nuages. . . .[2] Une clarté faible commence à percer la nuit étendue sur toutes les nations, et se répand de proche en proche. Les habitants de la Chaldée, plus voisins de la source des premières traditions, les Égyptiens, les Chinois, paraissent devancer le reste des peuples; d'autres les suivent de loin; les progrès amènent d'autres progrès. L'inégalité des nations augmente: ici les arts commencent à naître; là ils avancent à grands pas vers la perfection. Plus loin ils s'arrêtent dans leur médiocrité; ailleurs les premières tenèbres ne sont point encore dissipées; et, dans cette inégalité variée à l'infini, l'état actuel de l'univers, en présentant à la fois sur la terre toutes les nuances de la barbarie et de la politesse, nous montre en quelque sorte sous un seul coup d'œil les monuments, les vestiges de tous les pas de l'esprit humain, l'image de tous les degrés par lesquels il a passé, l'histoire de tous les âges.'[3]

The essays and notes from which the foregoing passages have been quoted testify to the greatness of the student of History who was put out of action on the threshold of his intellectual career by the great civil servant whose life-work was to conjure the Ideas of 1789 out of his creative administration of a decrepit *ancien régime*. Re-reading in A.D. 1951 the essays and notes[4] in which this lost Western historian has sketched the ground-plan of a mighty intellectual edifice, and recalling that Turgot was only twenty-three years old when he wrote these luminous fragments in A.D. 1750, a latter-day Western historian who had spent ten years of his working life as a temporary civil servant could not forbear to cry 'Qualis artifex periit'[5] when he read in a notice of the great eighteenth-century philosopher civil servant's career that he had entered the public service on the 5th January, 1752, hardly more than eighteen months after the delivery of the first, and twelve months after the delivery of the second, of his two epoch-making discourses at the Sorbonne.

que'.—Turgot, A. R. J.: *Second Discours en Sorbonne, sur les Progrès Successifs de l'Esprit Humain* (ibid., vol. ii, p. 602).—A.J.T.

[1] Turgot, A. R. J.: *Plan du Premier Discours, sur la Formation des Gouvernements et le Mélange des Nations* (ibid., vol. ii, p. 628). [2] Ibid., vol. ii, p. 628.

[3] Turgot, A. R. J.: *Second Discours, sur les Progrès de l'Esprit Humain*, prononcé le 11 Décembre, 1750 (ibid., pp. 598–9). In perceiving that the past conditions of the more advanced living societies could be reconstructed from a study of the actual conditions of their more backward contemporaries, Turgot had, of course, been anticipated by Thucydides in his introduction to *A History of the Atheno-Peloponnesian War* (Book I, chaps. 5–6).

[4] Premier Discours en Sorbonne, 'Sur les Avantages que l'Établissement du Christianisme a Procurés au Genre Humain', prononcé le 3 Juillet, 1750; Second Discours en Sorbonne, 'Sur les Progrès Successifs de l'Esprit Humain', prononcé le 11 Décembre 1750; 'Géographie Politique: Idées Générales', 1750; 'Esquisse d'un Plan de Géographie Politique'; Plan de Deux Discours sur l'Histoire Universelle: 'Idées de l'Introduction', 1750; Plan du Premier Discours, 'Sur la Formation du Gouvernement et le Mélange des Nations'; Plan du Second Discours, dont l'objet sera 'Les Progrès de l'Esprit Humain'; Autre Plan du Discours 'Sur les Progrès et les diverses Époques de Décadence des Sciences et des Arts', 1750; Pensées et Fragments qui avaient été jetés sur le papier pour être employés dans un des trois ouvrages sur l'Histoire Universelle, ou sur les Progrès de la Décadence des Sciences et des Arts (printed in *Œuvres de Turgot*, ed. cit., vol. ii, pp. 586–675).

[5] Suetonius: *The Lives of the Caesars*, 'Nero', chap. xlix, § 1.

Ibn Khaldūn

Ibn Khaldūn al-Hadramī of Tunis (*vivebat* A.D. 1332–1406)[1] was inspired by the same social milieu as the Sayyid Ibn al-Tiqtaqā al-Hillawī and as Ibn Khaldūn's fellow civil servant Rashīd-ad-Dīn al-Hamadānī to give to the historian's elemental question 'How has this come out of that?' the same particular application. 'How has this derelict Dār-al-Islām come out of that once flourishing Dār-al-Islām?' was the form in which the question presented itself to Arab and Persian alike, in the Maghrib[2] as well as in the two 'Irāqs,[3] on the morrow of the dissolution of a Syriac Society which, in its last phase, had been embodied politically in the Caliphate.

'We have heard with our ears, O God—our fathers have told us[4]—what Thou hast done in their time of old: How Thou hast driven out the heathen with Thy hand, and planted them in; how Thou hast destroyed the nations and cast them out. For they gat not the land in possession through their own sword, neither was it their own arm that helped them, but Thy right hand and Thine arm and the light of Thy countenance, because Thou hadst a favour unto them. . . .

'But now Thou art far off and puttest us to confusion and goest not forth with our armies. Thou makest us to turn our backs upon our enemies, so that they which hate us spoil our goods. Thou lettest us be eaten up like sheep and hast scattered us among the heathen. Thou sellest Thy people for naught and takest no money for them. Thou makest us to be rebuked of our neighbours, to be laughed to scorn and had in derision of them that are round about us. Thou makest us to be a byword among the heathen, and that the people shake their heads at us.'[5]

How has the bright dawn of the first generation of Islam thus faded away into the dreary darkness of a social interregnum? A question evoked in Ibn al-Tiqtaqā's mind by the contrast between the Present and the Past in 'Irāq was evoked in Ibn Khaldūn's mind by the same contrast in the Maghrib; and, though the barbarians by whose hands a paradise had been turned into a wilderness were not the same in the two halves of this devastated world, the Banu Hilāl's handiwork west of the Libyan Desert was indistinguishable from the Mongols' handiwork east of the Euphrates, and an identical tragedy presented the same intellectual problems. 'What was this society that has suffered this downfall?' was the first question with which Ibn Khaldūn, as well as Ibn al-Tiqtaqā, found himself confronted; and a question that the 'Irāqī Sayyid-historian had answered by writing *Al-Fakhrī* was answered by Ibn Khaldūn in *A History of the Berbers*.

Like an 'Irāqī Ibn al-Tiqtaqā's Persian contemporaries 'Alā-ad-Dīn al-Juwaynī and Rashīd-ad-Dīn al-Hamadānī, a Maghribī Ibn Khaldūn set the history of the Islamic Commonwealth within a wider frame; and he, too, found that even the broadest regional framework would not provide him with an intelligible field of study. Like Rashīd-ad-Dīn, Ibn Khaldūn was thus constrained, in answering one question, to ask an-

[1] See III. iii. 321–8.
[2] North-West Africa and Andalusia.
[3] 'Irāq 'Arabī, *alias* Babylonia or the land of Shinar, and 'Irāq Ajamī, *alias* the Jabal or Media.
[4] Cp. Psalm lxxviii. 3.
[5] Psalm xliv. 1–4 and 10–15 (as in *The Book of Common Prayer*).

other. 'What is this *Oikoumenê* whose provinces—an Islamic World or an Iran or a Barbary—have discovered their kinship with one another through the common experience of a supreme calamity?' Like Rashīd-ad-Dīn's regional history of Iran, Ibn Khaldūn's regional history of the Berbers was incorporated by its author into a *Universal History*;[1] but this achievement, in which Rashīd-ad-Dīn had reached his intellectual 'ceiling', moved Ibn Khaldūn to climb on into a higher intellectual sphere by asking himself the further question: 'How comes it that empires suffer the decline and fall exemplified in the history of the Islamic Commonwealth?'; and he gave his answer to this question in his Prolegomena (*Muqaddamāt*).[2] An analysis of this answer has been attempted in a previous passage of this Study[3] which need not be recapitulated here. In this place we need only recall that he set out to explain the declines and falls of empires in sociological terms, but discovered that this would-be strictly scientific explanation did not account for all the phenomena.

Though Ibn Khaldūn, like Rashīd-ad-Dīn, had won an intuition of Universal History, the Maghribī's actual range of historical vision was not so wide. It was virtually limited to the history of the rise and fall of Ibn Khaldūn's own Islamic Commonwealth, and the narrowness of this field deluded the Maghribī historian into two erroneous beliefs. He believed that an *esprit de corps* (*'asabīyah*) which was manifestly the psychological cement of all political communities was a monopoly of Nomad peoples in their pristine habitat and that, in virtue of possessing this politically indispensable psychological asset, the Nomads had also enjoyed a monopoly in the business of empire-building. Since he correctly recognized the historical truth that the *ci-devant* Nomad's *esprit de corps* becomes a wasting asset when once its possessor has drifted into becoming a parasitical shepherd of men, instead of remaining the providential shepherd of sheep that it is his proper vocation to be, Ibn Khaldūn's first essay in trying to account for the declines and falls of empires was to explain them as being the necessary consequence of the inevitable demoralization of the *ci-devant* Nomad conquerors through their social intercourse with their sedentary subjects. Knowing of no sedentary peoples except the tax-paying population of the Roman and Sasanian empires whom the Primitive Muslim Arab conquerors had taken over as the most valuable part of their spoils of war, Ibn Khaldūn fell into the further erroneous belief that, *ex officio*, all sedentary peoples must be destitute of *esprit de corps*; and, from this misleading combination of three false premises with one true premise, it followed logically that all empires must decline and fall within the number of generations that it would take for empire-builders who, *ex hypothesi*, were *ci-devant* Nomads to lose their politically creative ancestral virtue through acquiring their sedentary subjects' politically destructive ancestral vice.

This simple explanation of the declines and falls of empires was

[1] See III. iii. 324, n. 1.

[2] See III. iii. 322. The contents of Ibn Khaldūn's whole work are presented by de Slane in his translation of the *Muqaddamāt* (*Les Prolégomènes d'Ibn Khaldoun*, traduits en français et commentés (Paris 1863–8, Imprimerie Impériale, 3 vols.), vol. i. pp. xcv–cv).

[3] In III. iii. 473–6: 'The Relativity of Ibn Khaldūn's Historical Thought'.

borne out by all the historical evidence within Ibn Khaldūn's ken, and it would serve equally well to account for the transitoriness of the work of other *ci-devant* Nomad empire-builders whose histories were beyond Ibn Khaldūn's horizon. Yet, in our list of empire-builders in our table of universal states in this Study,[1] only five will be found in fact to have had a Nomad ancestry.[2] We may infer that, if Ibn Khaldūn had happened to command the wider horizon that was within any twentieth-century Western historian's purview, he would have recognized that his sociological hypothesis would not serve to explain more than a fraction of the phenomena; and, even within a horizon limited to the confines of the Maghrib, there was in fact one crucial piece of evidence that was refractory to Ibn Khaldūn's sociological explanation of declines and falls.

The derelict state of the Maghrib in Ibn Khaldūn's day, which had been the Maghribī inquirer's point of intellectual departure, was known by him to have been the consequence of ravages committed by two Arab Nomad tribes, the Banu Hilāl and the Banu Sulaym, who had been let loose against a rebellious Maghrib by the 'Fātimid' rulers of Egypt and Syria in A.D. 1051;[3] but, if the historian was right in holding that the rises and falls of empires were simply functions of the strength and weakness of the *esprit de corps* of Nomad empire-builders, then, *ex hypothesi*, the Banu Hilāl and Banu Sulaym ought to have brought upon the Maghrib, not the disaster which they had admittedly brought in fact, but the prosperity which had followed in the train of the Primitive Muslim Arab conquerors of the Maghrib some four hundred years before the date of the Banu Hilāl's devastating westward trek in the wake of that fertilizing previous wave of Arab conquest. These two invading hosts had both been Arab, both been Nomad, and both therefore been endowed with the sovereign social virtue of *esprit de corps*. Why, then, had the social effects of these two Arab Nomad invasions been, not identical, but antithetical? This failure of Ibn Khaldūn's sociological theory to explain North-West African historical facts led Ibn Khaldūn to the conclusion[4] that a Nomad *esprit de corps*, which (as he saw it) was a *sine qua non* for the social enterprise of empire-building, was at the same time not enough in itself to ensure success.

Why was it that an eleventh-century Arab Nomad invasion had worked havoc in a Maghrib where a seventh-century Arab Nomad invasion had proved a blessing? The answer must be that the second wave of Arab Nomad invaders had lacked some essential qualification, other than their

[1] Printed in vol. vi, on p. 327, and in vol. vii, on p. 769.

[2] These five *ci-devant* Nomad empire-building peoples are the Amorite restorers of the Sumeric Empire of Sumer and Akkad, the Chaldaean founders of a Neo-Babylonian Empire, the Arab reconstructors of a Syriac universal state, the Mongol founders of a universal state for the main body of the Far Eastern Society, and the 'Osmanlī founders of a universal state for the main body of Orthodox Christendom. The Timurids who founded a universal state for the Hindu World were not of Nomad origin, notwithstanding their assumption of the name 'Mughals'. They were descended from a champion of the sedentary population of Transoxania who had been his countrymen's leader in a war of liberation from a Nomad yoke (see II. ii. 144–150). The Manchu reconstructors of a Far Eastern universal state were, not Nomads, but sedentary highlanders who, before they had taken to agriculture, had made their living by hunting in the forests, not by stock-breeding on the Steppe.

[3] See III. iii. 323.

[4] See III. iii. 474–5.

common *esprit de corps*, which the first wave had possessed; and the chapter-headings in Ibn Khaldūn's Prolegomena[1] record the movement of his thought on this point. 'It is impossible', this train of thought begins, 'to establish a domain or to found a dynasty without possessing the support of a people animated by *esprit de corps*', and 'an enterprise which aims at securing the triumph of the religious principle can only succeed if it finds a strong party to support it.' *Esprit de corps* is, in fact, indispensable; but at the same time—and this is the new and crucial point—*esprit de corps* is not sufficient in itself. 'In general, the Arabs are incapable of founding an empire *unless* they have received a tincture of Religion of a certain strength from some prophet or saint'; 'the religious teaching of a prophet or a preacher of the Truth is the only basis on which a great and powerful empire can be founded'; and 'a dynasty which starts its career by placing itself on a religious basis will thereby double the effectiveness of the *esprit de corps* which is the means of its establishment.' It will be seen that the failure of a secular sociological explanation of the rises and falls of empires to account for the course of history in the Maghrib has led Ibn Khaldūn to introduce a new actor on to the stage of History and, in doing so, to give History itself a new dimension. His conclusion is that human affairs do not constitute an intelligible field of study so long as the inquirer is attempting to study them in isolation from the action of Man's Creator; and this is equivalent to saying that Man's *Oikoumenê* only becomes intelligible when it is recognized as being a fragment of God's Universe.

Saint Augustine

Ibn Khaldūn is here saying, in effect, that Man on Earth is a denizen of two worlds and a citizen of two commonwealths simultaneously. Man has a franchise in a mundane commonwealth in virtue of a human *esprit de corps*, and at the same time a franchise in a supra-mundane commonwealth thanks to divine revelations. This ultimate answer to a series of questions evoked by the tragic spectacle of the downfall of a civilization had already been given, a thousand years before Ibn Khaldūn's time, by another Maghribī man of genius who was of native Berber, not of immigrant Hadramī, origin, and whose Semitic *lingua franca* was, not Arabic, but Canaanite.[2] It is virtually certain that Ibn Khaldūn had never read Saint Augustine's *De Civitate Dei*, and perhaps improbable that he had ever even heard of it; and we may also guess that Augustine himself, when he propounded his transcendental thesis of Man's dual citizenship, was hardly conscious that he was applying, in a new and larger context, a concept which, from the fourth century B.C. down to the second century of the Christian Era, had been the constitutional keystone of the mundane commonwealth built up by the Romans.[3]

The inquiry which Augustine carried to a transcendental altitude had been initiated in his mind by an experience of mundane disaster that also moved Ibn Khaldūn, Rashīd-ad-Dīn, Juwaynī, and Ibn al-Tiqtaqā to ask their creative questions. These four Muslim historians were inspired

[1] Book I, § 2, *ad finem*, and § 3, *ad initium*.

[2] See III. iii. 138 n. 3.

[3] See IV. iv. 307–13.

by the portentous downfall of an Islamic Commonwealth, and three out of the four had personally suffered the shock which had shaken Dār-al-Islām from end to end when Baghdad had been sacked, and the Caliph Musta'sim been put to death, by the Mongol barbarian conqueror Hūlāgū in A.D. 1258. Augustine in his day had lived to suffer the comparable shock administered to all then living citizens of the Roman Empire by Alaric's sack of Rome in A.D. 410;[1] and this harrowing common experience had precipitated a controversy between the pagan and the Christian factions into which the Hellenic body social was divided in this last phase of Hellenic history. The pagans, who had been discomfited in their long struggle with their Christian opponents without having been yet either voluntarily converted or forcibly *gleichgeschaltet*, had seen and taken their opportunity of making capital out of a common calamity for use in their pursuit of a domestic feud. They had insinuated that the cause of Rome's fall in A.D. 410 was to be seen in the antecedent suppression of the rites of the traditional pagan official religion of the Roman Commonwealth through the intolerance of the Christian Roman Emperors Gratian (*imperabat* A.D. 367–83) and Theodosius I (*imperabat* A.D. 378–95).[2] Was it not to be expected that Rome's tutelary deities would cease to give the Roman Commonwealth their customary protection when their former protégés had ceased to pay them the customary worship that was their due? This tendencious pagan Roman explanation of the fall of Rome in A.D. 410 was the challenge that provoked Saint Augustine—as he has recorded in a passage of his *Reconsiderations*[3]—to write his own alternative answer to the question: 'What is the cause of this crushing public calamity that has overtaken our world in our time?'

'When we experienced the shock of the disastrous overthrow of Rome through the irruption of the Goths under the leadership of their king Alaric, the "pagan" worshippers of gods who are as false as they are numerous attempted to fasten the blame for this overthrow upon the Christian Religion and took this opportunity to import an unprecedented degree of acerbity and bitterness into their blasphemies against the One True God. This fired me with such zeal for the house of the Lord against blasphemies which were at the same time fallacies that I began to write a treatise *On the Commonwealth of God*.'

As Augustine here states, his initial purpose was to refute the pagans on a controversial issue in the terms in which this issue had been formulated by his adversaries; and, in execution of this purpose, he duly wrote the tract that occupies the first five out of the twenty-two books to which the *De Civitate Dei* was eventually to run.

'The first five books are devoted to a refutation of the thesis that the practice of the pagans' traditional polytheism is a condition *sine qua non* for the assurance of human welfare, and that the prohibition of this cult accounts for the incidence of the sea of troubles that has overwhelmed us.'[4]

This tract, which was the original crystallization-point of Augustine's eventual *magnum opus*, exhibits the forensic ability that was to be expected of a powerful intellect, exercised by a traditional Hellenic train-

[1] See V. v. 223, with n. 2.
[2] See IV. iv. 226–7 and V. vi. 89.
[3] *Retractationes*, Book II, chap. 69.
[4] *Retractationes*, ibid.

ing in rhetoric, when it had at last found a theme that appealed to the sophist's heart besides commending itself to his head. The author has made some telling points which his pagan opponents might have found it hard to rebut. Would these pagan Romans who insinuate that Christianity has been responsible for Rome's fall be alive today to make this insinuation if, during the sack of the city, they had not stooped to take sanctuary in Christian places of worship? And how was it that they were able to find asylum there? It was because the barbarian conquerors, being converts to Christianity themselves, had voluntarily abstained from despoiling or enslaving any of the conquered population who had sought refuge in Christian fanes. More than that, some of them had even robbed themselves of their legitimate spoils by personally conducting to these voluntarily conceded places of safety the potential victims whom they had encountered in the streets.[1] Had any previous conquerors, barbarian or Roman, ever shown such merciful forbearance in times past?[2] Or (to make the same point in other terms) had any pagan Hellenic temple ever secured to refugees the effective asylum that had been provided by Christian places of worship in Rome in A.D. 410?[3] Why had the Romans ever imagined that Rome would be saved by divinities who had been constrained to migrate to Rome by their failure to save Troy?[4] And why, if Paganism was the talisman of political and military success, had the devoutly pagan Goth war-lord Radagaisus lost, in marching on Rome, both his war-band and his life, whereas the Christian Goth war-lord Alaric had achieved the sensational success of capturing the Imperial City? Is not the One True God's hand manifest in this signal contrast between the respective fortunes of a pagan barbarian assailant, who would have been merciless to pagan and Christian alike, and a Christian barbarian assailant who showed mercy to pagan as well as Christian refugees in Christian sanctuaries?[5]

This nuclear *De Civitate Dei* is a masterpiece of controversial literature; but its forensic virtuosity would have left the hearts of Posterity cold, when once the artificial literary tradition of an already moribund Hellenic Paganism had become extinct, if the author had allowed the numerous other imperative calls on his time and energy[6] not merely to interrupt this literary enterprise but to terminate it. Happily Saint Augustine found himself unable to answer the controversial question raised by the dispute over the cause of the fall of Rome without being led into asking other questions. In the first place, his intellectual integrity forbade him to reply to the particular school of pagan Hellenic thought which had indicted the Christian Church without also dealing with a different pagan doctrine that was inconsistent with a belief in the efficacy of the pagan divinities' protection yet was equally incompatible with a Christian theology; and, in pursuit of this second battalion of pagan adversaries, Augustine was led into writing a second batch of five books to supplement his first essay.

1 *De Civitate Dei*, Book I, chaps. 1 and 7, quoted in V. v. 224.
2 Op. cit., Book I, chaps. 2, 5, and 6.
3 Op. cit., Book I, chap. 4.
4 Op. cit., Book I, chap. 3.
5 Op. cit., Book V. chap. 23, quoted in V. v. 224–5.
6 See *Retractationes*, ibid.

'The five books that follow [i.e. Books VI–X inclusive] argue against a thesis in which the practice of Polytheism is likewise defended in spite of its being conceded in this alternative pagan doctrine that troubles such as we have experienced have never failed, and never will fail, to beset Mankind, and that the variations in the severity of the incidence of these troubles are attributable to differences of place, time, and personality. The doctrine against which I argue in this part of the work is that a Polytheism expressing itself in rites of sacrifice has its utility for a life after Death, though not for our life in This World.'[1]

In this second instalment of the *De Civitate Dei*, Augustine has thus exceeded the limits of the initial question that had been set for him by his pagan adversaries. After asking himself 'Is it because Rome has ceased to be pagan that Rome has come to grief?' he has gone on to ask himself: 'Can a Paganism which has failed to prove its mundane utility prove that it has any greater utility for an after life?' And, if he had come to a halt after he had given his answer to this second question, his work might have been remembered as an interesting critique of a pair of varieties of pagan Hellenic religious experience. Indeed, considering that these two varieties, between them, cover virtually the whole gamut of Hellenic Paganism, Saint Augustine, in arriving at the end of his tenth book, would have given a substantially complete Christian answer to the question: 'What was this pagan Hellenic way of life that has suffered such dire disaster in our day?' Manifestly this is a far larger and more momentous question than the controversial issue raised in the forensic debate which had originally moved the combative Numidian apologist for Christianity to take up his powerful pen; but Augustine's second question was pregnant with a third; and this ultimate question, which is the subject of the last twelve books of the *De Civitate Dei* out of the eventual total of twenty-two, is the theme that has given Augustine's great work not only its title but its immortality.

After asking himself 'What was this mundane commonwealth that has fallen?' Augustine has risen to the height of the implicit consequent question: 'What is this other commonwealth that remains standing now that the mundane commonwealth has bitten the dust?' And thus the Christian theologian-historian's 'obstinate questionings'[2] have opened up to him, at the end of his long quest, the vision of a glorious Commonwealth of God which is living in two spiritual dimensions simultaneously. In the flow of Time it is living by faith while it is running the gauntlet of the ungodly on its earthly pilgrimage; and in the stability of its eternal home, for which it is now waiting with patience[3] 'until Righteousness turn again unto Judgement',[4] it is already participating in God's own peace and felicity.[5] We need not enlarge here upon Saint Augustine's conception of the relations between the Mundane and the Supra-Mundane Commonwealth; for we have touched upon it already in another context,[6] and no summary by an alien hand can dispense a reader from going to drink at the fountain-head. In this place we have

[1] *Retractationes*, Book II, chap. 69.
[2] Wordsworth: *Ode on Intimations of Immortality*.
[3] Romans viii. 25.
[4] Psalm xciv. 15 (as in *The Book of Common Prayer*).
[5] Saint Augustine: *De Civitate Dei*, Book I, Preface.
[6] In V. vi. 365–9.

only to observe that, in passing to the second part of the *De Civitate Dei* from the second instalment of the first part, Saint Augustine is being carried by the Human Mind's impulse to investigate the relations between the facts of History into embarking on the Human Heart's quest to find a meaning behind them.

A Twentieth-Century Western Student of History

The intellectual histories of no less than eleven out of the thirteen historians whom we have just been passing in review[1] indicate that shocking public events are apt to be fecund of intellectual inspirations for historians. On this showing, the generation into which the writer of this Study had been born in a post-Modern Western World could not plead that its own social milieu had been unconducive to historical thought; and the writer himself could testify (if he might venture once again to draw upon the only first-hand experience at his command) that, by the time when he found himself in his sixty-fourth year, the subjects for at least nine historical works of diverse ranges had been presented to him by questions arising from catastrophic events that he had lived to witness.

An historian born in A.D. 1889 who was still alive in A.D. 1952 had indeed already heard a long peal of changes rung on the historian's elemental question 'How has this come out of that?' How, first and foremost, had it happened that he had lived to see the immediately preceding generation's apparently reasonable expectations so rudely disappointed? In liberal-minded middle-class circles in democratic Western countries in a generation that had been born round about the year A.D. 1860, it had seemed evident by the close of the nineteenth century that a triumphantly advancing Western Civilization had now carried human progress to a point at which it could count upon finding the Earthly Paradise just round the next corner. This *fin-de-siècle* liberal Western hope had been a secularized version of Christ's promise in the Gospels: 'Verily I say unto you that there be some of them that stand here which shall not taste of death till they have seen the Kingdom of God come with power.'[2] How was it that this hapless generation had lived to see, instead, not the second coming of the Son of Man, but the advent of Antichrist? What fell miscarriage had overtaken the world-wide and perpetual peace that had been confidently augured in A.D. 1851 at the opening of a Great Exhibition in London and had then apparently been achieved twenty years later, after the end of the Franco-Prussian War of A.D. 1870–1? How had this peace come to be shattered in A.D. 1914 and A.D. 1939 by the successive explosions of two world wars in one lifetime? How had the twentieth century of the Christian Era come to see the eighteenth century's 'laws of civilized warfare' thrown to the winds? How had Human Nature prevailed upon itself to perpetrate the atrocities which Turkish hands had committed against the Armenians, and German hands against the Belgians, the Jews, the Poles, and all their other victims? Such

1 These eleven are Clarendon, Procopius, Josephus, Thucydides, Rhodes, Polybius, Ibn al-Tiqtaqā, 'Alā-ad-Dīn Juwaynī, Rashīd-ad-Dīn Hamadānī, Herodotus, Saint Augustine.

2 Mark ix. 1. Cp. Matt. xvi. 28 and Luke ix. 27.

wickedness, if not incompatible with Human Nature, was at least irreconcilable with a Western Civilization's moral heritage from Christianity; and, if Turkish atrocities could be explained as anachronistic outcrops of a residual savagery in the hearts of recent proselytes to a Western way of life, how was a Western historian to explain the apostasy of Germans who were native-born children of the Western household? How, through this welter of war and crime, had the political map of the *Oikoumenê* come to be changed beyond all recognition? How had the Ottoman Empire, the Danubian Hapsburg Monarchy, and the British Rāj in India come to be replaced by a litter of successor-states? How had the number of the Great Powers in a Western World come to be reduced, within a period of thirty-two years, from the figure of eight at which it had stood at the outbreak of a First World War in A.D. 1914 to the figure of two at which it stood at the close of a Second World War in A.D. 1945? How was it that these two survivors, the Soviet Union and the United States, were, both of them, located outside Western Europe? How had this West European peninsula of Asia, which had dominated the entire *Oikoumenê* for 231 years ending in A.D. 1914, come, by A.D. 1945, to be dwarfed by an outer ring of new countries conjured into life by West European enterprise? How had distance come, for human purposes, to be annihilated by the invention of the art of flying? And how had Mankind's conquest of the Air come to be enslaved to the service of a subsequently invented atomic weapon which threatened to annihilate the Western Civilization and perhaps Life itself on this planet?

Here were contemporary themes enough to occupy the time, energy, and genius of all those eleven great historians in our catalogue who, in other times and places, had been moved to show their mettle by the challenge of questions similarly presented by the history of their time; and the writer was aware that, if he had not had an Hellenic classical education, he might have been tempted into expending his stock of intellectual ammunition on an attack upon one or other of the historical targets that had been offered to him and his contemporaries by their own social milieu in their own day. The disappointment of his elders' secularized messianic expectations might have moved a twentieth-century Western historian to study the history of the quest for an Earthly Paradise upon which the Western Society had embarked towards the end of the seventeenth century of the Christian Era in its recoil from the Early Modern Western Wars of Religion. The shattering breach of the forty-three years' peace (*duraverat* A.D. 1871–1914), which had resulted in the dwarfing of Western Europe and the polarization of military and political power in the World round two non-European centres, might have moved him to study the history of a Modern Western Balance of Power. The atrocities committed by Turkish hands against Armenian victims in A.D. 1915–16 might have moved him to study the history of the effects of an impact of Western technique, institutions, ideas, and ideals—particularly the exotic Western ideal of nationally homogeneous parochial states—upon the geographically intermingled Islamic, Eastern Orthodox Christian, and Monophysite Christian societies. The German people's apostasy from the secularized faith of a Modern Western Civilization might have moved him to study the peculiarities in the ethical development of the German contingent in the Western Society since the Thirty Years War and also the weaknesses in the ethical development of a Late Modern Western Society which had purchased religious toleration at the price of dissevering Christian ethics from their historical roots in the soil of Christian beliefs. The break-up of the Ottoman and Hapsburg empires and the British Rāj might have moved him to devote his working life to a dissection of the political anatomy of one or other of these three polities. The conversion of the 'temperate and undecisive contests' of Gibbon's day[1] into wars of annihilation by the conquest of the Air and the splitting of the Atom might have moved him to study the history of the human consequences of the technological triumphs of a Late Modern Western science.

Thanks to his professional good fortune in being born into a Time of Troubles that was, by definition, an historian's golden age, the present writer was, in fact, moved to interest himself in each of these historical questions that were flung at him by current events; but his professional good fortune did not end here; for he had also been as fortunate as Turgot in his education. Like Turgot, he had been born into a civilization that had not sprung straight from the primitive level but was affiliated to a predecessor of its own species; and in England in A.D. 1896–1911, as in France in the mid-eighteenth century, the Western middle class not only recognized its Hellenic cultural heritage but set so high a value upon this spiritual heirloom that it made the Greek and Latin classics the staple medium of its higher education. Born, though he was, 162 years later than the great French historian civil servant, the writer, happening also to be born in an intellectually more conservative Western country, had been born just in time to receive in England a there then still undiluted Early Modern Western education in Hellenism. By the summer of A.D. 1911, when he had been studying Latin for nearly fifteen years and Greek for more than twelve, the languages, literature, history, and êthos of the Hellenic Civilization had become, as they were to remain, more familiar, and far more congenial, to him than any cultural treasures that his own native post-Hellenic society had to offer him; and this traditional education had the wholesome effect of rendering its recipients immune against the malady of corporate self-worship in the insidious form of cultural chauvinism. An Hellenically-educated Westerner could not easily fall into the error of seeing in Western Christendom the best of all possible worlds, nor, *a fortiori*, into the grosser error of equating a post-Western Christian Civilization with 'Civilization' *sans phrase*;[2] and no Hellenically-educated Western historian could consider the historical questions that his own contemporary Western social milieu was putting to him without referring them to the oracles of a Hellas in which he had found his spiritual home.

To illustrate this intellectual consequence of an Early Modern Western classical education from the cases in point, the present writer

[1] Gibbon, E.: *The History of the Decline and Fall of the Roman Empire*, 'General Observations on the Fall of the Roman Empire in the West', in chap. xxxviii, *ad finem*.

[2] The misconception of 'the Unity of Civilization' has been examined in I. i. 149–71.

could testify that he was unable to observe the disappointment of his liberal-minded elders' expectations without being reminded of Plato's disillusionment with a Periclean Attic democracy. He could not live through the experience of the outbreak of war in A.D. 1914 without realizing that the outbreak of war in 431 B.C. had brought the same experience to Thucydides. As he found his own experience revealing to him, for the first time, the inwardness of Thucydidean words and phrases that had meant little or nothing to him before, he realized that a book written in another world more than 2,300 years ago might be a depository of experiences which, in the reader's world, were only just beginning to overtake the reader's own generation. There was a sense in which the two dates A.D. 1914 and 431 B.C. were philosophically contemporaneous with one another;[1] and this philosophical truth was manifestly more significant than the arithmetical fact that the two dates happened to be 2,345 years apart on a chronological chart. Moreover, when the Hellenically-educated Western historian lived on to see war break out again in A.D. 1939, he could not taste this less shocking, but more harrowing, repetition of the experience of A.D. 1914 without being reminded that Thucydides' Great Atheno-Peloponnesian War had likewise taken the form of a tragedy in two acts separated by an interval of illusory peace, and that the Great Romano-Punic War of 264–201 B.C. and Great Romano-Persian War of A.D. 572–628 had each, again, been a double war on the Thucydidean pattern.[2] At the crisis of the first World War in the spring of A.D. 1918, when his country's fate had trembled in the balance, the poetry that had kept running through his mind had been no English verse; it had been the lines in which Lucretius had conveyed the indelible impression that had been made on Roman minds by Rome's dire struggle with Hannibal,

> ad confligendum venientibus undique Poenis
> omnia cum belli trepido concussa tumultu
> horrida contremuere sub altis aetheris oris.[3]

When he felt the shock and bewilderment that every non-German Western soul was bound to feel when faced with the portent of the Germans' apostasy from a common Western Civilization, he found himself reminded of the apostasy of Tiglath Pileser III's Assyrians from a Babylonic civilization that Assyria had previously shared with the Babylonians, Elamites, and Urartians—a moral catastrophe whose social consequences had given the Hellenes their opportunity to contend with the Iranians for an hegemony over devastated Babylonic, Syriac, and Egyptiac worlds. When he studied the appalling communal conflicts in a contemporary Turkey, Palestine, India, South Africa, and United States, he was reminded of such grim episodes in the history of a post-Alexandrine Hellenic World as Mithradates' massacre of Roman citizens and protected persons in Asia Minor in 88 B.C. and the extermination of Hellene and Jewish local minorities by Jewish and Hellene local majorities throughout Syria upon the outbreak of the Great Romano-Jewish

[1] The philosophical contemporaneity of all societies of the species known as civilizations has been discussed in I. i. 172–4.

[2] See XI. ix. 236.

[3] Lucretius: *De Rerum Naturâ*, Book III, ll. 833–5.

War in A.D. 66. The foundering of the Ottoman Empire and the Danubian Hapsburg Monarchy in the First World War recalled to his mind the catastrophes of Macedon, the Seleucid Monarchy, and other *peritura regna*[1] that had collided with Rome. The reduction in the number of a contemporary Western World's Great Powers from eight to two within the thirty-two years A.D. 1914–45 recalled the reduction in the number of a post-Alexandrine Hellenic World's Great Powers from five to one within fifty-two years and a quarter (219–168 B.C.).[2] The dwarfing of Western Europe, in a post-Modern Age of Western history, by a circle of giant Powers that had sprung up around her on the fringes of an expanding Western World, reminded him of the dwarfing of a pre-Alexandrine Hellas, in a post-Alexandrine Age of Hellenic history, by Macedonian successor-states of the Achaemenian Empire, a Carthaginian thalassocracy in the Western Mediterranean, and a Roman Commonwealth in Italy which had found their battlefields in Ionia, the Aegean, Continental European Greece, and Sicily.[3]

It will be seen that in the present writer's social milieu there were two factors—neither of them personal to himself, but both of them properties of the rock from which he had been hewn—which, between them, had a decisive influence on his approach to a study of History. The first of these factors was the current history of his own Western World in his own lifetime; the second was an Hellenic education that was the precious legacy of a fifteenth-century Western renaissance of Hellenic life and letters. By perpetually interacting with one another, as they did, these two factors worked together to make the writer's view of History binocular. When the historian's elemental question 'How has this come out of that?' was put to him by some current catastrophic event, the form which the question was apt to assume in his mind was not 'How has this come out of that state of affairs in the history of an un-Hellenic Western World in which I am a stranger and a sojourner?'[4] A current event so seldom failed to evoke a reminiscence of some comparable event in Hellenic history that, in an Hellenically-educated Western historian's mind, the stock form of the question came to be: 'How has this come out of that state of affairs in Western as well as in Hellenic history?' Two divergent forces in the historian's social milieu—current events and an Hellenic education—were thus always simultaneously exerting themselves upon his line of thought, and these divergent forces found their resolution in his mind in a habit of looking at History as a series of comparisons in two terms.

This binocular view of History might have been appreciated and approved by Far Eastern contemporaries of the writer's in whose then likewise still traditional education the classical language and literature of an antecedent civilization had played a no less predominant part. The English writer's experience would assuredly have been shared by any Chinese litteratus who had been fortunate enough to have completed his education before the abandonment, in A.D. 1905, of the public

1 Virgil: *Georgics* II, l. 498.
2 See the passage of Polybius's *Oecumenical History* quoted on p. 64, above.
3 See III. iii. 310–16.
4 Psalm xxxix. 12 (14 in *The Book of Common Prayer*). Cp. Hebrews xi. 13.

examinations in the classics which had previously been the obligatory avenue for gaining entry into the Imperial Civil Service. The Confucian litteratus, likewise, would have found himself unable to encounter any passing event without being reminded by it of some classical allusion, reminiscence, or parallel that would have, for him, a greater value and, indeed, perhaps even a greater reality than the post-classical occurrence that had set his mind working on its congenial task of chewing the cud of a familiar Sinic classical lore. The principal difference in mental outlook between this Late Ch'ing Confucian-minded scholar and his Late Victorian Hellenic-minded English contemporary might prove to be that a Chinese born into this generation could still remain content to make his historical comparisons in two terms only, whereas the Late Victorian Englishman, when once he had begun to think historically in two terms, could no longer rest till he had extended his cultural gamut to a wider range.

For a Chinese receiving his traditional classical education at the turn of the nineteenth and twentieth centuries of the Christian Era, it would still be a novel idea that any civilization other than the Sinic and its living Far Eastern successor could be deserving of any serious consideration; for, by this date, little more than half a century had elapsed since the Chinese had had their first experience of finding themselves defenceless against the assaults of 'south-sea barbarians' armed with new-fangled weapons. An invincibly Sinic-minded Chinese contemporary of the writer's might perhaps still have contrived to ignore the existence of any civilizations beyond the two which, between them, had meant everything to his forebears; but a similarly blinkered vision was impossible for any Westerner of the same generation.

It was impossible because, within the last four hundred years, a Western Society which had conquered the Ocean had thrust itself into contact with no less than eight other representatives of its own species in the Old World and the New;[1] and it had since become doubly impossible for Western minds to ignore the existence or to deny the significance of other civilizations besides their own and the Hellenic because, within the last century, these Westerners who had already conquered a previously virgin Ocean had gone on to conquer a previously buried Past. Within the fifty years following Napoleon's arrival at Alexandria, three hundred years after Vasco da Gama's arrival at Calicut, a new Western science of Archaeology had added to the number of the civilizations within the ken of Western minds by disinterring at least four buried civilizations—the Egyptiac, the Babylonic, the Sumeric, and the Mayan —and the writer was to live to see this list extended by the rediscovery of the Hittite and Minoan civilizations and the Indus and Shang cultures. In a generation which had acquired this wide historical horizon, a Western historian who had been led by his traditional Hellenic education to make historical comparisons in two terms could not be content till he had converted this dual into a plural. He was bound to go on to

[1] The eight civilizations in question were the Orthodox Christian and its offshoot in Russia, the Islamic, the Hindu, the Far Eastern and its offshoot in Japan, the Central American, and the Andean.

collect, for comparative study, as many specimens as he could find of the species of Society of which the Hellenic Society and the Western Society were merely two representatives. The twenty or thirty specimens collected and utilized in the present Study were the fruits of the field-work which the writer had been moved to carry out when it had dawned upon him that, for a comparative study of History, the intellectual resources within the reach of a Western historian in his day were of an unprecedented richness.[1]

When he had thus succeeded in multiplying his terms of comparison more than tenfold, he could no longer ignore a supreme question which his original comparison in two terms had already threatened to raise. The most portentous single fact in the Hellenic Civilization's history was the eventual dissolution of a society whose breakdown had been registered in 431 B.C. by the outbreak of the Great Atheno-Peloponnesian War; and, if there was any validity in the writer's habitual procedure of drawing comparisons between Hellenic history and Western, it would seem to follow that the Western Society, for its part, must at any rate be not immune from the possibility of coming to a similar end in its turn, even though there might be no *a priori* necessity that its history should take, sooner or later, this tragic Hellenic course. The consideration of so dire a possibility could, however, be kept at bay so long as the history of the Hellenic Civilization remained the only other term of comparison in the writer's mental field, since the rules of Logic did not exact the inference of a general and inexorable law of History from a single case which might, after all, perhaps have been a *lusus Naturae*. When, however, a Western student of History had collected as many as twenty-six specimens of societies of the species 'Civilizations' which had duly come to birth, without reckoning in four others which had been abortive, and when he had gone on to observe that, of these twenty-six, no less than sixteen were already dead by the time of writing,[2] he was bound to infer from this wider range of instances that death was indeed a possibility which confronted every civilization, not excluding the still living society into which he himself happened to have been born.

> Haud igitur leti praeclusa est ianua caelo
> nec soli terraeque neque altis aequoris undis,
> sed patet immane et vasto respectat hiatu.[3]

What was this 'door of Death' through which sixteen out of twenty-six civilizations within a twentieth-century Western historian's ken had disappeared already? In setting out to answer a question that had thus been forced upon him by an illuminating multiplication of an originally binocular view of History, the writer was led into a study of the breakdowns and disintegrations of civilizations; and through studying their breakdowns and disintegrations he was led on into a complementary study of their geneses and growths.

It will be seen that no less than three influences emanating from the writer's native Modern Western social milieu had worked together to

[1] An attempt to survey this rich field of historical study has been made in I. i. 63–129.
[2] See IV. iv. 1–2 and XII. ix. 411–12.
[3] Lucretius: *De Rerum Naturâ*, Book V, ll. 373–5, quoted in IV. iv. 4.

present him with the set of questions that had moved him to write the present work. The fifteenth-century Italian humanists who had raised the ghost of an extinct Hellenic culture in a post-Hellenic Western Christian World had compelled him to see History in two terms, *more Sinico*. The fifteenth-century Portuguese and Spanish mariners who had brought Western Christendom into touch with all the other living civilizations in the *Oikoumenê*, and the nineteenth-century French and English archaeologists who had disinterred a number of dead civilizations which had not only passed away but had also subsequently fallen into oblivion, had compelled him to break the bounds of a classical outlook by increasing the number of his terms from a bare two to more than twenty. These three goodly companies of creative Modern Western spirits had thus co-operated to educate one of the latter-day heirs of their cumulative intellectual achievements, and his consequent work had been produced under the auspices of these inspired and inspiring Modern Western pastors and masters.

2. *Inspirations from Personal Experiences*

Gibbon

If we now pass on to consider inspirations that have come to historians, not from their social milieux, but from personal experiences, we shall find a classic example in the genesis of *The History of the Decline and Fall of the Roman Empire* from Gibbon's experience at Rome on the 15th October, 1764.

Edward Gibbon's lifetime (*vivebat* A.D. 1737–94) was not barren of historic events. The English historian was thirty-eight years old at the outbreak of the American Revolution and fifty-two years old at the outbreak of the French Revolution; he lived to see his own country involved in no fewer than four wars; and, though he was still a child at the time of the War of the Austrian Succession and its Anglo-Spanish naval prelude (*gerebantur* A.D. 1739–48), he was in the full vigour of his intellectual powers when the Seven Years War (*gerebatur* A.D. 1756–63) and the American Revolutionary War (*gerebatur* A.D. 1775–83) were fought and when the French Revolutionary War broke out (*erupit* A.D. 1792). Yet—though Gibbon elicits a smile from his reader by suggesting that 'the captain of the Hampshire Grenadiers . . . has not been useless to the historian of the Roman Empire'[1]—it is patent that neither the Seven Years War nor any other contemporary public catastrophe was the source of Gibbon's inspiration. *L'Essai sur l'Étude de la Littérature* written in A.D. 1758–9, the abortive fragment of a history of the rise of the Swiss Confederation, written (likewise in French) in A.D. 1767–8, and *The History of the Decline and Fall of the Roman Empire*, which he began to sketch out in the rough at least as early as A.D. 1771[2] and finished writing

[1] *The Autobiographies of Edward Gibbon*, edited by John Murray (London 1896, Murray), pp. 190 (Memoir B) and 401–2 (Memoir D).

[2] See chap. xxx, n. 86: 'The Count de Buat is satisfied that the Germans who invaded Gaul were the *two-thirds* that yet remained of the army of Radagaisus. See the *Histoire Ancienne des Peuples de l'Europe* (tom. vii, pp. 87–121, Paris 1772): an elaborate work, which I had not the advantage of perusing till the year 1777. As early as 1771, I find the same idea expressed in a rough draft of the present History.'

in A.D. 1787, as well as the six drafts for an autobiography, written between A.D. 1788 and A.D. 1793, were all inspired by experiences that were personal to the author.

In the *Essai* (begun at Lausanne in March 1758) the language and the subject alike were acknowledgements of a personal debt to the contemporary French current in the stream of a Late Modern Western Society's intellectual activity; and this debt had been contracted by the author as a consequence of one private action of his own and another which this had evoked from his father. Gibbon's father had responded to Gibbon's conversion to Roman Catholicism at Oxford in A.D. 1753 by packing him off to Lausanne to complete his education there in the house of a Calvinist Protestant minister during the years A.D. 1753–8. A personal interest in Swiss institutions, as well as in French ideas, which had been aroused in Gibbon's mind by this five-years-long residence, at an impressionable age, in a French-speaking subject territory (as the Vaud then was) within the miniature empire of the Canton of Berne, explains Gibbon's tentative choice of the history of the Swiss as his next subject, after the publication of the *Essai* in A.D. 1761; and he set to work on his preparations for this second self-assigned task in the summer of A.D. 1765 for personal reasons again. He himself had then just returned to England from his grand tour on the Continent (*peregrinabatur* January 1763–June 1765); and his Lausannois friend Georges Deyverdun had simultaneously arrived in England to spend four consecutive summers (those of the years A.D. 1765–8)[1] with Edward Gibbon at his father's house at Buriton.

'The two historical designs which had balanced my choice were submitted to his taste, and, in the parallel between the revolutions of Florence and Switzerland, our common partiality for a country which was *his* by birth and *mine* by adoption inclined the scale in favour of the latter. . . . The assistance of Deyverdun seemed to remove an insuperable obstacle. The French or Latin memorials, of which I was not ignorant, are inconsiderable in number and weight; but in the perfect acquaintance of my friend with the German language I found the key of a more valuable collection.'[2]

As for *The History of the Decline and Fall of the Roman Empire*, we have Gibbon's own thrice-declared testimony that this was inspired by another personal experience of his which far surpassed all the rest in the fertility of its creative effects.

The failure of contemporary public events to bring into action the creative genius to which Gibbon's *magnum opus* bears irrefutable witness is the more remarkable considering that the historian was in truth (as might have been expected) neither insensitive nor indifferent to the current history of his day. The sureness of his historical intuition was, indeed, displayed in the diversity of his reactions to the divers contemporary public events mentioned above.

He was deeply impressed and gravely perturbed by the French

[1] See Low, D. M.: *Edward Gibbon, 1737–1794* (London 1937, Chatto & Windus), pp. 197–8.

[2] Gibbon, E.: *Autobiographies*, ed. cit., pp. 275–6 (Memoir C). Cp. pp. 407–8 (Memoir D).

Revolution; for, though he did not live to see it complete its course, he at once divined that it was an epoch-making new departure in the Western Society's history which sharply challenged the complacent view of a Late Modern Western Civilization's prospects to which he had committed himself so magisterially in *The History of the Decline and Fall of the Roman Empire* in his 'General Observations on the Fall of the Roman Empire in the West' at the end of Chapter xxxviii.[1] But, when the shock thus administered to Gibbon by the French Revolution did overtake him, nearly two years had already passed since he had written the last sentence of his great work; and, though he lived for more than four and a half years after the advent of an earth-shaking mundane apocalypse that had upset his lifelong *Weltanschauung*,[2] he was not moved by this revolutionary change in his social milieu to embark on any fresh creative intellectual enterprise. After the completion of *The Decline and Fall*, his only noteworthy literary achievements were the six draft autobiographies;[3] and, though these fragments are literary masterpieces which rank with *The Decline and Fall* itself as monuments of the writer's inimitable style, their contents are personal reminiscences which ring no new changes on the historian's elemental question 'How has this come out of that?' though they throw a flood of light on the personal circumstances which had led Gibbon to address himself to this question three times within the thirty years A.D. 1758–87.

As for the American Revolutionary War, Gibbon showed his historical discernment here again in dismissing it, together with the Seven Years War, the War of the Austrian Succession, and the foregoing hostilities between Great Britain and Spain, as one of those 'temperate and undecisive contests' that might produce continual fluctuations in the Balance of Power without deserving to be regarded as anything more than 'partial events' which could not 'essentially injure' the Western World's 'general state of happiness'.[4] This series of wars through which Gibbon had lived between A.D. 1739 and A.D. 1783 had, in truth, been different in kind from the war which he lived to see break out in A.D. 1792; for, as we have observed in another context,[5] the Western wars of A.D. 1739–83 were the relatively mild aftermath of the Western General War of A.D. 1672–1713, whereas the war that broke out in A.D. 1792 proved to be another general war, comparable in magnitude to the conflict that had been precipitated, 120 years earlier, by the ambitions of Louis XIV.

The failure of the Seven Years War to inspire Gibbon is nevertheless remarkable; for, though his historical insight may have inhibited him from overrating the historical importance of this 'temperate and undecisive' exercise of the European forces, his literary ambition might have tempted him to try to turn a current public event to personal

[1] See XII. ix. 741–57.

[2] Gibbon finished writing *The Decline and Fall* on the 27th June, 1787; the session of the French States General was opened at Versailles on the 5th May, 1789; Gibbon died on the 16th January, 1794.

[3] *The Autobiographies of Edward Gibbon*, edited by John Murray (London 1896, Murray).

[4] Gibbon: 'General Observations on the Fall of the Roman Empire in the West', quoted in IV. iv. 148 and in XII. ix. 424.

[5] In XI. ix. 252–3 and 255 (Table I).

account, since, at the outbreak of war in A.D. 1756, Gibbon was nineteen years old, and between March 1758 and February 1759, while the war was in progress, his already awakened literary ambition was leading him to write the first of his published works: *L'Essai sur l'Étude de la Littérature.*[1] From the moment when he started writing this juvenile essay till the moment, nearly ten years later, when he broke off work on his second literary project—a history of the Swiss—in the winter of A.D. 1767–8, Gibbon was painfully casting about for subjects with an obvious lack of inspiration which, to a twentieth-century Western historian's mind, was reminiscent of the deplorable attitude prevalent among latter-day candidates for post-graduate degrees in their desperate search for subjects for theses to be offered up to captains of intellectual industry whose fiat was law in the industrialized academic economy of the Western universities in a post-Modern Age.[2] Gibbon's choice of the histories of Switzerland and Florence as two possible alternative themes on which he might employ his pen had been the sequel to an unrewarding prospector's tour of other arid deposits of possibly metalliferous ore.

'In the summer of 1761, after consid ring the potentialities of Charles VIII's expedition into Italy, Richard I's crusade, the war of King John and the Barons, the Black Prince, a comparison of Titus and Henry V, lives of Sir Philip Sidney or Montrose, he had at last fixed on Sir Walter Raleigh. But in the following summer he felt obliged to drop his hero. He found that he could add little to the existing life by Oldys, poor performance though that might be, while he would hesitate to eke out his work by digressions into contemporary history which had already occupied such men as Walpole, Robertson, and Hume.'[3]

Indeed, from the time when Gibbon had completed his education until the winter of A.D. 1767–8, when, after abandoning the history of the Swiss, 'I more seriously undertook,' as he himself records, 'to methodise the form and to collect the substance of my Roman decay',[4] he was afflicted with a barrenness of intellectual creative power which he frankly confesses.

'Between [the publication of] my Essay and [the publication of] the first volume of *The Decline and Fall*, fifteen years (1761–1776) of strength and freedom elapsed without any other publications than my criticism on Warburton[5] and some articles in the *Mémoires Littéraires.*'[6]

It is astonishing that, after this long inauspicious prelude, Gibbon should have been continuously occupied, throughout a period of some nineteen and a half years, ending on the night of the 27th June, 1787, in producing a masterpiece of historical research, construction, and writing

1 See Low, D. M.: *Edward Gibbon, 1737–1794* (London 1937, Chatto & Windus), p. 102.

2 This attempt to apply the technique of the Division of Labour to a post-Modern Western World's intellectual activities has been noticed in I. i. 2–8.

3 Low, op. cit., p. 118, summarizing four passages, dating from the 14th April, 1761, to the 26th July, 1762, in Gibbon's journal, quoted in *Autobiographies*, ed. cit., pp. 193–7 (Memoir B).

4 Gibbon, *Autobiographies*, ed. cit., p. 284 (Memoir C). Cp. p. 411 (Memoir D).

5 Gibbon, E.: *Critical Observations on the Sixth Book of the Aeneid* (originally published in 1770, and reprinted in *The Miscellaneous Works of Edward Gibbon Esq.*, new edition, vol. iv (London 1814, John Murray), pp. 467–514).—A.J.T.

6 Gibbon, *Autobiographies*, ed. cit., p. 411 (Memoir D). Cp. pp. 283–4 (Memoir C).

which had no superior in its own genre in any literature known to Western scholars in A.D. 1952. It is, however, more astonishing still that, as soon as he had completed this supremely creative piece of intellectual work, Gibbon should have relapsed, for the remaining six and a half years of his life, into the intellectual barrenness from which he had suffered in his youth.

Gibbon did not even produce a final complete version of his autobiography out of his six successive fragmentary drafts; and the new literary enterprise to which he addressed himself between his return from Lausanne to England in the early summer of A.D. 1793 and his death on the 16th January, 1794, had not been his own idea, but had been undertaken at the suggestion of 'a young Scottish antiquary', John Pinkerton, who had audaciously rushed in where Gibbon's defaulting muse had forborne, this time, to tread.[1] A presentiment that this muse was now to desert him as arbitrarily as she had made her epiphany to him on the 15th October, 1764, not much less than twenty-three years back, can indeed be read between the lines of the elegiac passage in which the historian has recorded his feelings after writing the last sentence of his supremely great work.

'It was on the day, or rather the night, of the 27th June, 1787, between the hours of eleven and twelve, that I wrote the last lines of the last page in a summer-house in my garden. After laying down my pen I took several turns in a *berceau*, or covered walk of acacias, which commands a prospect of the country, the lake, and the mountains. The air was temperate, the sky was serene, the silver orb of the Moon was reflected from the waters, and all Nature was silent. I will not dissemble the first emotions of joy on the recovery of my freedom, and, perhaps, the establishment of my fame. But my pride was soon humbled, and a sober melancholy was spread over my mind by the idea that I had taken my everlasting leave of an old and agreeable companion, and that, whatsoever might be the future date of my history, the life of the historian must be short and precarious.'[2]

Gibbon's gift to his fellow men is indeed all contained in one immortal work which it took him some fifteen years (A.D. 1773–87) to write, some nineteen and a half years (A.D. 1768–87) to produce, including some four and a half years (A.D. 1768–72) spent on systematic study and on preliminary drafting,[3] and nearly twenty-three years (15th October, 1764–27th June, 1787) to create, including three years and more during which the already dedicated historian of the decline and fall of Rome 'still contemplated at an awful distance'[4] the subject that had been vouchsafed to him[5] by his heavenly visitant on an historic site at a memorable hour in

[1] 'A young Scottish antiquary approached him with a scheme for publishing the English chronicles from Gildas to the accession of the House of Tudor. Gibbon reflected, approved, took fire: he promised first his interest, then his assistance, and finally his collaboration' (Young, G. M.: *Gibbon*, 2nd ed. (London 1948, Hart-Davis), p. 175). 'He agreed to write a general preface and introductions for Pinkerton's projected edition of early English historians' (Low, D. M.: *Edward Gibbon, 1737–1794* (London 1937, Chatto & Windus), p. 345).

[2] Gibbon, *Autobiographies*, ed. cit., pp. 333–4 (Memoir E).

[3] See Gibbon, *Autobiographies*, ed. cit., pp. 284–6 (Memoir C) and 411–12 (Memoir D), and compare these passages with *The Decline and Fall*, chap. xxx, n. 86, cited on p. 98, n. 2, above.

[4] *Autobiographies*, p. 275 (Memoir C).

[5] See IV. iv. 59–60 and VI. vii. 9.

circumstances which the recipient of this divine inspiration has recorded in words that rise to the height of the occasion.

'It was on the fifteenth of October, in the gloom of the evening, as I sat musing on the Capitol while the barefooted fryars were chanting their litanies in the Temple of Jupiter,[1] that I conceived the first thought of my history.'[2]

This imaginative experience was the sole flash of inspiration with which Gibbon was ever visited. Without it, that wonderful genius might never have come to flower, and that famous name might have found no place in the record of Mankind's intellectual history. In chronological terms the psychic event which had these momentous consequences may have occupied no more than a fraction of one second out of the thirty-six years or so of the great historian's adult intellectual life; yet his watchful muse did not fail to see and seize her fleeting opportunity of gaining access to a mind which was normally rendered impervious to her divine promptings by a carapace of innate scepticism that had been case-hardened in an all too congenial eighteenth-century Western mental climate. Perceiving that her chosen vessel's usually inhibited soul had been momentarily softened by the cumulative emotional influences of a sight which recalled the greatness of a dead Past and a sound whose faintly floating strains conveyed the measure of the gulf between Past and Present, the goddess had made her dazzling instantaneous epiphany from the depths of a Subconscious Psychic Abyss in order to release the springs of a mighty mind's intellectual power by the annunciation of a theme which, at last, was fully worthy of the ready writer.[3]

'How has this come out of that?' It would be hard to find another instance in which the historian's stark elemental question had generated so fecund a germ of creative thought. The favoured recipient himself did not immediately apprehend more than a fragment of the mental wealth that had suddenly been poured into his lap, and even the incomparably great work that he eventually made of it was no more than a gleaning from the huge potential harvest.

'My original plan', Gibbon tells us,[4] 'was confined to the decay of the City; my reading and reflection pointed to that aim'; and this project was duly achieved in the essay that eventually found its place as the last chapter of the completed work, in which Gibbon surveys the ruins of Rome in the fifteenth century of the Christian Era and discusses the

[1] The pagan temple that had been replaced by the Christian church of Santa Maria in Arâ Coeli, served by the 'Zoccolanti' Franciscan Friars Minor, was actually the Temple of Juno Moneta, at the northern end of the Mons Capitolinus. The Temple of Jupiter Capitolinus had occupied the south-western end of the hill.—A.J.T.

[2] *Autobiographies*, pp. 405–6 (Memoir D). This experience is also recorded in two other of Gibbon's drafts for an autobiography. The account in Memoir E (ibid., p. 302) does not differ in any point from that in Memoir D, quoted above. The account in Memoir C (ibid., p. 270) gives 'the place and moment of conception' of *The History of the Decline and Fall* as 'the fifteenth of October 1764, in the close of evening, as I sat musing in [*sic*] the Church of the Zoccolanti or Franciscan fryars, while they were singing Vespers in the Temple of Jupiter on the ruins of the Capitol'. The other two accounts give the impression—though they do not expressly state—that Gibbon was sitting in the open air, with the ruins of Ancient Rome before his eyes, while the sound of the friars' voices was reaching his ears from inside the Christian Church on the site of a former pagan temple.

[3] Psalm xlv. 1 (2 in *The Book of Common Prayer*).

[4] In *Autobiographies*, ed. cit., p. 406 (Memoir D).

causes of the physical decay and destruction of a city which had reached the apogee of its material splendour in the second century. The last words of this chapter, written in the last hour of the 27th day of June, 1787, at Lausanne, nearly twenty-three years after the Muse's epiphany at Rome, are:

'It was among the ruins of the Capitol that I first conceived the idea of a work which has amused and exercised near twenty years of my life, and which, however inadequate to my own wishes, I finally deliver to the curiosity and candour of the public.—Lausanne, June 27, 1787.'

But in the meanwhile the growth of the original germ of thought had kept pace with the passage of Time; for, by the date at which Gibbon indited these closing words, this chapter was numbered, not 'Alpha and Omega', but lxxi. In the course of its elephantine gestation, the germ planted in Gibbon's mind on the 15th October, 1764, had grown more than seventyfold beyond the modest compass of its primal nucleus.

'My original plan was circumscribed to the decay of the City rather than of the Empire; and, though my reading and reflexions began to point towards that object, some years elapsed, and several avocations intervened, before I was seriously engaged in the execution of that laborious work.'[1]

The historian goes on to tell us[2] that he 'had yet a very inadequate notion' of the 'limits and extent' of his theme, even when he did start his serious labours on it in A.D. 1768.

'I gradually advanced from the wish to the hope, from the hope to the design, from the design to the execution, of my historical work. . . . Through the darkness of the Middle Ages I explored my way, in *The Annals and Antiquities of Italy* of Muratori, and compared them with the parallel or transverse lines of Sigonius and Maffei, of Baronius and Pagi, till I almost grasped the ruins of Rome in the fourteenth century, without suspecting that this final chapter must be attained by the labour of six quartos and twenty years.'[3]

By the 27th June, 1787, this labour had extracted a history of the Decline and Fall of the Roman Empire out of a theme which, on the 15th October, 1764, had been enunciated by the Muse merely as a history of the physical decay of a city that Trajan, Hadrian, and the Antonines had bequeathed to unworthy epigoni. 'How has this come out of that?' The labour of twenty years and six quarto volumes had expanded the field of Gibbon's answer to the historian's elemental question from the *pomoerium* of an imperial city to the *limites* of the universal state of which Rome had been the foundress and first capital; yet, immense though this progressive expansion of Gibbon's historical horizon was, it was prevented from expanding right up to 'the natural frontiers' of even a mundanely intelligible field of study by the narrowness of the original nucleus of the germinating idea.

The tragically dramatic contrast that had fired Gibbon's imagination

[1] Gibbon, E.: *Autobiographies*, ed. cit., pp. 270–1 (Memoir C).
[2] Ibid., p. 284 (Memoir C).
[3] Ibid., p. 411 (Memoir D). Cp. p. 284 (Memoir C).

among the ruins of the Capitol on the 15th October, 1764, had been the physical contrast between these present ruins and the past magnificence of those buildings when they had stood intact; and Gibbon had been right in seeing in the second century of the Christian Era the physical city of Rome's architectural *floruit*. In setting out to trace the history of the city's subsequent physical decay, he had therefore likewise been right in taking the death of Marcus Aurelius and accession of Commodus as his chronological starting-point. He had, however, failed to perceive that the geographical enlargement of his subject from an *Urbs Roma* to an *Orbis Romanus* demanded of him a concomitant extension of his chronological limits. He did not take Bacon's point[1] that the Roman Empire's mission and significance had lain in serving as a universal state for the whole of the Hellenic Society, and that the *orbis* which had been arrogantly styled *Romanus* by citizens of the city-state which had happened to serve as History's instrument for bringing this world into political unity was in truth an Hellenic World whose decline and fall had already been in full train before the rise of Rome had begun, and whose principal pre-Roman polities—Sparta, Athens, Olynthus, Macedon, and Syracuse—had given Rome her opportunity by failing to solve for the Hellenic Society betimes the political problem that Rome had solved for it eventually too late. The episode of mundane history that had been the implicit theme of Gibbon's flash of inspiration on the 15th October, 1764, was in truth the decline and fall, not just of a Roman Hellenic universal state, but of the Hellenic Civilization itself; and the 'beginning of great evils for Hellas',[2] in which the historian of the Decline and Fall ought to have found his chronological starting-point, was, not the accession of Commodus in A.D. 180, but the outbreak of the Great Atheno-Peloponnesian War in 431 B.C.[3]

This was not, however, either the only or the greatest spiritual treasure latent in Gibbon's fecund experience on the Capitol which the subject of the experience failed to harvest. The antiquarian approach which misled Gibbon into entering upon his story at a point more than six hundred years after its true beginning was not so grave a limitation as the sceptical temperament and the eighteenth-century Western bent of mind which inhibited him from apprehending the ultimate theme with which this marvellous revelation was pregnant. The ultimate theme was not a decline and fall of the Hellenic Civilization—occupying a somewhat longer span in the Time-dimension than the decline and fall of that society's Roman universal state after the death of Marcus Aurelius. It was not either this or any other episode of merely mundane history. It was a drama in which the action was raised to a higher spiritual dimension through an invasion of Time by Eternity. The heart of the revelation conveyed by the sound of a Christian liturgical chant impinging on the sight of the ruins of a Trajanic Rome was the truth that Man's mundane failures are seized by God as His hell-sent opportunities for offering to human souls a chance of finding spiritual salvation.[4]

[1] See the passage quoted from Bacon's essay 'Of the True Greatness of Kingdoms and Estates' in VI. vii. 110.

[2] Thucydides, Book II, chap. 12.

[3] This point has been made already in IV. iv. 58–63.

[4] See II. i. 271–99.

This truth that Man's failure, sin, and suffering in This World may serve Man, through God's grace, as a chariot on whose wings the Soul can soar heavenward[1] is an apocalypse in which History works together with Theology to lift a corner of the veil that shrouds from human vision the mystery of Human Nature and Destiny; for, in giving us an inkling of the good of Evil, this truth gives us a glimpse of the self-consistency and goodness of God's providence.

This is the ultimate meaning of 'the triumph of Barbarism and Religion' which Gibbon, in the closing seventy-first chapter of his work, claims to have described in the seventy chapters that precede it; and it is a meaning that had been duly divined by a Roman in whose person 'Religion and Barbarism' appeared, to Gibbon's unsympathetic eye, to be repulsively combined.[2] Not much less than twelve hundred years before the date of Gibbon's experience, Saint Gregory the Great, preaching a sermon to his Roman flock in the selfsame physical surroundings, had perceived and proclaimed the hollowness of this Trajanic Rome's outward grandeur;[3] and on the 15th October, 1764, Gibbon's visitant muse must have been fain to convey the Christian saint's inspiration to the post-Christian historian; for this visitant was a greater spiritual power than the Clio in whose garb she had presented herself in order to put her would-be chosen vessel to the test. Gibbon had in truth been visited in that ineffable moment by the Hokmah—God's Holy Wisdom[4]— who had once been recognized unerringly for what she was by the physically blind eyes of an English poet when his unquenched voice had hailed her as 'offspring of Heaven first-born'.[5] But Gibbon's heart had not known how to respond to the epiphany of this Celestial Light with Milton's prayer:

> Shine inward, and the mind through all her powers
> Irradiate, there plant eyes, all mist from thence
> Purge and disperse, that I may see and tell
> Of things invisible to mortal sight.

Instead of asking the historian's elemental question 'How has this come out of that?' with the spiritual humility that would have allowed his answer to expand to the full measure of its potential dimensions, the

[1] See II. ii. 210, n. 1; VII. vii. 420–9; and XII. ix. 627.

[2] Gibbon's treatment of Gregory the Great is a monument of the historian's virtuosity in the unamiable art of bestowing praise in terms that are more devastating than a candid censure:

'The pontificate of Gregory the Great . . . is one of the most edifying periods of the history of the Church. His virtues, and even his faults, a singular mixture of simplicity and cunning, of pride and humility, of sense and superstition, were happily suited to his station and to the temper of the times. . . .

'Experience had shown him the efficacy of these pompous rites. . . . and he readily forgave their tendency to promote the reign of priesthood and superstition. . . .

'The most abject ideas must be entertained of their [the sixth-century Italians'] taste and learning, since the epistles of Gregory, his sermons, and his dialogues are the work of a man who was second in erudition to none of his contemporaries.'

These are three fair samples of the laudatory arrows with which Gibbon has nailed his mighty victim to his sarcastic page in the forty-fifth chapter of his work.

[3] Saint Gregory the Great: *Homiliae Quadraginta in Evangelia*, No. xxviii (Migne, J. P.: *Patrologia Latina*, vol. lxxvi, col. 1212), quoted in IV. iv. 60–61.

[4] See Meyer, E.: *Ursprung und Anfänge des Christentums*, vol. ii (Stuttgart and Berlin 1921, Cotta), pp. 104–5; Dodd, C. H.: *The Bible and the Greeks* (London 1935, Hodder & Stoughton), pp. 217–18.

[5] Milton: *Paradise Lost*, Book III, l. 1.

self-assured child of a post-Christian Western secular enlightenment cramped the fruitful question from the outset by introducing into it a specious qualification. 'How on Earth has this come out of that?' was the form in which Gibbon recast, in his own style, the question that had been planted in his mind by its heavenly visitant; and, in thus automatically ruling the supra-mundane dimension of Reality out of his reckoning, he was unconsciously precluding himself from finding the treasure hid in his field,[1] though he sifted the soil with a diligence that could hardly have been surpassed by a twentieth-century Western archaeologist.

Volney

This personal experience of which Gibbon made so much or made so little, according to the standard by which we measure his achievement, was, of course, in any case not unique. We have already taken note[2] of the comparable personal experience that inspired Gibbon's younger contemporary Volney (*vivebat* A.D. 1757–1820) to write *Les Ruines, ou Méditations sur les Révolutions des Empires*; and, though Volney's tale of a visitation that overtook him while he sat musing on a fallen column among the ruins of Palmyra[3] may be apocryphal, there can be no doubt that this myth, if such it is, is a literary artifice for conveying a genuine experience. Volney on his travels in Egypt and Syria, like Gibbon on his visit to Rome, was inspired to write a great work on human affairs by a personal experience of a dramatic contrast between a miserable Present and a magnificent Past; and the inspiration that he had received *en voyage* in A.D. 1783–5 bore fruit in the publication of *Les Ruines* in A.D. 1791,[4] as Gibbon's inspiration *en voyage* in A.D. 1764 had borne fruit in the publication of *The History of the Decline and Fall of the Roman Empire* between A.D. 1776 and A.D. 1788.

Peregrinus Wiccamicus

The writer of the present Study had an authentic minor personal experience of the kind on the 23rd May, 1912, as he sat musing on the summit of the citadel of Mistrà, with the sheer wall of Mount Taÿgetus bounding his horizon in the western quarter of the compass, towards which he was bound, and the open vale of Sparta stretching away in the opposite eastern quarter, from which he had made his way that morning.

Though he had sat there, musing and gazing (and prosaically taking the edge off his hunger by consuming slabs of Pavlídhis' chocolate) through most of a long summer's day, till the gloom of evening constrained him reluctantly at last to move on in search of supper and a bed at Trýpi, he cannot pretend that he was inspired during his reverie on the summit by any strains from the throats of the nuns serving the church

[1] Matt. xiii. 44.

[2] On pp. 7–8, above.

[3] See *Les Ruines*, chaps. 1–4.

[4] Volney's fortuitous chronological advantage over Gibbon in being his junior by twenty years enabled him to profit mentally by a public catastrophe from which his senior had proved unable to derive any intellectual inspiration. The outbreak of the French Revolution, which had devastated Gibbon, stimulated Volney to bring the fruits of his Levantine experiences to harvest—though he had to pay for this stimulus by spending the last ten months of the Terror as a prisoner in irons.

of the Pandánassa, for he had left this far below in his spiral ascent of the miniature purgatorial mount that the citadel crowned like a Dantean Earthly Paradise. The sensuous experience that activated his historical imagination was not a sound of liturgical chanting; it was the sight of the ruins among which he had wound his way upwards to the peak; and this spectacle had been appalling; for, in this shattered fairy city, Time had stood still since that spring of A.D. 1821 in which Mistrà had been laid desolate, and in the spring of A.D. 1912 the nuns (rare birds in a Greek Orthodox Christendom) were the solitary inhabitants of a kástro that, for some six hundred years ending in the final catastrophe, had been the capital of Laconia under a series of successive régimes. Founded by the Franks *circa* A.D. 1249, recovered by the Byzantines in A.D. 1262, conquered by the 'Osmanlis in A.D. 1460, wrested from Ottoman hands by the Venetians in A.D. 1687,[1] and recovered by the 'Osmanlis in A.D. 1715, Mistrà had continued, through all these political, religious, and cultural vicissitudes, to reign for those six hundred years as the queen of the broad landscape that could be surveyed from her topmost battlements; and then, one April morning, out of the blue, the avalanche of wild highlanders from the Máni had overwhelmed her; her citizens had been forced to flee for their lives and had been despoiled and massacred as they fled; her deserted mansions had been sacked; and her ruins had been left desolate from that day to this.

Gazing across the plain which stretched away from this ruined hill-town's foot to her trim and respectable lowland successor near the banks of the Eurotas where he had passed the previous night, and reading in the guidebook in his hand that 'the present Sparta . . . founded in A.D. 1834 under King Otho after the War of Independence . . . is of entirely modern origin',[2] he was convicted of a horrifying sense of the sin manifest in the conduct of human affairs. Why should this lovely medieval eyrie have to be put to the sack in order that a commonplace modern townlet might be laid out on a different site to serve the selfsame public purpose?[3] The history of Laconia between A.D. 1821 and A.D. 1834 had been a typical sample of human history in general. *Quam parvâ sapientiâ mundus regitur*![4] A Gibbon might well find it difficult to decide whether Man's most damning vice was his brutality or his irrationality.

Needless to say, the writer of this Study had made no progress towards reading the cruel riddle of Mankind's crimes and follies by the time

[1] See Hammer, J. de: *Histoire de l'Empire Ottoman*, French translation, vol. xii (Paris 1838, Bellizard, Barthès, Dufour, et Lowell), p. 227.

[2] Baedeker, K.: *Greece*, 4th revised edition (Leipzig 1909, Baedeker). This old campaigner, which had been in the writer's hand at Mistrà on the 23rd May, 1912, was on his table in London on the 31st May, 1951, while he was writing these words.

'Even now, when it is abandoned to the tortoises and the sheep, the hill of Misthrà looks down, as it were, with feudal pride upon the brand-new streets and hideous cathedral of the modern Sparta'.—Miller, W.: *The Latins in the Levant* (London 1908, John Murray), p. 100.

[3] Bureaucracy had completed in cold blood the work of destruction that had been started in hot blood by war. 'The government of King Otho having transferred the residence of the official authorities to the new town of Sparta, the inhabitants of Misithra have followed, and the town of the Frank princes is sinking into a village'.—Finlay, G.: *A History of Greece from its Conquest by the Romans to the Present Time*, new ed., vol. iv (Oxford 1877, Clarendon Press), p. 198.

[4] Axel Oxenstierna, quoted in I. i. 463, n. 2.

when he was forced down from the heights of Mistrà by the twofold pressure of hunger and nightfall. Yet, before his reluctant descent, the binocular historical vision which he had acquired from a Late Medieval Italian classical education at Winchester and Oxford had won from the Laconian landscape an intuition that was the germ of the present work.

As he brooded over the catastrophe through which a Sparta founded under the auspices of a Bavarian king of Greece had usurped the role of a Mistrà that had been founded by a French prince of the Morea, it was borne in upon him that the nineteenth-century performance of this historical tragedy was not the only one within his knowledge. After all, every Western schoolboy knew that the present town of Sparta was not the first to have occupied that site and borne that famous name; and, indeed, only yesterday the dreamer himself had been taking cognizance of one corner of an Hellenic Sparta which had recently been excavated by other members of the British Archaeological School at Athens. 'Dorian' hands had anticipated Modern Greek hands in founding 'the city on the sown-land' (*spartâ*) at some date perhaps little less than three thousand years earlier than A.D. 1834. But if the history of a latter-day Western Society into which the Modern Greeks had forced their way out of an Ottoman prison-house was an antitype of the history of an antecedent Hellenic Civilization—and this was the aspect in which the Western Society's history presented itself to an Hellenically-educated Western mind—then the Hellenic Sparta that was the historic counterpart of the present city in the plain must be presumed to have been preceded by some pre-Hellenic counterpart of the Frankish and Ottoman Mistrà on whose topmost pinnacle the latter-day Western classical scholar was at this moment perched. An Hellenic Sparta's fortunes must have been founded on some previously regnant hill-town's catastrophe.

Had Hellenic Sparta in truth had such a predecessor? And, if so, where was the hill on which this hapless victim of that Hellenic Sparta had been set? 'A city that is set on a hill cannot be hid'.[1] 'I will lift up mine eyes unto the hills, from whence cometh my help';[2] and, raising his eyes as these texts shot through his mind, the gazer saw staring him in the face, on the crown of the bluff that overhung the farther bank of the Eurotas just opposite the all but coincident sites of Sparta the First and Sparta the Second, a monument that signalled to him the location of the pre-Hellenic counterpart of the Frankish and Ottoman citadel over whose battlements he was looking out. That white masonry that was flashing over there like a heliograph in the sunlight was 'the Menelaïon' to which he had hastened to make his pilgrimage upon his arrival at Sparta three days back; and this ruined shrine was reputed to stand on the site of Therapnê, the hill-city that was said to have been the capital of Laconia in a Mycenaean last phase of Minoan history. Here, at a strategic point equivalent to Mistrà's situation on the opposite side of the vale, had stood Frankish Mistrà's pre-Hellenic double whose overthrow had made the first Sparta's fortune; and the historic tragedy of Mistrà had thus in truth been played at least twice in this rock-bound amphitheatre of everlasting hills.[3]

[1] Matt. v. 14. [2] Psalm cxxi. 1. [3] Gen. xlix. 26.

Before the gazer descended from Mistrà that night, the impact of the Laconian landscape on his classical *Weltanschauung* had impressed on his mind two lasting lessons—one concerning the historical geography of Continental European Greece and the other concerning the morphology of the history of civilizations.[1]

He had learnt that, in this Mediterranean peninsula, the physical environment lent itself to two possible alternative social and political régimes which had in fact alternated with one another here at least twice over. The lie of the land and the set of an insinuating sea had decreed that in this country there should be a perpetual tug-of-war between the shepherds in the highlands which covered all but a fraction of the *terra firma* and the husbandmen, artisans, and mariners in the fruitful patches of plain and in the profitably situated ports; and the fluctuations in a perpetual struggle between these two elements in the population, who divided the territory so unevenly between them, were bound to be reflected in corresponding fluctuations in the fortunes of geographical sites and in the currency of political institutions. When the seafaring and farming population of the ports and plains was on the defensive—as it was apt to be particularly when it consisted of alien intruders who had thrust their way in from overseas—it could do no more than maintain a precarious hold over the plains, and over the passes leading from one plain to another, from fortified eyries. One such eyrie had been planted on the pinnacle of Mistrà by Frankish invaders in the thirteenth century of the Christian Era, and another on the bluff at Therapnê by Minoan invaders in the second millennium B.C., and the eventual catastrophe in which both these variations on the same historical theme had ended was manifestly the denouement that was to be expected from the inherent insecurity of this type of régime.

The exotic castle might pass, time and again, from one set of alien hands to another—as Mistrà had passed through French, Byzantine, Ottoman, Venetian, and, once again, Ottoman hands, and Therapnê through Cretan, Pelopid, and Achaean—but, sooner or later, the *tour de force* was likely to end in the same way. The perilously exposed outpost of an alien civilization would be overwhelmed by a social cataclysm in which the native wild highlanders, who had been kept at bay by the intruders without ever being either subjugated or assimilated, would descend upon the plains in a devastating spate; and this recurrent catastrophe, whenever it occurred, would be apt to result in a *peripeteia* that would inaugurate a spell of the alternative régime. For, when once the native highlanders had thus possessed—or repossessed—themselves of the plains, the ports, and the passes, their children would come to adopt the corresponding agricultural and maritime way of life without ceasing to be a match in warfare for their cousins who had stayed among the mountains to continue there to pursue the highlanders' two traditional avocations of shepherding and brigandage.[2] In contrast to the

[1] These two lessons implicit in the historical geography of Laconia have been noticed already in IX. viii. 491–5.

[2] In Macedonia, where the social *peripeteia* accompanying a transfer of sovereignty from the Ottoman Empire to the Kingdom of Greece had taken place ninety-one years later than in Laconia, the writer once had the good fortune to obtain a vivid sidelight on

alien intruders from overseas, the native highlanders who had ousted them from the plains, and who, in consequence, had taken to husbandry, manufacture, and seafaring, would have it in them to break the residual wild highlanders' spirit; and the visible symbol of the effective ascendancy that, under this indigenous régime, would be established over conservative highland shepherds by *ci-devant* highlanders who had now become lowlanders and husbandmen, would be the replacement of a fortified citadel of Therapnê or a fortified citadel of Mistrà by an open city on 'the sown-land'—a Sparta that could dispense with city-walls because the martial prowess of her disciplined citizen soldiers would have effectively struck terror into the cowed surviving highlanders' hearts.[1]

This lesson in the historical geography of Greece which the writer had learnt on the citadel of Mistrà on the 23rd May, 1912, had been treasured by him ever since; yet it had not proved so valuable for his then still unconscious future purposes as the simultaneous lesson in the morphology of the history of civilizations. A notion of the philosophical contemporaneity and philosophical equivalence of chronologically non-contemporary representatives of this species of Society had, it is true, been implanted in his mind by his Hellenic classical education,[2] and this tentative idea was to be ripened into conviction, little more than two years later, by the light that was to be thrown for him upon the vocabulary and the psychology of Thucydides by the outbreak of a First Western World War.[3] Yet these influences from the social milieu into which a classically-educated post-Modern Western historian had been born might not have availed, by themselves, to initiate him into a synoptic view of History if this synoptic view had not unfolded itself physically before his eyes from the summit of Mistrà on the 23rd May, 1912, in an experience that had been personal to the spectator.

Yosoburo Takekoshi

An experience that is personal in the sense of not being imparted by the subject's social milieu may also inspire an historian even when he experiences it at second-hand—as is attested by a twentieth-century

it from a living beneficiary. Waiting for an omnibus at Sorovich on the 4th September, 1921, he fell into conversation with a bystander who turned out to be a Slovene, born in Klagenfurt, Carinthia, who had emigrated as a boy to the United States, had come to Macedonia as a chauffeur for the American Red Cross, and was now driving a tractor in the service of three Greek brothers who were joint owners of a large estate in the neighbourhood of Sorovich, besides owning a whole block of houses just across the road from the railway station. Like the property itself, the present owners' up-to-date Western method of farming was a legacy from their father, who had died only four months since. In answer to a question about his enterprising deceased employer's antecedents, the Slovene mechanic volunteered: 'Well, he hadn't owned this property for very long. Before "the war" [meaning the Balkan Wars of A.D. 1912–13], when the Turks owned the land, he was just one of those "Christians"—what is the English word for them? . . . O, now I remember it: "brigands"—up in the mountains. But, when the Greek Army marched in, the Turks cleared out and the brigands came down from the mountains and seized the land. So that is how my employer got his property, and how I got my job.'

[1] This is perhaps the answer to a question that has been raised by a Modern Western historian. 'One wonders, on visiting Villehardouin's castle to-day, how the Ancient Spartans can have neglected a strategic position so incomparably superior to their open village down in the plain by the Eurotas.' Miller, W.: *The Latins in the Levant* (London 1908, John Murray), p. 100.

[2] See pp. 93–95, above.

[3] See p. 94, above.

Japanese historian, Yosoburo Takekoshi, in his preface to his book *The Economic Aspects of the History of the Civilisation of Japan.*[1]

'When Viscount Motono, who was Japanese Ambassador in Paris between 1901 and 1906, met Monsieur Gustave Le Bon, a distinguished evolutionist, the latter referred to the recent rise of Japan as marvellous and unparalleled in the World's history, and compared her progress to that of a comet which flashes across the sky, but pursues an irregular orbit, is dangerous to approach, and [is] extremely uncertain as to its appearance and disappearance. Japan, he further commented, like the comet, may some day abruptly pass away from sight yonder beneath the horizon. In reply, Viscount Motono pointed out that Japan had not appeared on the sky with any such abruptness as Monsieur Le Bon appeared to think; that, on the contrary, she had, through her long history, passed through various stages of progress till finally she emerged on the stage of the World's theatre fully prepared and ready to play her part. Her rise had only followed its natural course. Monsieur Le Bon thereupon urged the publication of a work dwelling upon Japan's progress; and, when subsequently Viscount Motono was home on leave, he told me of his interview with Monsieur Le Bon, and suggested that I should write a Japanese history to enlighten not only Monsieur Le Bon himself but many others in Europe who might entertain a similar idea regarding Japan.'

This suggestion of Viscount Motono's, arising out of his account of his conversation with Le Bon, duly sowed in his interlocutor's mind the seed of an intellectual enterprise which was retarded, without being choked, by the thorny political career in which the future author of the suggested work was involved for the next nine years or more. As soon as Yosoburo Takekoshi had been compulsorily discharged from political life through his failure to retain his seat in the Japanese Diet at the General Election of A.D. 1915, he took up in earnest the long delayed project and completed it in the course of the five years ending on the 25th November, 1920, when he wrote the preface in which he has recorded the book's genesis. The muse's part in this case had been played neither by a catastrophic public event nor by a poignant personal experience at first-hand, but by a report of a personal encounter between two other living minds.

[1] London 1930, Allen & Unwin, 3 vols.

D. THE FEELING FOR THE POETRY IN THE FACTS OF HISTORY

IN our foregoing inquiry into the impulse to investigate the relations between the facts of History, we have struck the springs of action of a number of historians. Some of those springs prove to have been released by personal experiences and others by events or circumstances in an historian's social milieu, while the historians whom we have constrained to abide our question have ranged in repute from the most eminent to the most obscure. This variety in the evidence which we have cited in dealing with one subject on our agenda gives point to the remarkable concordance of these divers witnesses' incidental uninvited testimony on our next subject. Our survey of responses to the challenging intellectual question 'How has this come out of that?' reveals in retrospect the significant truth that, in their attempts to answer it, historians have been drawn on to go deeper and to look farther.

When we are investigating the relations between the facts of History, we are trying to see God through History with our intellects. The sorting out of facts is essentially an intellectual activity. The Intellect, however, is only one faculty of the Soul. When we think about something, we are apt also to have feelings about it, and our impulse to express our feelings is still stronger than our impulse to express our thoughts. Feelings about History, as well as thoughts about it, have inspired historical works, and similar feelings, evoked by similar facts, have also been expressed in imaginative works in the divers genres of literature. There is, for example, a lyrical genre, an epic genre, a narrative genre, and a dramatic genre; and the feeling for the poetry in the facts of History has availed itself of all of these.

The lyrical genre—to begin with that—is one that has many facets. It may present itself in rejoicings at a dawn, in exultations over a liberation, in celebrations of an achievement, in praises of heroism, or in elegies over the sorrows of Human Life.

The joy of dawn is the emotional charge in some of the most famous scenes in Western history—the Latin Christian warriors' shout of 'Deus le volt' in response to Pope Urban II's preaching of the First Crusade, the ministry of Saint Francis of Assisi seen through Giotto's and through Saint Thomas of Celano's eyes, the landfalls of the *Pinta*[1] and the *Mayflower*, the signing of the Declaration of Independence, the taking of the Tennis Court Oath—and the poetry in some, at least, of these historic events has been uttered in lines that speak more eloquently than volumes. The poetry in the American Revolutionary War has been distilled by Emerson into one quatrain:

> By the rude bridge that arched the flood,
> Their flag to April's breeze unfurled,
> Here once the embattled farmers stood
> And fired the shot heard round the World.[2]

[1] Though the first member of Columbus's first expedition to sight land was a sailor on board the *Pinta*, this vessel's name had not won equal renown with the *Santa Maria*, which was the Admiral's flagship.

[2] Emerson: *Concord Hymn*, stanza 1.

The poetry in the French Revolution has been distilled by Wordsworth into two lines:

> Bliss was it in that dawn to be alive,
> But to be young was very Heaven.[1]

It is no wonder that, in these rejoicings at a dawn, the historians should have had to let the poets be their spokesmen; for the joy awakened by the dawn of a new era of History is the Soul's response to an epiphany that is something more than a merely temporal event. The dawns that awaken such joy as this are irruptions into Time out of Eternity. What has happened on these historic occasions likewise happens at the birth of every child:

> 'A woman when she is in travail hath sorrow, because her hour is come; but, as soon as she is delivered of the child, she remembereth no more the anguish, for joy that a man is born into the World.'[2]

In a mother's joy the Soul hails an incarnation; and, since 'alles Vergängliche ist nur ein Gleichnis',[3] the dawns of mundane eras that have this poetry in them are antitypes of cosmic dawns in which a Divine Light breaks into This World. A radiance which shines in upon us through Botticelli's picture, in the National Gallery in London, of the birth in the stable at Bethlehem is likewise manifest in the enlightenment under the Bodhi Tree, in the descent of the Dove at the baptism in Jordan, in the transfiguration on the mountain, in the vision on the road to Damascus, and in the imprinting of the stigmata in the wilderness; and, as Milton's voice strikes up in a Franciscan ode on the morning of Christ's nativity, Gibbon's voice dies away.

The thrill of liberation is the emotional charge in the historic events conveyed in the words Marathon, Salamis, Befreiungskrieg, Risorgimento, Renaissance; and these mundane historical events that have this poetry in them are antitypes of the Resurrection on Easter Morning. The bliss of achievement is the emotional charge in the recollection of Athens and Florence; in the spectacle of the Altar and Temple of Heaven, the frieze from the Parthenon, the church of the Ayía Sophía, and the Green Mosque;[4] and in the reading of *La Divina Commedia*; and these human achievements that have this poetry in them are antitypes of the ministries of Christ and the Buddha and the missions of all the bodhisattvas, prophets, and saints, down to a John Wesley and a Mahatma Gandhi, who have come and gone already and will be followed, through the ages, by later members of their goodly fellowship.[5] The glory of heroism is the emotional charge in the memories of the Three Hundred at Thermopylae, the Six Hundred at Balaclava, the Four Thousand at Waterloo,[6] and the Fifteen Thousand at Gettysburg; and

[1] Wordsworth: *The Prelude*, Book XI, ll. 108–9, incorporating *The French Revolution as it appeared to Enthusiasts at its Commencement.*

[2] John xvi. 21.

[3] Goethe: *Faust*, ll. 12104–5.

[4] A writer who had also seen the Dome of the Rock and the Tāj Mahal would, no doubt, mention these, too, at this point. By A.D. 1952 the present writer had already thrice visited Brusa, but he had not yet set foot in either Jerusalem or Agra.

[5] *Te Deum*, verse 8.

[6] If this was in truth the strength of the battalions of the French Imperial Guard that took part in the final assault and the subsequent last stand at Waterloo (see Rose, J. H.: *The Life of Napoleon I* (London 1904, Bell, 2 vols.), vol. ii, pp. 506–8).

these martial heroes are subjects for the poetry of a Tennyson or a Simonides in so far as they are antitypes of the Noble Army of Martyrs.[1]

'They were stoned, they were sawn asunder, were tempted, were slain with the sword; they wandered about in sheepskins and goatskins, being destitute, afflicted, tormented (of whom the World was not worthy); they wandered in deserts and in mountains, and in dens and caves of the Earth.'[2]

As for the *lacrimae rerum*,[3] these are as innumerable as the drops of water in the sea, since sorrow is the web of Man's mortal life. This is the emotional charge in Hesiod's elegy on Homer's heroes[4] and in Ch'ü Yüan's and Angilbert's elegies on the victims of fratricidal warfare.

> The warriors are all dead: they lie on the moor-field.
> They issued but shall not enter: they went but shall not return.
> The plains are flat and wide: the way home is long.
> Their swords lie beside them: their black bows, in their hand.
> Though their limbs were torn, their hearts could not be repressed....
> Steadfast to the end, they could not be daunted.
> Their bodies were stricken, but their souls have taken Immortality—
> Captains among the ghosts, heroes among the dead.[5]

The same voice that speaks these lines written in a Sinic Time of Troubles also makes itself heard in lines written during a post-Carolingian interregnum.

> Albent campi vestimentis mortuorum lineis
> Velut solent in autumno albescere avibus....
> Maledicta dies illa, nec in anni circulo
> Numeretur, sed radatur ab omni memoriâ,
> Iubar Solis illi desit, Aurora crepusculo,
> Noxque illa, nox amara, noxque dura nimium,
> In quâ fortes ceciderunt, proelio doctissimi,
> Pater, mater, soror, frater, quos amici fleverant.[6]

The chord of feeling that is touched by the pathos of the warriors' death in battle also sounds in response to the tragedy of the failure of a life-work. The tragedy of the extinction of a forlorn hope that had glimmered like a will-o'-the-wisp over Julian the Apostate's brief career has been conveyed by Libanius in two hexameters, of which the second is a Homeric reminiscence:

> *Ἰουλιανὸς μετὰ Τίγριν ἀγάρροον ἐνθάδε κεῖται,*
> *ἀμφότερον, βασιλεύς τ' ἀγαθὸς κρατερός τ' αἰχμητής.*[7]

The Apostate was, in spite of himself, an imitator of Christ; for such dedicated lives and tragic deaths as his are antitypes of Christ's passion,

1 *Te Deum*, verse 9.
2 Hebrews, xi. 37–38.
3 Virgil: *Aeneid*, Book I, l. 462.
4 Hesiod: *Works and Days*, ll. 156–73, quoted in VIII. viii. 75.
5 Ch'ü Yüan (*vivebat* 332–295 B.C.), translated by Arthur Waley in *A Hundred and Seventy Chinese Poems* (London 1920, Constable), pp. 23–24.
6 Angilbert's elegy on the Battle of Fontenoy (*commissum* A.D. 841), in *The Oxford Book of Medieval Latin Verse*, chosen by Stephen Gaselee (Oxford 1928, Clarendon Press), pp. 45–46.
7 Attributed to Libanius in *Anthologia Palatina*, Book VII, No. 147, but quoted without attribution by Zosimus in his *Historiae*, Book III, chap. 34. The second of the two lines is taken from the *Iliad*, Book III, l. 179, in which Helen is describing Agamemnon.

and the poetry in those elegies moves our hearts because our ears are catching the tones of the liturgy for Good Friday and our inward eye is beholding the Agony in the Garden—perhaps in the visual renderings of it that are presented in the pictures by Bellini and Mantegna which, in June 1951, were hanging side by side in the National Gallery in London.

The epic genre expresses the sense of romance that is evoked by conquests and defeats, by treks and voyages, and by the musical flow of the all-embracing ocean of History.

The dazzling personal triumphs of a Cyrus, Alexander, Caesar, Chingis, Timur, Cortés, Nādir Shāh, Clive, Wellesley, or Napoleon and corporate triumphs of the Macedonian, Arab, Mongol, Castilian, or British *conquistadores* have their dark reverse side in the agonies of their victims; and the sympathies of Mankind are revealed in the poets' choice of epic themes. Among the poets there is a consensus—which is impressive because it is tacit and manifestly undesigned—in feeling that the poignant woes of the conquered offer to the imagination a more promising subject than the conquerors' prosaic successes; and the victims are thus apt to win a posthumous revenge for their historical defeats on physical battlefields by rising from the dead to be crowned with a literary immortality.[1]

Even a violent death by Brutus's hand at the high tide of his career could not recapture for Pompey's conqueror the pathos with which Pompey's death had been invested by his foregoing defeat—as witness Plutarch's inability to move us by his account of Caesar's end as we are moved by the corresponding passage in *The Life of Pompeius Magnus*.[2] The sordid liquidation of a war-lord who has outlived his prime has been transfigured by the victim's suffering into a symbol of a sorrow that is at the heart of Human Life. On the same poetic plane, Yazdagird has had the last word against S'ad b. abī Waqqās, Roderick against Tāriq, Jalāl-ad-Dīn Mankubirnī against Chingis, and Constantine Dhrágasis against Mehmed Fātih. Even Musta'sim the unready and Atahualpa the usurper and fratricide are redeemed by the wanton cruelty with which their conquerors put them to death; and, if any laurels had sprung from Hūlāgū's sack of Baghdad or from Pizarro's rape of the Empire of the Four Quarters, these would not have adorned the murderer's brow. As for the Aztecs and the Assyrians, nothing became these bloodthirsty militarists so well as the last stands in which they gloriously displayed the courage of their abominable convictions. The no less abominable spirit and conduct of Homer's Achilles would be likewise beyond bearing if the listener were not all the time conscious that this egotist-savage knew full well that he was doomed to die in the flower of his youth. The true hero of the Iliad is, of course, not a conquering Achilles but a conquered Hector; and, though the triumphant war-lord Agamemnon's return home had the power to inspire a consummate work of art, Aeschylus's play had a superhuman theme in the awful irony of Divine Retribution. Even the pitiful crumbling of the Achaean

[1] This compensation for historical fact in 'heroic' tradition has been noticed in V. v. 607–14.

[2] Chaps. 77–80.

Power on the morrow of the Achaeans' ruthless sack of Troy evoked no poetry to match Euripides' *Troades* or the second book of Virgil's *Aeneid* or Abū'l-Baqā of Ronda's elegy on the *excidium* of Andalusia.

> As a fond lover weeps at parting from his beloved, bitterly weeps the Glorious Religion of Abraham
> For desolate countries forsaken by Islam and peopled only by Infidelity.
> Their mosques have become churches: there is nothing in them but bells and crosses,
> So that the mihrābs[1] weep, though lifeless, and the minbars[2] mourn, though wooden. . . .
> Oh, who will come to the help of a people once mighty but now abased, once flourishing but now oppressed by Unbelievers?
> Yesterday they were kings in their dwelling-places, and to-day they are slaves in the land of the Infidel.
> And what if thou couldst see them stricken with consternation, with none to guide them, wearing the garments of ignominy!
> Couldst thou but see them weeping when they are sold, the sight would dismay thee and throw thee into a frenzy of grief.
> Ah, betwixt many a mother and child comes such a sundering as when souls are parted from bodies!
> And many a young girl, beauteous as the new-risen Sun, blushing like rubies and coral,
> The barbarian drags to shame by force, her eyes weeping, her mind distraught.
> A sight like this melts the heart with anguish, if in the heart there be a Muslim's feeling and faith.[3]

The sorrows of the conquered must be the theme of the epic of Andalusia, since the triumphs of military conquerors—Achaean or Castilian—are not the stuff out of which poetry is made.

> Only the actions of the just
> Smell sweet and blossom in their dust.[4]

The only conquerors who court no literary nemesis are the victorious missionaries of higher religions whose epic deeds have been hymned in the Acts of Buddhist, Christian, and Muslim Apostles.

The poetry in treks and voyages likewise flows in the epic vein. It wells up in the Völkerwanderungen of the barbarians; in the 'Crusades' of the ex-barbarian Medieval Western Christian Latins and Primitive Muslim Arabs; in the Winning of the West by Sinic Pioneers in the second century B.C. and by North American pioneers in the nineteenth century of the Christian Era; in the Winning of the East by John of Piano Carpini, William of Rubruck, Niccolò, Maffeo, and Marco Polo and the other intrepid thirteenth-century Latin travellers who made the iron journey to Qāraqorum and Xanadu across the breadth of the Great Eurasian Steppe; in the prowess of Cossack watermen who pushed their way over tundra and through forest from the Urals to the Pacific

[1] Niches pointing towards Mecca.—A.J.T.

[2] Pulpits.—A.J.T.

[3] Written *circa* A.D. 1250 by Abū'l-Baqā of Ronda, and translated by R. A. Nicholson in *Translations of Eastern Poetry and Prose* (Cambridge 1922, University Press), pp. 168–9.

[4] Shirley: *Death the Leveller*, the closing lines.

within the brief Time-span of some fifty years;[1] in Colaeus's voyage to Tarshish between the Pillars of Hercules[2] and Columbus's passage of the Atlantic from Tarshish to the Antilles; in the fifteenth-century exploration of the Indian Ocean by Far Eastern mariners[3] who all but anticipated, from east to west, Vasco da Gama's subsequent feat of circumnavigating Africa from west to east; in the conquest of the Pacific by eastward-faring canoes and (perhaps) by westward-faring balsa-rafts;[4] in the conquest of the North Pole, South Pole, Air, Stratosphere, and Mount Everest by Western adventurers within the lifetime of the writer and reader of this Study; and in the pilgrimages of all pilgrims to Holy Places.

As for the grand epic whose theme is History herself, this stands in two rival versions which cannot be reconciled, though both of them can be deduced from Watts' picture of Chaos or from Sophocles' paean[5] on human achievement:

> Wonders are many, but none there be
> So strange, so fell, as the Child of Man.[6]

H. G. Wells in *The Outline of History* has written an epic poem on the theme 'Man Makes Himself' which is explicit in the title of a subsequent book from the pen of an eminent Western archaeologist of the next generation.[7] This bleak assertion is a post-Christian Western Man's defiant answer to the Psalmist's joyful assurance that 'the Lord He is God' and that 'we are His People and the sheep of His pasture' because 'it is He that hath made us and not we ourselves';[8] and that verse enunciates the theme of History as a series of encounters between Man and his Creator in which a Paradise that has been lost through a Fall is regained through a Redemption, and in which this deliverance[9] of God's creature is achieved at the cost of a passion that Christ has suffered 'for the means of grace and for the hope of glory'.

The opening lines of this *Divina Commedia* are to be found in another psalm:

> I will give thanks unto Thee, for I am fearfully and wonderfully made; marvellous are Thy works, and that my soul knoweth right well.
>
> My bones are not hid from Thee, though I be made secretly and fashioned beneath the Earth.
>
> Thine eyes did see my substance, yet being imperfect, and in Thy book were all my members written,
>
> Which day by day were fashioned when as yet there was none of them!
>
> How dear are Thy counsels unto me, O God; O how great is the sum of them!
>
> If I tell them, they are more in number than the sand; when I wake up, I am present with Thee.[10]

[1] See II. ii. 157 and V. v. 206–7.
[2] See Herodotus, Book IV, chap. 152.
[3] See Duyvendak, J. J. L.: *China's Discovery of Africa* (London 1949, Probsthain).
[4] Read Heyerdahl, Thor: *Kon-Tiki* (Chicago 1950, Rand McNally); *American Indians in the Pacific* (London 1952, Allen & Unwin).
[5] Sophocles: *Antigonê*, ll. 332–75.
[6] Gilbert Murray's translation.
[7] Childe, V. Gordon: *Man Makes Himself* (London 1936, Watts).
[8] Psalm c. 2.
[9] Romans viii. 21.
[10] Psalm cxxxix. 14–18 (13–18 in *The Book of Common Prayer*).

When we pass on to the story-teller's genre of literary art, we find the novelist vying with the diarist, the biographer, and the letter-writer to determine whether 'Fiction'[1] or 'Fact' is the more propitious medium for bringing out the poetry in the private affairs of ordinary people. In this competition between two rival forms of the art of distilling poetry out of a story, a Pepys, Saint Simon, Boswell, Manucci,[2] Cicero, and Horace Walpole are arrayed against an Herodotus,[3] the anonymous authors of *The Three Kingdoms*,[4] and a Modern Western school of historical novelists.[5]

The dramatic genre of literary art has the power of conveying the poetry in the facts of History in an ascending order of degrees. It may content itself with a bare rehearsal of the drama that is inherent *ipso facto* in any reversal of roles (*peripeteia*),[6] or it may present the drama as an act of Poetic Justice, or it may interpret justice as an inexorable operation of the laws of Destiny or grinding of the mills of God.

Classic examples of the reversal of roles in the histories of civilizations are the successive overthrows of the Achaemenian Empire by Macedon and of Macedon by Rome,[7] the triumph of Christianity over Paganism in the Roman Empire, the change in the fortunes of the Southern States of a North American Union through the outcome and aftermath of an American Civil War, and 'the Chain of Destruction', traced in a previous Part of this Study,[8] in which one ephemeral military technique after another had been dramatically discomfited by a successor which had then suffered the same fate in its turn. On the plane of personal encounters, as contrasted with institutional relations, we may cite one example from the realm of 'Fact' and another from the realm of 'Fiction'.

The sheer drama of *peripeteia* is Polybius's theme in his account of the feelings experienced by the Seleucid King Antiochus III on a night in the year 214–213 B.C. in which his dissident cousin Achaeus, whom he had been besieging in the citadel of Sardis, was suddenly delivered into his hands.

'Since early in the night, the King had been in such a fever of anxious

[1] In so-called 'works of fiction', the element of fiction never amounts to more than a small percentage of the whole matter, and this authentically fictitious ingredient is capable of conveying philosophic truth that is less easy to convey in citations of so-called 'matters of fact' (see I. i. 448–50 and 452–3).

[2] Manucci, Niccolao: *Storia do Mogor, or Mogul India, 1652–1708*, translated by William Irvine (London 1906–8, John Murray, 4 vols.).

[3] e.g., in his tales of Mycerinus (Book II, chaps. 129–33), Rhampsinîtus (Book II, chap. 121), Gyges (Book I, chaps. 8–13), Croesus (Book I, chaps. 28–56 and 85–91), Cyrus (Book I, chaps. 107–30), Polycrates (Book III, chaps. 39–43 and 120–5), Dêmocêdês (Book III, chaps. 129–38), and Scylês (Book IV, chaps. 78–80).

[4] *San Kuo Chih Yen I*, a romantic legend of the Han Empire's three turbulent local successor-states, which developed through the ages till it attained its definitive form in the time of the Ming Dynasty (English translation by Brewitt-Taylor, C. H. (Shanghai 1925, Kelly & Walsh)).

[5] See the citations in the present writer's 'Acknowledgements and Thanks' on p. 225, below.

[6] The problem of *peripeteia* has been discussed, apropos of the nemesis of Creativity, in IV. iv. 245–60.

[7] See Polybius: *Oecumenical History*, Book XXIX, chap. 21, in which the historian of Macedon's overthrow by Rome comments on a passage, commenting on Macedon's triumph over Persia, which he quotes from the work of his predecessor Demetrius of Phalêrum.

[8] In IV. iv. 431–65.

expectancy, while he was waiting to see how the plot [to kidnap Achaeus] would work out, [that he had been unable to sleep; so] he had dismissed his suite and had sat up in his tent on the alert, with no one in attendance save for two or three aides-de-camp. And now, when Cambylus and his party entered and deposited Achaeus, [captive and] bound, on the floor, the amazingness of this spectacle gave Antiochus such a shock that he was smitten with aphasia. It was a long time before he could utter a word, and, when his feelings did at last find vent, their first manifestation was a surge of sympathy which made him burst into tears.

'If we are to try to interpret this psychological reaction of Antiochus's, my own diagnosis would be that he was overwhelmed by a conviction of Man's impotence to guard against, or even reckon with, the deadly strokes of Fortune. Here lay Achaeus, nephew of Laodicê [II] the wife of Seleucus [II], husband of Laodicê the daughter of King Mithradates [III of Pontic Cappadocia], and ruler *de facto* till yesterday of all [the dominions of the Seleucid Dynasty] north-west of Taurus. The citadel of Sardis, in which he had established himself, was deemed to be the strongest fortress in the World by the common consent of his own troops and his adversaries. And now here he was, lying bound on the floor, absolutely in the power of his enemies, before the news of this extraordinary event had had time to reach a soul beyond the immediate participants.'[1]

This account of a matter of historical fact which occurred in the Hellenic World in the third century B.C. has an unmistakable fictional companion piece in the following passage near the close of a post-Modern Western novel which, as its author tells us in his preface, was finished by him in July 1908. The *mise-en-scène* here is not a tent but a bedroom, and the prone figure is not a prisoner, alive tonight, who will be put to death tomorrow, but a corpse from which the life has already departed. The figure standing silent and unnerved is, in this tableau, not a man's but a woman's, and she is not the prone figure's rival for a crown; she is his deserted wife who 'had not seen him for thirty-six years'. But the shock is no less great, and its elemental cause is the same overwhelming sense of Man's defencelessness against Fate.

'That was no conventional, expected shock that she had received. It was a genuine unforeseen shock, the most violent that she had ever had. In her mind she had not pictured Gerald as a very old man. She knew that he was old; she had said to herself that he must be very old, well over seventy. But she had not pictured him. This face on the bed was painfully, pitiably old. . . . The body, whose outlines were clear under the sheet, was very small, thin, shrunk, pitiable as the face. And on the face was a general expression of final fatigue, of tragic and acute exhaustion; such as made Sophia pleased that the fatigue and exhaustion had been assuaged in rest, while all the time she kept thinking to herself horribly: "Oh! how tired he must have been."!

'Sophia then experienced a pure and primitive emotion, uncoloured by any moral or religious quality. She was not sorry that Gerald had wasted his life, nor that he was a shame to his years and to her. The manner of his life was of no importance. What affected her was that he had once been young, and that he had grown old, and was now dead. That was all. Youth and vigour had come to that. Youth and vigour always came to that. Everything came to that. He had ill-treated her; he had abandoned her;

[1] Polybius: *Oecumenical History*, Book VIII, chap. 20.

he had been a devious rascal; but how trivial were such accusations against him! The whole of her huge and bitter grievance against him fell to pieces and crumbled. She saw him young, and proud, and strong, as for instance when he had kissed her lying on the bed in that London hotel—she forgot the name—in 1866; and now he was old, and worn, and horrible, and dead. It was the riddle of Life that was puzzling and killing her.'[1]

In this riddle of Life the change from Life to Death is, of course, the supreme *peripeteia*. 'All men are born with halters round their necks; but it is only when caught in the swift, sudden turn of death that mortals realise the silent, subtle, ever-present perils of life.'[2] This total change that deprives Life of Life itself must be of the same absolute magnitude for every creature.

> The poor beetle that we tread upon
> In corporal sufferance finds a pang as great
> As when a giant dies;[3]

and Death the Leveller brings Gerald Scales' tragedy to a parity with Achaeus's.

> Sceptre and Crown
> Must tumble down
> And in the dust be equal made
> With the poor crookèd scythe and spade.[4]

Yet the direness of the reversal of Fortune is, if not more evident, at least more ironic, in the deaths of mortals who, in this transitory life, have been invested with an ephemeral show of power and wealth.

> Mortality, behold and fear
> What a change of flesh is here!
> Think how many royal bones
> Sleep within these heaps of stones.
> Here they lie, had realms and lands,
> Who now want strength to stir their hands,
> Where from their pulpits seal'd with dust
> They preach 'In greatness is no trust.'
> Here's an acre sown indeed
> With the richest, royallest seed
> That the Earth did e'er suck in
> Since the first man died for sin.
> Here the bones of birth have cried
> 'Though gods they were, as men they died!'
> Here are sands, ignoble things,
> Dropt from the ruin'd sides of kings:
> Here's a world of pomp and state
> Buried in dust, once dead by Fate.[5]

The drama of *peripeteia*, which has been given these classic expressions by great artists in the twin realms of 'Fact' and 'Fiction', and which is

[1] Bennett, Arnold: *The Old Wives' Tale*, Book IV: 'What Life is', chap. 4: 'End of Sophia'.
[2] Melville, Herman: *Moby Dick*, chap. lx.
[3] Shakspeare: *Measure for Measure*, Act. III, scene i, ll. 79–81.
[4] Shirley: *Death the Leveller*, stanza i, ll. 5–8.
[5] Beaumont: *On the Tombs in Westminster Abbey*.

the theme of Edmund Spenser's fluttering stanzas on Mutability,[1] reaches its acme in the realm of 'Myth', where the Truth can be uttered whole and entire because 'the ineffable is here accomplished'.[2] In the encounters between David and Goliath, Solon and Croesus, Jesus and Pilate, the mystery is progressively revealed to the initiate's understanding.

The Poetic Justice whose judgements this drama executes is most familiar in the realm of brute force.

> 'When a strong man armed keepeth his palace, his goods are in peace; but, when a stronger than he shall come upon him and overcome him, he taketh from him all his armour wherein he trusted, and divideth his spoils.'[3]

'All they that take the sword shall perish with the sword';[4] and the justice that ever lies in wait for 'the slayer' who 'shall himself be slain'[5] has overtaken the sons of Cratos and Bia[6] in a long procession, headed by Hesiod's Race of Bronze,[7] in which the Aztecs tread on the heels of the Assyrians, while the rear is brought up by Prussians marching to their own destruction into lands that they have invaded in cold blood.

> *Οὐδ' ὅστις πάροιθεν ἦν μέγας,*
> *παμμάχῳ θράσει βρύων,*
> *οὐδὲ λέξεται πρὶν ὤν·*
> *ὃς δ' ἔπειτ' ἔφυ, τρια-*
> *κτῆρος οἴχεται τυχών.*[8]

Yet the doom of liquidation is not the heaviest sentence that can be passed by Justice on an unconscionable militarist. She may stay the hand of the external 'enemy and avenger'[9] in order to give a triumphant victor time and occasion to emulate a demented Cleomenes' fearful vengeance upon himself.

> 'When he had gained possession of the edged tool, Cleomenes began to mutilate himself from below the knees upwards by slashing his flesh into strips. He began below the knees, and went on from there to his thighs and from his thighs to his hips and his flanks untıı ne reached his stomach and died in the act of cutting this to ribbons.'[10]

Such long-drawn-out acts of *hara-kiri* have been the self-inflicted dooms of militarists collectively as well as individually.

> Ergo inter sese paribus concurrere telis
> Romanas acies iterum videre Philippi.[11]

The century of Roman domestic revolutions and civil wars (*saeviebant* 133–31 B.C.) was the nemesis of a half-century of wars of conquest in which Rome had made herself the unchallengeable mistress of the Hel-

[1] See the stanzas from *The Faerie Queen*, cantos vii and viii, quoted in V. vi. 100, n. 1.

[2] Das Unbeschreibliche
Hier ist's getan.
Goethe: *Faust*, ll. 12108–9.

[3] Luke xi. 21–22. Cp. Matt. xii. 29 and Mark iii. 27.

[4] Matt. xxvi. 52.

[5] Macaulay: *Lays of Ancient Rome*, 'The Battle of the Lake Regillus', section 10.

[6] These two cosmic powers appear among the dramatis personae in Aeschylus's *Prometheus Vinctus*.

[7] See Hesiod: *Works and Days*, ll. 143–55, quoted in VIII. viii. 74.

[8] Aeschylus: *Agamemnon*, ll. 168–72.

[9] Psalm xliv. 16.

[10] Herodotus, Book VI, chap. 75.

[11] Virgil: *Georgics* I, ll. 489–90.

lenic World.[1] Rome, and Rome only, was left to bring Rome to justice; and, within the hundred years opening with the year of Tiberius Gracchus's tribunate, Rome duly measured to herself again with the same measure that she had meted withal—'good measure, pressed down, and shaken together and running over'.[2] The dragon's-tooth seed of plantation slavery sown in areas devastated by the Hannibalic War produced an unintended crop of 'mean freemen'; and no less terrible examples of a self-inflicted nemesis were to be found in the post-Christian chapters of a Modern Western Society's history. A crop of 'mean Whites' had been the unintended harvest wherever the ubiquitous pioneers of a West European Civilization had sown the seed of Negro slavery, while the trade-union spirit and the civil service spirit had been the fruits of the enslavement of souls to machines in a Modern Western Industrial Revolution.[3]

The inexorability of the mills of God in grinding out the sentences passed by Justice was borne in upon the soul of Scipio Aemilianus in the last hour of Rome's once formidable rival and adversary, Carthage, according to the first-hand testimony of the Roman commander's Megalopolitan friend and companion, Polybius.

'When Scipio saw this great and ancient city meeting her end for ever in utter annihilation, he is said to have burst into tears and not to have concealed the fact that he was weeping for the enemy. For a long time he remained wrapped in his own thoughts; he realised that cities and nations and empires were destined, by God's providence, to pass away; he remembered that this had been the fate of Ilion, a city prosperous in its day; the fate of the Assyrian and Median and Persian empires which, each in turn, had once been the greatest in the World; and the fate of the Macedonian Empire, the most recent and most brilliant of them all. Then, whether deliberately or unconsciously, he recited aloud the lines:

> A day of doom shall dawn, and on that day
> Shall Holy Ilion's city pass away,
> And Priam, that great spearman, and the host
> Of Priam's people in their proud array.[4]

Polybius, whose pupil Scipio had been, asked him in so many words what he intended by the quotation, and Scipio is said to have thrown aside all reserve and to have uttered the name of his own country, on whose behalf he was filled with foreboding by his vision of the destinies of Man. This has been recorded at first hand by Polybius himself.'[5]

This spiritual experience of Scipio's convicts him of having been under the dominion of a doctrine of doom which was of the essence of the Hellenic *Weltanschauung* and which worked no less potently in Hellenic souls in which it was unavowed than in those in which it was explicit. This doctrine is enunciated starkly in Herodotus's stock formula

[1] See Polybius: *Oecumenical History*, Book I, chap. 1, quoted on p. 64, above.
[2] Luke vi. 38. Cp. Matt. vii. 2; Mark iv. 24.
[3] See XII. ix. 561–604 (especially 565–6, 572–4, 587). [4] *Iliad*, Book IV. ll. 164–5.
[5] Polybius: *Oecumenical History*, Book XXXVIII, chap. 22. The original text has been lost, but the sense of it has been preserved in the paraphrase, here quoted, by a latter-day Hellenic historian, Appian of Alexandria (*vivebat circa* A.D. 90–160), who was writing in the deceptive sunlight of an Antonine 'Indian Summer'. The passage will be found in Appian's *Roman Studies*: 'The Book of Africa', chap. 132.

'Evil had to befall so-and-so, and therefore' there followed the action, whatever it might be, that brought this doom to pass.[1] A classical situation in which this doctrine seems to be true to life is the apparently inexorable approach of a civil war which everyone can foresee yet no one can avert because no one can—or will—exorcise the besetting sin which is the root of the evil. In the bosom of a post-Scipionic Roman Commonwealth the awful civil war of 90–80 B.C. duly broke out and continued to rage until it had burnt itself to ashes, though its advent had been foreseen and dreaded in advance for at least forty-three years (133–90 B.C.). In the bosom of a North American Union the no less awful civil war of A.D. 1861–5 arose and ran its dreadful course notwithstanding the efforts to avert it that had been made by statesmen on both sides for at least forty-one years running from the negotiation of 'the Missouri Compromise' in A.D. 1820. The drama of inexorability which these tragic passages of History exemplify can be conveyed in poetry better than in prose—as witness two masterpieces of post-Modern Western literature: Stephen Vincent Benèt's poem *John Brown's Body* and Thomas Hardy's 'epic drama' *The Dynasts*. There is a veritably Hellenic order in the economy of the English poet's two-storied stage, on which the actions of human beings on Earth who seem to themselves to be freely exercising their wills appear at a supra-mundane level to be determined by the fiat of principalities and powers whose activities are invisible to their human puppets.

At this level the poetry in the facts of History raises the question of the meaning behind the facts with an insistence that it is impossible to ignore. If Necessity is queen of the last act of the play, can Freedom have ever reigned at any stage? If sinners are powerless to elude their punishment, was it ever in their power to avoid committing the sin for which this punishment is the nemesis? And, if the sin has been as inevitable as the punishment is inexorable, how can the doom which the pitiless mills grind out be identified with Justice? If we are to salvage our theodicy,

'we require a theory of human motives which will allow of our conceiving them, simultaneously, both as supernatural causes coming from without and also as integral parts in the working of the agent's mind.'[2]

When these words were written by a prescient-minded Western classical scholar in or before A.D. 1907, he declared what was the truth at the time when he added that 'Modern Psychology is, of course, not equal to the task of this reconciliation'. Within the forty-six years, however, that had elapsed between the publication of Francis Cornford's book and the time of writing of these lines, a post-Modern school of Western psychologists had rehabilitated as a scientific hypothesis the Hellenic religious belief that Cornford had diagnosed and expounded. In the 'autonomous complex' erupting from the abyss of a Subconscious Psyche to challenge the sovereignty of a Conscious Will that must

[1] See, for example, Herodotus, Book I, chap. 8; Book IV, chap. 79; Book V, chap. 33 [in the negative]; Book V, chap. 92δ; Book VI, chap. 64; Book VI, chap. 135; Book VII, chap. 11; Book VII, chaps. 17–18; Book VIII, chap. 35; Book IX, chap. 109.

[2] Cornford, F. M.: *Thucydides Mythistoricus* (London 1907, Edward Arnold), pp. 154–5.

either subdue the intruder or suffer the consequences of becoming its slave, we are manifestly presented with a 'scientific' name for the *kêr* or *daimon* that assails the hero of an Attic tragedy.[1] In both these expressions of the identical idea of spiritual 'possession', the linguistic resources at a Time-bound mind's disposal are misleadingly inadequate; for, if the full-blooded language of Hellenic mythology falls wide of the truth in portraying these dread principalities and powers as conscious and wilful personalities, the anaemic language of Western science falls equally wide in classifying them as inanimate abstractions. Yet, through either glass, we see the same truth darkly.

This problem of the relation between Law and Freedom, which is presented by the phenomenon of *Peripeteia*, must not, however, detain us at this point from completing the course of our Study. We have wrestled with it at least twice already at earlier points,[2] and we should gain nothing now by stepping aside to try a fall with it again. Our present, and concluding, subject is the inspirations of historians.

[1] 'Internally, temptation takes the form of a violent passion, uncontrollable if its victim is unguarded and secure. The conquerors of Troy are beset by Erôs, the spirit of rapine; but this passion is not conceived [of] as a natural state of mind determined by a previous state—the effect of a normal cause; it is a spirit (δαίμων) which haunts, swoops down, and takes possession of the Soul when Reason slumbers and keeps no watch. Erôs is constantly spoken of by the Greeks as a disease (νόσος); but that word had not the associations merely of a wasting and painful bodily corruption. Diseases were caused by invading spirits, those malignant *kêres* of whom Age and Death are the chief, and who seize as much upon the Soul as upon the Body. . . . This to the Greeks was a very familiar idea.'—Cornford, op. cit., pp. 157–8.

[2] e.g. in IV. iv. 245–61 and in XI. ix. 167–405, *passim*.

E. THE QUEST FOR A MEANING BEHIND THE FACTS OF HISTORY

The meaning behind the facts of History towards which the poetry in the facts is leading us is a revelation of God and a hope of communion with Him; but in this quest for a Beatific Vision that is visible to a Communion of Saints we are ever in danger of being diverted from our search for God to a glorification of Man; and this sin of associating the creature with the Creator[1] precipitates the man-worshipper into a continuing fall from idolatry through disillusionment to an eventual depreciation of Man which is almost as excessive as the adulation to which it is the inevitable sequel.

From morn
To noon he fell, from noon to dewy eve.[2]

An idolization of Man by Man himself, which is patently ridiculous when the idol is some individual mannikin, may be more specious when the blasphemous worship is paid to some collective Leviathan. Yet the state-worship that a post-Christian Western Society commended as 'patriotism' and the church-worship that it denigrated as 'fanaticism' both turn as bitter on the palate as the hero-worship of an Alexander, Hitler, Caesar, or Napoleon. In whatever form this anthropolatry may be practised, it stultifies itself by passing over into irony. 'Plus ça change, plus c'est la même chose.'[3] 'Any man of forty who is endowed with moderate intelligence has seen—in the light of the uniformity of Nature—the entire Past and Future.'[4] And what a spectacle is presented by 'the best of all possible worlds' with which Voltaire makes play, at Leibnitz' expense, in *Candide*. 'Recordare, mi fili, quam parvâ sapientiâ mundus regitur.' An aphorism attributed to a seventeenth-century Western statesman is matched by an eighteenth-century Western historian's sardonic description of History as being 'little more than the register of the crimes, follies, and misfortunes of Mankind'.[5] 'All is vanity' is the refrain of Ecclesiastes; and, from this disillusioning anthro-

[1] The judgement on 'association' (*shirk*) in the Qur'ān has been noticed in I. i. 9, n. 3.
[2] Milton: *Paradise Lost*, Book I, ll. 742–3.
[3] Karr, Alphonse: *Les Guêpes*, January 1849.
[4] Aurelius, Marcus: *Meditations*, Book IX, chap. 2, quoted in V. vi. 137. Marcus's melancholy view of Human Life was brought home to the writer by two repetitive experiences—one consummated when he was fifty-one and the other when he was fifty-seven. One day in May 1940, as he was approaching the corner of the Cornmarket and George Street in Oxford, his eye caught a poster in a newspaper-vendor's hand announcing: 'Liége falls: Forts held impregnable smashed by German guns', and, for an instant, he was at a loss to know whether he was living in A.D. 1940 or in A.D. 1914, because, at that same corner in August 1914, he had been given the same shock by a poster displaying the same words. His second experience of the kind occurred on a day in April 1946, when, as the official train carrying the British Delegation to the Peace Conference of Paris halted at a point between Calais Harbour and Calais Town, it occurred to him that this was the point where the Delegation had been given lunch when they had been travelling this way on this train on a day in December, 1918. Looking out of the railway-carriage window to identify the building, he found that this time it had been rased to the ground.
[5] Gibbon, E.: *The History of the Decline and Fall of the Roman Empire*, chap. iii, echoing Bayle, P.: *Dictionaire*, 3rd. ed., iii. 1899^b, s.v. Manichéens.

pocentric angle of vision, Life presents the mirage of a wilderness, not only for Mankind but for the gods.

'The Sun hides not Virginia's Dismal Swamp, nor Rome's accursed Campagna, nor wide Sahara, nor all the millions of miles of deserts and of griefs beneath the Moon. The Sun hides not the Ocean, which is the dark side of this Earth and which is two-thirds of this Earth. So, therefore, that mortal man who hath more of joy than sorrow in him, that mortal man cannot be true—not true, or undeveloped. . . . The Gods themselves are not for ever glad. The ineffaceable sad birth-mark in the brow of Man is but the stamp of sorrow in the signers.'[1]

Happily Man can find no rest in this spiritual *cul-de-sac*, and his disillusionment with his grotesquely deified Self drives him back into the narrow way which leadeth unto Life[2] across a bridge built for him by the saving irony of the Gospels.

'Thou fool, this night thy soul shall be required of thee.'[3]

'For whosoever will save his life shall lose it, and whosoever will lose his life for My sake shall find it. For what is a man profited if he shall gain the whole World and lose his own soul? Or what shall a man give in exchange for his soul?'[4]

When 'Dominus illuminatio mea' is taken in lieu of 'Man is the measure of all things'[5] as Man's key to the riddle of Human Life, the vanity of Man is transfigured in this divine light.

'Lord, what is Man that Thou takest knowledge of him, or the Son of Man that Thou makest account of him? Man is like to vanity; his days are as a shadow that passeth by.'[6]

This divine concern with Man's vanity, which for the Psalmist is an enigma, is for Job one of the aggravating circumstances of Man's intolerable plight.

'Let me alone, for my days are vanity. What is Man that Thou shouldest magnify him and that Thou shouldest set Thine heart upon him? And that Thou shouldest visit him every morning and try him every moment? How long wilt Thou not depart from me, nor let me alone till I swallow down my spittle?'[7]

But there is another psalm in which Job's petulant question finds its answer.

'What is Man that Thou are mindful of him? And the Son of Man, that Thou visitest him? For Thou hast made him a little lower than the angels, and hast crowned him with glory and honour. Thou madest him to have dominion over the works of Thy hands; Thou hast put all things under his feet. . . . O Lord our lord, how excellent is Thy name in all the Earth.'[8]

A spectacle in which no meaning can be found, so long as the meaning

[1] Melville, Herman: *Moby Dick*, chaps. xcvi and cvi.
[2] Matt. vii. 14.
[3] Luke xii. 20. Cp. Psalm xxxix. 6 (7 in *The Book of Common Prayer*).
[4] Matt. xvi. 25–26. Cp. Mark viii. 35–37 and Luke ix. 24–25. Cp. also Matt. x. 39; Luke xvii. 33; John xii. 25.
[5] This aphorism, which is attributed to Protagoras, is to be found in Plato's *Theaetêtus*, 183 B.
[6] Psalm cxliv. 3–4. Cp. Psalm xxxix. 4–6 (5–7 in *The Book of Common Prayer*).
[7] Job. vii. 16–19.
[8] Psalm viii. 4–6 and 9.

of it is sought in the creature's vain endeavours, proves to be meaningful as soon as the meaning of it is sought in the Creator's indwelling purpose. 'Seek, and ye shall find; knock, and it shall be opened unto you'[1] is the message of salvation from the Dweller in the Innermost.

'Les grandeurs et les misères de l'homme sont tellement visibles qu'il faut nécessairement que la véritable religion nous enseigne et qu'il y a quelque grand principe de grandeur en l'homme, et qu'il y a un grand principe de misère. Il faut donc qu'elle nous rende raison de ces étonnantes contrariétés.'[2]

In Pascal's vision, it is part of the paradox of Human Nature that

'L'homme n'est qu'un roseau, le plus faible de la Nature, mais c'est un roseau pensant';[3]

and the purpose for which this 'thinking reed' has been created is proclaimed by Jalāl-ad-Dīn Rūmī in the opening lines of the *Mathnawī*.

Hearken to this reed forlorn
Breathing, even since 'twas torn
From its rushy bed, a strain
Of impassioned love and pain. . . .

'Tis the flame of Love that fired me,
'Tis the wine of Love inspired me.
Wouldst thou learn how lovers bleed,
Hearken, hearken to the reed.[4]

While 'the Heavens declare the glory of God, and the Firmament showeth His handiwork',[5] this singing reed reveals God's purpose. As the Sun, when he 'rejoiceth as a giant to run his course',[6] is the source from which 'the things that are seen'[7] derive not only their visibility but their genesis and their growth and their sustenance,[8] so God is the source from which Man derives his significance as well as his consciousness and his life, and the purpose of God that is the reason for Man's existence is that the creature should re-enter into communion with its Creator.

When Man's quest thus finds its true *qiblah*, Man's spirit rises to the full height of its powers, and at this spiritual altitude the Soul's feeling for the poetry in the facts of History is transfigured into a sense of awe in the presence of an Almighty God (*'azza wa jalla*) who is also God the Merciful and the Compassionate: Allāh ar-Rahmān ar-Rahīm. The lyrical feeling is transfigured into awe at 'the tender mercy of our God whereby the dayspring from on high hath visited us';[9] the epic feeling into awe at God's execution of His providential designs. 'This is the Lord's doing, and it is marvellous in our eyes';[10] and the psalmist's eager acclamation is involuntarily endorsed by a Laodicean historian when, in writing the last lines of *The History of the Decline and Fall of the Roman Empire*, Gibbon is moved to describe his subject as 'the greatest,

[1] Matt. vii. 7. Cp. Luke xi. 9.
[2] Pascal: *Pensées*, No. 430 in Brunschvicg's arrangement.
[3] Ibid., No. 347.
[4] Rūmī, Jalāl-ad-Dīn: *Selections from his Writings*, translated by R. A. Nicholson (London 1950, Allen & Unwin), p. 31.
[5] Psalm xix. 1.
[6] Psalm xix. 5.
[7] 2 Cor. iv. 18.
[8] Plato: *Respublica*, 509 B.
[9] Luke i. 78.
[10] Psalm cxviii. 23.

perhaps, and most awful scene in the history of Mankind'. Awe lends wings even to the pedestrian poetry of the story-teller. 'I have been young and am now old, and yet saw I never the righteous forsaken, nor his seed begging their bread.'[1] But the drama in the facts of History is the province of poetry in which Awe comes into its kingdom. 'He hath put down the mighty from their seat and hath exalted the humble and meek'[2] is a Christian theme that, even in a pagan rendering,[3] brings the Soul within a bow-shot of God's awful presence. This presence makes itself felt behind the human figures of the prophets who deliver the burden of Nineveh and the burden of Babylon.[4]

> The might of the Gentile, unsmote by the sword,
> Hath melted like snow in the glance of the Lord.[5]

And the doom of the militarist is only the most dramatic application of a sentence that has been passed on all the shadowy unsubstantial glories of our blood and state.

> Some men with swords may reap the field
> And plant fresh laurels where they kill,
> But their strong nerves at last must yield:
> They tame but one another still.
> Early or late
> They stoop to Fate,
> And must give up their murmuring breath
> When they, pale captives, creep to death.[6]

When the feeling for the poetry in the facts of History is thus transmuted into awe at the epiphany of God in History, the historian's inspiration is preparing him for an experience that has been described as 'the Beatific Vision' by souls to whom it has been vouchsafed. In this experience, God is seen face to face, and no longer through a glass darkly;[7] and this means that the vision carries the Soul beyond the limits of History or of any other avenue of approach towards God through His revelation of His nature in His works. Yet, for every seeker after God, his own God-given glimpse of the marvels of the Created Universe—narrow-verged though his human horizon is bound to be—is a lamp unto his feet and a light unto his path;[8] and the historian's path ascends from a feeling for the poetry in History through a sense of awe at God's action in History to a participation in Man's fellowship with Man which brings him to the threshold of the saint's communion with God.

In this process of progressive initiation, the first stage in an historian's spiritual pilgrimage is the experience of a communion on the mundane

[1] Psalm xxxvii. 25.

[2] Luke i. 52.

[3] An echo of the verse here quoted from the Gospel according to Saint Luke strikes a Christian ear in the account of the activity of Zeus that is ascribed to Aesop, in colloquy with Chilôn, by Diogenes Laertius in *The Lives, Doctrines, and Sayings of the Philosophers of Repute*, Book I, chap. iii, § 2. Between Diogenes' τὰ μὲν ὑψηλὰ ταπεινῶν τὰ δὲ ταπεινὰ ὑψῶν and the Lucan ὕψωσε ταπεινούς there is a verbal correspondence that points to a common literary source.

[4] See Nahum iii. 2–3 and 18, and Isaiah xiv. 4–12, quoted in IV. iv. 468–9, n. 2, and compare Ezekiel xxxi. 3–17.

[5] Byron: *The Destruction of Sennacherib*, closing lines.

[6] Shirley: *Death the Leveller*, middle stanza.

[7] 1 Cor. xiii. 12.

[8] Psalm cxix. 105.

plane with persons and events from which, in his usual state of consciousness, he is sundered by a great gulf[1] of Time and Space that, in ordinary circumstances, is impassable for all his faculties except his intellect. A tenuous long-distance commerce exclusively on the intellectual plane is an historian's normal relation to the objects of his study; yet there are moments in his mental life—moments as memorable as they are rare—in which temporal and spatial barriers fall and psychic distance is annihilated; and in such moments of inspiration the historian finds himself transformed in a flash from a remote spectator into an immediate participant, as the dry bones take flesh and quicken into life.

The hand of the Lord was upon me and carried me out in the Spirit of the Lord, and set me down in the midst of the valley which was full of bones, and caused me to pass by them round about; and, behold, there were very many in the open valley; and, lo, they were very dry. And He said unto me: 'Son of Man, can these bones live?' And I answered: 'O Lord God, Thou knowest.' Again He said unto me: 'Prophesy upon these bones, and say unto them: "O ye dry bones, hear the word of the Lord. Thus saith the Lord God unto these bones: Behold, I will cause breath to enter into you, and ye shall live; and I will lay sinews upon you and will bring up flesh upon you and cover you with skin and put breath in you, and ye shall live; and ye shall know that I am the Lord."' So I prophesied as I was commanded; and as I prophesied there was a noise, and, behold, a shaking, and the bones came together, bone to his bone. And, when I beheld, lo, the sinews and the flesh came up upon them and the skin covered them above, but there was no breath in them. Then said He unto me: 'Prophesy unto the Wind, prophesy, Son of Man, and say to the Wind: "Thus saith the Lord God: Come from the four winds, O Breath, and breathe upon these slain, that they may live."' So I prophesied as He commanded me, and the breath came into them, and they lived and stood up upon their feet, an exceeding great army.[2]

'Debout les morts!' The spark that fires an historian's imagination to become a vehicle for this miracle of resurrection may be a quickening encounter with some passage in an historical record or a quickening sight of some historic monument or landscape, and this memorable experience, which is the historian's human reward for his professional labours, may be kindled in the most apparently unpromising tinder.

The present writer, for example, still retained, some forty years after one experience of the kind, an abiding sense of personal participation in the war of 90–80 B.C. between Rome and her Italian allies as a lasting consequence of the instantaneous effect on him of a passage in the table of contents (*periocha*) of the eighty-ninth book of Livy's history upon which he had stumbled one day when, during his reading as an undergraduate for the school of *Literae Humaniores* at Oxford, he was unexpectantly ploughing his way through the surviving précis of the lost books of Livy's work in the faint hope of gleaning some additional scraps of knowledge of the appalling history of the Hellenic World in the last two centuries B.C.

'Mutilus, one of the proscribed [leaders of the Italian Confederacy], succeeded, by muffling his countenance, in making his way undetected to

[1] Luke xvi. 26. [2] Ezekiel xxxvii. 1–10.

the back of his wife Bastia's house—only to be refused admittance: she taxed him with having a price on his head. His retort was to plunge his blade into his breast and spatter his wife's door with his blood.'[1]

As the student read this quickening passage of an arid epitome, he was transported, in a flash, across the gulf of Time and Space from Oxford in A.D. 1911 to Teanum in 80 B.C.,[2] to find himself in a back yard on a dark night witnessing a personal tragedy that was more bitter than the defeat of any public cause. He saw the Sidicine fugitive, expelled from Nola by craven Samnite comrades-in-arms for fear of Roman retribution if they continued to harbour him,[3] stealing up to his own home in his own city in the confident expectation that here, at least and at last, he could count on finding love, loyalty, and shelter; and then, in answer to his low call, a woman's head appears at the window, and one short colloquy informs him that his wife is as heartless as his comrades-in-arms. In an instant, the blade rasps in the scabbard, the body falls with a thud, and the splashing blood irrevocably seals the traitor-wife's infamy.[4] Already the beat of the avenging Furies' wings can be heard in the air as the twentieth-century eye-witness is caught up again and replaced in a trice in his normal locus in Time and Space.

A stop-watch would, no doubt, have registered that the duration of this transport had been infinitesimally brief; yet, in virtue of the poignancy of the experience, the momentary posthumous spectator's imagination was able, ever after, to recapture the atmosphere of that dire reunion of husband and wife; and this one scene in the tragic drama of a civil war between a Roman Republic and an Italian Confederacy would call up, before his mind's eye, a series of dramatic incidents running back past the climax of the catastrophe to its eve. Through the eyes of a Velleius he could see the Samnite leader Pontius Telesinus lying, on the evening of the 1st November, 82 B.C., at the threshold of the Colline Gate, 'wearing in death the countenance of a victor'[5] (the Samnite hero was indeed *felix opportunitate mortis*[6] by comparison with his unhappy surviving Sidicine colleague and comrade Mutilus). Through the ears of Marcus Tullius Cicero, the young recruit, he could hear the parley between the Roman consul Gnaeus Pompeius Strabo and the Marsian

1 'Mutilus, unus ex proscriptis, clam capite adoperto ad posticas aedes Bastiae [*sic*] uxoris cum accessisset, admissus non est quia illum proscriptum diceret; itaque se transfodit et sanguine suo fores uxoris respersit.'—Livy: *Epitomê Libri* LXXXIX.

2 Gaius Papius Mutilus met his tragic end in the year before that in which Volaterrae capitulated to Sulla (see the passage quoted from Granius Licinianus's history in footnote 3, below), and Volaterrae capitulated (see ibid.) in the consulship of [Publius] Servilius [Vatia] and [Appius] Claudius [Pulcher], i.e. in the year 79 B.C.

3 'Et Volaterrani se Romanis dediderunt . . . et proscriptos ex oppido dimiserunt, quos equites a consulibus Claudio et Servilio missi conciderunt. Iam ante [anno superiore] et Samnites qui Nolae erant idem fecerant metu obsidionis. Papiusque Mutilus inde fugiens, cum ne ab uxore quidem Bassia noctu Teani reciperetur, quod erat in proscriptorum numero, usus est pugionis auxilio.'—Granius Licinianus, Book XXXVI (*Granii Liciniani quae supersunt*, ed. by Flemisch, M. (Leipzig 1904, Teubner), p. 32).

4 Bassia's infamy was the more heinous, considering that, during a soul-testing century of Roman history (133–31 B.C.), when 'a man's foes' were verily 'they of his own household' (Matt. x. 36. Cp. Matt. x. 21 and 35; Mark xiii. 12; Luke xii. 52–53 and xxi. 16), 'id . . . notandum est, fuisse in proscriptos uxorum fidem summam, libertorum mediam, filiorum nullam.'—Velleius Paterculus, C.: *Historia Romana*, Book II, chap. 67.

5 'Victoris magis quam morientis vultum praeferens'—Velleius Paterculus, C.: *Historia Romana*, Book II, chap. 27.

6 Tacitus: *Agricola*, chap. 45.

leader Publius Vettius Scato. 'How am I to address you?' the Roman spokesman asks. 'As a would-be friend who is an involuntary enemy' the insurgent spokesman answers.[1] At that moment, perhaps, it was still not too late to arrest the Furies' flight; and there had been a time before that, again, when statesmanship might even have averted a catastrophe which, for a decade, was to turn all Italy into one vast gladiatorial amphitheatre. In the picture conjured up by Plutarch's words a twentieth-century English student could recapture a scene in the Roman politician Marcus Livius Drusus's house in the capital, towards the close of the first decade of the last century B.C., when Drusus's Marsian friend Quintus Pompaedius Silo was spending a few days with him as his guest. He could watch the distinguished visitor making friends with his host's nephews and then saying to them, half in joke and half in whimsically tragic earnest: 'Do plead for us with your uncle; do beg him to make our cause his own in our struggle to win the franchise.'[2]

This resurrection, in a twentieth-century English student's experience, of souls that had striven and suffered and died in Italy in the second decade of the last century B.C. was noteworthy inasmuch as the bones which had been brought back to life were, in this instance, no perfect skeletons, but mere casual bits and fragmentary pieces. In conjuring up out of these scanty relics an exceeding great army, the historian's awe-inspired imagination was performing, on its own plane, something like an equivalent of the miracle performed on the intellectual plane by contemporary Western palaeontologists who knew how to reconstruct a megatherium from a single vertebra and a pithecanthropus from a single tooth. If the Imagination could strike fire from such tinder as surviving tables of contents of lost books and surviving entries in pedestrian chronicles, it was not surprising that it should be able to make as much of the intact works of gifted historians; and the same experience of a magical translation to a distant point-moment in Space-Time, which had overtaken the present student of History when he was reading the tables of contents of the lost books of Livy in A.D. 1911, was to overtake him again in A.D. 1951 when he was reading Bernal Diaz's description of his first sight of the approaches to Tenochtitlan.

'During the morning we arrived at a broad causeway and continued our march towards Iztapalapa; and, when we saw so many cities and villages built in the water and other great towns on dry land, and that straight and level causeway going towards [the city of] Mexico, we were amazed and said that it was like the enchantments they tell of in the legend of Amadis, on account of the great towers and *cues* [temples] and buildings rising from the water, and all built of masonry. And some of our soldiers even asked whether the things that we saw were not a dream. . . . I stood looking at it and thought that never in the World would there be discovered other lands such as these, for at that time there was no Peru, nor any thought of it. Of all these wonders that I then beheld, to-day all is overthrown and lost, nothing left standing. . . .

1 'Quem cum Scato salutasset, "Quem te appellem?" inquit. At ille "Voluntate hospitem, necessitate hostem".'—Cicero: *Philippicae*, Speech XII, chap. xi, § 27.

2 '"Ἄγε," εἶπεν, "ὅπως ὑπὲρ ἡμῶν δεήσεσθε τοῦ θείου συναγωνίσασθαι περὶ τῆς πολιτείας." — Plutarch: *Cato Minor*, chap. 2.

'Gazing on such wonderful sights, we did not know what to say, or whether what appeared before us was real; for on one side, on the land, there were great cities, and in the lake ever so many more, and the lake itself was crowded with canoes, and in the causeway were many bridges at intervals, and in front of us stood the great city of Mexico, and we—we did not even number four hundred soldiers! And we well remembered the words and warnings given us by the people of Huexotzingo and Tlaxcala, and the many other warnings that had been given that we should beware of entering [the city of] Mexico, where they would kill us as soon as they had us inside.'[1]

The sense of personal participation in the Castilian expedition to Mexico in A.D. 1519, which the present writer experienced while he was reading this passage in Bernal Diaz's record of his reminiscences, had been anticipated when, in A.D. 1949, he was reading accounts of 'the Fourth Crusade' written by a gifted French and a cultivated Byzantine participant in that sordid transaction between two mutually antipathetic Christendoms.

At one moment he found himself on board a thirteenth-century French ship catching a thrilling first sight of Constantinople through Geoffrey de Villehardouin's eyes.

'Or poez savoir que mult esgarderent Costantinople cil qui onques mais ne l'avoient veue; que il ne pooient mie cuidier que si riche vile peust estre en tot le monde, cum il virent ces halz murs et ces riches tours dont ele ere close tot entor à la reonde, et ces riches palais et ces haltes yglises, dont il i avoit tant que nuls nel poist croire, se il ne le veist à l'oil, et le lonc et le lé de la vile qui de totes les autres ere soveraine. Et sachiez que il n'i ot si hardi cui la chars ne fremist; et ce ne fut mie mervoille; que onques si granz affaires ne fu enpris de nulle gent, puis que li monz fu estorez.'[2]

At another moment the twentieth-century reader found himself in Nikítas Khoniátis' shoes, striding back, with his heart in his mouth, into the jaws of Death on the forlorn hope of trying to rescue a girl who had just been kidnapped by a Frankish soldier from among a party of Byzantine refugees that was heading for the Golden Gate in a perilous attempt to make an exodus from the ravished City.

'Our chief anxiety was for the women, so we had put them in the middle of our party with a cordon of men outside and had instructed the girls to smear their faces with dirt [in order to conceal their sexual attractions from the Frankish soldiery's eyes]. . . . We were bound for the Golden Gate; but, when we had got about as far as the church of Mocius the Martyr, a barbarian . . . snatched a beautiful girl from among us. She was a judge's daughter . . . and her father, whose stamina had been broken by old age and sickness, had slipped and fallen in a puddle and was now lying there crumpled up, lamenting aloud and plastered with mud. He kept on looking at me as if he were expecting at least some show of assistance from me, and he began to call upon me by name to do anything that I could to help him to retrieve his daughter. So I turned back there and then,

[1] Bernal Diaz del Castillo: *The Discovery and Conquest of Mexico, 1517–1521*, translated by A. P. Maudslay (London 1928, Routledge), pp. 269–71.

[2] Geoffroi de Villehardouin: *Conquête de Constantinople*, chap. xxvi, § 128 (3rd ed. of N. de Wailly's text and translation (Paris 1882, Didot), p. 72).

without more ado, and started to follow at the kidnapper's heels, weeping and denouncing at the top of my voice the crime that had just been committed. As I went, I made supplication to any passing soldiers of the Frankish army who were not altogether ignorant of our [Modern Greek] tongue—trying to induce them to come to the rescue and taking some of them by the hand, till I had managed to work upon the feelings of some of them so far as to prevail upon them to form a posse for the pursuit of that lecherous beast. I led the way with my posse behind me; we arrived at the villain's billet; and then he pushed the girl inside and took his stand at the gates in a truculent posture. . . . When my companions told him with some vigour to give the girl back, his first reply was an insolent refusal. Two imperious passions—lust and rage—had him fast in their grip; but, when he saw that the men were losing their tempers, and heard them threatening him with impalement for misconduct aggravated by contumacy, and when he was convinced that they were really in earnest, he reluctantly yielded and gave the girl up.'[1]

If the imagination could be fired not only by the Champenois adventurer's winged words but even by a narrative in a Byzantine historical work whose pages had been damped by the mildew of an affected style in a pedantic classical diction, it was still less surprising that the same miracle could also be evoked by the sight of monuments and landscapes that were visual echoes of the Past. In A.D. 1952 the writer of this Study had a vivid recollection of six such experiences in which he had found himself participating in an historic past event through a momentary annihilation of the intervening time on the hypnotizing spot.

On the 10th January, 1912, as he sat musing on one of the twin summits of the citadel of Pharsâlus, with his eyes ranging away to the peaks of Pelion, Ossa, and Olympus over the downs of Cynoscephalae —the crouching Dog's Heads—the middle distance of a sunlit landscape came, in the brooding gazer's imagination, to be overcast with the sinister mist that, on a morning 2,109 years back in the Past, is blindfolding the patrols of two armies as these nervously grope their way towards one another on those fog-bound slopes. When the parting of the mist reveals to the posthumous spectator's sight the right wing of the Macedonian phalanx already carrying all before it in the momentum of its charge downhill, he instantly feels the stab of anxiety that, at this moment, pierces King Philip's heart as he glances back over his left shoulder to look for the left wing of the phalanx that should have been following his own right wing up. 'O form front, Nîcânôr! Form front! And cover my left flank. Close the gap, Elephant, close the gap, for God's sake!' But the fate of Macedon's last army is already sealed. Don't you see what that hawk-eyed Roman field-officer is doing over there on the triumphant Roman right? He is not missing his chance of striking a decisive blow by waiting for orders from Titus. Look, he has already withdrawn two battalions from the victorious Roman attack on Nîcânôr's unready wing and has wheeled them, left-about, at the double to take Philip's exposed wing in the rear. And now it is no battle; it is a massacre—for these uncouth Italian troops have never been

[1] Nikítas Khoniátis: *Narrative of Events after the Capture of the City* [by the Franks], chap. 3, on pp. 779–82 of Immanuel Bekker's edition (Bonn 1835, Weber).

drilled in the humane rules governing the 'temperate and undecisive contests' in which the regular forces of a civilized Hellenic World are more or less innocuously exercised. Look, the outmanœuvred phalangites are raising their pikes—they are making the signal that they surrender—but those murderous Roman swords callously complete their cruel work.

As the harrowed participant from another world averts his eyes from an unbearable spectacle, they catch a glimpse of a despairing commander riding off, *ventre à terre*, with no more than a handful of life-guards still attending him. Is this fleeing horseman Titus Quinctius Flamininus's defeated adversary Philip Demetriou? Or is he Gaius Julius Caesar's defeated adversary Gnaeus Pompeius Magnus? Before the dreamer has time to refocus his diffracted historical vision, it all vanishes abruptly into thin air, and the landscape flickers back into a pastoral present in which the sounds floating up from the slopes of Cynoscephalae to the heights of the acropolis of Pharsâlus are, not the din of sword-blades nor the shrieks of wounded men, but the tinkling of goat-bells and the bleating of sheep peacefully grazing, to the strain of their shepherds' pipes, over the site of a doubly historic battlefield. Can the dreamer really have sunk, for that instant, those twenty-one centuries deep below the current surface of Time's waters on which he now finds himself riding, once again, in his normal waking life? He might doubt it if the poignancy of the momentary experience had not left a sequence of Greek elegiac verses running persistently through his head.

Αἴλινον αἴλινον εἰπέ, κατήριπε δῶμα Φιλίππου·
αἴλινον, ἐξ ἐδάφους ὤλετο γῆ Μακεδών.
ἡ δὲ φάλαγξ ἔστρωται ἀνὰ στίχας, ὡς ὅτ' ἀμητὴρ
ἐστόρεσεν δρεπάνῳ Θεσσαλικὰς στάχυας—
ὣς ὄγμος κατὰ κόσμον ἐλήλαται αἰχμητάων,
οὐδ' αὐτὸς κείνων τάξιν ἔλυσ' Ἀΐδης.
ἴσχει χεὶρ ἀμενηνὸς ἑῆς ἔτι θραῦμα σαρίσης,
ἀσπίδα δ' ἀργυρέην λυθρὸς ἔβαψε μέλας.
τῶνδ' Ἀσίην πρόγονοι μὲν ἐπικρατέως ἐρατεινὴν
εἷλον, ὑπερφιάλοις κῆρες Ἀχαιμενίδαις·
νῦν δ' αὐτοῖς ἀτηρὸς ἀπὸ ζόφου ἦλθε τριακτήρ,
αἰετὸς αἰπολίοις, 'Οσκὸς ἀμαιμάκετος.
ἡ δ' Ἑλλὰς τρὶς ὄλωλ', αὐτόχθονος οὔκετι χειρὶ
κοιράνου ὀψομένη σκῆπτρον ἀνασσόμενον.[1]

[1] The following translation of this Greek has been made for the writer by his friend Mr. John Lodge:

Ah! woe is me for Philip's house made void,
And woe for Macedonia's land destroy'd!
In swathes the phalanx fell, like ears of corn
By sickle of Thessalian reaper shorn:
So sank the warrior host, in strict array,
And Death himself shook not their ranks astray.
The nerveless hand its shatter'd pike retains,
And crusted gore the silver buckler stains.
Their fathers, born for Persians' overthrow,
Wrested fair Asia from that haughty foe;
But these, with western pow'r ill-match'd in fight,
Perish'd, as goats beneath an eagle's might.
Thrice fall'n is Hellas, never to behold
Her realm again by native prince controll'd.

At the east end of the Island of Crete on the 19th March, 1912, as he rounded the shoulder of the last mountain on his path from Khandrà to Palaíkastro, the same twentieth-century Western student of History suddenly sighted the ruins of a baroque villa[1]—built, by the look of it, for one of the last of the Venetian governors of Candia—which, had it been erected on English and not on Cretan soil, would probably then still have been inhabited by the descendants of its original occupant, but which in Crete in A.D. 1912 was already a relic of 'Ancient History' on a par with the ruins of the Minoan imperial palace at Cnossos which the twentieth-century English wayfarer had been visiting a week since. As he stood staring at this Jacobean country house, where the Modern Western Civilization in which he himself lived and moved and had his being had suffered the pangs of death on Cretan soil a quarter of a millennium ago, the spectator had an experience which was the counterpart, on the psychic plane, of an aeroplane's sudden deep drop when it falls into an air-pocket. On that spot on which Time had stood still since the eviction of the Venetians by the 'Osmanlis in the War of Candia (*gerebatur* A.D. 1645–69),[2] the spectator was suddenly carried down in a 'Time-pocket' from a day in the year A.D. 1912 to a day in the fifth decade of the seventeenth century on which History, in that house, had come abruptly to an end in an evacuation without any sequel except solitude and decay.

'The spider has wove his web in the imperial palace, and the owl hath sung her watch-song on the towers of Afrasiab.'[3]

On the east coast of Laconia on the 23rd April of the same year 1912 the same wayfarer had a similar experience when he scaled the citadel of Monemvasía—'the Little Gibraltar' that had won this name from the isthmus which was its sole link with the mainland and had lent the same name to the 'malmsey' wine which had once been exported to Western Christendom from its quays. As he scaled those miniature Heights of Abraham and scrambled through a breach in the ramparts that crowned the summit, he fell again into the deep trough of Time as he beheld the antique bronze cannon lying tossed about at all angles among the jagged outcrops of limestone and the thorny macchia and the quietly browsing goats. There lay the guns as they had been left on a day on which Time had stood still at Monemvasía. They had lain there till their wooden carriages had rotted away, and no one had ever troubled to remount them or to carry them off. In that instant the spectator was transported to the evening of the day—whatever date that day

[1] This experience has been mentioned in this Study already, in different contexts, in XII. ix. 431, n. 2, and IV. iv. 282.

[2] See IV. iv. 278.

[3] 'From Saint Sophia he [Mehmed the Conqueror] proceeded to the august but desolate mansion of an hundred successors of the Great Constantine, but which, in a few hours, had been stripped of the pomp of royalty. A melancholy reflexion on the vicissitudes of human greatness forced itself on his mind, and he repeated an elegant distich of Persian poetry.'—Gibbon, E.: *The History of the Decline and Fall of the Roman Empire*, chap. lxviii.

In a footnote, Gibbon observes that 'this distich, which Cantemir gives in the original, derives new beauties from the application. It was thus that Scipio repeated, in the sack of Carthage, the famous prophecy of Homer. The same generous feeling carried the mind of the conqueror to the Past or the Future.'

may have borne in Archbishop Ussher's chronological chart[1]—on which this historic fortress had been stranded on the flowing Time-stream's motionless marge.

This experience of the present writer's at Monemvasía on the 23rd April, 1912, was duplicated on the 24th November, 1929, at the opposite end of the Continent, on a larger rocky peninsula, jutting out like a dagger into the Gulf of Chihli, which at that date was held on a lease from China by Japan.

'The strategic and commercial ports of the Leased Territory are not very distant from one another in Space. They stand on two notches, near the dagger's point, that form their harbours; and from notch to notch it is only about two hours' drive in a car. In "ideal" or "philosophic" time, however, they are far apart, and the distance between them is always widening. [While] Dairen is reaching out its hands towards a prosperous bourgeois future, Port Arthur stands fixed in one tragic moment of the Past. . . .

'As I stood on the heights along which the defences of the fortress had run, and let my eyes range over the landscape, I felt as I had felt when, on my way out to the Far East, my route had led me through Verdun a few months before. That landscape had never seen Mankind engaged on their normal works of peace. It had seen war, and war alone; and, now that the tide of war had ebbed away, the landscape had somehow ceased to be part of the actual living world. It was a landscape with no present, no future, and no function except to bear silent testimony to the tragedies of which it had been the scene in its great days, now for ever past.

'At Port Arthur there was one height in particular which commanded a magnificent view in both directions: inwards over the city and the harbour with its slit of an entrance guarded by bluffs on either hand; outwards over the open country across which the Japanese attack had been delivered. The Japanese had carried that height at fearful cost, and the Russians had lost it to their undoing, for, when once the Japanese artillery had opened fire from there, it had shot . . . the Russian fleet in the harbour and the whole Russian garrison to pieces, and the Russian commandant had had no choice but to capitulate.

'On the morrow of that capitulation, Time at Port Arthur had stood still. The place was still living—or lying dead—in that morrow when I

[1] At the time the spectator had taken it for granted that the spectacle which he was beholding in A.D. 1912 was the tableau of Monemvasía as the fortress had been left on the morrow of its recovery from the Venetians by the 'Osmanlis in A.D. 1715 (see IV. iv. 279); but investigation showed that Monemvasía had changed hands through a peacefully negotiated capitulation, and not through being taken by storm, both on the 7th–10th September, 1715, when the Venetians had surrendered it to the 'Osmanlis, and on the 5th August, 1821, when the 'Osmanlis had surrendered it to the Moreot Greek insurgents. The transactions that resulted in the surrender of Monemvasía on the 7th–10th September, 1715, are recorded by Brue, B.: *Journal de la Campagne que le Grand Vesir Ali Pacha a faite en 1715 pour la Conquête de la Morée* (Paris 1870, Thorin), pp. 53–7. The surrender of the fortress on the 5th August, 1821, is noticed in Finlay, G.: *A History of Greece from its Conquest by the Romans to the Present Time, B.C. 146–A.D. 1864*, vol. vi (Oxford 1877, Clarendon Press), p. 213. This testimony is explicit; yet, on the 23rd April, 1912, the citadel of Monemvasía wore the appearance of having been taken by assault at the moment when Time had come to a halt there. The writer could only conjecture that, either in A.D. 1715 or in A.D. 1821, the victors, after making their peaceful entry, had breached the wall and dislodged the guns from the embrasures in order to put the fortress permanently out of commission as an insurance against the risk of a reoccupation by enemy naval forces. An expert on Modern Western military technology would, no doubt, be able to tell at a glance whether these guns were of late seventeenth-century or of late eighteenth-century make.

visited it the other day. Nothing had happened at Port Arthur in between to break the spell and make the hands of the clock move forward again; and I remembered having had precisely that sensation long ago in another famous fortress far away.'[1]

This experience of communion with a tragic past event, which was imparted to one spectator at Monemvasía in A.D. 1912 and at Port Arthur in A.D. 1929, can hardly be escaped by any visitor to the battlefields of Chattanooga and Gettysburg, where Time's spontaneous halt has been seconded by Man's artifice. At Gettysburg on the 21st April, 1947, when the same spectator was reconnoitring that tragic landscape, the guns that had been in action there on the 1st–4th July, 1863, were once more standing in battery in their authentic stations; for in this field the wooden gun-carriages which at Monemvasía had rotted away had been providently replaced by replicas in rustless metal. Gazing from the summits of the two Round Tops across no-man's-land to the Confederate lines, and then gazing across the same deadly intervening space in the opposite direction—from the point where Lee had stood to the clump of trees in the Federal lines which had been indicated to Pickett as his objective—the spectator felt once again a sensation which he had known in Liaotung and in the Morea. He was in momentary personal communion with his fellow human beings who had struggled and suffered and died on that field long ago; and, on the evening of the same day, he heard the story of a far more poignant experience than his own on the same enchanted spot. That evening Mrs. Hanson,[2] the wife of the President of Gettysburg College, who, like her husband, was of Southern birth, told him that, when, after her husband's appointment, she had found herself in Gettysburg for the first time and had been taken to see the battlefield, she had burst into tears at the sight. The emotion that had found this vent had welled up from deep springs; for this lady had had an uncle who had been one of the survivors of Pickett's charge. No description of the battle had ever come to her ears from this first-hand source, since her kinsman could never bring himself to speak of what he had witnessed in that terrible passage of arms; but his pregnant silence had initiated his niece in her childhood into a personal communion with the tragedy of the 3rd July, 1863; and, when, at last, years after, as a grown woman, she first set eyes on the scene of her uncle's and his fallen comrades' unspeakable ordeal, it was no wonder that her feelings should have overcome her.

The most vivid of the present writer's experiences of the local annihilation of Time in a place where Time had stood still had overtaken him at Ephesus on the 11th February, 1921.

'I approached Ancient Ephesus from the slopes of a limestone hill spangled with crimson anemones, gashed with the quarries from which the stones of the city were hewn, and crowned with the remnants of towers and curtain walls. I had chosen my direction so as to descend upon the theatre from above, and the view, suddenly disclosed, of the vast cavity, with the seats still in place and the stage buildings standing, was

[1] Toynbee, A. J.: 'Life and Life-in-Death', in *A Journey to China* (London 1931, Constable), pp. 200–6.

[2] Mrs. Elizabeth Trimble Painter Hanson.

as impressive as I had expected it to be. Beyond it the great central thoroughfare of the city, a streak of marble pavement showing up against the green of the plain, led down to the ancient harbour, now a reed-bed, yellow and brown. Parallel to the thoroughfare on our left stood the mountain of Coressus, with Lysimachus's fortifications on the sky-line. Beyond, on a separate and lower hill of limestone, stood "the Prison of Saint Paul", a tower in a salient of the city's defences. Beyond that again lay the sea, deep blue against the horizon, and to our right stretched the plain of alluvium which has choked the harbour and driven the sea away. The River Caÿster, which built the plain and co-operated with the folly of Man to the city's undoing, wound like a snake in spiteful loops and curves through the feverish levels which it has laid down.'[1]

At the instant at which this historic panorama impinged on the spectator's eyes, the empty theatre peopled itself with a tumultuous throng as the breath came into the dead and they lived and stood up upon their feet. 'Some . . . cried one thing and some another; for the assembly was confused, and the more part knew not wherefore they were come together.'[2] Those two dishevelled figures must be Gaius and Aristarchus; that ineffectual-looking creature must be Alexander. What is this rhythmic roar into which the babel of tongues is resolving itself? Will Gaius and Aristarchus escape with their lives? Thank Heaven for the intrepid town clerk's promptness and presence of mind. But at the moment when the cries of 'Great is Diana' are dying down and the clerk is beginning to reason tactfully with the crowd, the life flickers out of the scene as the spectator is carried up again instantaneously to the current surface of the Time-stream from an abyss, nineteen centuries deep, into which the impact of the sight of the theatre at Ephesus had plunged him.

On each of the six occasions just recorded, the writer had been rapt into a momentary communion with the actors in a particular historic event through the effect upon his imagination of a sudden arresting view of the scene in which this long-past action had taken place. But there was another occasion on which he had been vouchsafed a larger and a stranger experience. In London in the southern section of the Buckingham Palace Road, walking southward along the pavement skirting the west wall of Victoria Station, the writer, once, one afternoon not long after the end of the First World War—he had failed to record the exact date—had found himself in communion, not just with this or that episode in History, but with all that had been, and was, and was to come. In that instant he was directly aware of the passage of History gently flowing through him in a mighty current, and of his own life welling like a wave in the flow of this vast tide. The experience lasted long enough for him to take visual note of the Edwardian red brick surface and white stone facings of the station wall gliding past him on his left, and to wonder—half amazed and half amused—why this incongruously prosaic scene should have been the physical setting of a mental illumination. An instant later, the communion had ceased, and the

[1] Toynbee, A. J.: *The Western Question in Greece and Turkey* (London 1922, Constable), pp. 148–9: 'Two Ruined Cities', written at Smyrna on the 21st February, 1921.
[2] Acts xix. 32.

dreamer was back again in the every-day cockney world which was his native social milieu and of which the Edwardian station wall was a characteristic period piece.

A sense of personal communion with all men and women at all times and places, which outranges the gamut of an historian's prose, is articulate in a poem which was already familiar and dear to the writer of this Study at the time when that ineffable experience travelled through him.

> Men laughed in Ancient Egypt, long ago,
> And laughed beside the Lake of Galilee,
> And my glad heart rejoices more to know,
> When it leaps up in exultation too,
> That, though the laugher and the laugh be new,
> The joy is old as is the ancient sea.
>
> Men wept in noble Athens, so they say,
> And in great Babylon of many towers,
> For the same sorrows that we feel to-day;
> So, stranded high upon Time's latest peak,
> I can with Babylonian and with Greek
> Claim kinship through this common grief of ours.
>
> The same fair moon I look upon to-night,
> This shining golden moon above the sea,
> Imparts a richer and more sweet delight
> For all the eyes it did rejoice of old,
> For all the hearts, long centuries grown cold,
> That shared this joy which now it gives to me.
>
> Whate'er I feel I cannot feel alone.
> When I am happiest or most forlorn,
> Uncounted friends whom I have never known
> Rejoicing stand or grieving at my side,
> These nameless, faceless friends of mine who died
> A thousand years or more e'er I was born.[1]

'Wherefore, seeing we also are compassed about with so great a cloud of witnesses, let us lay aside every weight, and the sin which doth so easily beset us, and let us run with patience the race that is set before us.'[2] The runner has not yet reached his goal; for the experience, which only poetry can convey, of the unity of the spirit in the bond of peace[3] is the revelation of a fellowship which is not the work of men[4] but is an act of God; and God's presence and participation transfigure a precarious Brotherhood of Man into a Communion of Saints in which God's creatures are united with one another through their union with their Creator.[5]

> Quae fessis requies, quae merces fortibus,
> Cum erit omnia Deus in omnibus![6]

[1] Rosalind Murray.
[2] Hebrews xii. i.
[3] Eph. iv. 3.
[4] Acts v. 38.
[5] Saint Augustine: *De Civitate Dei*, Book XIX, chaps. 13, 17, and 20, quoted in V. vi. 166 and in V. vi. 367.
[6] Abelard: *O quanta qualia sunt illa sabbata . . .*

'Vere Jerusalem est illa civitas';[1] for, in this full and perfect communion, man is reconciled with man, and Mankind with Non-Human Nature.

O happy living things! No tongue
Their beauty might declare:
A spring of love gushed from my heart,
And I blessed them unaware.[2]

In this rapture with which the love of God transfigures a human heart, Saint Francis preaches the Gospel to the birds and finds in the Sun and Moon his brother and his sister.

Luna, dies et nox et noctis signa severa
noctivagaeque faces caeli flammaeque volantes,
nubila sol imbres nix venti fulmina grando[3]—

this spectacle of the majesty of the stellar cosmos, which captivates a poet's imagination, racks a philosopher's mind with anxiety for fear lest the awe which this sight will inspire in unsophisticated human hearts may re-subdue these to the tyranny of mischievous divinities whom a Philosophy Militant has interned in the intermundia after banishing them from a world which they have malevolently infested.[4]

Nam cum suspicimus magni caelestia mundi
templa, super stellisque micantibus aethera fixum,
et venit in mentem solis lunaeque viarum,
tunc,[5]

while the philosopher is shaking his head, the saint breaks out into jubilation.

Altissimu onnipotente bon Signore,
Tue so le laude, la gloria e l'honore e onne benedictione.
Ad Te solu, Altissimu, se confanno,
Et nullu homo ene dignu Te mentovare.
Laudatu si', Mi Signore, cum tucte le Tue creature,
Spetialmente messor lu Frate Sole,
Lo quale lu jorno allumeni per nui;
Et ellu è bellu e radiante cum grande splendore:
De Te, Altissimu, porta significatione.
Laudatu si', Mi Signore, per Sora Luna e le Stelle;
In celu l'ai formate clarite e pretiose e belle.
Laudatu si', Mi Signore, per Frate Ventu,
E per aere e nubilo e sereno e onne tempu,
Per le quale a le tue creature dài sustentamentu.[6]

The Heavens declare the glory of God, and the Firmament showeth his handiwork.

One day telleth another, and one night certifieth another.

There is neither speech nor language, but their voices are heard among them.

Their sound is gone out into all lands, and their words into the ends of the World.

1 Abelard, ibid.
2 Coleridge: *The Rime of the Ancient Mariner*, Part IV *ad finem*.
3 Lucretius: *De Rerum Naturâ*, Book V, ll. 1190–2.
4 See the whole passage in *De Rerum Naturâ*, Book V, ll. 1183–1240.
5 Ibid., ll. 1204–7.
6 Saint Francis of Assisi: *Laudes Creaturarum*, ll. 1–14.

In them hath He set a tabernacle for the Sun, which cometh forth as a bridegroom out of his chamber, and rejoiceth as a giant to run his course....

The Law of the Lord is an undefiled law, converting the Soul; the testimony of the Lord is sure, and giveth wisdom unto the simple.[1]

O All ye Works of the Lord, bless ye the Lord; praise Him, and magnify Him for ever. . . .

O ye Heavens, bless ye the Lord; praise Him, and magnify Him for ever. . . .

O ye Sun and Moon, bless ye the Lord; praise Him, and magnify Him for ever.

O ye Stars of Heaven, bless ye the Lord; praise Him, and magnify Him for ever.

O ye Showers and Dew, bless ye the Lord; praise Him, and magnify Him for ever.

O ye Winds of God, bless ye the Lord; praise Him, and magnify Him for ever. . . .

O ye Nights and Days, bless ye the Lord; praise Him, and magnify Him for ever. . . .

O all ye Whales and all that move in the waters, bless ye the Lord; praise Him, and magnify Him for ever.

O all ye Fowls of the Air, bless ye the Lord; praise Him, and magnify Him for ever.

O all ye Beasts and Cattle, bless ye the Lord; praise Him, and magnify Him for ever.

O ye Children of Men, bless ye the Lord; praise Him, and magnify Him for ever. . . .

O ye spirits and souls of the Righteous, bless ye the Lord; praise Him, and magnify Him for ever.

O ye holy and humble men of heart, bless ye the Lord; praise Him, and magnify Him for ever.[2]

Nostrum est interim mentem erigere
Et totis patriam votis appetere.[3]

We praise Thee, O God; we acknowledge Thee to be the Lord.
All the Earth doth worship Thee, the Father Everlasting.
To Thee all angels cry aloud, the Heavens and all the Powers therein....
Heaven and Earth are full of the majesty of Thy glory.
The glorious company of the Apostles praise thee.
The goodly fellowship of the Prophets praise thee.
The noble army of Martyrs praise thee.
The Holy Church throughout all the World doth acknowledge Thee.[4]

As these diverse yet concordant voices awoke in the heart of a twentieth-century Western historian who had been born and brought up in London, their human rendering of the heavenly language of a Communion of Saints called up before his inward eye a human presentation of the Beatific Vision in a picture in the National Gallery in Trafalgar Square which had printed itself on his imagination before the current century of the Christian Era had begun to run. On the altarpiece

[1] Psalm xix. 1–5 and 7.
[2] *The Song of the Three Holy Children*, vv. 1, 3, 6–9, 15, 23–26, 30–31.
[3] Abelard, ibid.
[4] The *Te Deum*, vv. 1–3 and 6–10.

painted by Fra Angelico for the Church of San Domenico at Fiesole the Angels, Patriarchs, Prophets, Saints, and Martyrs stand in their companies,[1] *prasiai prasiai*,[2] worshipping Christ in His glory in their midst.

Das Unzulängliche,
Hier wird's Ereignis;[3]

and the Communion of Saints thus made visible is an unspoken call to prayer.

Christe, audi nos.

Christ Tammuz, Christ Adonis, Christ Osiris, Christ Balder, hear us, by whatsoever name we bless Thee for suffering death for our salvation.

Christe Jesu, exaudi nos.

Buddha Gautama, show us the path that will lead us out of our afflictions.

Sancta Dei Genetrix, intercede pro nobis.

Mother Mary, Mother Isis, Mother Cybele, Mother Ishtar, Mother Kwanyin, have compassion on us, by whatsoever name we bless thee for bringing Our Saviour into the World.

Sancte Michael, intercede pro nobis.

Mithras, fight at our side in our battle of Light against Darkness.

Omnes Sancti Angeli et Archangeli, intercedite pro nobis.

All ye devoted bodhisattvas, who for us your fellow living beings and for our release have forborne, aeon after aeon, to enter into your rest, tarry with us, we beseech you, yet a little while longer.

Sancte Joannes Baptista, intercede pro nobis.

Noble Lucretius, who, in spite of thyself, art also a forerunner of the Saviour, instil thy poetry into our hearts and thy sincerity into our understandings.

Omnes Sancti Patriarchae et Prophetae, intercedite pro nobis.

Valiant Zarathustra, breathe thy spirit into the Church Militant here on Earth.

Sancte Petre, intercede pro nobis.

Tender-hearted Muhammad, who art also one of the weaker vessels of God's grace, pray that His grace may inspire us, like thee, to rise above our infirmity in our zeal for His service.

Sancte Paule, intercede pro nobis.

Blessed Francis Xavier and Blessed John Wesley, continue Paul's work of preaching the Gospel in all the World.

Sancte Joannes, intercede pro nobis.

Blessed Mo-ti, disciple of Christ before Christ's epiphany in a far country, transmit thou too the message of Love that an Unknown God hath revealed to thee.

Omnes Sancti Apostoli et Evangelistae, intercedite pro nobis.

Strong Zeno, help us to find God by playing the man. Pious Confucius, help us to do our duty towards God by doing it towards our neighbours.

[1] Mark vi. 39. [2] Mark vi. 40. [3] Goethe, *Faust*, ll. 12106–7.

Sancte Stephane, intercede pro nobis.

Blessed Socrates, also a martyr, show us, like Stephen, how to suffer death in perfect charity towards those that despitefully use us.

Omnes Sancti Martyres, intercedite pro nobis.

All ye who have been persecuted for righteousness' sake without leaving a memorial, teach us too to suffer without expectation of even a posthumous earthly reward.

Sancte Gregori, intercede pro nobis.

Blessed Açoka, who, like Gregory, didst serve God by feeding His sheep, teach us also to bear one another's burdens.

Sancte Augustine, intercede pro nobis.

Jalāl-ad-Dīn Mawlānā, singing reed, make heavenly music for us as the breath of God's spirit pours through thee.

Sancte Pater Benedicte, intercede pro nobis.

Epicurus, who wast likewise the revered founder of a spiritual family, impart to us thy gracious gifts of sweetness and light.

Sancte Antoni, intercede pro nobis.

Marcus, recluse in the palace and hermit in the camp, teach us too to make the flight of the Alone to the Alone amid the bustle of this busy World.

Omnes Sancti Monachi et Eremitae, intercedite pro nobis.

All ye who have also served God, though ye were uncloistered and unwithdrawn, teach us too how to be in the World yet not be of it.

Sancta Maria Magdalena, intercede pro nobis.

Blessed Francis, who for Christ's sake didst renounce the pride of life, help us to follow Christ by following thee.

Omnes Sancti et Sanctae Dei, intercedite pro nobis;

For *ilayhi marji'ukum jamī'an*: to Him return ye every one.[1]

Finis

London, 1951, June 15, 6.25 p.m., after looking once more, this afternoon, at Fra Angelico's picture of the Beatific Vision.

[1] Qur'ān x. 4.

XIII. B (iii), ANNEX

A BUSINESS SCHOOL OF INTELLECTUAL ACTION

If, as has been argued in the chapter to which this annex attaches, action is the Alpha and Omega[1] of scholarship, no less than of 'practical' affairs, this accounts for the remarkable fact that a high proportion of an effective minority of scholars in divers fields, including the field of History, has been recruited, not from among the professional Scribes and Pharisees in an orthodoxly academic walk of life, but from publicans and sinners who have taken their intellectual action as amateurs after having served a laborious apprenticeship in such 'practical' trades as war, law, politics, and, notably, commerce. If the essence of scholarship is action, the first and last requirement for success in scholarship is to be *aktionsfähig*; and, accordingly, a 'practical' profession in which a neglect to take action spells instant disaster is a surer training in the essentials of scholarship, as well as in those of 'practical' business, than an academic profession in which the nemesis of inactivity is not immediately brought home to a hesitant soul by a disastrous event.

In a previous context[2] we have already taken note of the careers of a pleiad of historians and a band of poets, sages, and saints who returned to a life of action on the spiritual plane after having withdrawn from it on the 'practical' plane on which they had served their apprenticeship. Clarendon and Ibn Khaldūn were lawyer-statesmen in retreat. Polybius was a politician who had been deported and interned, Dante one who had been sentenced to exile, and Ollivier one who had fallen into disgrace. Machiavelli was a rusticated, Confucius an unemployed, and Saint Gregory the Great a retired, civil servant. Josephus was a prisoner-of-war and Saint Ignatius Loyola an invalided soldier, while Thucydides and Xenophon were soldiers in exile. Muhammad and Solon were retired business men. Our previous observations on these men of action who had qualified for entering on their spiritual activities by first going through a 'practical' apprenticeship need not be recapitulated here; but it is pertinent to our present inquiry to remind ourselves that the personal careers of seven out of the eight eventual historians on our previous list all follow one uniform pattern. Their withdrawal, temporary or permanent, from 'practical' life had, in every case save Ibn Khaldūn's, been involuntary. Every one of them had taken to History as a *pis aller* to occupy an enforced and unwelcome vacation from some form of 'practical' activity;[3] and, when, thanks to their 'practical' training in action,

[1] Rev. i. 8 and 11.

[2] In III. iii. 263–332.

[3] This statement needs some qualification in its application to Thucydides, since he tells us himself in the first sentence of his work (in Book I, chap 1) that he 'started work on it immediately after the outbreak of war, in the expectation that this war would not only be a great one but would be the most important that had ever yet been fought'. The historian's subsequent active service was, no doubt, a public duty which he took as a matter of course. Yet we can also feel sure that he did not welcome the twenty years' period of full-time leisure for concentrating on his historical work to which he was

they made a conspicuously greater success on the intellectual plane of action than they had formerly made in 'practical' life, we may guess that most of them were surprised to find that an activity which had been thrust upon them by a personal misfortune had won them fame besides bringing them consolation. We may now go on to take note of another set of eventual historians recruited from the world of 'practical 'affairs—the business world in four cases and the world of law and politics in the fifth—whose careers, in three instances out of the five, conform to the same pattern externally, but prove, when we probe beneath the outward events to the inner psychic realm of ideals, aims, motives, and feelings, to have been, not congruent with, but actually antithetical to, the careers of the seven historians-in-spite-of-themselves whom we have already taken into account.

Outwardly there is a striking correspondence in pattern between the careers of Thucydides, Xenophon, Polybius, Josephus, Machiavelli, Clarendon, and Ollivier and the careers of George Grote (*vivebat* A.D. 1794–1871), Heinrich Schliemann (*vivebat* A.D. 1822–90), and James Ford Rhodes (*vivebat* 1848–1927). These three careers, like those seven, can all be analysed into a strophe, in which a 'practical' profession makes the first call—and this an exacting one—upon the hero's time and energy, and an antistrophe, in which he devotes himself to scholarship; and in these cases again, as in those, the break between the two symmetrically balanced chapters of personal history is likewise marked by a caesura. It is significant, however, that, in the broken careers of a Rhodes, a Grote, and a Schliemann, the caesura is one of the hero's own making.

Though Schliemann's career can challenge comparison, on the score of eventfulness, with that of any other hero known to History, neither the Victorian London banker Grote nor the post-Bellum Cleveland coal and iron merchant Rhodes was ever in danger of having his life-caesura cleft for him by so sensational an intervention of History in action as Josephus's experience of being taken prisoner, Polybius's of being deported, Thucydides', Xenophon's, and Clarendon's of being exiled, or even Machiavelli's and Ollivier's milder mishaps of being rusticated and of falling into political disgrace. Like Schliemann, Grote and Rhodes had to contrive for themselves an indispensable *vitai pausa*[1] that was never provided for them, ready-made, by the alarums and excursions of contemporary public life. Schliemann, as we have already noticed,[2] insulated his strophic accumulation of a fortune from his antistrophic excavation of Troy and Mycenae by spending two years, after he had wound up his business at St. Petersburg in A.D. 1864, on travelling round the globe and writing, *en voyage* across the Pacific, a book that had for its subject neither self-help nor Homer, but China and Japan.[3] Grote's equivalent step, after he had refrained in A.D. 1841 from

condemned through being exiled from Athens as his penalty for having failed in 424 B.C. (see Book IV, chaps. 104–7) to prevent the capture of Amphipolis-on-Strymon by a Lacedaemonian expeditionary force under Brasidas' command.

[1] Lucretius: *De Rerum Naturâ*, Book III, l. 860.

[2] On p. 16, n. 1, above.

[3] See Ludwig, E.: *Schliemann of Troy* (London 1931, Putnam), pp. 117 and 118–19.

standing again for Parliament[1] and had made up his mind to concentrate on the writing of *A History of Greece* in the country, was to arrange—though he did not find this easy—to absent himself from his bank in the City of London between October 1841 and April 1842 and to spend the interval on visiting Italy for the first time in his life[2]—a temporary release from a 'chain'[3] of public and private 'practical' duties which was made absolute when he retired from business in the summer of A.D. 1843.[4] Rhodes, after retiring from business at Cleveland, Ohio, in A.D. 1886, spent a year in Europe before settling down to write, first at Cambridge, Massachusetts, and afterwards, on the other side of the same Charles River, in Boston, *A History of the United States from the Compromise of 1850 to the Final Restoration of Home Rule at the South in 1877*.

'If this seemed a singular way of starting literary work, it was certainly shrewd; it effaced the office from his mind; it made a complete break between the two widely different halves of his life and enabled him to launch upon the second section with a fresh, free mind. Incidentally too, while abroad, he translated a French novel, writing it out carefully with the design of shaping his style and familiarising himself with the art of composition. Then upon his return he entered at once upon the real work of his life.'[5]

Thus the careers of our three *ci-devant* business men resembled those of our seven *ci-devant* soldiers and statesmen in being symmetrically divided into strophes and antistrophes by caesuras; but, in noticing that the three business men's caesuras had to be induced artificially because they were not imposed by events beyond the hero's control, we have already put our finger on the inner antithesis between two patterns of life that are congruent only outwardly. For Schliemann and for Grote, as for Rhodes, 'the real work of his life' was the creative intellectual work that he achieved mainly or entirely during the post-caesuran chapter, and the 'practical' affairs to which he had been indentured during the pre-caesuran chapter had been a 'chain' that had held him back from devoting himself to the work on which his heart was set, whereas each of our seven soldiers and statesmen had found 'the real work of his life' in the pre-caesuran chapter of it and would never have abandoned 'practical' affairs for historiography if his creative destiny had not been imposed upon him by the ruthless stroke with which his 'practical' activities had been cut short by the shears of the cosmic weaver at the humming loom of Time.[6] Each of our seven soldiers and statesmen became an historian in spite of himself during the second half of his career, while

[1] See Grote, H.: *The Personal Life of George Grote* (London 1873, John Murray), pp. 140–1, for the text of Grote's letter, announcing his decision not to stand again, to J. Travers, and Travers' letter to W. E. Hickson, testifying that 'Grote's retirement is *his own* act, and he is *inexorable* upon the point'. How happy Ollivier, Clarendon, Machiavelli, and Thucydides would have counted themselves if any of their supporters could have given the same account of the circumstances in which they had taken their departure from public life.

[2] See Grote, H., op. cit., pp. 143–51.

[3] George Grote in a letter of the 14th September, 1841, to Senior, quoted ibid. (see p. 144).

[4] See Grote, H., op. cit., p. 153.

[5] Morse Jr., J. T.: 'Memoir of James Ford Rhodes', in the *Proceedings of the Massachusetts Historical Society*, October 1926–June 1927, vol. lx (Boston 1927), p. 179.

[6] Goethe: *Faust*, ll. 501–9, quoted in II. i. 204 and in V. vi. 324.

each of our three business men remained a business man in spite of himself during the first half of his career.

On the criterion of the hero's own intentions, desires, and feelings, the antithesis is extreme; and the cosmic weaver's performance in eventually making a great scholar out of every one of these raw souls is all the more impressive. The conclusions to be drawn from this performance are clear. For a scholar who desires nothing better than to be one, just as much as for a scholar who has been made into one by *force majeure*, 'practical' affairs must be a magnificent apprenticeship for creative intellectual work; and the reason why they have this virtue must be because they give the future historian an effective preliminary training in a life of action which is the scholar's true life as well as the business man's, the statesman's, and the soldier's.

This sovereign virtue of being men of action was shared by our three *ci-devant* business men, not only with our seven *ci-devant* soldiers and statesmen, but also with two lawyer-statesmen-historians, Ibn Khaldūn (*vivebat* A.D. 1332–1406) and Lord Bryce (*vivebat* A.D. 1838–1922), and with a banker-scholar, Walter Leaf (*vivebat* A.D. 1852–1927), who, in contrast to all the others, managed to drive 'practical' activities and creative intellectual work in double harness throughout their working lives.[1] 'Schliemann was always more of a fighter than a thinker, a man of action rather than of contemplation; and so, even in later life, his letters and speeches were more arresting than his books. . . . He was entirely a man of action and not of letters.'[2] 'The very next morning' after his first arrival in Ithaca in July 1868, 'his inborn impulse towards action came to the fore; about 5 a.m. he climbed the peak' of Mount Aëtos 'with four workmen. . . .'[3] 'Bryce, with his boundless energy and his ubiquity, had the general characteristics of a man of action rather than of a scholar. Even his books were planned and sketched in the open air and on the move more than in the study'[4]—and indeed we have noticed already[5] that Bryce's perennial curiosity to add to his ever growing fund of information was harnessed to a self-set yet faithfully followed agenda in which the writing of books, and not the reading of them, was the scholar-statesman's business. As for Walter Leaf, his recognition of the truth that intellectual, as well as commercial, work is action is on record in his own words. 'Until the thought is definitely

[1] In Leaf's life this contemporaneous pursuit of a pair of diverse activities was a conscious and deliberate policy, as he has recorded in the opening paragraph of an unfinished autobiography printed at the beginning of his wife Charlotte M. Leaf's book *Walter Leaf* (London 1932, John Murray), p. 1:

'I have always been conscious of a double strain in my own mental make-up: a double strain which it has been my conscious aim to foster and to realise in a fair and even balance throughout my whole life. . . . The markedly contrasted characters of my two grandfathers . . . typified . . . the combination, in one of their descendants, of two sides of active life: the administrative and the studious or reflective. It has always been my desire to prove myself true to the tradition of my father's family—Yorkshire men of action, successful men of business—and at the same time not to lose hold of the literary and scholastic vein which seems to have been handed down to me by the inheritance of my maternal grandfather, who was, a hundred years ago, one of the best Greek scholars of his day.'

[2] Ludwig, E.: *Schliemann of Troy* (London 1931, Putnam), pp. 113 and 25.

[3] Ibid., p. 136.

[4] E. I. Carlyle in *The Dictionary of National Biography, 1922–1930* (Oxford 1937, University Press), p. 134.

[5] On p. 21, n. 1, above.

formulated, it is nothing', he once wrote in a posthumously printed paper;[1] and, after he had accepted in A.D. 1878 an invitation from the publishing house of Macmillan to finish the work on an edition of Homer that had been left incomplete owing to the death by misadventure of a friend of his who had begun it, 'he lost no time in starting'[2] and wrote in his diary:[3] 'It is a comfort to me to think that I am at length employed . . . on something that somebody wants done, and not merely on the dilettante acquisition of knowledge.'

It is noteworthy that, in this vital point of emerging from an apprenticeship in business as effective men of action, the two Homerists Leaf and Schliemann should have been kindred souls, because the native temperament of the indigo merchant who took Life by storm presents a piquant contrast to that of the silks and ribbons merchant who, while admitting *sotto voce* that, 'if a task is forced upon me, and I am convinced of its rightness, I can carry it out with a good deal of executive capacity',[4] declares, with a characteristic modesty, that 'I have never had a real ambition except to try to carry out to the best of my power the duty which was present to me at the moment.'[5]

The flair for action which inspired these 'practical men' in their intellectual activities, as well as in their businesses, reveals itself in the methods of self-education that they worked out. Schliemann, for example, who would have been a prodigy as a linguist alone, even if he had neither excavated Troy nor made a financial fortune, succeeded in mastering at least twelve foreign languages—though, so he declares, 'my memory was bad, since from my childhood it had not been exercised upon any object'—by always making some active use of the language that he was studying.

> 'Necessity taught me a method which greatly facilitates the study of a language. This method consists in reading a great deal aloud without making a translation, taking a lesson every day, constantly writing essays upon subjects of interest, correcting these under the supervision of a teacher, learning them by heart, and repeating in the next lesson what was corrected on the previous day. . . . I never went on my errands, even in the rain, without having my book in my hand and learning something by heart.'[6]

Thus Schliemann was preaching what he himself had practised when he advised a friend not to retire from business unless he had a hobby.

> 'You will make an enormous mistake if you think that good reading will give you adequate occupation. You will get sick of it. But, now I remember, you are a violinist, bravo! bravissimo! That will make it all right. Only you must devote yourself passionately to music, play at concerts, compose, practise day and night.'[7]

On this principle Schliemann, when he dared at last to allow himself to learn Greek, taught himself by learning passages of the classics by heart and then composing in the language himself.

[1] See Leaf, C. M., op. cit., p. 167.
[2] Ibid., p. 149.
[3] See ibid., p. 150.
[4] Walter Leaf in C. M. Leaf, op. cit., pp. 115–16.
[5] Ibid.
[6] Schliemann, H.: *Ilios* (London 1880, Murray), pp. 9–10. Cp. pp. 10–11 and 14–16.
[7] Quoted in Ludwig, op. cit., p. 283.

'I learnt Ancient Greek [he tells us] as I would have learnt a living language. I can write in it with the greatest fluency on any subject I am acquainted with.'[1]

Schliemann's biographer Ludwig subsequently tested Schliemann's claim by obtaining, from a specialist in Oriental languages, an expert opinion[2] on the extant books of exercises in manuscript by which Schliemann had taught himself, not only Greek, but, shortly after, Persian, Arabic, and Turkish. The specialist found, to his astonishment and admiration, that Schliemann's self-taught method of learning a new language enabled him, after six weeks' study, 'to express his thoughts both orally and in writing'. In the first letter[3] that he wrote in Greek, Schliemann writes of it as 'the language of my waking thoughts and of my dreams'; and his biographer afterwards found in these Greek exercise-books—which 'represent the veritable monologue of a merchant who longed to escape into the realm of the ideal'—'documents of greater psychological value than any that are to be found in the whole accumulation of thousands of papers which Schliemann collected and preserved'.[4]

In short, Schliemann's prescription for learning a language was to do something with it, and it is significant that his method should have been adopted independently by Grote and by Rhodes. Rhodes, as we have noticed,[5] deliberately prepared himself, when the time came, for his long-since intended enterprise of literary composition in his mother tongue by translating a French book into English. As for Grote,

'it was . . . a surprise to me [Mrs. Grote records in her account of their first day at Verona in A.D. 1841] when I heard Grote suddenly break forth in a new language, which he apparently employed with facility, questioning our attendant on all the points which attracted his curiosity . . . Within a day or two of our arrival in Rome . . . Grote engaged a master in order to familiarise himself with the Italian tongue—to which end he translated, as best he could, English comedies into Italian, *vivâ voce*, for an hour daily.'[6]

Though Grote's respect for what Schliemann called 'the tedious rules of grammar'[7] was characteristically greater[8] than Schliemann's, he was at one with his younger contemporary in habitually going into action in his studies as well as in his business, and, for him as for Schliemann, the method that he employed in learning a language was merely an application of a constant habit that seems never to have deserted him save once, in the critical winter of A.D. 1833–4.[9] 'The amount of notes, scraps, extracts, and dissertations which he wrote . . . attests the eager appetite for knowledge which devoured him';[10] and his wife's observation is borne out by her future husband's own record in her extracts[11]

1 Schliemann, *Ilios*, p. 15.
2 Printed in Ludwig, op. cit., on pp. 104–5.
3 Written to his uncle the pastor of Kalkhorst. See the quotation in Ludwig, op. cit., on p. 103.
4 Ludwig, op. cit., pp. 107–8. See the passages quoted, in an English translation, ibid., on pp. 108–12.
5 On p. 147, above.
6 Grote, H., op. cit., pp. 146–7.
7 Schliemann, *Ilios*, p. 15.
8 See Grote, H., op. cit., p. 146.
9 See p. 152, below.
10 Grote, H., op. cit., p. 41.
11 Ibid., pp. 29–37. Cp. p. 134.

from his diary between the 22nd September, 1818, and the 28th March, 1819.

The story of George Grote is not the least remarkable of our ten instances in which an outstanding piece of creative intellectual work has been the outcome of a 'practical' training; for, in the temperament of this banker-historian, there was perhaps enough of 'the leaven of the Pharisees'[1] to have inhibited him from intellectual achievement if his father had not been so selfish as to plant him, before he was sixteen years old,[2] at a desk in the family bank in Threadneedle Street instead of allowing him to complete his academic education by going up to the University. Indeed, Grote's native tendency towards intellectual dissipation was evidently so strong that it may be doubted whether even his enforced apprenticeship in banking would have secured him his intellectual salvation if his wife had not joined forces with his business to induce him to persevere in a self-discipline which is the prerequisite for effective action in any field.

After his father had forced him into the family banking-business, Grote divided the small margin of time still left to him for cultural activities, in which he had not ceased to put his treasure, between learning to play the violoncello, learning German, and studying Economics, History, and Metaphysics;[3] not content with this, he threw himself into the movement for establishing the University of London and became, in A.D. 1827, one of the original members of the Council;[4] and, though he did give up the 'cello in A.D. 1830,[5] the liberty that he took with the personal freedom that was bequeathed to him before the end of the same year by the death of his selfish and tyrannical father[6] was to allow himself to be sucked into parliamentary politics on the wave of the contemporary movement in Great Britain for parliamentary reform, and not to retire from business in order to concentrate upon the writing of a history of Greece which he had adopted, perhaps as early as A.D. 1822, as the theme for a future *magnum opus*.[7] From the time of his plunge in A.D.

[1] Matt. xvi. 12; Luke xii. 1.
[2] See Grote, H., op. cit., pp. 8 and 10.
[3] See ibid., pp. 11–12.
[4] See ibid., p. 55. 'He sometimes would return from the meetings of Council quite overwearied' (ibid., p. 57).
[5] See ibid., p. 41.
[6] See ibid., pp. 61–62.
[7] Mrs. Grote claims that the decision to write a history of Greece was taken by her husband, at her suggestion, late in A.D. 1823:

'Towards the autumn of the year 1823, Mrs. Grote, hearing the subject of Grecian history frequently discussed at their house in Threadneedle Street, and being well aware how attractive the study was in her husband's eyes, thought it would be a fitting undertaking for him to write a new History of Greece himself. Accordingly she propounded this view to George Grote: "You are always studying the ancient authors whenever you have a moment's leisure; now here would be a fine subject for you to treat. Suppose you try your hand!" The idea seemed acceptable to the young student, and, after reflecting for some time, he came to the resolution of entering upon the work. His studies became chiefly directed towards it from that time forward. The quantity of materials which he accumulated in the form of "notes" and extracts during his preparation for the History (which have been preserved by the care of his wife), give evidence of his industry, and of the deep interest he felt in his self-appointed task' (Grote, H., op. cit., pp. 49–50).

This account of the genesis of Grote's great work is contradicted, however, by another piece of evidence that also comes from Mrs. Grote's pen. In a letter to G. Warde Norman, written by her in October 1823, she mentions that 'the Grecian History prospers, and G. is more absorbed in it than ever. He has nearly concluded the account of the Greek colonies'—i.e. chapters 22 seqq. of the Second Part of the History as eventually

1830 into politics down to the time of his eventual retirement first from politics in A.D. 1841 and then from business in A.D. 1843, the wife who was also the Egeria of the historian *in posse* was in constant anxiety for fear lest her husband might throw away an intellectual destiny that had long been manifest to her eyes by an intemperate dissipation of his energies.

'The "History of Greece", she wrote in her note-book on the 1st February, 1831, a few weeks before Grote's acceptance of an invitation from the Lord Mayor of London to stand for one of the seats in Parliament allocated to the City, '*must* be given to the public before he can embark in any active scheme of a political kind. . . . His reputation must be created by the "opus magnum" (as John Mill calls the "History").'[1]

And her failure to prevail upon her husband to give his literary work priority over politics was followed by a realization of her fears. After Grote's election to Parliament in December 1832, 'the History was laid on the shelf',[2] and on the eve of the parliamentary session of A.D. 1834 Mrs. Grote wrote in her notebook:

'G. did not apply himself, as I earnestly besought him, to the furtherance of his History during the winter, but permitted himself to graze about the field of letters—a propensity with which he is not in general reproachable, having usually had distinct objects in view in his studious hours. This winter he has indulged in all manner of promiscuous reading, and has written fewer memoranda in connection with books than I ever recollect him to have done in the same period. I very much apprehend that he will continue this desultory habit of reading, and feel it painful to resume the old labours to which he once applied himself with fond attention and sustained energy. I see, too, a growing demand in his mind for the acquisition of Physical Science, Geology and Chemistry in particular.'[3]

In thus taking alarm at the eruption, in the potential historian's mind, of an unregulated appetite for an aimless omniscience, this indomitable woman of action by proxy was not at fault; for her husband's symptoms were veritably those of a soul that is on its way to intellectual perdition. The cause of this intellectual calamity was, of course, not far to seek. The strain that Grote had imposed on himself by playing an active part in the parliamentary session of A.D. 1833 while continuing to be the responsible managing partner in the family banking business had exhausted, in these 'practical' activities, even the exceptional capacity for action with which this banker-politician-historian had been endowed by nature; and, after this excessively severe ordeal, his intellect's overtaxed bow instinctively protected itself by refusing to be rebent for overtime employment on intellectually creative work. But the diagnosis of the malady did not make it any the less alarming. 'This unremitting labour towards public objects made me', his wife recalls,[4] 'complain not infrequently of the sacrifice; but Grote was inflexible' till his gradual disillusionment with practical politics became at last sufficiently acute to move him to write, as he wrote in February 1838: 'I now look wistfully

printed (see Momigliano, A.: *George Grote and the Study of Greek History* (London 1952, Lewis), p. 7, with n. 12 on p. 21).

[1] Grote H., op. cit., p. 67.

[2] Ibid., p. 75.

[3] Ibid., p. 87.

[4] Ibid., p. 101.

back to my unfinished Greek history. I hope the time will soon arrive when I can resume it.'[1]

The notable feature of the sequel was not that Grote eventually recoiled from the politics of which he had, by then, had his fill to the historiography at which, by A.D. 1843, he had been shying for at least twenty years; the feature that made the ending of Grote's story a happy one after all was that, during the last twenty-nine years of his life (A.D. 1842–71), he proved himself to be a Solomon by duly building his temple after having, for the preceding twenty years, been doing his worst to incapacitate himself for playing the intellectual man of action's part by lingering over David's preliminary task of assembling Solomon's building materials.[2] Grote and his wife had no sooner returned to England from their caesuran five months' visit to Italy in A.D. 1841–2 than Grote 'now methodically laid out the scheme of his first two volumes, as the real basis of his long-contemplated "History of Greece"'.[3] During the first half of the year 1843, when he was still responsible for the affairs of the bank, 'few days passed in which he did not devote at least eight hours to the composition of the "History"'.[4] The winter of A.D. 1845 found him 'getting the first two volumes through the press, whilst continuing the writing of the third and fourth'.[5] 'Grote never deviated from his system of daily labour; he retired, after breakfasting at 9.0 a.m., to his library, whence he rarely emerged until the afternoon hours.'[6] The last proofs of the twelfth and concluding volume were returned to the printer on the 23rd December, 1855.[7]

The honours for the historian's eventual attainment of a goal that he had set for himself more than thirty-two years back have to be divided between the hero, his wife, and his banking business in proportions which could have been assessed only, perhaps, by Mrs. Grote; and she has not divulged this information; but the spectator of a Victorian drama whose denouement was the eventual triumph of intellectual purposiveness over intellectual dissipation in the hero's soul can see that the happy ending was the fruit of discipline—whatever the source from which this discipline may have been derived. When, in A.D. 1864, Grote went on, without a pause, to start work upon his book on Aristotle as soon as he had sent his book on Plato to the press,[8] a friend said to Mrs. Grote, on hearing from her of this,

> 'Grote's intellectual course always seems to me to resemble the progress of a planet through the firmament: never halting, never deviating from its onward path, steadfast to its appointed purpose; it quite impresses one with wonder!'[9]

Discipline is, indeed, the key-note of the lives of all these successful men of intellectual action, and it shows itself to the greatest effect in their disciplined use of their time. They displayed a capacity for persisting, over periods amounting to as much as half or three-quarters of a normal working lifetime, in the pursuit of long-term intellectual

[1] Ibid., p. 127.
[2] 2 Sam. vii; 1 Chron. xxii; 1 Chron. xxviii. 3.
[3] Grote, H.: op. cit., p. 152.
[4] Ibid., p. 153.
[5] Ibid., p. 162.
[6] Ibid., p. 170, referring to the historian's regimen in A.D. 1846–7.
[7] See ibid., p. 224.
[8] See p. 20, above.
[9] Grote, H., op. cit., p. 277.

objectives; and, meanwhile, they wrung from a working life that was mainly occupied with 'practical' duties a modicum of leisure for employment in gradually approaching a distant intellectual goal by teaching themselves how to lay out and economize their time to best advantage in the daily round.

Even Grote, who was perhaps the weakest vessel among these iron wills, was able, after all, to summon up the staying-power to abide by his decision to write a history of Greece for at least twenty years before he began to put it into execution and for twelve years more before the work was complete. James Ford Rhodes held to his purpose for twenty-six years before setting to work in A.D. 1887 on the writing of his *History of the United States from the Compromise of 1850*, and for no less than sixty-one years till the publication, in A.D. 1922, of a final volume carrying the story down to A.D. 1909, if it is true

> 'that even in school days he had conceived the purpose of writing American history, and, as the Civil War was then waging, he saw tempting material in rapid and exciting creation around him, whereby the scheme inevitably took ever more and more powerful hold upon his imagination.'[1]

In Schliemann's life a Time-interval of thirty-nine years separated the date of his resolve, in A.D. 1829, to excavate Troy from the date of his first assault upon the mound at Hisārlyq in A.D. 1868. Bryce lived to accomplish the writing of the most ambitious of all his works, *Modern Democracies*, though the unforeseen interruption of the work on his literary agenda by the calls of public duty during the First World War had prevented him from putting pen to paper on this long-since planned and persistently cherished literary project till he was eighty years old. And these heroically self-disciplined characters showed the same steadfast patience in biding their time for taking their principal intermediate steps towards the achievement of their eventual objectives as in pushing forward their saps and traverses, decade by decade, towards these ultimate goals.

Schliemann, for example, could have put his marvellous linguistic gift to work in mastering the Ancient Greek language at any time after that memorable day in A.D. 1837[2] on which he had listened, spell-bound, to the recitation of Homeric verses which were then still unintelligible to him; and Greek was, in fact, 'the first language he learnt for other than practical purposes',[3] though it was the tenth out of the twelve that he taught himself from first to last.[4] Yet, just because his craving to drink

[1] Morse Jr., J. T.: 'Memoir of James Ford Rhodes', in the *Proceedings of the Massachusetts Historical Society*, October 1926–June 1927, vol. lx (Boston 1927), p. 178. The memoir continues: 'Now Mr. Rhodes was, by his nature, a very wise man. Already, while still so near to the outset of life, he showed that sound good sense and wideness of vision which come to most of us, when fortunately they come at all, so many years later. He had no notion of being too eager, of making a start before he was sure of being able to hold on. So he held his ardour well in hand until all desirable preparations were fully completed and he could devote all his mind and all his hours to his writing.'

[2] See p. 15, above.

[3] Ludwig, E.: *Schliemann of Troy* (London 1931, Putnam), p. 104. At the bank for buying gold-dust which Schliemann set up at Sacramento, California, in A.D. 1851, he conducted, according to his own account, in eight languages a business at which he was working every day from 6.0 a.m. to 10.0 p.m. (Ludwig, op. cit., p. 90).

[4] See p. 15, above.

of this cup was so strong, Schliemann deliberately refrained, for nearly nineteen years, from raising it to his lips.

'My wish to learn Greek had always been great, but before the Crimean War I did not venture upon its study, for I was afraid that this language would exercise too great a fascination over me and estrange me from my commercial business, and during the war I was so overwhelmed with work that I could not even read the newspapers, far less a book. When, however, in January 1856, the first tidings of peace reached St. Petersburg, I was no longer able to restrain my desire to learn Greek, and at once set vigorously to work.'[1]

Even, however, after he had thus, at long last, opened the flood-gates, his iron will still availed to regulate the aperture.

'My recreation [he wrote to his sister] is languages, to which I am bound by a consuming passion. During the week I am continuously occupied in my counting-house, but on Sundays I sit from early morning until late at night over Sophocles, whom I am translating into Modern Greek.'[2]

The same hero of the life of intellectual action showed a comparable self-restraint in postponing his indulgence in a visit to the land of Troy. The business man who commanded the financial means of transporting himself from St. Petersburg to California as early as A.D. 1850 manifestly had it in his power financially to visit the Troad, from that year onwards at latest, at any time that he might choose. Yet he deliberately postponed his first visit till A.D. 1868, when his self-equipment with the financial and intellectual sinews of archaeological war was at last complete, though in the meantime he had travelled round the globe in A.D. 1864–5[3] and had previously come as close to Troy as Smyrna and the Cyclades in A.D. 1859.[4] Walter Leaf, likewise, had it financially in his power to do his field-work in the Troad for at least as many years as Schliemann had had the same coveted archaeological objective within his financial reach before he had allowed himself to make his first pilgrimage to his poetic imagination's Mecca. Yet Leaf did not carry out his survey of the Troad till A.D. 1911, twenty years after his election in A.D. 1891 to be a director of the London and Westminster Bank had made him a man of means, and eight years after a first tantalizing glimpse of Troy on a three-weeks' holiday cruise in A.D. 1903 had left a mental wake of 'memories of Troy seething behind him'.[5] The obstacle that compelled this scholar-banker to draw these long drafts upon his patience was an inability to find, not the requisite financial means, but the requisite length of continuous spare time for temporary release from those day-to-day financial responsibilities in the City of London which were the scholar's penance for drawing the banker's remuneration;[6] and

[1] Schliemann, H.: *Ilios* (London 1880, John Murray), p. 14.

[2] Quoted by Ludwig in op. cit., p. 107.

[3] See Schliemann, *Ilios*, p. 18; Ludwig, *Schliemann*, pp. 118–19.

[4] See Schliemann, *Ilios*, p. 16; Ludwig, *Schliemann*, pp. 115–16.

[5] Leaf, C. M.: *Walter Leaf* (London 1932, John Murray), pp. 201 and 203. Leaf had a second brief glimpse of Troy in A.D. 1910 (see ibid., p. 325).

[6] This necessity, under which Leaf had found himself, of waiting for eight years in order to obtain the necessary leisure for making his survey of the Troad was mentioned by him casually in the course of a conversation with the present writer in A.D. 1913; and an exercise of patience, which the seasoned man of commercial and intellectual action

Leaf the scholar may perhaps have had moments of envying a Cambridge or Oxford don for his leisure as wistfully as a don with children to educate might at times have envied Leaf the banker for his income.

George Grote, in his day, had already met, in his own double life, with the same difficulty in obtaining leave of absence from the banker-spider's parlour for the scholar-fly. In A.D. 1827 Grote had, in fact, been compelled by the exigencies of his duties in Threadneedle Street to cancel a plan (for which another opportunity never afterwards presented itself) of visiting at Bonn the German historian B. G. Niebuhr;[1] and he continued to be thus tightly chained to business for the next fourteen years. 'Up to this time', writes Mrs. Grote, in chronicling their five-months' tour in Italy in A.D. 1841–2, 'the inexorable conditions of our position forbade the idea of distant travel';[2] and, even at this stage in his career, by when he had been at work in the family bank for thirty-one years and had been 'the real working partner' for twenty-five,[3] Grote had to make an advance-payment to his partners—a payment, not of money, but of time—for the luxury of a five-months-long vacation.

'In order to execute this (to us) vast programme, Grote had to earn the leisure required by giving a close attendance, during the months of July, August, and September [1841], at the banking house; his partners, William Prescott and Charles Grote, taking their respective holidays in the interval. This arrangement necessitated the passing much time in London, both George and his wife sleeping in town four or five nights of every week during the whole summer.'[4]

Even then, 'Grote was bound to be in England again early in April [1842] for the bank dividends'.[5]

The self-discipline that thus declared itself in a patient, as well as steadfast, pursuit of distant intellectual objectives would not, of course, have borne fruit if it had not also been exercised simultaneously in a day-to-day regimen that made it possible for the scholar business man to advance along his self-appointed intellectual path at the tortoise's slow but sure gait.[6]

Leaf, for example, ascertained by experiment in September 1875, at a moment when, on the threshold of his career in business, he was preparing himself for the second time to take the examination for a fellow-

manifestly took as a matter of course, made a deep impression on the mind of a young Oxford don on whose subjective Time-scale, in his twenty-fifth year, a span of eight years seemed a veritable aeon.

[1] Grote, H., op. cit., pp. 51–52.

[2] Grote, H., op. cit., p. 143. 'The annihilation of distance' through the progress of Western technology in an Industrial Age of Western history, into which Grote as well as Leaf had been born, did not proceed quite fast enough to shorten their periods of waiting to make their pilgrimages by shortening the length of the time required for 'the round-trip'. In A.D. 1841–2 there was not yet any through connexion by railway between Calais and Rome, and in A.D. 1911 not yet any through connexion by air between London and Constantinople.—A.J.T.

[3] George Grote had been 'the real working partner' since A.D. 1816 (Grote, H., op. cit., p. 46) and had gone into the bank before his sixteenth birthday, i.e. in A.D. 1810.

[4] Grote, H., op. cit., p. 143.

[5] Ibid., p. 151.

[6] 'Nothing surely is so potent as a law that may not be disobeyed. It has the force of the water-drop that hollows the stone. A small daily task, if it be really daily, will beat the labours of a spasmodic Hercules. It is the tortoise which always catches the hare. . . . Constancy in labour will conquer all difficulties.'—Trollope, Anthony: *Autobiography*, chaps. 7 and 20.

ship at Trinity College, Cambridge,[1] that he could do hard intellectual work for six hours a day but not for more.

'This I have always taken as a rule in after life. Needless to say that this does not apply to the ordinary round of more or less mechanical routine which, with most people, passes for work; I am speaking only of real attention, of real thinking, which is the most exhausting of all the occupations of life. . . . But there is a great relief if the attention is not solely concentrated on one subject, and if it is possible to divide it between two. By limiting my deliberate attention during the hours of business in the day and filling up my time with the amount of routine which is always coming in, I have always found it possible to turn in the evening with a fresh mind to study or writing for as much as two or three hours with profit; and it is this alternation of employments which has enabled me to carry on two interests side by side through all my life. . . . I used to retire to my study after dinner and read or write, often up till midnight, and I am inclined to think—though I never timed myself—that for considerable spells I managed to get through my maximum of six hours a day, divided between the office and the study, in addition to an uncertain amount of mere routine in the office which hardly counted.'[2]

Grote, at any rate in his twenties, found the time for his daily intellectual work mostly not after dinner but before breakfast, to judge by the extracts, printed by Mrs. Grote,[3] from a 'diary kept by George Grote, Junior, in order to keep Miss Lewin [the future Mrs. Grote] informed of his way of life during the early period of their engagement'. The consumption of an amazing quantity of formidably solid

[1] In October 1875 Leaf duly won, at this second attempt, an award which was the highest intellectual distinction open to a graduate of the University of Cambridge. With characteristic good feeling, he resigned his fellowship after a few months because he had a conscientious objection to drawing remuneration for a sinecure (see Leaf, C. M., op. cit., pp. 125 and 126).

[2] Walter Leaf, in the fragment of autobiography printed in C. M. Leaf, *Walter Leaf*, pp. 123–4. Cp. Mrs. Leaf's own observations ibid., on pp. 148 and 225. The advantages of an alternating regimen of intellectual work had likewise been discovered by John Stuart Mill, who served in the office of the Examiner of India Correspondence in the India House for thirty-five years (1823–58)—for the last two years as chief of the office—and then retired only because he was not in sympathy with Parliament's action in liquidating the East India Company and transferring its political and administrative functions to the Crown.

'I was in a few years qualified to be, and practically was,' Mill writes in the third chapter of his *Autobiography*, 'the chief conductor of the correspondence with India in one of the leading departments, that of the Native States. This continued to be my official duty until I was appointed Examiner, only two years before the time when the abolition of the East India Company as a political body determined my retirement. I do not know any one of the occupations by which a subsistence can now be gained, more suitable than such as this to anyone who, not being in independent circumstances, desires to devote a part of the twenty-four hours to private intellectual pursuits. . . . For my own part I have, through life, found office duties an actual rest from the other mental occupations which I have carried on simultaneously with them. They were sufficiently intellectual not to be a distasteful drudgery, without being such as to cause any strain upon the mental powers of a person used to abstract thought, or to the labour of careful literary composition.'

Anthony Trollope's concurrence on this point with John Stuart Mill is impressive, considering the diversity in temperament between these two good civil servants who both managed also to be distinguished men of letters in their very different lines.

'If it be necessary for you to live by your work, do not begin by trusting to literature. Take the stool in the office . . .; and then, in such leisure hours as may belong to you, . . . persevere in your literary attempts. . . . Such double toil, you will say, is severe. Yes; but, if you want this thing, you must submit to severe toil. . . . More than nine-tenths of my literary work has been done in the last twenty years, and during twelve of those years I followed another profession.'—Trollope: *Autobiography*, chaps. 11 and 20.

[3] In op. cit., pp. 28–37.

intellectual pabulum is recorded between the first entry—'*Tuesday, 22nd September, 1818*. Rose at 7. Read Say for a couple of hours'—and the last:

'*Sunday, 28th March, 1819*. Rose at ½ past 5. Studied Kant until ½ past 8, when I set off to breakfast with Mr. Ricardo. Met Mr. Mill [senior] there, and enjoyed some most interesting and instructive discourse with them, indoors and out (walking in Kensington Gardens), until ½ past 3, when I mounted my horse and set off to Beckenham. Was extremely exhausted with fatigue and hunger when I arrived there, and ate and drank plentifully, which quenched my intellectual vigour for the night. Bed at ½ past ten.'[1]

'The habits of work were not relaxed after Grote's settling in Threadneedle Street as a married man. . . . A bell was . . . fixed in our bedroom, and duly rung at 6.0 a.m. by the private watchman,[2] in order to secure Grote's getting up at that hour';[3] and, indeed, 'Rose at 6' are the opening words in six out of eight entries in Grote's journal chronicling his intellectual work before breakfast from the 3rd to the 10th December, 1822, inclusive.[4]

The nineteenth-century English banker-historian's daily regimen had been anticipated by a Persian contemporary of Dante's, Rashīd-ad-Dīn al-Hamadānī, who contrived, by making good use of a minimum of spare time, to write the *Jāmiʿ-al-Tawārīkh* ('A Comprehensive Collec-

[1] This day-long intellectual orgy of Grote's in Kant's, Ricardo's, and Mill's company on a Sunday was, of course, no more typical of the intellectual hero's normal time-table on a week-day than were Schliemann's Sunday revels in Sophocles' company. The following entry is a characteristic sample of Grote's regimen on a working day.

'*Saturday, 13th March* [*1819*]. Rose at ½ past 7, after a sleepless night. Read some of Hume's essay on the Academical Philosophy. Breakfasted, and rode to London, where I found a letter from my dearest H., which gave me great delight, as also one from Miss Hale. Went to Guildhall twice this day to prove some debts. Between 4 and 5 read some more Kant. Dined at ½ past 5; played on the bass; drank tea at ½ past 7; then passed the evening in studying Kant, and writing down some remarks which occurred to me. Journalised the last three days, and went to bed at 11' (ibid., p. 35).

[2] This regimen of the banker-historian Grote's was emulated by the civil servant novelist Anthony Trollope. 'It was my practice to be at my table every morning at 5.30 a.m., and it was also my practice to allow myself no mercy. An old groom, whose business it was to call me, and to whom I paid £5 a year extra for the duty, allowed himself no mercy. During all those years at Waltham Cross he was never once late with the coffee which it was his duty to bring me. I do not know that I ought not to feel that I owe more to him than to anyone else for the success I have had. By beginning at that hour I could complete my literary work before I dressed for breakfast.'—Trollope: *Autobiography*, chap. 15.

[3] Grote, H., op. cit., p. 48.

[4] See ibid., pp. 48–49. Edward Gibbon, during his voluntary spells of residence in his father's country house at Buriton, had likewise found himself goaded into making time for intellectual work by early rising, under pressure, not of a family business, but 'social' demands on his time.

'At home I occupied a pleasant and spacious apartment; the library on the same floor was soon considered as my peculiar domain, and I might say with truth that I was never less alone than when I was by myself. My sole complaint, which I piously suppressed, arose from the kind restraint imposed on the freedom of my time. By the habit of early rising I always secured a sacred portion of the day, and many scattered moments were stolen and employed by my studious industry. But the family hours of breakfast, of dinner, of tea, and of supper were regular and long: after breakfast Mrs. Gibbon expected my company in her dressing-room; after tea my father claimed my conversation and the perusal of the newspapers; and in the midst of an interesting work I was often called down to receive the visit of some idle neighbours. Their dinners and visits required, in due season, a similar return; and I dreaded the period of the full moon, which was usually reserved for our more distant excursions.'—*The Autobiographies of Edward Gibbon* (London 1896, Murray), Memoir B, pp. 162–3. Cp. Memoir C, p. 286.

tion of Histories') while he was Prime Minister in an Il-Khānī Mongol Government—'if we may accept as good evidence his own testimony, cited by Dawlatshah,[1] that the interval between dawn and sunrise was the only time when he was able, after having said his prayers and performed some religious exercises, to occupy himself with the writing of his history, since every other moment was consecrated to affairs of state'.[2] Rashīd-ad-Dīn has also put it on record that he accomplished a great deal of historical writing by turning to it in spare moments of his official working day.[3] 'He was so avaricious with his time that, even during journeys, when he was actually in the saddle, he did not cease to meditate on topics that were of sufficient importance to make it necessary for him to give them a mature consideration.'[4]

Leaf, in spite of his practice of sitting up late, was also, like Rashīd-ad-Dīn and Grote, an early riser—as witness the entry: '*2nd April, 1894*. . . . Up at 6, as usual, to look out of window.'[5] But this English banker-scholar of a younger generation than Grote's was tempted into rising early by the lure, not of Kant or Say, but of the sunrise and the birds.[6]

These business men who became eminent scholars were at the same time outstandingly successful in their businesses. Schliemann demonstrated his giftedness in this field by making his fortune in spite of having started without a penny; but Grote, Rhodes, and Leaf, who were not pricked by the spur of penury, all likewise made their mark in the business world. 'I have reason to know', Mrs. Grote records,[7] 'that the reputation of George Grote as a competent and wise banker became at this period [*circa* A.D. 1828–9] generally acknowledged, and that the result was an extension of the business of the house in Threadneedle Street.' Rhodes 'found himself possessed of a comfortable fortune, and absolutely free to do what he would',[8] by A.D. 1886, by when he had spent seventeen years in the family business; and during this commercial strophe of his life he made a strong enough impression on his

[1] In his *Tadhkirāt-ash-Shu'arā, man. persan* No. 250, fol. 83*r*., in the Bibliothèque Nationale (*ci-devant* Bibliothèque Royale) in Paris.

[2] E. M. Quatremère, in his life of Rashīd-ad-Dīn prefixed to his edition of the preface to the *Jāmiʿ-at-Tawārīkh* and the sections recording the history of Hūlāgū Khan, entitled *Histoire des Mongols de la Perse*, vol. i (Paris 1836, Imprimerie Royale), p. lxx.

[3] See Quatremère, ibid., p. lxii.

[4] Quatremère, ibid., pp. lviii–lix. Compare C. Plinius Secundus the Younger's account, in his *Epistulae*, Book III, Ep. v, of his uncle and namesake Pliny the Elder's habits of work. 'He used to begin to work by lamp light on the Volcanalia [23rd Aug.] . . . getting up while it was still pitch dark. In the winter he used to get up at 1.0 a.m. or, at the latest, at 2.0 a.m., and often at midnight. . . . Before daybreak he used to wait on the Emperor Vespasian (another night-worker) and then go straight on to his office. After getting home, he would devote what was left of his time to study. . . . On the road he would put all business out of his mind and would attend to his studies exclusively; at his elbow he would have a secretary armed with book and writing-pad, and in winter also with mittens to protect his hands, to make sure that even the inclemency of the season should be powerless to rob his master of any of his time for study. For the same reason my uncle used, in Rome, to go about in a sedan chair. I remember his once taking me to task for going on foot. "You might", he said, "have saved those hours". He counted all time lost that was not given to study. . . . So avaricious was he with his time.'

[5] Leaf, C. M., op. cit., p. 181.

[6] Like Grote, Leaf was fond of music, and mountaineering was another of his recreations. Grote, for his part, was a keen cricketer (see Grote, H., op. cit., p. 14).

[7] In op. cit., p. 59.

[8] Morse Jr., J. T., in the *Proceedings of the Massachusetts Historical Society*, October 1926–June 1927 (Boston 1927), p. 179.

business associates, by his prowess on ground shared by him with them, for one of them, long after the scholarly antistrophe to Rhodes' business career had made the *ci-devant* coal merchant famous in a world that was not theirs, to have 'remarked regretfully, when his name was mentioned: "I knew Mr. Rhodes very well in the old days. He was highly thought of. What a pity he dropped out, for he would have made his reputation."'[1] Walter Leaf, who in A.D. 1875 had taken on his shoulders the burden of an ailing family business immediately after finishing his education at Cambridge, did both make and keep his reputation in the City of London by the success with which he acquitted himself of his thankless initial task on Old Change. The perpetual growth of the esteem in which he was held in the business world was registered in his successive appointments to the chairmanship of the London Chamber of Commerce in A.D. 1887, to a directorship of the London and Westminster Bank in A.D. 1891, to the deputy chairmanship of the same bank in A.D. 1909, and finally, in A.D. 1918, to the chairmanship of this rapidly growing business concern.[2] So long as Leaf lived, no City man could ever have imagined that this eminent banker had 'dropped out' of the business world, though there may have been some City men who were no more alive than Rhodes' former business associate was to the versatile man of action's fame in a non-commercial sphere of activity. Conversely, Leaf may have had contemporaries in the world of classical scholarship who were unaware that he was anything more than one of themselves; for 'Walter Leaf was undoubtedly one of the outstanding figures among the classical scholars of his generation. . . . He became the recognized authority on his special subject, and his output, both in quality and [in] quantity, would have been remarkable even for a professional scholar with no other occupations; for a man busy all his life in other spheres it was little short of miraculous.'[3]

What was the secret of a miracle that was performed, not only by Walter Leaf, but likewise by George Grote, Heinrich Schliemann, James Ford Rhodes, and James Bryce? It was the old secret of a stuttering Demosthenes' miraculous self-transfiguration into a golden-mouthed public speaker. It was the response of a soul charged with a creative intellectual mission to the challenge of a 'practical' profession that must disappoint its apprentice of his hopes of attaining his intellectual objective if he did not take heroic measures to meet this threat of frustration. This was the life-story even of Bryce and Rhodes, who had embraced a 'practical' career deliberately without having been pushed into this by any external pressure. *A fortiori* it was the life-story of Schliemann, Grote, and Leaf, who were all victims, in various ways and degrees, of faults or failings of their fathers.

The Pastor Ernst Schliemann's sins against his son were more flagrant than the banker George Grote Senior's or the merchant Charles John

[1] Grant, Robert, in the *Proceedings of the Massachusetts Historical Society*, October 1926–June 1927 (Boston 1927), p. 125.

[2] The London and County Bank had been amalgamated with the Westminster Bank in A.D. 1909, and Parr's Bank was amalgamated with the London County and Westminster Bank in A.D. 1918 (Sir Montagu Turner in C. M. Leaf, op. cit., pp. 301–2).

[3] Bailey, Cyril in C. M. Leaf, op. cit., p. 317.

Leaf's. The pastor's profligacy cost his famous son Heinrich the loss of his childhood's sweetheart Minna Meineke by shocking the Schliemanns' neighbours into ostracizing the whole family after the premature death of Heinrich Schliemann's cruelly wronged mother; and it also cost Heinrich Schliemann the best part of the education which would have been a pastor's son's normal start in life. Yet this long debit column against Pastor Ernst Schliemann's name is partly offset by credits which neither George Grote Senior nor Charles John Leaf could claim. George Grote Senior 'had no sympathy with learning',[1] while the intellectual inspiration that Walter Leaf received from his father[2] was faint compared with that which Heinrich Schliemann received from his—not to speak of the automatic physical heritage of vitality which Pastor Ernst Schliemann expended on setting Nature at defiance by prolonging a dissolute life to the age of ninety,[3] leaving it to his son Heinrich Schliemann to employ a transmitted fund of energy in making his fortune, mastering twelve foreign languages, and excavating Troy and Mycenae.[4]

Of three business men who took intellectually promising sons into partnership—George Grote Senior, Charles John Leaf, and Daniel Pomeroy Rhodes—the last-named alone comes out of the transaction with credit. There is no suggestion that James Ford Rhodes' entry into the family business was anything but the young man's own spontaneous choice, and no suggestion, either, that, thereafter, the father exercised any cramping tyranny over his son's private life. (It is significant, for example, that, in A.D. 1872, only three years after his entry into the family business in A.D. 1869, James Ford Rhodes made the happy marriage for which Grote and Leaf were both constrained to wait.) On the other hand there is a piece of presumptive evidence suggesting that James Ford Rhodes' father may have done something to inspire his son with the resolve—which the future historian is said to have formed in his boyhood[5]—one day to write a history of his country's contemporary tragedy; for Daniel Pomeroy Rhodes had been one of the leading Douglasite delegates from the North-West at the fateful convention which the Democratic Party had held at Charleston, S.C., on the 23rd April–1st May, 1860.[6] As for the other two partner-fathers, George Grote Senior was a selfish tyrant and Charles John Leaf a pathetic invalid.

The historian-banker's father put George Grote Junior into the family business before his sixteenth birthday in order to make sure of being able to pass his own time in indulging his personal tastes by leading the conventional life of a country gentleman.[7] He obstructed for nearly five years (A.D. 1815–20) his son's wish to marry.[8] He then made his consent

[1] Grote, H., op. cit., p. 10.
[2] See Walter Leaf in Leaf, C. M.: *Walter Leaf*, pp. 17–19.
[3] See Schliemann, H.: *Ilios* (London 1880, Murray), p. 1, n. 1.
[4] 'The almost unswerving attachment of the son to the father, in spite of every form of provocation from the father's side, can be explained only by his instinctive sense of their kinship of spirit.'—Ludwig, E.: *Schliemann of Troy*, p. 39.
[5] See p. 154, above.
[6] See Nevins, A.: *The Emergence of Lincoln* (New York 1950, Scribner, 2 vols.), vol. ii, p. 206.
[7] See Grote, H., op. cit., pp. 8 and 9–10.
[8] See ibid., pp. 18 and 38.

conditional on the young couple's living in a house adjoining the bank in Threadneedle Street (a condition which, in Mrs. George Grote Junior's belief, was responsible for the premature delivery and swift death of her child and for an attack of puerperal fever that was all but fatal to its mother).[1] And, though the younger Grote had become 'the real working partner' in A.D. 1816,[2] his father, till his death in A.D. 1830, 'appropriated the greater portion of the profits which fell to the Grote family, allowing his eldest son no more than just sufficient to keep him from incurring debts.'[3] This paternal tyranny was odious, yet George Grote's tribulations under it were perhaps hardly more severe than the trials brought upon Walter Leaf by a breakdown of his father's health which exposed a dutiful son to the more exacting tyranny of his own scrupulous conscience and tender heart.

In the same year A.D. 1874 in which Walter Leaf's father's health gave way, Walter's uncle Frederick died of cancer, and, since his uncle William had already died in A.D. 1871, the family business unexpectedly found itself bereft of all three partners of the older generation.[4] In these tragic circumstances, which in themselves were enough to put crushing moral pressure upon a sensitive member of the rising generation, Walter Leaf's father appealed to him to come to the family's rescue; and the son 'deliberately accepted the offer of a place in the business with all the consequences', though he 'regarded it from the first as a disagreeable duty'.[5] The consequences were indeed severe for him; for, in contrast to George Grote Junior, who had taken over a family business at a time when the openings for it had been favourable, and who had then been left free by his father to use his opportunities and abilities in making a success of it, as he did, at his own discretion, so long as he provided his father with sufficient profits from it, Walter Leaf was taking over a family business which was already in decline and which, as was to be proved by the event, ought to have been sold at that stage, and he had to spend the first eighteen years of his business life (A.D. 1875–93) in bearing, as 'counting house partner', the brunt of a losing battle before his father—who did not forbear to interfere with his son's management after he had become incapable of exercising the responsibility himself[6]—could be induced to waive his sentimental objections to amalgamating with another firm.[7] It was not until he was invited in A.D. 1891, sixteen years after his first entry into the City, to join the Board of the London and Westminster Bank, that Walter Leaf found his way at last into a business career that was congenial to him. Meanwhile, his sense of duty towards his parents led him not only to spend eighteen years of his working life (A.D. 1875–93) on the thankless task of keeping the family business afloat, but also to refrain for nineteen years (A.D. 1875–94) from marrying.[8]

The painfulness of these frustrating sacrifices on the planes of per-

[1] See Grote, H., op. cit., pp. 39–40.
[2] See ibid., p. 46.
[3] Ibid., p. 51. Cp. p. 39.
[4] Walter Leaf in Leaf, C. M.: *Walter Leaf*, pp. 109–11.
[5] Walter Leaf, ibid., pp. 114 and 113.
[6] See Leaf, C. M.: *Walter Leaf*, pp. 145–7.
[7] See Walter Leaf, ibid., pp. 112–15.
[8] See Leaf, C. M., ibid., p. 159.

sonal and professional life drove both George Grote Junior and Walter Leaf to seek consolation in intellectual activities. 'Looking forward to a commercial course of life, certain to prove uninteresting in itself', Grote 'resolved to provide for himself the higher resources of intellectual occupation'.[1] 'I made no pretence of liking the drudgery', Walter Leaf wrote, in retrospect, of his entry into the family business in A.D. 1875, 'but it had to be faced; and from the very first day I determined that it should not make me forget the higher intellectual interests'.[2] 'My dead friends in *Calf and Russia*', George Grote Junior wrote to G. W. Norman in May 1819, 'still continue faithful and interesting, and, if it were not for them, life would be a very waste indeed'.[3] 'Only Homer keeps me going' and 'I have taken to work as some men would have taken to drink—to drive away my thoughts'—are two of the entries in Walter Leaf's diary in A.D. 1879.[4] 'These are they which came out of great tribulation';[5] for, in the event, Grote and Leaf were, not warped, but stimulated, by their ordeal.

'Soon the pruning of those years was to blossom out all the more vigorously for its ruthless suppression. Does not the gardener prune the rose tree? This same process, which in Walter's life meant a rigid cutting-back, strengthened every fibre of his being for what followed when once his wings were free to soar.'[6]

As for Schliemann,

'while . . . he had railed against the fate of a youth spoilt by his father's irregular life, he did not realise the strength of the impetus which a long artificially obstructed stream can gather before it at last breaks forth.'[7]

Nor are the intellectual benefits of personal and professional tribulations solely negative. An ordeal that stimulates the intellect by challenging it also gives it a positive schooling in open-mindedness, judiciousness, perceptiveness, and an art of communicating ideas to other minds which is an indispensable intellectual accomplishment for a human social animal and is at the same time the most arduous stage in the process of literary composition. Sir Arthur Evans[8] notices in Schliemann that 'his old intense faculty of self-repression came out again in his later campaigns at Troy, where, in spite of much inward repugnance, he at last submitted to "scientific methods"'; and Cyril Bailey[9] similarly notices in Leaf 'the eagerness with which, while retaining his general outlook, he would welcome every kind of new light, and the courage with which he could abandon any theory which he felt to be no longer tenable'. John Torrey Morse Junior, in his appreciation of James Ford Rhodes and his work,[10] notices that Rhodes never succumbs, as Macaulay does, to a temptation to embroider at inordinate length

[1] Grote, H., op. cit., p. 11.
[2] Leaf, C. M., op. cit., pp. 121–2.
[3] Grote, H., op. cit., pp. 21–22.
[4] Leaf, C. M., op. cit., p. 144.
[5] Rev. vii. 14.
[6] Leaf, C. M., op. cit., p. 161. Compare the simile of the pollarded willow that has been propounded in the present Study in I. i. 168; II. i. 273; II. ii. 209.
[7] Ludwig, op. cit., pp. 134–5.
[8] In Ludwig, op. cit., p. 19.
[9] In Leaf, C. M., op. cit., p. 319. Cp. p. 320.
[10] In the *Proceedings of the Massachusetts Historical Society*, loc. cit., pp. 181–2.

his descriptions of picturesque incidents, and he suggests an explanation of Rhodes' workmanlike sense of proportion.

'Is it possible that his cool self-restraint was indirectly due to the long years of his business training? . . . Business teaches what may be called a clean-cut way of thinking; impulse is absolutely discarded; an accurate knowledge of exact facts is essential; due weight must be allotted among colliding suggestions. In short, the study given to the matter in hand must be both exhaustive and dispassionate.[1] Such had been Mr. Rhodes' mental training for many years; and it had shaped the way in which he contemplated his subject matter. . . . I strongly incline to believe . . . that Mr. Rhodes' score of years in mere practical business were of substantial advantage to him when he came to write the annals of a great multitude of very hard and conflicting facts.'

Besides thus exercising the judgement, business practice can also sharpen the intuition. In noticing that Schliemann divined at first glance which was the true site of Troy, Emil Ludwig[2] cites Herder's remark to Goethe: 'With you the eye is everything'; and he goes on to comment:

'This rapid, keen, surveying, collating eye was characteristic of Schliemann; and it cannot be denied that a decade spent in looking over stocks, samples, steamships, and warehouses trains the eyes better than the study of the opinions of a hundred experts when, before digesting them, the archaeologist has never been himself to the place concerned.'

As for the training that business practice gives in the social art of conveying ideas, John Stuart Mill[3] observes, of his experience at the India house, that

'it was valuable to me by making me, in this portion of my activity, merely one wheel in a machine, the whole of which had to work together. As a speculative writer, I should have had no one to consult but myself, and should have encountered in my speculations none of the obstacles which would have started up whenever they came to be applied to practice. But, as a secretary conducting political correspondence, I could not issue an order or express an opinion without satisfying various persons, very unlike myself, that the thing was fit to be done. I was thus in a good position for finding out by practice the mode of putting a thought which gives it easiest admittance into minds not prepared for it by habit; while I became practically conversant with the difficulties of moving bodies of men, the necessities of compromise, the art of sacrificing the non-essential to preserve the essential. I learnt how to obtain the best I could, when I could not obtain everything.'[4]

This practical philosophy, into which Mill the logician was thus inducted by Mill the India House clerk, is more likely to inspire effective intellectual action than the impossibilism of the grammarian who, in

[1] In this respect, a practical career has the same effect in the province of public administration as in that of private business. 'The occupation accustomed me to see and hear the difficulties of every course, and the means of obviating them, stated and discussed deliberately with a view to execution' (Mill, J. S.: *Autobiography*, chap. 3 *ad finem*).—A.J.T.

[2] In op. cit., p. 140.

[3] In his *Autobiography*, ibid.

[4] Mill, J. S.: *Autobiography*, chap. 3 *ad finem*.

Robert Browning's poem, is carried to his grave *rê infectâ* as the penalty for his hybris in playing for 'all or nothing'.[1]

The value of a self-education in practical affairs had been borne in upon the present writer by an experience of his own that had made a deep and lasting impression on his mind. On the 18th–20th November, 1911, *en route* from Brindisi to Athens on his first visit to Greece, he had fallen into conversation with a young American of his own age who was one of his fellow-passengers on board the s.s. *Mykáli*. By that time the writer had been studying Latin for fifteen years, Greek for twelve and a half, and Hellenic history for two and a half intensively, and, on the last day of the voyage, as the boat steamed up the Gulf of Corinth and then through the canal into the Saronic Gulf, he was enjoying the thrill of identifying one feature in the landscape after another: the twin mountains Chalcis and Taphiassus, planted side by side like a pair of gigantic baetyls *vis-à-vis* Patras; Panachaïcus wreathed in clouds; Parnassus followed by Helicon and confronted by Cyllênê; Acrocorinthus standing erect at the head of the Gulf; and, as a climax to this perpetually shifting panorama, the sudden view, round the shoulder of Salamis, of the Acropolis of Athens with Hymettus rising up behind it. Yet this constantly recurring thrill of setting eyes, for the first time in his life, on famous and beautiful objects that had long loomed large on his mental horizon could not distract the Englishman from giving an increasing share of his attention to his conversation with his American contemporary who was leaning over the rail at his side; for, while the young Englishman had been making himself into a classical scholar, the young American had been doing half a dozen other things which were so different from the Englishman's personal experiences up to date that they could not fail to arouse his interest. In the brief course of his working life so far, the young American had already worked on a farm, in a bank, in a bakery, in a lawyer's office, and in a grocer's store; and he had confuted the proverb about the rolling stone by accumulating incidentally enough spare money to carry him round the World (he had already travelled three times to and fro through the Mont Cenis Tunnel). Today and tomorrow he would be in Greece; the day after tomorrow he would be moving on to Egypt. In comparison with his English travelling companion, he was a babe in his knowledge of Greece and an old hand in his knowledge of Life. When, as the ship came to anchor at the Peiraeus, the two 'Anglo-Saxons' discovered that their otherwise piquantly different educations had been identical in the negative point of sending them both out into the wide world unable to speak with the tongues of either men or angels,[2] it was the American who, in this emergency, made businesslike bargains for the pair of them with a boatman to row them ashore and with a cabman to drive them up to Athens. Two days after that, he sailed, in accordance with his schedule, for Alexandria; and, though the writer never heard from him thereafter, he never doubted that he duly arrived at a destination which, forty years on, the writer himself had not yet succeeded in reaching.

This brief encounter taught the Englishman a lesson in the cardinal

[1] See p. 38, above.

[2] 1 Cor. xiii. 1.

virtues of the practical life which made him appreciate one of the surviving fragments of the work of the statesman-historian Polybius.

'Plato says[1] that human affairs will never come right until "either the philosophers receive royal authority or the kings take to philosophy"; and, taking my cue from him, I should say, for my part, that the study of History will never come right until either one or other of two things happens. One of these alternatives is that the men of action (*οἱ πραγματικοὶ τῶν ἀνδρῶν*) should take up the writing of historical works—and take this up not just as a side-line (*παρέργως*), as they do now, but with so genuine a conviction that this is quite as important and quite as well worth doing [as any "practical" business] that they will be inspired with a life-long devotion to this pursuit and will refuse to allow themselves to be distracted from it. The other alternative is that would-be professional historians should take the view that history cannot be written effectively unless the writer has acquired an outlook that can be given only by actual experience of practical life. Until this happens, there will be "no hope of a cessation" of the ignorance of the present breed of historical writers.'[2]

[1] See Plato: *Respublica*, 473 D, quoted in III. iii. 93 and V. vi. 242.—A.J.T.

[2] Polybius: *Oecumenical History*, Book XII, chap. xxviii, §§ 2–5. In Book XII, chap. xxv, section *h* and section *i*, §§ 1–2, Polybius has already made the same point *ad hominem* apropos of his predecessor Timaeus of Tauromenium:

'Timaeus confesses that he stayed for fifty years on end at Athens as a visitor who, all that time, admittedly had no experience whatsoever of military service and made no first-hand acquaintance with the topography [of the scenes of the historical events that he was recording]. So it is no wonder that, when, in his narrative, he runs up against these topics, he should display gross ignorance and should get quite a number of things wrong. Moreover, when he does occasionally approach the truth, he is like one of those painters who use lay figures for their models. They sometimes succeed in reproducing the outline of the original, but they fail to catch the verisimilitude and vitality of real live creatures—fail, in fact, to do what is precisely the professional job of an artist. Timaeus, like all other bookish historians, comes to grief in the same way. They fail to catch the verisimilitude of historical events, because nothing but personal experience (*αὐτοπαθείας*) can enable the historian to achieve that. An historian who has not actually taken part himself in historical events will never succeed in effectually stimulating his readers. The historians of the classical school attached so much importance to achieving verisimilitude that, when they had to deal with politics, they would note that, as a matter of course, the writer has been a politician and has had practical experience of public affairs; when they had to deal with war, that he has seen active service and has been under fire; when they had to deal with life, that he has been a married man and has brought up a family; and similarly for all sides of life. But obviously this qualification for writing history will be found only in those historians who have mastered it by actually taking part themselves in historical events. . . . The moral is that a preoccupation with documentary materials is only one-third part of an historian's task—and this the third in order of importance.'

A NOTE ON CHRONOLOGY

(I) THE PROBLEM

IN the present work the first approach to the histories of the civilizations has been to make a comparative study of them as so many representatives of one species of Human Society, and this comparative treatment postulates that all representatives of the species are in some sense 'philosophically contemporary' with one another,[1] however far apart their locations may be on a chronological chart. In Parts II–V inclusive, which occupy the whole of volumes i–vi except for an introductory Part I, the chronological relation between one civilization and another has therefore not been a question of crucial importance; for a more or less correct knowledge of the internal chronology of each civilization is all that is required for attempting a comparative study of the geneses, growths, breakdowns, and disintegrations of the civilizations known to have existed up to date.

In the present concluding batch of volumes, however, the writer has been confronted with the task of trying to bring the respective internal chronologies of all the known civilizations into relation with one another by entering them all on a single Time-chart in so far as the historical evidence accessible in A.D. 1952 has allowed of this; for these volumes vii–x, containing Parts VI–XIII, are concerned in Parts VI–VIII with the relation of 'apparentation' and 'affiliation' between an antecedent and a posterior civilization, and in Parts IX–X with encounters between contemporaries in the Space-dimension and between non-contemporaries in the Time-dimension. Moreover, the inquiry into universal churches in Part VII has raised the question of the relation of these religious institutions to the civilizations that have preceded them and have followed them, and this has led to an analysis of the species of Society that we have called 'civilizations' into sub-varieties, representing different generations, which are distinguished from one another by differences in their historical relations to the higher religions.[2] It is evident that for these purposes we need to know how the several internal chronologies of our twenty-one civilizations (or whatever the number may be) stand to one another; and, as soon as we try to work out a single consolidated Time-chart, we find that the means at our disposal differ sharply in the degree of their adequacy or inadequacy in two different sets of cases.

For a student of the histories of civilizations who was working in the Western World in the twentieth century of the Christian Era, it was comparatively easy to correlate the Western Civilization's chronology with the chronologies of its living contemporaries (the Near Eastern Orthodox Christian, Russian Orthodox Christian, Iranic Muslim, Arabic Muslim, Hindu, Chinese Far Eastern, and Japanese Far Eastern societies) and also with the chronologies of antecedent civilizations (the

[1] See I. i. 172–4. [2] See VII. vii. 421–3.

Hellenic, Syriac, Indic, and Sinic) to which one or more of the living civilizations were affiliated. But the evidence in the twentieth-century Western historian's possession did not enable him to reconstruct with any degree of certainty the chronology of the earliest chapters in the histories even of those four civilizations belonging to a generation immediately preceding that of his own society and its living contemporaries; and the uncertainty was greater still in the cases of other civilizations—some belonging to the same immediately preceding generation and others to an earlier generation again—of whose history no continuous tradition has been preserved by any of the civilizations that were still alive in the twentieth century of the Christian Era.

These once forgotten civilizations had been buried mentally in oblivion, besides being buried physically underground, for some thousands of years before they had been disinterred by the Modern Western archaeologist's spade. Manifestly the difficulty of correlating their chronology with that of the living civilizations and the immediate predecessors of these was vastly greater than the difficulty of consolidating the chronology of these still living and these never yet forgotten civilizations; and it was almost as difficult to translate into years of the Christian Era the chronology of the pre-Columbian civilizations of the Americas which had been contemporaries of the Western Civilization of the Old World but had been overwhelmed and submerged by its impact after having been unknown to it before it fell upon them with this instantaneously destructive effect.

The translation into years of the Christian Era of the chronologies of the pre-Columbian civilizations of the New World and the disinterred civilizations of the Old World was a task which a student of History was bound to attempt, because he could not afford to ignore the invaluable new light that Archaeology had thrown on History within the Western field of vision by bringing these formerly unknown civilizations to the Modern Western historian's knowledge. Yet, in attempting to co-ordinate Archaeology's finds with his traditional store of historical information by locating the disinterred civilizations' chronologies on his own Western Time-chart, the Western historian was manifestly committing himself to a hazardous undertaking; and the hazard was more evident when the present writer started work again on this Study, after a seven-years-long interruption caused by the Second World War, than it had been during the years A.D. 1927–39, within which he had planned the whole book, written the first five Parts of it, and published these in the first six volumes.

During the years A.D. 1927–39 the present writer was well aware that the relation of the Mayan and the affiliated Yucatec Civilization's chronology to that of the Western Civilization was the subject of a still unsettled controversy among the experts,[1] but at that time he mistakenly believed that the chronologies of the disinterred civilizations of North-East Africa and South-West Asia—the Egyptiac, Minoan, and Sumeric civilizations and the Indus Culture in the first generation, and the Sumeric Civilization's Babylonic and Hittite successors in the

[1] See I. i. 124–5.

second generation—had been definitively correlated, more or less accurately, both with one another and with the chronology of the Western Civilization, in a Time-chart that had been worked out by Eduard Meyer. He felt no hesitation during those years in adopting the conclusions of this great authority, and indeed in A.D. 1952 these conclusions still appeared in retrospect to have been warrantable in the light of all the evidence forthcoming at the time.

Between A.D. 1939 and A.D. 1946, however, Meyer's conclusions had been thrown into the melting-pot as a result of the digestion, analysis, and discussion of fresh evidence that had been discovered in the nineteen-thirties. The writer returned to a study of History in A.D. 1946 to find that in Sumeric, Babylonic, and Hittite history the old chronological landmarks had been swept away and that no new landmarks had yet secured any general acceptance. The experts all agreed that the new evidence convicted Eduard Meyer's chronology of being too high; but here their consensus ended. There were now in the arena at least four rival new chronologies for South-West Asian history; and, while the most conservative of these reduced Meyer's dating of the First Dynasty of Babylon by only about one hundred years—from 2049–1750 B.C. to 1950–1651 B.C.—the most radical of the four reduced it, by nearly 250 years, to 1806–1507 B.C.

Meanwhile, in compensation, the former disagreement over Mayan and Yucatec chronology appeared to have been resolved by a victory of the lower over the higher of the two main former rival correlations of the internal chronology of the Mayan and Yucatec civilizations with years of the Christian Era.

(II) THE CASE FOR THE GOODMAN-MARTINEZ-THOMPSON CORRELATION OF THE YUCATEC AND MAYAN CHRONOLOGY WITH YEARS OF THE CHRISTIAN ERA

In the first five Parts and six volumes of this Study the present writer set out C. P. Bowdich's and H. J. Spinden's higher correlation and S. G. Morley's and J. E. S. Thompson's lower correlation side by side, without venturing to offer his readers any lead of his own towards making a choice.[1] Considering the blackness of his own ignorance of the subject, this suspension of judgement was the only attitude that he could have adopted without being guilty of intellectual impudence, though this agnosticism had the serious disadvantage of leaving the chronology in the air, since there was a discrepancy of some 260–70 years between the two systems.[2] Even an amateur, however, could see that Spinden's chronology for the Mayan, Yucatec, and Mexic civilizations had one ominous weakness in common with Meyer's chronology for the Sumeric, Babylonic, and Hittite civilizations. It required

[1] See, for example, I. i. 124–5.

[2] See the British Museum *Guide to the Maudslay Collection of Maya Sculptures* (London 1923, British Museum), p. 48, and Gann, T., and Thompson, J. E. S.: *The History of the Maya* (London 1931, Scribner), preface.

the assumption that, in the reconstructed record, there was a chronological gap in which History was a blank not occupied by any disinterred archaeological remains. This hypothetical interregnum in the archaeological record, which was about 150–200 years long in Eduard Meyer's chronology of South-West Asian history,[1] was about 350 years long in Spinden's chronology of Central American history;[2] yet in both cases the archaeological evidence, taken on its own merits, pointed, not to an interregnum, but to continuity;[3] and for this reason, among others, 'opinion has turned against it [the Spinden correlation] ... in recent years'.[4] J. E. S. Thompson advocates as 'the most acceptable' correlation, without claiming that the evidence in its favour is irrefutable, the Goodman-Martinez-Thompson correlation[5]—a refinement on Morley's correlation which was adopted by Morley himself.[6]

On the authority of Morley, Thompson, and other Mayan scholars associated with the Carnegie Institution of Washington, the conversion of Mayan years into Gregorian years of the Christian Era according to the Goodman-Martinez-Thompson correlation has been adopted in Parts VI–XIII of the present Study. Yet in A.D. 1952 the experience of the revolution in South-West Asian chronology between A.D. 1939 and A.D. 1946 gave warning that the further progress of archaeological discovery might lay Morley's and Thompson's apparently definitive chronological system in ruins, as it had already laid Eduard Meyer's. One inescapable weakness of any attempt to correlate the Mayan Time-count with years of the Christian Era in the existing state of Western knowledge of the Mayan calendrical system was that, before the Maya collided with the Spaniards, they had substituted a relatively imperfect 'Short Count', in which 'accuracy within a period of only 256 years could be achieved',[7] for a previously current 'Long Count' which 'was exact to the day over a period of 374,440 years'.[8] 'Thus the problem of correlating the Mayan "Long Count" with Christian chronology consists of two different operations: first of correlating the Gregorian calendar with the Maya "Short Count", and second of correlating the Maya "Short Count" with the Maya "Long Count".'[9] Disagreement over the method of performing this second operation had been one cause of the difference between the rival Western computations of Mayan

1 See I. i. 111.

2 See Thompson, J. E. S.: *Maya Hieroglyphic Writing: Introduction* (Washington, D. C. 1950, Carnegie Institution of Washington), p. 306, col. 2.

3 In the field of Hittite history the formerly postulated gap, 200 years broad, is pronounced 'artificial and incredible', in the light of the archaeological evidence, by Sidney Smith in *Alalakh and Chronology* (London 1940, Luzac), p. 17. Cp. Böhl, F. M. Th.: 'King Ḫammurabi of Babylon in the Setting of his Time (about 1700 B.C.)', in *Mededeelingen der Koninklijke Nederlandsche Akademie van Wetenschappen*, Afd. Letterkunde, Nieuwe Reeks, Deel 9, No. 10 (Amsterdam 1946, Nordhollandsche Uitgevers), p. 344.

4 Thompson, op. cit., p. 33.

5 See Thompson, op.cit., pp. 5 and 303, following his *Maya Chronology, The Correlation Question* (Washington, D.C., 1935, Carnegie Institution of Washington, Publication 456, No. 14, pp. 51–104). 'In the light of present evidence an open verdict must be returned' (*Maya Chronology*, p. 82. Cp. p. 75).

6 See Morley, S. G.: *The Ancient Maya* (Palo Alto 1946, Stanford University Press), p. 458.

7 Morley, op. cit., p. 291.

8 Ibid., p. 457; cp. pp. 288–9.

9 Ibid., p. 457.

chronology in Western terms; and, while the Goodman-Martinez-Thompson correlation might be confirmed by further discoveries in the calendrical province of Mayan studies, it might also be overthrown in its turn. Subject to this warning, it nevertheless seemed to be the best correlation to adopt in the circumstances of the time at which Parts VI–XIII of the present Study were being written and published.

(III) THE CURRENT CONTROVERSY OVER THE DATING OF THE FIRST DYNASTY OF BABYLON IN TERMS OF YEARS B.C.

The Overthrow of Eduard Meyer's Reconstruction of the Chronology of South-West Asian History.

In A.D. 1952 the correlation of Mayan with Western chronology in terms of the Goodman-Martinez-Thompson formula appeared at least to be better assured—pending some subversive fresh archaeological discovery in the Middle American field—than any of the four or more rival systems that, in the arena of South-West Asian chronological studies, were at this date in competition with one another for replacing a system, worked out by Eduard Meyer, which the progress of archaeological discovery had already discredited.

It was true that the internal chronology of the First Dynasty of Babylon had not been impugned. This dynasty was still believed to have been on the throne during eleven consecutive reigns whose severally recorded individual lengths added up to an aggregate period of 300 years ending in the overthrow of the eleventh king Samsu-ditana in a raid made on Babylon by the Hittite war-lord Muršiliš I. But there were now four or more rival substitutes for Eduard Meyer's correlation—adopted in Parts I–V of the present Study[1]—of these 300 years with the years 2049–1750 B.C.; and, even if one of these competing correlations, or some other again, differing from each and all of them, were eventually to be proved correct, it was now pointed out that 'the earlier dynasties' could 'not be dated exactly from the king-list because the period by which the reigns of Ishbi-Irra [the first king of the Dynasty of Isin] and Ibi-Sin [Ibbi-Sin, the last king of the Third Dynasty of Ur] overlapped' could 'not be fixed, and' because 'the same doubt' applied 'to the reigns of Ur-Nammu [previously transliterated as Ur-Engur, the first king of the Third Dynasty of Ur] and Utu-khegal [of Erech, Ur-Nammu's forerunner]'.[2] In A.D. 1952 there was, indeed, no consensus among scholars regarding the correlation of any date in South-West Asian history earlier than about 1450 B.C.[3] Nevertheless, the still inconclusive controversy over the dating of the First Dynasty of Babylon was evidently the potential key to a possibility of eventually reacquiring something like the approximate certainty that Eduard Meyer had believed himself to have attained; for the highest and lowest of the current rival datings

[1] e.g., in I. i. 106, 110, and 111, and in V. vi. 296–8.
[2] Smith, Sidney: *Alalakh and Chronology* (London 1940, Luzac), pp. 30–31.
[3] See Smith, op. cit., p. 1.

of this dynasty were not much less than 150 years apart; and, by comparison with a discrepancy of this order, the chronological uncertainties arising from the overlapping of Ishbi-Irra's reign with Ibbi-Sin's, and of Ur-Nammu's with Utu-khegal's, were narrowly circumscribed.[1] Thus, if the current controversy over the dating of the First Dynasty of Babylon could be settled, this would also settle, within narrow limits, the dates of previous chapters of South-West Asian history at least as far back as the days of Lugal-zaggisi of Erech and his victim Uru-kagina of Lagash, who had reigned some five or six hundred years before the First Dynasty of Babylon had been founded.[2]

In A.D. 1952 the rival datings of the First Dynasty of Babylon stood as follows in terms of years B.C.[3]:

Modern Western Advocates	*Period of the First Babylonian Dynasty*	*Reign of Hammurabi*
(*a*) Sidersky; Thureau-Dangin;[4] Goetze	1950–1651	1848–1806
(*b*) Ungnad; Sidney Smith[5]	1894–1595	1792–1750
(*c*) Albright;[6] Cornelius; Van der Waerden	1831/30–*circa* 1531/30[7]	1728–1686[8]
(*d*) Poebel; Böhl;[9] Dossin; Schubert	1806–1507	1704–1662

1 'There is new evidence to show that the margin of error for the overlap Ibbi-Sin/Ishbi-Irra does not amount to more than a year or two. See A. Falkenstein in *Z.A.*, xv (1949), pp. 59 ff., especially p. 76. Ishbi-Irra conquered Isin in about the twelfth year of Ibbi-Sin.'—Note by Mr. M. B. Rowton.

2 See I. i. 109.

3 This table has been taken from a paper read by Professor A. Goetze before the American Oriental Society at its meeting in Cincinnati at Easter time, 1950, which the author has kindly allowed the present writer to cite. See also Professor Goetze's paper on 'The Problem of Chronology and Early Hittite History' in *The Bulletin of the American Schools of Oriental Research*, No 122, April 1951, pp. 18–25, especially pp. 19–20.

4 See Thureau-Dangin, F.: 'Iasmaḫ-Adad', in *Revue d'Archéologie*, vol. xxxiv (1937), pp. 135–9.

5 See Smith, S.: *Alalakh and Chronology* (London 1940, Luzac); 'Middle Minoan I–II and Babylonian Chronology', in the *American Journal of Archaeology*, vol. xlix, No. 1 (Concord, N. H. 1945, Rumford Press), pp. 1–24.

6 See Albright, W. F.: 'A Third Revision of the Early Chronology of Western Asia', in *B.A.S.O.R.*, No. 88, December 1942, pp. 28–32, superseding a previous paper on the subject by the same scholar ibid.: 'New Light on the History of Western Asia in the Second Millenium B.C.', in No. 77, February 1940, pp. 20–32, and No. 78, April 1940, pp. 23–33. In this earlier paper Albright had adopted Dating (*b*), but the subsequent publication of Poebel's papers on the Assyrian King-List, discovered in A.D. 1932–3 at Khorsabad, led Albright to lower his dating for the First Dynasty of Babylon by 64 years—this precise figure for the amount of the reduction being determined by the astronomical exigencies of the tenth king Ammi-ṣaduga's Venus observations (see 'New Light', pp. 30–31). The position reached by Albright in his third revision (i.e. Dating (*c*)) is maintained by him in a review of Sidney Smith's *Alalakh and Chronology* in *A.J.A.*, vol. xlvii, 1943, pp. 491–2, and in a paper on 'An Indirect Synchronism between Egypt and Mesopotamia *circa* 1730 B.C.' in *B.A.S.O.R.*, No. 99, October 1945, pp. 9–18. On p. 10 of this paper Albright records that, in lowering his own original reduction of Eduard Meyer's chronology by another 64 years, he was 'combining the evidence of the Venus observations with the data of the Khorsabad List', and he goes on to express the opinion that 'this latest reduced chronology fits the archaeological and historical picture so exactly that it cannot be appreciably wrong, so far as I can see.'

7 In *B.A.S.O.R.*, No. 88, December 1942, p. 31, Albright had dated the First Babylonian Dynasty 1831/30–1550 (*sic*, not 1530) B.C., but this is, no doubt, merely a misprint, since in *A.J.A.*, vol. xlvii (1943), p. 492, he restores to this dynasty its well-established total span of approximately 300 years by placing its terminal date *circa* 1530 B.C.

8 According to Albright in *B.A.S.O.R.* No. 88, December 1942, pp. 30–31. In *A.J.A.*, vol. xlvii, 1943, p. 492, he makes Hammurabi reign for an additional ten years down to 1676 B.C. This is, no doubt, merely a misprint.

9 See Böhl, F. M. Th.: 'King Ḫammurabi of Babylon in the Setting of his Time

When the experts were in such signal disagreement with one another, it would manifestly have been impertinent in a layman to presume to put forward any opinion of his own; but the layman could at least examine, for himself, the new pieces of archaeological evidence on which all four rival datings alike were based; and he could also take note of certain at least relatively well-ascertained points in Assyrian and Egyptiac chronology and in Hittite history with which any revised version of South-West Asian chronology would have to reckon.

There were three new discoveries that were accountable, between them, for the overthrow of Eduard Meyer's reconstruction of the chronology of South-West Asian history.

The Stratigraphical Evidence from Sites in North Syria.

The first discovery was that, on sites in North Syria, especially at Ugarit (Rās ash-Shamrah) on the coast and at Alalakh ('Atshānah) on the River Orontes, which, in the second millennium B.C., were subject to cultural radiation from both the Sumeric and the Egyptiac World, objects of Sumeric provenance or style attributable to the time of the First Dynasty of Babylon were found to lie in later strata than objects of Egyptiac provenance or style attributable to the reigns of the Egyptiac Emperors of the Twelfth Dynasty down to Amenemhat III inclusive.

'A Ras Shamra les cylindres babyloniens gravés d'inscriptions du temps de la première dynastie et dont certains ont pu être attribués au temps d'Hammourabi se trouvent dans les strates ou dans les tombes de l'Ugarit Moyen 2, et non dans celles de l'Ugarit Moyen 1 (2100–1900), sauf remaniements. Ils y sont donc attribuables avec certitude à la période entre 1900 et 1750 en chiffres ronds. Dans plusieurs cas nous avons pu établir que les strates qui contiennent les cylindres en question sont postérieures aux monuments égyptiens commençant à Ugarit avec ceux de Sésostris I et se terminant avec ceux d'Aménemhat III; cela restreint encore davantage la date de certains des cylindres babyloniens provenant d'Ugarit et permet de les placer entre 1800 et 1700 environ.

'Ainsi, les monuments et les observations stratigraphiques et chronologiques de Ras Shamra s'accordent fort bien avec les dates proposées par Mr. Sidney Smith . . ., d'après lesquelles la première dynastie babylonienne ne venait au pouvoir que vers 1900 en chiffres ronds et s'écroulait vers 1600.[1] D'après la même chronologie, le règne d'Hammourabi s'étend de 1792 à 1750, c'est à dire qu'il est contemporain de la fin de la période correspondant à la prépondérance politique dont l'Égypte du Moyen Empire avait joui en Syrie et en Palestine.'[2]

This stratigraphical evidence from North Syria was of some importance

(about 1700 B.C.)', in *Mededeelingen der Koninklijke Nederlandsche Akademie van Wetenschappen, Afd. Letterkunde*, Nieuwe Reeks, Deel 9, No. 10 (Amsterdam 1946, Noord-Hollandsche Uitgevers), pp. 341–70, especially p. 352.

[1] 'Les dates exactes proposées par Mr. S. Smith sont 1894 pour le commencement, 1595 pour la fin de la dynastie.'

[2] Schaeffer, C. F. A.: *Stratigraphie Comparée et Chronologie de l'Asie Occidentale (iiie et iie millénaires)* (London 1948, Oxford University Press), pp. 29–30. Cp. Sidney Smith, *Alalakh and Chronology* (London 1940, Luzac), p. 15, where Smith quotes Schaeffer's more tentative statement of the same point in *Ugaritica*, i. 18, n. 2. Cp. Albright, 'New Light', in *B.A.S.O.R.*, No. 77, p. 29, and Neugebauer, O.: 'The Chronology of the Hammurabi Age', in the *Journal of the American Oriental Society*, vol. lxi (New Haven 1941, Yale University Press), p. 58.

in the history of the current 'Battle of the Dates', inasmuch as it had been one of the earliest of the new pieces of information that had cast doubt on the tenability of Eduard Meyer's previously acceptable chronology. Such evidence, however, suffered from the inherent weakness of being inevitably imprecise; and it was significant that the argument in favour of Dating (*b*), which had been founded upon it by Schaeffer and Smith, was contested both by M. B. Rowton, who was an advocate of Dating (*c*), and by Professor Albrecht Goetze, who was an advocate of Dating (*a*). Mr. Rowton comments:

'Little can be made of the seals found at Ras ash-Shamrah or elsewhere in the Aegean area.[1] It might be added that an exact dating of seals of the "Old Babylonian" period has yet to be established. That term is often applied rather loosely to all Mesopotamian seals between the end of Ur III and the Kassite period, a total of over 400 years. A seal that belongs to the beginning of that period can, of course, be clearly distinguished from one that belongs to the end of it. But the grading of those seals (the majority) which do not belong to either of these extremes has not yet been done (probably for lack of reliable chronological evidence). Consequently, as matters stand, it is hardly possible to say whether a seal of this period is to be dated, say, 50 years before or 50 years after the middle of Hammurabi's reign.'[2]

Professor Goetze, for his part, was of the opinion that, 'where an independent check is possible, the evidence, as far as published, does not bear out Schaeffer's claims';[3] and he expressed[4] the same doubts as those entertained by Mr. Rowton in regard to Dr. Schaeffer's datings and attributions of cylinder seals disinterred from North Syrian sites. Professor Goetze also challenged Dr. Sidney Smith's arguments,[5] on archaeological grounds, for dating the strata Alalakh VI and VII *circa* 1800–1600 and hence for adopting Dating (*b*) for the First Dynasty of Babylon. It seemed evident that the stratigraphical evidence from North Syria, though it might suffice for impugning Eduard Meyer's chronology, did not suffice for providing a criterion for judging between the relative merits of the rival new datings.[6]

The Evidence of the Mari Archives

A second revolutionary discovery was the disinterment, in A.D. 1935–8, of the archives of Zimri-Lim, King of Mari (Ma'er) on the Middle Euphrates. Twenty thousand documents—15,000 of them economic, but the other 5,000 political—were retrieved.[7] The political documents

[1] See Rowton, M. B., in the *Journal of Near Eastern Studies*, vol. x (Chicago 1951, University of Chicago Press), p. 202.

[2] Mr. M. B. Rowton, in a note for the writer of this Study. Cp. Porada, E., in the *Journal of Cuneiform Studies*, vol. iv (1950), pp. 155–62.

[3] A note by Professor Goetze, enclosed with a letter of the 13th November, 1951, to the writer of this Study.

[4] Ibid.

[5] In *Alalakh*, pp. 8–10.

[6] The utility of the archaeological evidence bearing on the period of South-West Asian history under consideration in the present Note on Chronology is appraised as follows by Dr. Sidney Smith in a letter of the 13th October, 1951, to the writer of this Study: 'Archaeological evidence is chronologically important only in establishing sequences. . . . Nothing about lengths of time is proved [by archaeological evidence] in Palestine. In Syria sometimes archaeological material is associated in different levels with dated documents—a very different state of affairs.'

[7] See Dossin, G., in *Syria*, vols. xix (1938), pp. 105–26, and xx (1939), pp. 97–113. and W. von Soden's résumé in *Die Welt des Orients*, Heft 3 (1948), pp. 187–204.

in this trove straddle a period of at least sixty-two years all told, including the last nine years of the reign of Zimri-Lim's father Yakhdun-Lim, twenty-one years of Assyrian domination, exercised by the King of Assyria Šamši-Adad I, and the thirty-two years of Zimri-Lim's own reign, ending in the year of the destruction of Mari by Hammurabi of Babylon,[1] which is known, from Hammurabi's records, to have occurred in the thirty-fifth year of Hammurabi's reign.[2] The historical and chronological implications of these Mari Archives, and of contemporary documents from other places in the South-West Asian World of the day, can be appreciated better if we postpone our consideration of them till after we have dealt with the third of our three revolutionary discoveries.

The Evidence of the Khorsabad List of Kings of Assyria

This third discovery was the disinterment at Khorsabad, in A.D. 1932–3, of a list of the Kings of Assyria which purports to record the complete consecutive series down to Asshur-Nirari V (*regnabat* 754–745 B.C.), beginning with the first king of all. This Khorsabad List also gives figures for the lengths of reigns from the reign of the thirty-third king, Êrišu I, except for eight effaced entries and eight reigns—the forty-second to the forty-seventh inclusive, and the eighty-fourth and eighty-fifth—where a figure is replaced by the formula *ṭ/duppīšu šarrūta ēpuš* ('He exercised kingship during his *ṭ/duppu*').[3]

Twenty years after its discovery, this list still remained unpublished; and, at the time of writing, information about it was still to be found only in an article that had been published by Professor A. Poebel in the *Journal of Near Eastern Studies* in three instalments.[4] Poebel's article presented the contents of the Khorsabad King-List in the form of an interpretation of them, and this method of presentation had evoked from other scholars the criticism to which it manifestly laid itself open.[5] Yet enough was now known about the Khorsabad King-List to make it plain at least that this was a tantalizing document.

Since the reign of the latest king enumerated in it, No. 107, Asshur-Nirari V, was already known with certainty to correspond to the years 754–745 B.C., and since one of the kings for the lengths of whose reigns figures are given in the list—No. 39, Šamši-Adad I—was now known,

[1] These were the figures given by G. Dossin in *Studia Mariana* (edited by Parrot, A.: Leiden 1950, Brill), pp. 51–61, especially p. 59, as was pointed out to the present writer by Professor Goetze. Dossin's figures superseded those given by Böhl, op. cit., p. 348, namely 58 years all told, including the last 8 years of Yakhdun-Lim's reign, 20 years of Assyrian domination, and a reign of 30 years for Zimri-Lim. It was possible that the total span of years would be further increased by the progress of research.

[2] See Böhl, op. cit., pp. 348 and 354. Hammurabi's conquest of Mari in his thirty-second year, which, according to Böhl, op. cit., p. 354, n. 18, was not the final settlement of accounts, is equated with the definitive conquest by Van der Meer, P.: *The Ancient Chronology of Western Asia and Egypt* (Leiden 1947, Brill), p. 21.

[3] See Smith, S.: 'Middle Minoan I–II and Babylonian Chronology', in the *American Journal of Archaeology*, vol. xlix, No. 1, p. 19, and Rowton, M. B.: '*Ṭuppu* and the Date of Hammurabi', in the *Journal of Near Eastern Studies*, vol. x (Chicago 1951, University of Chicago Press), pp. 184–204.

[4] In *J.N.E.S.*, vol. i, No. 3, July 1942, pp. 247–306 and 460–91, and vol. ii, January–October 1943, pp. 56–90.

[5] See, for example, Sidney Smith's strictures in 'Middle Minoan I–II and Babylonian Chronology', p. 18.

from the evidence in the Mari Archives, to have ruled Mari for twenty-one years between the end of Yakhdun-Lim's reign there and the beginning of the reign of Yakhdun-Lim's son Zimri-Lim, whom the evidence of the Mari Archives certified to have been a contemporary of Hammurabi's, the Khorsabad List of Assyrian Kings ought to have made it possible approximately to date Hammurabi's reign, and, with it, the whole period occupied by the First Dynasty of Babylon, in terms of years B.C. In order, however, to provide this eagerly desired information with entire certainty and exactness, the Khorsabad List would have had, from reign No. 39 onwards, to be unmutilated and undisputedly precise in its indications, and unfortunately neither of these two conditions was fulfilled. In the first place the figures for kings Nos. 61, 65, and 66 had been effaced; and, though the figure for No. 61 could be restored from a fragment of another copy of the list, the lengths of the reigns of Nos. 65 and 66 remained unknown quantities.[1] In the second place the meaning of the formula 'his period', which did duty for a figure in eight cases (Nos. 42–47 and 84–85), was in dispute. In the third place it was contended by at least one authority, Dr. Sidney Smith, that there was no warrant for taking it for granted that the years recorded in this list were, all the way back to the figure given for Šamši-Adad I's reign, Babylonian solar years calculated according to the system labelled 'Julian' in a latter-day Western World in allusion to its official adoption by the Roman Government under the dictatorship of Julius Caesar as from the beginning of the Babylonian year that eventually came to be known retrospectively as 45 B.C.

A study of Poebel's article made it evident, even to a layman, that the author had succumbed to a temptation to try to force the Khorsabad List to solve the riddle of South-West Asian chronology with complete precision and certainty in spite of all these three impediments. Poebel tacitly assumes that all the years recorded in the list are Julian years; he postulates[2] that the compiler of the list uses the formula 'his period' in the technical sense of meaning part of the fraction of the preceding-king's last regnal year that was still unexpired at the time of that preceding king's death or deposition; and—as a result of ingenious attempts to check the data given in the Khorsabad List by comparing them with isolated, and apparently mutually conflicting, chronological statements made by Shalmaneser I (*regnabat* 1272–1243, supposing that the solar year had already been adopted in Assyria by his time) and by Esarhaddon (*regnabat* 680–669 B.C.)—he comes to the conclusion that the lost figures for reigns Nos. 65 and 66 would also prove, if they had been preserved or recovered, to have occupied, between them, only a fragment of one single year which is already accounted for in the list. On this showing, he concludes that all the unknown quantities in the Khorsabad List, as we have it, amount, in the aggregate, to no more than zero, and that it is legitimate to use the figures of regnal years contained in the list as if they represented an unbroken series of Julian solar years.

Manifestly, in adopting this procedure, Poebel is courting a risk of

[1] See Smith, S.; 'Middle Minoan I–II and Babylonian Chronology', in *A.J.A.*, vol. xlix, no. 1, p. 18.

[2] In *J.N.E.S.*, vol. i, p. 296, n. 130.

unduly lowering the dating of Šamši-Adad I's reign in Assyria and Mari, and therefore, by implication, also the dating of Zimri-Lim's reign in Mari and of Hammurabi's at Babylon. Indeed, if Poebel's assumptions in regard to all the three points on which the Khorsabad List was impugned by other scholars had all proved equally vulnerable to attack, the result would have been, not only to discredit Poebel's reconstruction of Assyrian chronology on the basis of the Khorsabad List, but also to demonstrate that any reconstruction on this basis would be impracticable. As it happened, however, the point in Poebel's presentation of his case that proved to be the least convincing to his critics was the point that introduced the smallest margin of arithmetical uncertainty into a calculation based on the figures that the Khorsabad List furnished. If it had been demonstrated that the phrase *ṭ/duppīšu* meant, when used in this king-list, 'an indeterminate period' or 'an unspecified period', then the chronology of Assyrian history from reigns Nos. 84 and 83 upwards would have remained still subject to a considerable possibility of error, while from reigns Nos. 47–42 upwards it would have remained altogether incalculable. And a further element of uncertainty would have been added if it had also been demonstrated that the solar year had not been adopted for official purposes in Assyria until the reign of Tiglath-Pileser I (*regnabat* 1114–1076 B.C.), and that, before that, the 'years' recorded in the Assyrian annals had been lunar years which might or might not have been brought into step with the solar years from time to time by rough-and-ready intercalations. On these two latter points, however, Poebel's assumptions, while they were impugned by Dr. Sidney Smith, were approved by a preponderance of expert opinion, and the only point of the three in which Poebel had an impressive majority against him was his assumption that the pair of reigns for which the figures in the Khorsabad List had been lost through an accidental defacement would have been found to have a zero value if the figures had been preserved.

Dr. Sidney Smith's scepticism in regard to the use of solar years in Assyrian official chronology before the reign of Tiglath-Pileser I did not find favour with other contemporary scholars;[1] and it was also pointed out that, if Assyrian official years before that date were in truth lunar years, the automatic effect would be, not to raise, but to lower, the dating in solar years by about three years in each century, and that a hypothetical excessive correction of this hypothetical automatic reduction by occasional intercalations was the only expedient by which the lunar-year hypothesis could be made to serve as an argument in favour of a higher dating. Moreover, there was one piece of positive evidence which indicated both that *ṭuppīšu* had the numerical value of zero and

[1] According to Van der Meer, P.: *The Ancient Chronology of Western Asia and Egypt* (Leiden 1947, Brill), pp. 1–2, the Assyrians and the Babylonians both alike used lunar years, and both alike adjusted these to the Julian solar year—thus, both alike, using Julian solar years in practice. The Assyrians had had an automatic method of adjustment —'the month whose beginning was the nearest to the Spring Equinox was the first month of the year'—whereas the Babylonians made the necessary intercalations by decree. The only innovation that Tiglath-Pileser I of Assyria made, according to Van der Meer, was to replace the previous Assyrian method of adjustment by the Babylonian method.

that the Assyrian official years had in truth been solar years for at least a quarter of a millennium before Tiglath-Pileser I's day. The Assyrian King Asshur-Uballit I (No. 73 in the Khorsabad List) was known, on the evidence of the Tall-al-'Amarnah Archives, to have been a contemporary of the Egyptian Emperor Ikhnaton, whose reign was known, from the Egyptian evidence, to have fallen within the second quarter of the fourteenth century B.C. (in the years 1380–1362, according to J. A. Wilson's dating)[1]; and, on the basis of the figures in the Khorsabad List, Asshur-Uballit's reign would be dated 1362–1327 B.C.[2] if the lengths of the reigns of kings Nos. 84 and 85 (two *ṭuppu* reigns) were assumed to be zero and if the years in which the Khorsabad List was reckoning were assumed to be solar years. There thus seemed to be positive evidence in favour of making both these assumptions of Poebel's at least as far upwards as this point in the Khorsabad List, and no evidence against making Poebel's assumption that the years of the list were solar years right back to the reign of Šamši-Adad I.

Dr. Sidney Smith attacked Poebel's assumption that the formula *ṭ/duppīšu šarrūta ēpuš* was equivalent to zero for chronological purposes by impugning the philological contentions on which Poebel's assumption had been based by Poebel himself.[3] Smith had succeeded, in Rowton's opinion,[4] in demolishing Poebel's philological basis for the equation of *ṭuppīšu* with zero; but Rowton, for his part, proposed an alternative philological interpretation of the phrase which, like Poebel's interpretation, would equate it with zero in its usage in the Khorsabad List. The question was whether the formula used in the Khorsabad List meant, as Sidney Smith contended,[5] 'an indeterminate period', or whether it meant, as Rowton contended, an 'end-bit' required for bringing a measure of capacity up to its full volume or bringing a measure of time up to its full length. The answer turned on the interpretation of the meaning of the Akkadian word *ṭuppu* in other contexts; and on this matter no one who was not an Assyriologist, and an accomplished one, could presume to pass judgement. The issue was a crucial one for the chronological question that is the subject of the present note; for, if Smith's interpretation was right, the formula would mean that the compiler of the Khorsabad List either had not known or had not chosen to tell the length of the reign to which he was applying the formula; and, considering that the formula is applied to no less than eight reigns before we arrive (in a chronologically ascending order) at the reign of Šamši-Adad I, this would mean that Šamši-Adad I's reign was practically undatable on the basis of the Khorsabad List. On the other hand, if Rowton's interpretation was right, the formula, as used

[1] See Wilson, J. A.: *The Burden of Egypt* (Chicago 1951, University of Chicago Press), p. vii.

[2] Mr. M. B. Rowton, in *'Irāq*, vol. viii (1946), p. 96, had calculated that Asshur-Uballit's accession year was, not 1362, but 1356 B.C.; but there were also alternative datings of Ikhnaton's reign which brought the terminal date of this down to 1352 B.C. The contemporaneity of Ikhnaton and Asshur-Uballit was attested beyond dispute by the retrieval of correspondence between them in the Tall-al-'Amarnah Archives.

[3] See Smith, Sidney: 'Middle Minoan I–II and Babylonian Chronology', in *A.J.A.*, vol. xlix, No. 1, pp. 1–24.

[4] See Rowton, M. B.: '*Ṭuppu* and the Date of Hammurabi', in *J.N.E.S.*, vol. x (1951), p. 201.

[5] Ibid., p. 19.

in the Khorsabad List, would mean that the reign to which it applied fell within a fraction of time between the completion of a period already assigned in the list to a previous king and the antecedent actual date of that previous king's death.[1] And, on this interpretation, a reign characterized in the list by this formula would, after all, be chronologically equivalent to zero, as Poebel had assumed.

A layman who was incompetent to assess the philological pros and cons could at least appreciate Rowton's non-technical point that the formula was unlikely to be a circumlocution for a confession of ignorance or for a refusal to supply information, considering that, in recording the names of the first thirty-two of the kings in his series, the compiler of the Khorsabad List has frankly left a blank opposite each name, without giving either a figure for the length of the reign or a formula to cloak his ignorance of it. If he has thus frankly admitted his ignorance in these thirty-two cases, is it probable that he will have attempted to cloak it in eight other cases? The inference seems to be that the formula means, in Modern Western terms, not 'an unknown quantity', which presumably would have been indicated by a blank as before, but 'zero'.[2]

If we were to opt for Rowton's, as against Smith's, interpretation of the formula *ṭ/duppīšu šarrūti ēpuš*, as well as for the view that the compiler of the Khorsabad List was reckoning throughout in solar years, it would follow that the Khorsabad List could be used as evidence for an approximate reconstruction of Assyrian chronology as far back as King Šamši-Adad I's reign; for, on these assumptions, the only unknown quantity would be the aggregate length of the two reigns Nos. 65 and 66, for which the durations originally recorded in the list had been lost to Modern Western scholarship owing to the accident that the piece of the clay tablet on which this information had originally been inscribed had been broken away before the tablet had been disinterred. Poebel's proposal to equate these two missing figures likewise with zero was unconvincing for two distinct reasons. In the first place, it seemed, *a priori*, improbable that precisely these two entries that had been lost through a physical accident should have happened originally to have been either 'blanks' or 'zeros' and not to have been figures for numbers of years, considering that, out of the 68 intact entries on the list, from king No. 33, whose reign is the first to be dated, down to king No. 107, with whose reign the list ends, not one is marked 'blank' and only eight are marked 'zero'.[3] In the second place, if, in spite of this *a priori*

[1] This interpretation of the use of the *ṭuppu* formula in the Khorsabad King-List is advocated, not only by Rowton, but also by Van der Meer, P.: *The Ancient Chronology of Western Asia and Egypt* (Leiden 1947, Brill), p. 10.

[2] 'To express "zero" (meaning in this case that the missing figure is included in the figure given for the preceding king), an Assyrian scribe would have had to use a phrase of some sort, for the simple reason that he did not possess a sign for "zero" (see Neugebauer, O.: *The Exact Sciences in Antiquity* (Princeton 1951, University Press), pp. 16, 20, and 29.'—Mr. M. B. Rowton, in a note for the writer of this Study.

[3] Mr. M. B. Rowton comments, in a letter of the 22nd January, 1952, to the writer of this Study: 'Apart from the purely mathematical improbability of the two missing reigns being *ṭuppu* reigns (the odds against are at least 60:8), there is also the genealogical factor. If these two reigns Nos. 65 and 66 are to be counted zero, then kings Nos. 61–71 reigned a total of only 79 years in six generations on the showing of Poebel's list in *J.N.E.S.*, vol. ii (1943), pp. 86 seqq. So far as I know, there is no similar instance in World History.'

improbability, Poebel's equation of the sum of the two lost entries with zero were to be accepted, one effect, as we shall see at later points in this note,[1] would be to synchronize chapters of Sumeric history and chapters of Egyptiac history which, in the light of our historical knowledge, would seem unlikely to have been contemporary with one another in truth. On these two grounds, Albright[2] had made an aggregate allowance of 20 years—which he afterwards extended to 22–27 years[3]—for the two missing figures, while Rowton had suggested[4] an aggregate allowance of 32 years, on the ground that 'the average for a reign in the Ancient Near East is 16 years'. Albright's original allowance would raise Poebel's dating for Šamši-Adad I's reign from 1726–1694 B.C. to 1746–1714 B.C.; Rowton's would raise it to 1758–1726 B.C.

Since Šamši-Adad is known to have exercised a 21 years' domination over Mari immediately before the reign of Zimri-Lim there, and since Zimri-Lim is known to have been overthrown by Hammurabi of Babylon in the thirty-second year of Zimri-Lim's reign and in the thirty-fifth year of Hammurabi's, it will be seen that our choice between the alternative datings for Šamši-Adad's reign on the basis of the Khorsabad List will condition our choice between the alternative datings for Hammurabi's reign and in consequence for the whole epoch of the First Dynasty of Babylon. At the same time this synchronism would not suffice, in itself, to enable us to date Hammurabi's reign in terms of years B.C. with precision, since it was vitiated by two still unknown quantities. There was the unknown numerical value of the combined length of the two Assyrian reigns Nos. 65 and 66, which was assessed at 20 or 22–27 years by Albright and at 32 years by Rowton, and there was an uncertainty—not yet cleared up by any evidence forthcoming in the Mari Archives—about the synchronization of Šamši-Adad's reign (he reigned for 33 years as King of Assyria, according to the Khorsabad List) with Zimri-Lim's reign and with Hammurabi's.

The Chronological Significance of Ammi-ṣaduga's Venus Observations

In view of the failure of even the combined testimony of the Khorsabad List and the Mari Archives to yield a precise dating for Hammurabi's reign in terms of years B.C., it was fortunate that the approximate dating which, between them, they did yield could be narrowed down to the choice of a particular set of years B.C. by bringing to bear a piece of independent evidence—in the shape of observations of the planet Venus, recorded by Hammurabi's fourth successor, Ammi-ṣaduga, on tablets reporting omens—which restricted the possible choice of datings for the reigns of the kings of the First Dynasty of Babylon to a limited number of sets of years B.C. If these Venus observations had been the only evidence forthcoming, they would have been of no avail for chronological purposes. Dr. Sidney Smith points out[5] that 'omens . . .

[1] See pp. 194 snd 204, below.
[2] See Albright, W. F.: 'A Third Revision', p. 30, and his review of Dr. Sidney Smith's *Alalakh and Chronology* in *A.J.A.*, vol. xlvii, p. 491.
[3] In a letter of the 20th November, 1951, to the writer of this Study.
[4] In a note for the writer of this Study.
[5] In *A.J.A.*, vol. xlix, No. 1, p. 19.

can only fix dates if on other grounds the reign of Ammi-ṣaduga can be limited to a period within a year or two of a possible astronomical solution of the date of observation'; and Sidney Smith's judgement on this astronomical point is endorsed by O. Neugebauer's,[1] who points out that 'the Ammi-ṣaduga observations . . . are not sufficient to decide by astronomical means between . . . at least five [chronological] possibilities [for the dating of Hammurabi's reign]'.[2] Neugebauer concludes that, while 'Astronomy requires for Hammurabi one of the years 1856, 1848, 1792, 1736 (and perhaps a few more dates in between, if we rearrange a little the choice of dates from the Venus tablets), . . . Archaeology and king-lists alone must suffice to date both the First Babylonian and the Twelfth Egyptian dynasties'.[3]

On Albright's and Rowton's view of the Khorsabad List of Kings of Assyria, this list, taken together with the Mari Archives, does provide—in spite of the uncertainty arising from the loss of the figures for reigns Nos. 65 and 66 and from the lack of evidence for an exact synchronization of Šamši-Adad's reign with Zimri-Lim's and with Hammurabi's—the independent historical evidence required for making use of the astronomical evidence provided by the Venus tablets; and these two scholars' approximate datings of Šamši-Adad's reign lead them, on the evidence of the Venus tablets, to take the astronomically admissible dating 1726–1684 B.C.[4] as the exact dating of Hammurabi's reign. Sidney Smith, who is sceptical about the possibility of extracting chronological evidence from the Khorsabad King-List but finds alternative independent evidence in the stratification of artifacts disinterred on North Syrian and Aegean sites, opts, on this basis, for the likewise astronomically admissible dating 1792–1750 B.C.,[5] which would imply the dating 1814–1782 B.C., at the latest,[6] for the reign of King Šamši-Adad I of Assyria according to Dossin's interpretation, in A.D. 1950, of the internal chronology of the Mari Age.

This dating for this king would imply, in turn, on an interpretation of the Khorsabad List in which *ṭuppīšu* is taken to mean 'zero', that the two Assyrian reigns Nos. 65 and 66, for which the figures are missing in the Khorsabad List, had lasted for 88 years in the aggregate. This is not an impossible figure for the combined length of the reigns of a father and a son. A higher figure is credibly recorded as the length of the single reign of the Egyptiac Emperor Pepi II.[7] At the same time a hypothetical figure 88 is of so different an order of magnitude from the known average figure of 32[8] years for the average length of a couple of reigns in the Ancient Near East that, while not impossible, it does

[1] See Neugebauer, O.: 'The Chronology of the Hammurabi Age', in *J.A.O.S.*, vol. lxi, pp. 58–61.

[2] Ibid., p. 59.

[3] Ibid., p. 61.

[4] See p. 172, above.

[5] See p. 172, above.

[6] Dr. Sidney Smith, in a letter of the 13th October, 1951, to the writer of this Study. In *A.J.A.*, vol. xlix, No. 1. (1945), p. 23, Dr. Smith suggests the slightly lower dating 1812/1811–1780/1779 B.C. for Šamši-Adad I's reign.

[7] Dr. Smith, in a letter of the 13th October, 1951, to the writer of this Study, suggests that 'the reign of Asshur-rabi I [king No. 65] must have been a very long one to account for short reigns before and short reigns after'. Van der Meer, in op. cit., p. 11, suggests that Asshur-rabi I's reign must have been important, considering the posthumous references to it.

[8] See p. 180, above.

seem highly improbable. This improbable figure does not, of course, exist for Dr. Sidney Smith himself, because he does not accept the interpretation of the Khorsabad List—equating *ṭuppīšu* with 'zero'—from which the figure arises; and in any case the improbability of the numerical value '88 years' is not a conclusive argument—any more than the improbability of Poebel's numerical value 'zero' for the pair of missing figures is—in favour of Albright's and Rowton's dating of Hammurabi (i.e. Dating (*c*)), considering that the numerical value '88', as well as the numerical value 'zero', is not impossible, however unlikely.

The Relative Certainty of the Dating of the Egyptiac 'Middle Empire'

If neither the Babylonian King Ammi-ṣaduga's Venus observations nor the Khorsabad List of Kings of Assyria provided conclusive evidence for passing judgement between Datings Nos. (*b*) and (*c*) for the First Dynasty of Babylon, the next recourse would be to see whether a decision between them could be reached on the basis of the chronology of Egyptiac history in the same age. The profitableness of this quest clearly depended on the answers to two questions. Was it possible to establish synchronisms between the chronology of South-West Asian history in this age and Egyptiac chronology? And, if this should prove to be possible, would it also be enlightening? In other words, was the chronology, in terms of years B.C., of Egyptiac history less in doubt—or, at any rate, less in dispute—in the sixth decade of the twentieth century of the Christian Era than the chronology of South-West Asian history was at the same date? It may be prudent to look into this second question first, since, if the answer to it were to prove to be in the negative, the first question would then be hardly worth examining.

In the Egyptian, as in the South-West Asian, field the astronomical evidence, in and by itself, appeared to be indecisive. For example, the astronomical statements in the Kahun papyri would equally well fit rival chronologies for the Twelfth Dynasty of Egypt which differed from one another by as much as one hundred years.[1] Moreover,

'The chronology of Egypt before the Eleventh Dynasty remains completely uncertain; Eduard Meyer's system for the early period has collapsed, and, with it, must go all attempt to be precise till there is more evidence.'[2]

'For dates of the Sixth Dynasty and all earlier periods, the margin of uncertainty has to be reckoned in centuries.'[3]

On the other hand, it looked in A.D. 1937 as if

'the approximate dates of the Twelfth Dynasty and later periods in Egyptian history have been established with a degree of probability which

[1] See Neugebauer, O.: 'The Chronology of the Hammurabi Age', in *J.A.O.S.*, vol. lxi, pp. 60–61, and Wood, L. H.: 'The Kahun Papyrus and the Date of the Twelfth Dynasty', in the *Bulletin of the American Schools of Oriental Research*, No. 99, October 1945, pp. 5–9.

[2] Smith, S., in *A.J.A.*, vol. xlix, No. 1, p. 24.

[3] Edgerton, W. F.: 'On the Chronology of the Early Eighteenth Dynasty (Amenhotep I to Thutmose III)', in the *American Journal of Semitic Languages and Literatures*, vol. liii, No. 3, April 1937, pp. 188–97. The sentence quoted will be found on p. 197.

comes very close to certainty, [even though] exact dates—not only months and days but exact years—must still be taken *cum grano salis*.'[1]

This last statement can be verified by comparing Edgerton's, Wood's, and Parker's[2] datings for reigns of Twelfth-Dynasty Egyptiac emperors. Amenemhat (Amenemmes) I's first regnal year is placed by Edgerton[3] somewhere between 1995 B.C. and 1970 B.C. and is tentatively equated by him with 1989 B.C., while it is reckoned by Wood to have begun on the 3rd January, 1991 B.C.[4] and is equated by Parker with the year 1991 B.C. approximately.[5] Senwosret (Sesostris) III's first regnal year is placed by Edgerton[6] somewhere between 1882 B.C. and 1870 B.C. and is tentatively equated by him with 1876 B.C., while it is reckoned by Wood to have begun on the 6th December, 1879 B.C.,[7] and is equated by Parker[8] with the year 1878 B.C. approximately. A layman could have some confidence in feeling that he would not be very far astray from the correct correlation of the internal chronology of the Twelfth Dynasty of Egypt with years B.C. if he followed Albright[9] in accepting both Wood's correlations and Edgerton's internal chronology, and in making the consequently necessary small adjustments of Edgerton's tentative table of dates in terms of years B.C., and if he then went on to follow Albright, Rowton, and Sidney Smith in taking Parker's subsequent conclusions as being virtually definitive.[10] It was also reassuring to observe that these three Egyptologists, in papers published in A.D. 1942 and A.D. 1945 and in a book published in A.D. 1950, were in substantial agreement, not only with one another, but also with Eduard Meyer. Edgerton dates the total period of the Twelfth Dynasty *circa* 1989–1776 B.C.; Wood (by implication from his figures for the first years of Amenemhat (Amenemmes) I and Senwosret (Sesostris) III) *circa* 1991–1778 B.C.; Parker 1991–1786 B.C.; Meyer *circa* 2000–1788 B.C.[11] The conspicuously exceptional survival of Meyer's chronology[12] in this instance suggested

[1] Edgerton, ibid., p. 197.

[2] See Parker, R. A.: *The Calendars of Ancient Egypt* (Chicago 1950, University of Chicago Press), p. 69.

[3] See Edgerton, W. F.: 'Chronology of the Twelfth Dynasty', in the *Journal of Near Eastern Studies*, vol. i (Chicago 1942, University of Chicago Press), pp. 306–314. See the table on p. 314.

[4] See Wood, ibid., p. 8.

[5] In op. cit., p. 69.

[6] See Edgerton, ibid., p. 314.

[7] In op. cit., p. 8.

[8] In op. cit., p. 69.

[9] See Albright in *B.A.S.O.R.*, No. 99, p. 13.

[10] 'Parker's *The Calendars of Ancient Egypt* . . . not only far surpasses Meyer and Borchardt, but also reconstructs the chronology of the Twelfth Dynasty very solidly' (Professor Albright, in a letter of the 20th November, 1951, to the writer of this Study). 'I agree that Parker's work has settled the chronology of the Twelfth Dynasty in Egypt beyond reasonable doubt' (Mr. Rowton, in a note for the writer of this Study). 'Parker . . . has, to my mind, settled this question' [of lunar datings in Egyptiac documents] (Dr. Sidney Smith, in a letter of the 13th October, 1951, to the writer of this Study). For a layman this emphatic consensus of the experts in favour of Parker's conclusions was as encouraging as it was impressive.

[11] See the present Study, I. i. 137 and V. vi. 192.

[12] Meyer's chronology for both the foundation of the Twelfth Dynasty and the previous political reunification of the whole Egyptiac World by the prince Mentuhotep of the Eleventh Dynasty who commemorated this achievement by taking the title of 'Sam Tawi', 'the Uniter of the Two Lands', had been retained virtually unaltered by H. E. Winlock in 'The Eleventh Egyptian Dynasty' (*Journal of Near Eastern Studies*, vol. ii, No. 4, October 1943 (Chicago 1943, University of Chicago Press), pp. 249–83). In this paper, Winlock, like Meyer, equates Amenemhat I's first regnal year with 2000 B.C. (p. 283); he reckons that Mentuhotep 'Sam Tawi's' reunification of the Egyptiac World

to a layman's mind in A.D. 1952 that the evidence at the disposal of the Modern Western science of Egyptology for the dating of the Twelfth Dynasty in terms of years B.C. must have been more or less adequate since as far back as the beginning of the twentieth century of the Christian Era; and in this light it did not seem over-sanguine to take Parker's dating of the Twelfth Dynasty in terms of years B.C. as a more or less assured chronological landmark, and to go on to conclude that the chronology of all the subsequent chapters of Egyptiac history was likewise fairly well established in its main outlines—whatever doubts might still remain about the location and duration of some individual reigns or about the relations of certain reigns (especially Thothmes II's, Hatshepsut's, and Thothmes III's) to one another.

The Picture Presented by the Mari Archives and by Babylonian Documents dating from the Reign of Hammurabi

We may now look at the picture of South-West Asia as this presents itself to us in the Mari Archives, in Babylonian documents produced by, or during the reign of, Hammurabi, and in such other contemporary information about this chapter of South-West Asian history as had been disinterred by the middle of the twentieth century of the Christian Era. When we have seen what this picture is, we may be able to make out how the Age of Hammurabi and its sequel, the remaining 155 years of the life of the First Dynasty of Babylon from the first regnal year of Hammurabi's immediate successor Samsu-iluna down to the year in which his last successor Samsu-ditana was overthrown by the Hittite war-lord Muršiliš I, can or cannot be made to fit in with the apparently more or less secure framework of Egyptiac chronology in and after the Age of the Twelfth Dynasty of Egypt.

The picture of South-West Asia in the Age of Hammurabi is a clear one. At the opening of this age at the date, twenty-seven years before that of Hammurabi's accession, at which the Mari Archives begin, South-West Asia is still partitioned among successor-states of a universal state—'the Empire of Sumer and Akkad', *alias* 'the Empire of the Four Quarters'—which had been founded by Ur Nammu (formerly transliterated as Ur-Engur) of Ur and had broken up after the overthrow of Ur Nammu's fourth successor, Ibbi-Sin (Ibi-Sin), by Elamite rebels.[1] At the opening of the present chapter there are nine Great Powers in

was within sight of completion in 2061 B.C. (p. 266); and he dates this prince's total reign 2070–2019 B.C. (p. 261). In a later work, however, *The Rise and Fall of the Middle Kingdom in Thebes* (New York 1947, Macmillan), Winlock adopts Wood's chronology (see pp. 8–9, together with the chronological table on p. 2). In this work, Winlock dates Mentuhotep 'Sam Tawi's' accession 2061 B.C.; his reunification of the Egyptiac World 2052 B.C.; and his death 2010 B.C. Thus, in A.D. 1952, there appeared to be a consensus among Egyptologists in favour of a chronology for the Eleventh and Twelfth Dynasties of Egypt that put the initial dates nine years lower than they had been put by Eduard Meyer. The terminal date for the Twelfth Dynasty was, nevertheless, placed by R. A. Parker only two years lower than it had been placed by Eduard Meyer (i.e. was placed by Parker in 1886 B.C. instead of in 1888 B.C.), since Parker emended the Turin Papyrus's figure 213 years for the total span of the Twelfth Dynasty to the figure 223, and thus arrived at the figure 206 years for the net total span—reckoning that 17 regnal years out of the aggregate 223 were years in which two reigns were overlapping, in consequence of the Twelfth Dynasty's institution of co-regencies (see Parker, op. cit., pp. 68–69).

[1] See V. vi. 297.

the South-West Asian arena—Elam, Larsa, Eshnunna (in North-Eastern Shinar), Assyria, Isin (in Central Shinar), Babylon, Mari (on the Middle Euphrates, extending north-westward as far as the valley of the River Balikh), Carchemish (on the west bank of the westward elbow of the Euphrates), and Aleppo (alias Yamkhad)[1]—together with a number of lesser states for whose allegiance the Great Powers are in competition.[2] The Sumeric Great Powers of the day are concerned, not with any external threats to the Sumeric Society as a whole, either from a neighbouring civilization or from barbarians, but with a domestic rivalry with one another. The competition between them is intense; and the period culminates in a successful attempt to reintegrate Ur-Nammu's 'Empire of the Four Quarters' through the annihilation of all but one of the parochial Powers by a single victorious survivor which thereby attains to universal dominion.

This political reunification of the Sumeric World by force of arms, which is the work of the Amorite King Hammurabi of Babylon, is preceded by an abortive bout of aggression on a smaller scale in which the would-be empire-builders are the Amorite King Šamši-Adad I of Assyria (king No. 39 in the Khorsabad List) and his sons Išme-Dagan (No. 40) and Yasmakh-Adad.[3] They manage to dominate Mari for twenty-one years (the tenth to the thirtieth year inclusive of the years covered by the Mari Archives); and, on one interpretation of one piece of evidence, Eshnunna, too, is temporarily under their rule.[4] These Amorite war-lords' imperialism is frustrated by the reinstatement, at Mari, of the previous local dynasty in the person of King Zimri-Lim; but, after an Amorite ruler of Assyria has thus failed, an Amorite ruler of Babylon is subsequently successful in achieving wider ambitions. As early as the seventh and eighth years of his reign, King Hammurabi of Babylon has already conquered and annexed Isin;[5] and now, after having bided his time for twenty-two years, he proceeds to establish control over most of his other rivals in a series of nine successive annual campaigns, waged from his thirtieth to his thirty-eighth year inclusive.[6] Assyria (whose power it takes him two campaigns to bend), Larsa, Mari, and Eshnunna—in fact, all the surviving Powers in the South-West Asian arena except Aleppo (Yamkhad) in the extreme

[1] See Böhl, op. cit., pp. 346 and 353.

[2] See the letter, quoted by Böhl, ibid., pp. 352–3, and by Sidney Smith in *Alalakh*, p. 11, addressed to King Zimri-Lim of Mari by one of his subjects. This letter enumerates five Powers besides Mari—namely Babylon, Larsa, Eshnunna, Yamkhad (i.e. Aleppo), and Qatana. It explicitly makes the two points that each of these Powers has a number of satellites and that, among the Great Powers themselves, there is a Balance of Power which fluctuates in accordance with the success or failure of each Power in a perennial competition for winning the lesser states' allegiance.

[3] See Böhl, ibid., p. 346. King Šamši-Adad I of Assyria was, not an Assyrian, but, like Hammurabi, an Amorite (see Dossin G.: 'Šamši-Addu Ier, Roi d'Assyrie', in *Académie Royale de la Belgique: Bulletin de la Classe des Lettres*, 5e Série, tome xxxiv, p. 60).

[4] Professor Goetze comments: 'The opinion that Eshnunna was dominated by Šamši-Adad is based on the date found on tablets from Ashjaly which say "Year in which Šamši-Adad died." The argument is invalid, since in the same region whole series of dates commemorating the deaths of potentates have come to light. . . . One can only assume that it was a custom at this period to mention the passing of the ruler in a neighbouring state in a date formula.'

[5] See Böhl, ibid., p. 353.

[6] See ibid. pp. 346 and 353–4.

North-West[1] and Elam in the extreme South-East—fall under the control of Babylon within these nine years. Hammurabi rounds off these victories over other Sumeric Powers by subjugating Gutium,[2] the strategically vital section of the western mountain rim of the Iranian Plateau through which, between Elam to the south of it and Assyria to the north of it, runs the road (skirting the rock of Behistan) up which a conqueror from the Tigris-Euphrates Basin pushes his way eastward on to the plateau, and down which a barbarian perched on the plateau descends westward upon the lowlands.[3]

The Nemesis of Hammurabi's Imperialism

For a student of History, Hammurabi's feat of getting the better of four rival Powers within nine years is reminiscent of Ts'in She Hwang-ti's feat of overthrowing six rival Powers within ten years, while Hammurabi's inordinate sacrifice of blood and treasure on the altar of the archaistic ideal of re-establishing a universal state that has long since been in abeyance is reminiscent of the costly campaigns in North-West Africa, Italy, and the Iberian Peninsula that Justinian conducted in pursuit of the objective of recovering for the Roman Empire the outlying western provinces that had been lost by this Hellenic universal state after the death of Theodosius I. In view of the nemesis which overtook both Justinian's and Ts'in She Hwang-ti's achievement within a few years of the baneful world-conqueror's death, it is not surprising to see the same nemesis overtake the same perverse *tour de force* when Hammurabi is the hero—or villain—of the piece.

In fact, Hammurabi's, like Justinian's and Ts'in She Hwang-ti's, immediate successor reaped the whirlwind.

> 'These conquests did not last longer than half [*sic*] a dozen years: the last four years of Hammurabi himself and the first eight years of his successor Samsu-iluna.'[4]

The superficially reintegrated 'Empire of Sumer and Akkad' was disrupted from within, during Samsu-iluna's reign, by the secession of a 'Kingdom of the Sealand';[5] and

> 'the date-formula for the ninth year of Samsu-iluna, "Year that the Kassite Army . . . ," even in the abbreviated form which is all that is recorded, shows that a Kassite invasion, the only one mentioned in any document,[6] took place in Samsu-iluna's eighth year.'[7]

In invading Gutium without pushing on to a natural frontier, Hammurabi of Babylon had committed the same military and political error as his predecessor Naramsin of Akkad.[8] He had given the highland

[1] Mr. D. J. Wiseman, of the Department of Assyrian and Egyptian Antiquities in the British Museum, points out the importance of Yamkhad in the South-West Asia of this age as the Warden of 'the Fertile Crescent's' north-western marches against the barbarians from the Anatolian highlands.

[2] See Böhl, op. cit., p. 355.

[3] For this road, see VI. vii. 205–6 and 210, n. 3.

[4] Böhl, ibid., p. 354. Cp. pp. 346–7.

[5] See Smith, S.: *Alalakh*, pp. 18–19.

[6] Professor Albrecht Goetze notes: 'A Kassite invasion is also mentioned in the formula of the fourth year of Samsu-iluna's son Abi-ešuh; see now *J.C.S.*, vol. v (1951), p. 99.'

[7] Smith, op. cit., p. 24.

[8] See I. i. 109.

barbarians provocation without subjugating them effectively, and the sequel in both cases was a barbarian avalanche.[1] In the second millennium B.C. the Kassite barbarian highlanders reacted as the Gutaean barbarian highlanders had reacted in the third millennium. The Kassites were the beneficiaries of Hammurabi's work in Shinar, as the Lombards were of Justinian's work in Italy; and, when, after a social interregnum, the curtain rises in the fifteenth century B.C. on a nascent Babylonic World, we find the whole of Babylonia under Kassite domination.[2] Nor are these Kassite residuary legatees of Hammurabi's empire in its metropolitan provinces the only barbarians who have profited from the collapse precipitated by Hammurabi's excessive expenditure of a moribund Sumeric Society's remaining stock of energy. The Kassite successor-state of a momentarily restored Empire of Sumer and Akkad in Babylonia marches in the fifteenth century with a Mitannian successor-state in Mesopotamia, with its centre in the basin of the River Khabur; and, though Hammurabi's victim Assyria, unlike Hammurabi's own imperial Babylon, has succeeded in keeping herself free from direct barbarian rule, the fifteenth century finds Assyria standing at bay, almost encircled by Mitannian territory and perhaps at times compelled to acknowledge Mitanni's overlordship.[3]

An Egyptiac Chronological Framework for the 210 Years of South-West Asian History Running from the Earliest of the Letters in the Diplomatic Correspondence of King Šamši-Adad I of Assyria down to the Hittite War-Lord Muršiliš I's Raid on Babylon

We now have to examine how the more or less well-established framework of Egyptiac chronology will accommodate a phase of South-West Asian history covering, in the aggregate, a span of about 210 years, made up of the last 12 years covered by the Mari Archives before Hammurabi's first regnal year,[4] the 43 years of Hammurabi's reign, and the 155 years, ending in the year of Muršiliš's sack of Babylon, during which the First Dynasty of Babylon lingered on after Hammurabi's death. In order to fit into our approximately established correlation of Egyptiac chronology with years B.C., any correlation of these 210 years of South-West Asian history with years B.C. has to fulfil four conditions. The initial date (i.e. the date at which Šamši-Adad I's diplomatic

[1] Mr. M. B. Rowton comments: 'The military forces capable of defending [the Lower Tigris-Euphrates Basin] against the barbarians were the national armies of the major city-states. Hammurabi destroyed as many of these as he destroyed city-states. In place of them he had only his own troops to oppose the barbarians, and unavoidably these came to be over-extended. In the conquered territories a good part of the male population would have gone into slavery, and, among the remainder, bitterness would be too great, for at least a generation, to make it feasible for the Babylonian Government to take the risk of enlisting them on any large scale in its own forces.'

[2] See I. i. 116.

[3] See Götze (Goetze), A.: *Hethiter, Churriter und Assyrer* (Leipzig 1936, Harrassowitz), pp. 98–99 and 116–17.

[4] The Mari Archives extend backwards in time over the twenty-seven years preceding Hammurabi's first regnal year, but the particular correspondence in these archives that has a bearing on the current state of relations between the Sumeric World and the Egyptiac World is the diplomatic correspondence of King Šamši-Adad I of Assyria, and, while this appears to extend over at least the last ten years before Hammurabi's accession, there seems to be no warrant for supposing that any of the extant documents in this series date from much farther back than that.

correspondence begins) must be later than the latest date of the Twelfth Dynasty of Egypt's effective ascendancy over Syria; the terminal date (i.e. the date of Muršiliš I's sack of Babylon) must be earlier than the earliest date of the Eighteenth Dynasty of Egypt's continuous effective ascendancy over Syria; the date of this Hittite King Muršiliš I's reign must be sufficiently earlier than the date of Muršiliš I's eventual successor Suppiluliuma's Egyptiac contemporary Ikhnaton's reign to allow the necessary time for the series of known events in Hittite history between Muršiliš I's time and Suppiluliuma's; and the date of Hammurabi's death must be earlier than the date of the arrival of a Hyksos barbarian war-band at the north-eastern corner of the Nile Delta, if the Hyksos were by then already equipped with horse-drawn chariots. The grounds for postulating these conditions must be explained and justified before the conditions can be used as criteria for trying to judge between the four rival datings of the First Dynasty of Babylon that were in the arena in A.D. 1952.

The Twelfth Dynasty's Ascendancy over Syria and the Dating of Šamši-Adad I's Diplomatic Correspondence

Most scholars who had studied the Mari Archives down to A.D. 1952 seemed to have been struck by the absence in them of references to Egypt, and to have taken the view that in this case an *argumentum ex silentio* was a legitimate inference.[1] Considering that cuneiform tablets, discovered in the Balikh Valley and dating from the period of Šamši-Adad's ascendancy over Mari, testified that the domain of this principality in this chapter of its history had come as close to Syria as this,[2] the date at which Šamši-Adad I's diplomatic correspondence begins—and, *a fortiori*, the date at which this King of Assyria, who was master of Mari from the tenth to the thirtieth of the sixty-two years that the Archives cover, marched across Syria to the Mediterranean[3]—must, it might seem, have been later than the latest date at which the Twelfth Dynasty of Egypt's ascendancy over Syria had still been effective.

[1] See, for example, W. F. Albright, 'New Light', in *B.A.S.O.R.*, No. 77, pp. 27 and 31, and O. Neugebauer in *J.A.O.S.*, vol. lxi, p. 58. This negative testimony of the Mari Archives appeared to be supported by the positive evidence of Archaeology.

'Si Hammourabi avait été un contemporain des premiers pharaons de la xiie dynastie, comment les Sésostris et Amenémhat qui avaient envoyé des cadeaux diplomatiques à Ugarit, à Qatna et même plus loin au Nord, en Asie Mineure, auraient-ils pu ignorer des centres de culture et de politique aussi importants que ceux de Babylone et de Mari? Comment expliquer aussi que ces centres, qui selon les textes de Mari avaient acheté des produits originaires de pays aussi éloignés que la Crète, soient restés dans l'ignorance de la grande culture de la vallée du Nil au temps du Moyen Empire? Enfin, comment expliquer qu'à l'occasion de l'importation des produits égéens à Mari et en Babylonie par l'intermédiaire d'Ugarit alors saturée d'influences égyptiennes, aucun monument égyptien du Moyen Empire ne soit parvenu dans ces pays, alors qu'ils y furent importés du temps du Nouvel Empire?'—Schaeffer, C.F.A.: *Stratigraphie Comparée et Chronologie de l'Asie Occidentale (iiie et iie millénaires)* (London 1948, Oxford University Press), p. 29.

[2] This piece of information was given to the writer by Mr. M. B. Rowton on the 6th October, 1952.

[3] See Smith, S.: *Alalakh*, pp. 12 and 15. 'The peak of Šamši-Adad's power, evidenced by his raid to the Mediterranean, will probably have been reached toward the end of his reign.'—Professor Albrecht Goetze, in a note enclosed with a letter of the 13th November, 1951, to the writer of this Study.

This conclusion was rejected by Professor Goetze:

'The argument that Egypt ought to be mentioned in the Mari documents [if these are contemporary with the Twelfth Dynasty] does not impress me. If the fact [that Egypt is not mentioned in them] is to be acknowledged, it simply confirms [the evidence indicating] the limitations of Egyptian power, which falls short of the expectations of many among us. I personally feel that not even Sesostris (Senwosret) III exercised political power in Syria, and that his influence on towns like Ugarit was merely diplomatic and cultural. . . . The deductions made by Sidney Smith, *Alalakh*, pp. 13 ff., from certain Egyptianizing seals are completely unconvincing. There is no evidence which would show to my satisfaction that any pharaoh of the Twelfth Dynasty ruled over Alalakh or Yamkhad/Aleppo. . . . My scepticism concerning the Twelfth Dynasty has steadily mounted.'[1]

Professor Goetze pointed out that Wilson[2] took the view that the Twelfth Dynasty of Egypt had gained its influence in Syria, not by military conquest, but by 'peaceful penetration', and that Wilson was not alone in holding that opinion.[3] This account of the nature of the Twelfth Dynasty's standing in Syria was, however, contested by Professor Albright.[4]

'Goetze, as you know, places the reign of Z mri-Lim (the Mari period proper) roughly about 1850–1820 B.C. This cannot be squared with the Theban Empire of Senwosret (Sesostris) III and Amenemhat (Amenemmes) III. It is true that some scholars want to depress the estimates held by many of us with respect to Egyptian power and prestige during this period, insisting that there was no real empire. They forget that (except for the Execration Texts and a few other items) our knowledge of the Theban imperial domination of Nubia comes chiefly from discoveries in Nubia and the region of the First Cataract. Similarly our knowledge of the Egyptian empire in Asia will have to come from excavations in Palestine and Syria. Very few strata of this period have actually been uncovered, but, where they have been reached, Egyptian objects invariably turn up. This is true of Gezer, Megiddo, &c., in Palestine, and also of Byblos, Qatna, and Ugarit in [Northern] Syria. As the Posener Execration Texts prove (and you mention),[5] the northern limit of Egyptian suzerainty (however desultory the defence of this line may have been) ran approximately along the Eleutherus Valley inland, dipping south to pass around the northern border of the territory of Damascus. Even in the time of the Thirteenth Dynasty there was still some semblance of unity under the first kings and under the kings from Sebek-hotep II to Sebek-hotep IV, including especially Nefer-hotep, who was still nominal overlord of Byblos about 1740–1730 B.C.[6] In fact there were only a few years before about 1720 B.C. in which Egypt was actually in a state of anarchy and from which no monuments are preserved. This was a flourishing period in literature,

[1] Remarks enclosed with a letter of the 13th November, 1951, from Professor Goetze to the writer of this Study.

[2] In *The Burden of Egypt*, p. 134.

[3] 'Similar views have recently been expressed by A. Scharff in Scharff, A., and Moortgat, A.: *Äegypten und Vorderasien im Altertum* (Munich 1950, Bruckmann), pp. 106 ff., and by R. Dussaud in *L'Art Phénicien du IIe Millénaire* (Paris 1949, Geuthner), pp. 25 ff.' —Professor Goetze, ibid.

[4] In a letter of the 20th November, 1951, to the writer of this Study.

[5] See p. 191 below.—A.J.T.

[6] See Albright, W. F.: 'An Indirect Synchronism between Egypt and Mesopotamia *circa* 1730 B.C.,' in *B.A.S.O.R.*, No. 99 (1945), pp. 9–18.—A.J.T.

and the art of the period was not entirely negligible. Certainly Egyptian wares were still being exported (e.g., scarabs). If we follow Sidney Smith's chronology[1] and date the Mari period proper about 1790–1760 B.C., we shall find ourselves in the last decade or so of the Twelfth Dynasty and the first generation of the Thirteenth. It is incredible that Egypt should not be mentioned and that Egyptian objects should not be found in Mari during this period (when Egyptian influence was so strong at Byblos, just before and after the end of the Twelfth Dynasty). The Mari records mention Ugarit and Qatna often, Byblos and Hazor in Galilee less often, Cyprus and Crete frequently; they would simply have to mention Egypt unless this period was precisely the generation when Egyptian influence had been reduced to zero by the nomadic Semites who had seized power in the Delta and Lower Egypt generally (no monuments of the later kings of the Thirteenth Dynasty appear north of Upper Egypt).'

It will be seen that the advocates of Dating (*c*) and of Dating (*a*) differ *in toto* in their respective estimates of the degree of an Egyptiac 'Middle Empire's' visibility above the horizon of a Power bestriding the Middle Euphrates as far north-westwards as the valley of its tributary the Balikh. Whereas Goetze estimates that 'the Middle Empire's' presence in Syria might have been ignored at Mari even at the height of the Twelfth Dynasty's power, Albright estimates that it could never have been ignored till a stage in the decline and fall of the Twelfth Dynasty's epigoni which was not reached till more than a hundred years after the date of Senwosret (Sesostris) III's death. Böhl, for his part, apparently cannot satisfy himself that Egypt could have been ignored at Mari before the arrival of the Hyksos barbarian invaders of Egypt at the north-east corner of the Nile Delta;[2] and this seems to be one of his grounds for his dating of Hammurabi's reign as late as 1704–1662 B.C. (i.e. for his adoption of Dating (*d*)).

Böhl's post-Hyksos dating of the Mari Archives is a *reductio ad absurdum* if, as is argued below, there are other considerations that might indicate that the Hyksos could hardly have made their first lodgement in the Delta while Hammurabi was still alive.[3] Moreover, even Dating (*d*) would not have the effect of making Šamši-Adad's diplomatic correspondence posterior to the establishment of the Hyksos in the Delta unless we accepted, for this event in Egyptiac history, the earliest of several alternative datings for it that range over a Time-span of more than fifty years (between *circa* 1730 and *circa* 1675 B.C.).[4] An amateur observer of this chronological controversy might feel inclined to reject both the two extremes represented by Böhl's and Goetze's respective theses; and he would also notice that the one point on which there seemed to be some agreement among otherwise dissentient experts was a prevalent impression that the decline in 'the Middle Empire's' standing in Syria had been a gradual process. At what stage in the process had the decline reached a degree at which it would be credible that, in the diplomatic correspondence of a Power astride the

[1] i.e. Dating (*b*). This argument of Professor Albright's would, of course, militate, *a fortiori*, against Dating (*a*), which Professor Goetze advocates.—A.J.T.
[2] See Böhl, op. cit., pp. 348 and 352.
[3] See p. 198, below.
[4] See p. 197, below

Middle Euphrates, the Egyptian factor in international affairs would make no mark? In A.D. 1952 most of the experts seemed to agree that 'the Middle Empire's' standing in Syria (whatever its precise status there may have been) was already past its zenith at least as early as the morrow of Amenemhat (Amenemmes) III's death *circa* 1797 B.C. but was still at its height down to the date of Senwosret (Sesostris) III's death *circa* 1843 B.C. The open question, on which there was as yet no consensus, was that of the political situation in Syria during the reign of Amenemhat (Amenemmes) III (*imperabat circa* 1842–1797 B.C.).

At its apogee, the ascendancy of the Egyptiac Middle Empire had extended over the North Syrian principalities of Byblos on the coast, Alalakh on the Orontes, and Yamkhad between the elbows of the Orontes and the Euphrates, as was attested by the evidence of the disinterred monuments.[1] Before the end of Amenemhat (Amenemmes) III's reign, however, Byblos—and therefore presumably *a fortiori* the interior of North Syria—had become independent.[2] On the other hand the effective maintenance of Egyptian rule over South and Middle Syria during at least the earlier years of Amenemhat (Amenemmes) III's forty-nine-years-long reign seemed to be attested by lists of place-names and personal names inscribed on figurines, preserved at Brussels, which Albright dates in the third quarter of the nineteenth century B.C.; for the place-names here mentioned cover Western Palestine and Phoenicia as far north as the River Eleutherus (*Arabicè* Nahr-al-Kabīr) —i.e. farther north than Byblos—on the coast, and Northern Gilead, the Hawrān and Damascus in the interior, while in the Baqā' they extend as far north as Rās Ba'lbak, forty miles south of Homs.[3] Sidney Smith concedes[4] that 'the recession of Egyptian power was slow. The monuments at Rās ash-Shamrah imply [Egyptian] control of Ugarit in the time of Amenemhat III. There is no valid ground for believing that Egyptian weakness began till the dynastic troubles set in after his death, and Egypt's footing in Asia was not completely lost till about twenty years after the death of Nefer-hotep.' He comes to the conclusion that 'the domination of the Twelfth Dynasty of Egypt in Syria ceased some time in the reign of Amenemhat III'.[5] Goetze, however, while admitting, in deference to the *argumentum a silentio*, that the initial date of the Mari Archives must be later than the end of the reign of Senwosret (Sesostris) III, maintains[6] that the absence in them of any reference to the Egyptiac World is compatible with a dating of them that would place their beginning as early as the beginning of Amenemhat (Amenemmes) III's reign.

In face of this disagreement among the experts, the most prudent course in A.D. 1952 for a layman was to assume provisionally that the

[1] See Smith, S.: *Alalakh*, pp. 13–15.

[2] See Albright, F. W.: 'The Land of Damascus between 1850 and 1750 B.C.', in *B.A.S.O.R.*, No. 83 (New Haven, October 1941), p. 32; *eundem*: 'An Indirect Synchronism between Egypt and Mesopotamia *circa* 1730 B.C.', ibid., No. 99, October 1945, p. 17, n. 52.

[3] See Albright, in *B.A.S.O.R.*, No. 83, pp. 32–33.

[4] In a letter of the 13th October, 1951, to the writer of this Study.

[5] *Alalakh*, p. 29.

[6] In the paper read by him before the American Oriental Society at Cincinnati at Easter time, 1950.

most probable approximate upper limit for the dating of our problematical 210 years of South-West Asian history was the mid-point of Amenemhat (Amenemmes) III's reign *circa* 1820–1819 B.C., while recognizing that, alternatively, this upper limit might be as high as 1842 B.C. or as low as 1797 B.C. This would make 1792–1750 B.C. (Dating (*b*)) the highest probable of the several astronomically possible datings for the reign of Hammurabi, since, on this dating, the earliest letters in Šamši-Adad's diplomatic correspondence would be dated *circa* 1804 B.C.; and 1595 B.C. would then be the date of Muršiliš I's raid on Babylon, though, as far as the Twelfth-Dynasty Egyptiac evidence went, these dates might be either as high as 1842 B.C. for the beginning of Šamši-Adad's correspondence, 1830–1788 B.C. for Hammurabi's reign, and 1623 B.C. for the raid on Babylon, or as low as 1797 B.C., 1785–1743 B.C. and 1588 B.C., if we were to agree that the moment at which Egypt disappeared from view below Mari's diplomatic horizon might have been at any point in Amenemhat (Amenemmes) III's forty-six-years-long reign (*circa* 1842–1797 B.C.).

It will be seen that, even if we were to admit the feasibility of dating Šamši-Adad's correspondence at the very opening of Amenemhat III's reign, this would still rule out Dating (*a*), whereas we could set the date of Šamši-Adad's correspondence as late as a median point in Amenemhat III's reign without thereby ruling out Dating (*b*). On the other hand, if we were to hold that Šamši-Adad's correspondence, in which Egypt is ignored, could not have begun till after Amenemhat III's death, this judgement would rule out Dating (*b*) as well as Dating (*a*), as was pointed out by Rowton.[1]

'The highest theoretical limit is, as you say, 1842 B.C., since Amenemhat III is attested at Ras ash-Shamrah. Goetze's chronology would place the accession of Hammurabi *circa* 1850 B.C. and the end of Egyptian domination in Syria not later than 1860 B.C. Smith's chronology yields *circa* 1805 B.C. for the latter event, and therefore comes within the limits, as you point out. But it requires the postulate that the Egyptian domination in Syria ended during the reign of the powerful Amenemhat III (cp. *Alalakh*, p. 29). There is no evidence for this, and it certainly cannot be regarded as *a priori* probable. The fact that at Ras ash-Shamrah the monuments of Amenemhat III (and others) were deliberately damaged shows that his domination there was resented and was therefore very real.'

If Dating (*b*), as well as Dating (*a*), was held, on these grounds, to be inadmissible, Dating (*c*), by contrast, would be compatible with the longest estimate of the duration of 'the Middle Empire's' influence in Syria; for, according to Dating (*c*), Šamši-Adad's correspondence would not have started before *circa* 1740 B.C., i.e. about half a century after Amenemhat III's death.

The Eighteenth Dynasty's Ascendancy over Syria and the Dating of Muršiliš I's Raid on Babylon

How early was the Eighteenth Dynasty's ascendancy over Syria effectively established? A dominion extending to the Euphrates is

[1] In a note enclosed with a letter of the 20th November, 1951, to the writer of this Study.

claimed by Thothmes (Tuthmosis) I in an inscription dated in the second year of his reign; and, since he does not expressly claim to have won this dominion for himself, it is possible that he may have inherited it from one of his predecessors. While it is held to be improbable that any permanent lodgement in Asia, any farther north than Palestine, had been made by the cautious founder of the Eighteenth Dynasty, Amosis, there is no evidence to disprove, though there is also none to prove, that the ascendancy over the whole of Syria up to the Euphrates, which Thothmes I claims to be exercising, was achieved by Amosis' immediate successor and Thothmes I's immediate predecessor Amenhotep (Amenophis) I.[1] If we take Thothmes I's claim at its face value, and if we adopt Wilson's datings of these reigns[2] (and his datings were among the lowest estimates current at the time of writing), we can take it as certain that Muršiliš I's raid on Babylon cannot have been later than Thothmes I's accession in 1525 B.C., and possible that it was not later than some date in the reign of Amenhotep I, who, according to Wilson, was on the throne from 1545 to 1525 B.C. Muršiliš I's sack of Babylon cannot have occurred after the establishment of a continuous effective ascendancy over the north of Syria by the Eighteenth Dynasty of Egypt, since, in this dynasty's records, there is no mention of that historic Hittite campaign and indeed no mention of Muršiliš I at all; and, considering that Muršiliš I not only sacked Babylon but claims to have overthrown the Kingdom of Aleppo,[3]

'it is incredible that . . . when Egypt was in nominal control of Syria as far as the Euphrates . . . the Egyptian inscriptions should fail to mention the Hittites at a time when, under Muršiliš I, the latter had conquered Syria and Western Mesopotamia.'[4]

This would mean that, if Thothmes (Tuthmosis) I did in truth exercise even a nominal control over Syria as far as the Euphrates, the lowest correlation of our 210 years of Sumeric history with years B.C. that our Eighteenth Dynasty Egyptiac chronological framework would allow would be 1733–1524 B.C. (i.e. the 210 years immediately preceding Thothmes I's second regnal year according to Wilson's reckoning). It would also mean that, as far as the evidence of Egyptiac history went, we should not be entirely sure of our ground unless we dated our 210 years of South-West Asian history as high as 1755–1546 B.C. (i.e. the 210 years immediately preceding the accession of Amenhotep (Amenemmes) I, according to Wilson's reckoning).

There seemed, however, to be no warrant for taking Thothmes (Tuthmosis) I's claim seriously enough to venture to use it confidently as evidence for chronological purposes. The only piece of corroborative evidence known to Western scholars in A.D. 1952 was Thothmes (Tuthmosis) III's statement, in his record of the campaign in the thirty-third year of his own reign in which he reached the westward elbow of

[1] See the discussion of this point in Drioton, E., and Vandier, J.: *L'Égypte* (Paris 1946, Presses Universitaires de France), p. 381.

[2] See Wilson, J. A.: *The Burden of Egypt* (Chicago 1951, University of Chicago Press), p. vii.

[3] See Smith, S.: *Alalakh*, pp. 12–13.

[4] Albright, W. F., in *A.J.A.*, vol. xlvii, p. 492.

the Euphrates and made a raid across the river, that he set up a stele on the west bank side by side with a stele of Thothmes I's which he found standing there. This testimony of Thothmes III's would prove that Thothmes I, or one of his lieutenants, had once penetrated thus far into Asia and had staked out a boundary for the Egyptian Empire at the 'natural frontier' provided by the course of the Euphrates where it approaches nearest to the shore of the Mediterranean. But this would be no evidence that either Thothmes I himself or any successor of his before Thothmes III had ever held this line effectively or continuously. Indeed, the systematic conquest of Syria which Thothmes III carried out by stages over a total period of twelve years, running from the twenty-second to the thirty-third year of his reign, is presumptive evidence that Syria was not under effective Egyptian control during at any rate the immediately preceding chapter of history, when the Empress Hatshepsut was in power; and, on this showing, while we need not doubt that the Euphrates had once been reached by an expeditionary force led or sent by Thothmes I, we cannot be sure that North Syria, up to the line of the Euphrates, had ever been effectively occupied or continuously held by the New Empire of Egypt at any date before the thirty-third year of the reign of Thothmes III. Since Wilson dates Thothmes III's reign 1490–1436 B.C., this means that the evidence of Egyptiac history does not unequivocally preclude our dating our 210 years of South-Western Asian history as low as 1668–1458 B.C. (i.e. the 210 years immediately preceding the thirty-third year of the reign of Thothmes III).

It will be seen that the ascendancy of the Eighteenth Dynasty of Egypt over Syria fails to provide us with a decisive chronological criterion for the dating of our 210 years of South-West Asian history because the facts about this episode of Egyptiac history that had been brought to light by Western scholars were, down to A.D. 1952, still so fragmentary that there was at that time a margin of no less than eighty-seven years between the earliest (1546 B.C.) and the latest (1459 B.C.) theoretically possible datings for the latest year B.C. in which Muršiliš I's raid on Babylon might fall without conflicting with Egyptiac chronological data. If the Eighteenth Dynasty's ascendancy over Syria up to the Euphrates was the work of Amenhotep I at the beginning of his reign *circa* 1545 B.C., this would rule out the two Datings (*d*) and (*c*) of the four rival datings of South-West Asian history, which date Muršiliš I's raid 1507 B.C. and 1531/30 B.C. respectively, but would not be incompatible with either Dating (*b*), which dates the raid 1595 B.C., or, *a fortiori*, with Dating (*a*), which dates it 1651 B.C. If, on the other hand, the Eighteenth Dynasty's dominion in Syria had been extended up to the Euphrates only just before the second year of Thothmes I's reign *circa* 1523 B.C., this would still rule out Dating (*d*), but would now just allow of Dating (*c*), and would, indeed, provide some presumptive evidence in favour of Dating (*c*) by suggesting that there might have been a relation of cause and effect between these two closely consecutive events; for, if the date of Muršiliš I's raid did immediately precede the date of the extension of the Eighteenth Dynasty's dominion up to the

Euphrates, it would be a plausible conjecture that *post hoc* signified *propter hoc* in this case. The Hittite raid on Babylon via Aleppo would have been the event that stimulated the Imperial Government at Thebes (so we might reconstruct the story) to push its frontier forward from some point in Palestine to a 'natural frontier', along the western elbow of the Euphrates, where the Theban Power would be in a position to prevent any repetition of the Hittite Power's alarming performance.[1]

Moreover, even if the Egyptian ascendancy in North Syria in Thothmes I's reign was little more than nominal, it seemed unlikely that, once the claim to it had been asserted in an official inscription and been staked out on the spot by the erection of a stele, it could have been flouted at any subsequent date in Thothmes I's reign by a Hittite raid on Aleppo without this producing reactions on the Egyptian side which would have left some trace on the disinterred Egyptiac records of the period, defective though these records were. We cannot, however, feel so confident that Muršiliš I's raid would have left a mark on the Egyptiac records if it had occurred neither during Thothmes I's reign nor before it, but after it, during the period (dated 1486–1468 B.C. by Wilson) when the Empress Hatshepsut was in power, since it seems to have been the Empress's deliberate policy to ignore Egypt's interests in Asia; and, on this account, we cannot exclude, on the strength of the Egyptiac evidence alone, without reference to other considerations, the possibility that Muršiliš I's raid did occur in Hatshepsut's time and that it was the stimulus that provoked, not Thothmes I's occupation of North Syria, but Thothmes III's.

A dating as low as this for the raid is, of course, highly improbable on other grounds. It would be lower than even Poebel's dating (the fourth and lowest of the four rival schemes), and Poebel's is the lowest that the figures in the Khorsabad List of Kings of Assyria allow of, even when all the unknown quantities in this list are given (as they are given by Poebel) the numerical value of zero. Moreover, a dating of Muršiliš I's reign in the second quarter of the fifteenth century B.C. would make nonsense of the known facts of Hittite history by reducing the interval between Muršiliš I's reign and Tutkhaliya II's to less than thirty years. Yet the theoretical possibility on the Egyptiac evidence—however improbable in the light of the other evidence—that Muršiliš I's raid may have occurred in Hatshepsut's time disqualifies the Eighteenth Dynasty's ascendancy over Syria from serving as a decisive criterion for judging between the four rival datings of South-West Asian history, since, if the date of the raid had been in truth as late as this, it would have been too late to be compatible with any of those four datings, and thus would give us no guidance for deciding between their relative merits.

The Contemporaneity of Ikhnaton's Reign with Suppiluliuma's and the Dating of Muršiliš I's Raid on Babylon

There was, however, another chronological point of reference in the chronology of the Eighteenth Dynasty of Egypt which might perhaps

[1] This point is made by Professor Albright in a letter of the 20th November, 1951, to the writer of this Study.

be made to yield some indirect evidence regarding the date of Muršiliš I's raid. Ikhnaton (*imperabat* 1380–1362 B.C. according to Wilson) was known to have been a contemporary of the Hittite war-lord Suppiluliuma; Suppiluliuma was one of the successors of Muršiliš I; and it might be possible to estimate the Time-interval between the reigns of these two Hittite Kings by making conjectural allocations of time for the known intervening events in Hittite history. This alternative approach to the dating of Muršiliš I's raid was, however, highly problematical at the time of writing, since, down to A.D. 1952, the information about this period of Hittite history that was at the disposal of Western scholars was still fragmentary, and the interpretation of what there was of it was still in dispute.

Professor Albrecht Goetze, who was the pioneer of this approach,[1] sought to pave his way by establishing an additional Hittite-Egyptiac synchronism to reinforce the synchronism between the reigns of Suppiluliuma and Ikhnaton. Goetze submitted that the reign of Suppiluliuma's great-grandfather Tutkhaliya II could not have begun earlier than *circa* 1449 B.C., since the renascence of Hittite power in Tutkhaliya II's reign made itself felt in an expansion of the Hittite empire into Syria, and it was inconceivable that this expansion could have started so long as the Egyptiac Emperor Thothmes (Tuthmosis) III was alive.[2] From this concordant pair of synchronisms between Hittite and Egyptiac chronology it would follow that the raid on Babylon by the Hittite King Muršiliš I must be dated early enough to allow for the transaction, between that event and the accession of Tutkhaliya II, of the intervening events of Hittite history which had been brought to light by the disinterment of the Boghazqal'eh Archives. From an examination of the evidence about these intervening events that was known to Western scholars up to date, Goetze concluded[3] in A.D. 1951 that the sack of Babylon by Muršiliš I was

'separated from [the renascence of Hittite power under the predecessors of Suppiluliuma] by no less than nine reigns, of which at least two . . . were fairly long. The nine kings in question represent 5+x, most likely seven, generations. In terms of years, this should mean a period of roughly 200 years. Since Event II is fixed at *circa* 1450 B.C., we would on this basis place Event I around 1650 B.C. Thus, of the four proposed solutions of the problem of Babylonian chronology, (*c*) and (*d*) prove impossible, (*b*) is unlikely, leaving (*a*) the one that is to be preferred.'

Professor Goetze's reconstruction of this chapter of Hittite history, and consequently also his chronological conclusions from it, were, however, rejected by the advocates of all the three rival datings, including Dr. Sidney Smith,[4] whose dating was the next highest to Goetze's own. Albright[5] challenged Goetze's duplication of the series of three

[1] See Goetze, A.: 'The Problem of Chronology and Early Hittite History,' in *B.A.S.O.R.*, No. 122, April 1951, pp. 18–25.
[2] This second point is made by Goetze ibid., pp. 19 and 20. Wilson's date for Thothmes III's death was, however, not 1449 B.C. but 1436 B.C.
[3] Ibid., p. 23.
[4] e.g. in a letter of the 13th October, 1951, to the writer of this Study.
[5] In a letter of the 20th November, 1951, to the writer of this Study.

Hittite kings: Hantili, Zidanta, and Huzziya. 'There is nothing about these kings', he suggested, 'to support the view that there were two of each.' Rowton[1] attacked Goetze's chronological conclusions on the basis of statistical evidence drawn from the histories of South-West Asia and Egypt. On this basis, he contended that 1432 B.C. was a more probable date than 1449 B.C. for the accession of Tutkhaliya II; that the average span of a generation in royal families in this aeon was, at longest, 25·2 years and perhaps no longer than 23, as against Goetze's allowance of 28; and that, in a politically turbulent age, the known events of Hittite history down to the beginning of Tutkhaliya II's reign from the beginning of Muršiliš I's reign do not require an allowance of more than 120 years, as against Goetze's allowance of 200. On the reckoning that Tutkhaliya II came to the throne *circa* 1430 B.C., this would bring Muršiliš I's accession to *circa* 1550 B.C. A corollary of this Rowtonian revision of Goetze's figures would be that the evidence furnished by known facts of Hittite history would be compatible with a dating of Muršiliš I's raid at 1531/30 B.C. (the date of it according to Dating (*c*)), instead of constraining us to date the raid at 1651/50 B.C.—a date which, if accepted, would rule out not only Datings (*d*) and (*c*) but Dating (*b*) as well, and would thus leave Goetze's Dating (*a*) in undisputed possession of the field.

Rowton's critique of Goetze's thesis[2] seemed, however, to show that, while the argument from Hittite history did tell against Dating (*d*), it did not avail to rule out either Dating (*c*) or, *a fortiori*, Dating (*b*). In other words, Hittite history fails, like the history of the Eighteenth Dynasty of Egypt's ascendancy over Syria, to provide us with the decisive criterion that we are seeking.

The Hyksos Conquest of Egypt and the Dating of the Reign of Hammurabi

Another date in a relatively well-established Egyptiac chronology which might provide a point of reference for a relatively uncertain South-West Asian chronology was, as we have observed, the date of the arrival of Hyksos barbarian invaders at the north-eastern corner of the Nile Delta. In A.D. 1952 this event was diversely dated by Egyptologists in terms of years B.C. at dates ranging from *circa* 1730 B.C.[3] through *circa* 1720–1715 B.C.,[4] 1710 B.C.,[5] and 1682 B.C.,[6] to *circa* 1675 B.C.[7] The choice

[1] In *B.A.S.O.R.*, No. 126, April 1952, pp. 20–24.

[2] A reply to Mr. Rowton by Professor Goetze will be found in *B.A.S.O.R.*, No. 127 (1952), pp. 21–26. See also, ibid., pp. 27–30, Albright, W. F.: 'Further Observations on the Chronology of the Early Second Millennium B.C.'

[3] See Drioton, E., and Vandier, J.: *L'Égypte* (Paris 1946, Presses Universitaires de France), pp. 282–4. Cp. Säve-Söderbergh, T: 'The Hyksos Rule in Egypt', in *The Journal of Egyptian Archaeology*, vol. xxxvii, December 1951 (London 1951, The Egypt Exploration Society), p. 55, with n. 1.

[4] On the evidence of 'the Stele of the Year Four Hundred' (which Drioton and Vandier interpret as pointing to a date *circa* 1730 B.C. for the first lodgement of the Hyksos in the Delta) Sidney Smith, in *Alalakh*, p. 1, n. 1, dates this lodgement between 1720 and 1715 B.C.

[5] See Böhl, op. cit., p. 348, following Stock, H.: *Studien zur Geschichte und Archäologie der 13 bis 17 Dynastie Ägyptens*, in *Ägyptische Forschungen*, Heft 12 (Glückstadt-Hamburg 1942).

[6] Sewell, J. W. S., on the evidence of 'the Stele of the Year Four Hundred', in *The Legacy of Egypt* (Oxford 1942, Clarendon Press), p. 10.

[7] Mr. M. B. Rowton, in a communication to the writer of this Study.

of dates, within this range of about fifty-five years, for the advent of the Hyksos at the Asian fringes of the Egyptiac World would have a bearing on South-West Asian chronology if it were to be established that the Hyksos barbarian invaders of Egypt, like the contemporary Mitanni and Kassite barbarian invaders of Mesopotamia and of Shinar, included at least a contingent of Sanskrit-speaking warriors who were of Central Asian Nomad origin; for it would follow that this contingent, at any rate, must have reached Syria from Central Asia via Mesopotamia, and from this it would follow, in turn, that they could not have traversed Mesopotamia till after Hammurabi's death, since the Upper Tigris Basin, and therefore, *a fortiori*, the basins of the Khabur and the Balikh, had been proved to have been included in Hammurabi's dominions by the discovery, at Diyārbakr, of a monument bearing a portrait of Hammurabi carved in relief.[1] It was true that, in A.D. 1952, the effectiveness of Hammurabi's authority over the several principalities which he claimed to have subjugated was being called in question by the results of recent progress in the discovery and interpretation of contemporary documents. Yet, even when Hammurabi's own account of his achievements had been discounted in the light of this new knowledge, it would still seem hardly credible that, if a Eurasian Nomad war-band had broken through the northern frontier of Hammurabi's empire within Hammurabi's lifetime, no reference to this shattering event should have been found among Hammurabi's disinterred records.

Accordingly, if the Hyksos barbarian invaders of Egypt should prove to have included a contingent of Nomads from Central Asia, the establishment of the date of their invasion of Egypt would furnish a criterion for judging between the four rival datings of Hammurabi's reign. In A.D. 1952, however, this view of the Hyksos war-band's composition and provenance was being disputed by critics of it who maintained that in truth there was no evidence for the Hyksos having been anything but local Semitic-speaking barbarians from the immediate neighbourhood of the north-east corner of the Nile Delta, and also no evidence for the Hyksos invasion having been a sudden overwhelming cataclysm and not a gradual infiltration. If this alternative account of the Hyksos were to prove to be the right one, then manifestly there would be no criterion for South-West Asian chronology to be obtained from the date of the Hyksos invasion of Egypt, whatever this date might be, and whether it was to be equated with some single year B.C. or with a period extending, perhaps, over more than half a century; for a gradual infiltration into Egypt of local barbarians from the Sinai Peninsula, or, at the farthest, from Palestine or Transjordan, might have occurred during Hammurabi's lifetime without having made any mark on the records of his reign. It will be seen that the current controversy over the composition and provenance of the Hyksos, and over the circumstances of the establishment of their ascendancy in Egypt, governed the question whether the date of the Hyksos invasion of Egypt could or could not be used as a criterion for the dating of South-West Asian history. We must therefore look into the pros and cons of this Egyptological controversy

[1] See Böhl, op. cit., p. 354.

before attempting to apply this criterion for our South-West Asian purposes; and, in then proceeding to consider how the four rival datings of South-West Asian history would respond to this test, we must never forget that the test would be a valid one only if the view that the Hyksos included a contingent of Sanskrit-speaking Central Asian Nomads were to hold its ground against the view that the Hyksos were nothing but local Semitic-speaking barbarians from the Asian borderlands of the Nile Delta.

The controversy over the composition and provenance of the Hyksos turned on three points: the language that they spoke, the weapons that they used, and the manner in which they made themselves masters of Egypt.

The belief that the Hyksos included a Sanskrit-speaking contingent was based on two considerations: first, the philologically well-attested presence of a Sanskrit-speaking contingent among the more or less contemporary Mitanni barbarian invaders of Mesopotamia and Kassite invaders of Shinar, and, second, the conjecture that this element among the Hyksos was represented by the element in the fifteenth-century population of Syria that bore the title 'mariannu', and that the word 'mariannu' was an Indo-European word signifying 'males' and thence 'warriors'.

The Mitanni and the Kassites did appear to have been composite hordes in which local transfrontier barbarians from just beyond the northern and eastern borders of Hammurabi's empire had been reinforced by contingents of Nomads from Central Asia who spoke an Indo-European language. The Kassites seem to have consisted of Gutaean highlanders from the Zagros reinforced by Sanskrit-speaking Nomads; the Mitanni, of Hurrian highlanders from Armenia reinforced by Sanskrit-speaking Nomads. If the Hyksos should prove to have consisted of Palestinian or Sinaitic Semitic-speaking barbarians, reinforced by Sanskrit-speaking Nomads and perhaps by Hurrians as well, this would be all of a piece with the rest of the picture of the Völkerwanderung in the eighteenth and seventeenth centuries B.C.

The geographical distribution of the descendants of the Indo-European-speaking intruders from Central Asia into South-Western Asia, as we find them distributed in and after the fifteenth century B.C., accords with at least one piece of archaeological evidence[1] to suggest that a wave of Sanskrit-speaking invaders which had broken out of the Eurasian Steppe on to the Iranian Plateau had split into a left wing which had swept over Eastern Iran into the domain of the Indus Culture and a right wing which had poured westwards through the Caspian Gates into Azerbaijan and thence across Armenia into Anatolia and across Mesopotamia into Syria and eventually into Egypt—as, in the eleventh century of the Christian Era, the Turkish-speaking Nomad invaders of the 'Abbasid Caliphate divided into a left wing that descended on the Caliphate's dominions in the Indus Valley and a right wing that, from a new base of operations in Azerbaijan, invaded the dominions of the East

[1] The affinity between swords brought to Mohenjo-daro by the Sanskrit-speaking barbarian destroyers of the Indus Culture and swords of the Hyksos Age found in Palestine is pointed out by Stuart Piggott in his *Prehistoric India* (London 1950, Pelican), pp. 228–9.

Roman Empire in Anatolia in and after A.D. 1037, Syria in and after A.D. 1071, and finally Egypt in A.D. 1164–9. On this historical analogy we might also infer that, in the age of the First Dynasty of Babylon, South-West Asia played the same role as in the age of the ʿAbbasid Caliphate in acting as a lodestone that drew Nomad invaders out of their distant Central Asian cattle-ranges, and that, in both ages alike, the Nomads' eventual invasions of Anatolia, Syria, and Egypt were incidental consequences of an attack that had been directed towards the Tigris-Euphrates Basin and the Indus Basin as its first objectives.[1]

As against this suggestion that the Hyksos are likely to have been all of a piece with the Mitanni and the Kassites in their composition and their provenance, Albright makes the point that

> 'The Hyksos royal names are, after all, predominantly Canaanite or Amorite, so that the irruption of the Indo-Iranians and Hurrians [into South-Western Asia] seems largely to have spent itself before reaching the Egyptian frontiers.'[2]

Säve-Söderbergh[3] pronounces in the same sense still more categorically. 'Most of the Hyksos names are pure Semitic, and those which cannot be thus explained are in any case hardly Hurrian.[4] . . . Names of a Hurrian type are conspicuously absent among the Hyksos.'[5]

The inconclusiveness of this reasoning is exposed by the possibility of concluding, on the same grounds, that the irruption of the Scandinavians into Western Christendom in the Dark Ages of Western history must have spent itself before reaching Normandy, since the names borne, and the language spoken, by the Norman conquerors of Apulia, Sicily, and England were, after all, predominantly French. In this instance we happen to know for a fact that, notwithstanding this linguistic evidence, the forebears of the eleventh-century Norman masters of a province on the Channel Coast of France had come thither in the tenth century from Scandinavia. On this showing, Säve-Söderbergh's and Albright's *argumentum a silentio* might have been overridden if the progress of discovery and research had confirmed Eduard Meyer's two theses that surviving epigoni of the Hyksos were to be seen in the 'mariannu' who are found in Syria in the fifteenth century B.C., and that the word 'mariannu' is Indo-European.[6]

In the fifteenth-century B.C. the mariannu in Syria were echeloned immediately in front of the Mitanni just across the Euphrates in Mesopotamia, and the apparent survival of the name 'mariannu', a thousand years later than that, in Anatolia looks like another indication that the mariannu had been associated with the Mitanni in a Völkerwanderung which had reached Anatolia from a starting-point in Central Asia in the eighteenth or seventeenth century B.C. Mâres (whose name was still per-

[1] This point has been made in I. i. 104–9.

[2] Albright, W. F., in *B.A.S.O.R.*, No. 78, April 1940, p. 33.

[3] Säve-Söderbergh, T.: 'The Hyksos Rule in Egypt', in *The Journal of Egyptian Archaeology*, vol. xxxvii, December 1951 (London 1951, The Egypt Exploration Society), pp. 53–71.

[4] Ibid., p. 58.

[5] Ibid., p. 58, n. 3.

[6] See Meyer, E.: *Geschichte des Altertums*, vol. ii, Part I, 2nd ed., pp. 33–38, cited in I. i. 105.

petuated in A.D. 1952 in the district of Georgia called Imerethia) are located by Herodotus[1] in the mountainous hinterland of the south-east corner of the Black Sea, while the Mariandyni[2] who were eventually enslaved by the Hellenic colonists of Heraclea Pontica, on a westerly stretch of the Anatolian shore of the Black Sea, testify by the 'hyphenated' structure of their name that at this point the mariannu had met and mingled with Thynian invaders from South-Eastern Europe, as, in the hinterland of the Mediterranean coast of Spain, Celts similarly met and mingled with Iberians to form the mixed community known as the Celtiberi. Similar evidence shows that a detachment of the Mitanni found its way into Anatolia at the heels of the mariannu, as in the seventh century B.C. the Scythians found their way into Anatolia at the heels of the Cimmerians.[3] Herodotus[4] locates a community of 'Matieni' on the right bank of the River Halys (Qyzyl Irmāq) opposite the Phrygians, and records[5] that, in Xerxes' expeditionary force, these 'Matieni' were brigaded with the Paphlagonians and were equipped like the Paphlagonians, the Ligyes, the Mariandyni, and the Cappadocians. Hecataeus[6] perhaps records the presence of an advance guard of these 'Matieni' on the left (i.e. west) bank of the Halys in his mention of a town named Hyopê, near Gordii, inhabited by 'Matieni' who wore Paphlagonian dress, while his 'Matieni' who are neighbours of the Moschi[7] would be identical with Herodotus's Anatolian 'Matieni' if the Moschi in question are those who contended with the Assyrians in Lycaonia in the eighth century B.C., but would be neighbours of the Mâres, in the hinterland of the south-east corner of the Black Sea, if the Moschi associated with them are, as Hecataeus implies in this passage, the remnant of the Moschi that had survived in this secluded area.[8]

This geographical association of the name 'mariannu' with the name 'Mitanni' might commend the thesis that the mariannu, like the Mitanni, included an Indo-European-speaking element if there were also some philological warrant for this. Eduard Meyer's conjectural Indo-European etymology for the word was, however, rejected by more recent scholars. According to Dr. Sidney Smith,[9] the 'mar-' in 'mariannu'

[1] In Book III, chap. 94, and Book VII, chap. 79.

[2] See Herodotus, Book I, chap. 28; Book III, chap. 90; Book VII, chap. 72.

[3] Hrozný hazards the conjecture that the Midianites were the epigoni of a detachment of these Mitanni who had accompanied or anticipated a left wing of the mariannu in their invasion of Syria and had broken from there upon the highlands of North-Eastern Arabia. See Hrozný, B.: *Die Älteste Geschichte Vorderasiens und Indiens* (Prague 1943, Melantrich), pp. 134, 152, 213–14. Hrozný points out in op. cit., p. 134, that his equation of Midian with Mitanni is borne out by the presence of the Mitannians' associates the Hurrians astride the King's Highway immediately to the north of Midian, in the highlands east of the Wadi ʿArabah that were subsequently taken from these 'Horites' by the Edomites (see VI. vii. 102, n. 1). Hrozný's identification of the names 'Midian' and 'Mitanni' was, however, rejected by Goetze.

[4] In Book I, chap. 72.

[5] In Book VII, chap. 72.

[6] Hecataeus, Fragment 287 in Jacoby's arrangement.

[7] Hecataeus, Fragment 288 in Jacoby's arrangement.

[8] The evidence about the Anatolian Matieni is presented by F. H. Weissbach in Pauly–Wissowa: *Real-encyklopädie*, new edition, vol. xiv (Stuttgart 1930, Metzler), cols. 2203–4. On the Hellenic map of Anatolia, 'Matianê' (*Turcicè* Machan) also figures as the name of a station, just to the south of the southernmost bend of the River Halys, on the road between Soandus (Nevshehir) and Sacasena (Süksün).

[9] In a personal communication to the writer of this Study. See also *The Antiquaries' Journal*, vol. xix, p. 43.

was derived from a Sumerian word meaning wagon, while 'the -annu could be an afformative of the Hurri language, not Indo-European'. According to Mr. D. J. Wiseman,[1] no Indo-European personal names were to be found among more than 2,100 personal names of mariannu that were known to Modern Western scholars by June 1953. Mr. Wiseman concurred with Dr. Sidney Smith in holding that 'mariannu' was a Hurrian word; and this would be what was to be expected, considering that, at Alalakh, about 90 per cent. of the personal names were Hurrian in the fifteenth century B.C., while, on the same site in the eighteenth century B.C., some of these fifteenth-century Hurrian names had already been current.[2] The Hurrian word 'mariannu' seems to have been, not an ethnikon, but a class-designation. There was, for example, a fifteenth-century writ, issued by Niqmepa, making Gabia a 'mariannu' in perpetuity. In North Syria in the fifteenth-century B.C. the mariannu seem to have been the highest of three classes into which the population was divided,[3] and they seem also to have been distinguished by the possession of wheeled transport, considering that the entries 'has a chariot/wagon' and 'has no chariot' were placed against the names of mariannu in a disinterred list. A record of one-year-old horses being put to 'mariannu work' had also been found.[4]

This association of the mariannu with horses in the fifteenth century B.C. looks like another indication that, even if they did not share with the Mitanni an Indo-European element in their racial composition, they did share with them the mastering of a military technique that had been ascribed, by one school of Modern Western scholars, to the Hyksos as well. The Hyksos had been credited with the possession of two new-fangled weapons, the horse-drawn chariot[5] and the composite bow,[6] and these two new weapons had been held to have been introduced to South-West Asia suddenly by eighteenth-century or seventeenth-century Sanskrit-speaking Nomad invaders from Central Asia.[7] This thesis, however, had latterly been contested. According to Säve-Söderbergh,[8] for example, 'the horse was known in Mesopotamia long before we find any traces of Indo-Iranians[9][3] and . . . there is not the slightest evidence that the Hyksos used the horse until the very latest part of their rule in Egypt'. Among the material relics of life in Egypt during the period of the Hyksos ascendancy there, 'not even a bone of a horse'

[1] In a personal communication to the writer of this Study. See now also D. J. Wiseman: *The Alalaḫ Tablets* (London 1953, British School of Archaeology at Ankara: Occasional Papers, No. 2), pp. 9–10.

[2] In the eighteenth century B.C. the names of the most common implements were also Hurrian at Alalakh, and this suggested that, by that date, Hurrian had become the prevailing language of Northern Syria (note by Mr. Wiseman).

[3] 'Alalakh has 34 mariannu, who seem to be the leading citizens in all walks of life. One of them is the mayor. Neighbouring villages have fewer' (note by Mr. Wiseman).

[4] Note by Mr. Wiseman.

[5] See Winlock, H. E.: *The Rise and Fall of the Middle Kingdom in Thebes* (New York 1947, Macmillan), pp. 152–8.

[6] See ibid., pp. 158–9.

[7] See VIII. viii. 17.

[8] Ibid., p. 59.

[9][3] 'Cp., for example, Götze, *Kleinasien*, 72 (inter alia, a *rabi sīsē* in the Cappadocian tablets from the nineteenth century); horses and chariots in Mari under Zimri-Lim (*Syria*, No. xix, p. 125); Mallowan, *Iraq*, No. ix, p. 216 ("the chariot was already widely used in the Early Dynastic-Sargonid III periods, and . . . the chariot warfare so freely practised in the middle of the second millennium B.C. was then a comparatively modern exploitation of an invention which had been made more than a thousand years earlier").'

had been found in any Egyptian tomb of that age; no picture of a horse had been found; and in hunting-scenes the hunter is depicted on foot.[1] Among all the allegedly Hyksos earth-work fortresses, once supposed to be the characteristic laagers of an army of charioteers, only two had been identified in Egypt itself, and these two had turned out to be probably not fortresses but temple-foundations.[2] As for the Hyksos' new-fangled weapons, Säve-Söderbergh contends[3] that

'it is only towards the end of their rule in Egypt that they introduce a number of improvements in military technique in an attempt to uphold their political power against the growing Egyptian opposition. Then first the horse-drawn chariots, new types of daggers and swords, bronze weapons, the strong compound Asiatic bow, &c., are imported from Asia.'

The opposing view that the Hyksos had brought these new-fangled weapons with them at their first appearance and, in virtue of them, had conquered Egypt at one stroke might seem to be supported by the late and second-hand, but sole surviving, literary record of the Hyksos conquest. Manetho, in a passage quoted from his work by Josephus in his *Contra Apionem*,[4] writes:

'The story is an almost incredibly fantastic one. A people from the East, of obscure origin, had the audacity to march against Egypt, and they conquered it at one stroke; it was child's play for them; they met with no resistance. And then, when they had overcome the previous government of Egypt, they behaved atrociously; they burned down the cities and rased the temples to the ground, and the whole of the native population suffered cruelly at their hands: the males were massacred; the women and children were enslaved.'

In this passage, which was the sole surviving piece of literary evidence for the event, the note of unexpectedness, suddenness, surprise, and speed is unmistakable and, indeed, emphatic. But against this reading of Manetho's testimony, whatever it may be worth, Säve-Söderbergh pits archaeological evidence for the thesis that the conquest was a gradual one and that it consisted merely in the substitution of local Semitic-speaking rulers for Egyptian rulers, and not in the immigration of a horde of strange barbarians from the back of beyond. In the Eastern Delta, dynasts with Semitic names begin to make their appearance perhaps as early as 1730 B.C.[5] The term which has been transliterated into Greek as 'Hyksos', and which means 'rulers of foreign countries', 'gives us the impression that the Hyksos were only a little group of foreign dynasts rather than a numerous people with a special civilization'.[6] 'There are a great many tombs from the Hyksos period in Egypt, but there is nowhere a clear indication of an invasion of a foreign people from the North. . . . There is nowhere a sudden change in the burial customs',[7] and the alleged evidence in the style of Egyptian pottery of the Hyksos Age for an immigration of a foreign people into Egypt in this period will not hold water.[8]

[1] See ibid., pp. 59–60.
[2] See ibid., p. 60.
[3] Ibid., p. 61.
[4] Josephus: *Contra Apionem*, Book I, chaps. 75–82.
[5] See Säve-Söderbergh, ibid., pp. 55, n. 1.
[6] Ibid., p. 56.
[7] Ibid., pp. 56–57.
[8] Ibid., pp. 57–58.

Thus, by A.D. 1952, the thesis that the Hyksos included a contingent of Sanskrit-speaking Central Asian Nomads had come under heavy fire; and, though, in the still inconclusive state of the controversy, this thesis could not be held to have been driven off the field as yet, it was already clear that any attempt to use it as a criterion for dating the reign of Hammurabi was subject to the possibility that it might prove a broken reed. With this reservation in our minds, we may now go on to consider how the date of the Hyksos invasion of Egypt would affect the choice between the four rival reconstructions of South-West Asian chronology if the Hyksos should, after all, turn out to have included a Central Asian contingent who could not have driven their chariots across South-Western Asia while Hammurabi was still alive.[1]

If, on these grounds, we could take it as being certain that Hammurabi's death must have been earlier than the Hyksos invasion of Egypt, this would rule out Dating (*d*), which dates Hammurabi's death 1662 B.C., i.e. thirteen years later than the very latest of the divers rival datings, ranging from 1730 B.C. to 1675 B.C., for the Hyksos invasion of Egypt that were in the field in A.D. 1952.[2] This event in Egyptiac history cannot, however, be used as a criterion for deciding between Datings (*c*) and (*b*) for Hammurabi's reign unless we are able to come to some conclusion regarding the date of the Hyksos invasion itself; for in A.D. 1952 the current rival datings of it splayed out, as we have seen, over a span of no less than fifty-five years extending from 1730 B.C. to 1675 B.C., and, whereas the earlier of these two extreme datings would rule out not only Dating (*d*) for Hammurabi's reign but also Dating (*c*), which dates Hammurabi's death 1686 B.C., the later of the two extreme datings would be compatible with Dating (*c*), as well as with Dating (*b*). It will be seen that the acceptability of Dating (*c*) for the reign of Hammurabi was at stake in the current controversy over the dating of the Hyksos invasion of Egypt—on the assumption, of course, that a contingent of barbarians from Central Asia was included in the Hyksos war-band.

For the establishment of the date of the Hyksos invasion there were two mutually independent approaches in the light of the Egyptiac information at the disposal of Western scholars up to date. Since the dates of the Twelfth Dynasty and the date of the expulsion of the Hyksos from Egypt by Amosis were already more or less well assured, the chronology of the intervening age could be reconstructed on the basis of the Egyptiac king-lists and of the names, the regnal years, and

[1] Goetze, in a paper read before the American Oriental Society at Cincinnati at Easter 1950, maintained that an invasion of Egypt by barbarians from Central Asia could not have taken place so long as Hammurabi's successor Samsu-iluna was on the throne, since during his reign Babylon still maintained her hold on the Middle Euphrates. But might they not have ridden from east to west across the plains of Northern Mesopotamia and have crossed the Euphrates at its westward elbow, at some point to the north of Carchemish? This route would hardly have trespassed on the domain of the Babylonian Empire in the territory of the former Kingdom of Mari.

[2] Professor W. F. Albright comments, in a letter of the 5th January, 1952, to the writer of this Study: 'Certainly a storm broke over Mesopotamia and Syria-Palestine in the years immediately following the death of Hammurabi, and, since this storm is hard to separate from the rise of the Fifteenth Dynasty in Egypt [i.e. from the establishment of the Hyksos domination—A.J.T.], one would apparently be compelled to date the latter event as late as after 1660 B.C., which does seem highly improbable.'

the acts of individual kings that were recorded in disinterred documents. If the collapse of the Hyksos Power in Egypt was to be dated *circa* 1567 B.C., the figure of 108 years, given by the Turin Papyrus for the total duration of the Hyksos Fifteenth Dynasty,[1] would place the Hyksos invasion of Egypt at 1675 B.C., and this dating of that event would allow sufficient time both for five or six Fifteenth-Dynasty Hyksos war-lords who exercised a domination over Egypt[2] and for the preceding pharaohs, bracketed together in the king-lists as the Thirteenth Dynasty, who had reigned between the end of the Twelfth Dynasty, dated 1786 B.C. by Parker, and the Hyksos irruption.

This dating accorded so well with all interpretations of all the extant evidence, save for one single item, that it would hardly have been questioned if this other piece of evidence had not turned up in the shape of 'the Stele of the Year Four Hundred'.[3]

This monument had been discovered on the site of the Deltaic city of Tanis (*alias* Ramses), to which the capital of 'the New Empire' had been transferred from Thebes in the time of the Nineteenth Dynasty.[4] The inscription on the stele states that it was erected by order of Ramses (Ramesses) II (*imperabat* 1301–1234 B.C. according to Wilson) to commemorate a state visit paid to Tanis by Ramses (Ramesses) II's father, Seti (Sethos) I—at some date, to judge by the styles and titles employed in this context, that was anterior to both Seti I's and his father Ramses I's accession to the Imperial Throne—for the celebration of the reign of 'Seth-the-Great-of-Strength, the Son of Re, His Beloved'. Since Seth was the local tutelary divinity of Tanis, and since the four-hundredth year of his reign was the occasion that had led to the erection of the stele, the initial year of this four-hundred-years-long span was presumably some date at which Tanis had, for some reason, become a place of importance. On the supposition that Tanis was identical with 'Avaris', the city in which the Hyksos war-lord who had been the conqueror of Egypt had established his military headquarters and his summer residence according to the passage of Manetho's work quoted by Josephus in his *Contra Apionem*,[5] it was conjectured by Western scholars that the selection of the city by the Hyksos for this important role was the event in the history of Tanis which had been taken as the initial date of an era whose four-hundredth year had given occasion for the erection of Ramses (Ramesses) II's stele. This conjecture might appear to be supported by the representation of the god Seth on the stele in Asiatic dress, since the Hyksos were known to have identified the autochthonous Egyptiac divinity Seth with an imported tutelary divinity of their own. If it were further to be assumed that the four-

[1] Manetho gives the figure of 104/3 years for the same epoch, i.e. for the duration of his Fifteenth Dynasty. Säve-Söderbergh, in loc. cit., p. 66, prolongs the total duration of the Hyksos Rāj in the north of Egypt and in Southern Palestine by reckoning that the Hyksos rulers of the Fifteenth Dynasty were followed by 'a second group . . . which we may call the Sixteenth Dynasty'.

[2] Six names of Hyksos pharaohs of the Fifteenth Dynasty were recorded by Manetho; five names (four of them corresponding to four of Manetho's) had been recovered by Modern Western archaeologists (see Drioton and Vandier, op. cit., p. 285).

[3] English translation in Pritchard, J. B.: *Ancient Near Eastern Texts* (Princeton 1950, University Press), pp. 252–3.

[4] See II. ii. 112 and 114.

[5] Book I, chaps. 75–82, partially translated on p. 203, above.

hundred-years period was to be reckoned back, not from the date of the erection of the stele, but from the date of Seti's state visit to Tanis at some date before the end of the reign of Horemheb (*imperabat circa* 1349–1319 B.C.), the cumulative result of this pile of assumptions would indicate, for the Hyksos conquest of Egypt, a date round about 1730–1720 B.C.

Unless it were assumed, as it was by Säve-Söderbergh,[1] that the Hyksos Fifteenth Dynasty had been followed by a Hyksos Sixteenth Dynasty, this interpretation of 'the Stele of the Year Four Hundred' was the sole basis for any dating of the Hyksos conquest of Egypt earlier than *circa* 1675 B.C., which, as we have seen, was the date indicated by the Turin Papyrus's figure of 108 years for the duration of the Fifteenth Dynasty.

An acceptance of even the lowest of the dates for the Hyksos conquest that could be reconciled with this interpretation of 'the Stele of the Year Four Hundred' would have the chronologically awkward effect of allowing too little time for the aggregate length of the reigns known to have occurred between the end of the Twelfth Dynasty and the beginning of the Hyksos Fifteenth Dynasty.[2] Some of the scholars who pinned their faith on the stele sought to meet this difficulty by assuming that the reigns of some of the pharaohs of the Thirteenth Dynasty were contemporaneous with one another, while others sought to meet it by assuming that the latest of these reigns were contemporaneous with the first stage of the Hyksos conquest of Egypt, which, on this hypothesis, was assumed to have been accomplished in successive stages.

There might be something to be said for the first of these two suggested ways out of the chronological difficulty, considering that, at least in the last stage of all before the Hyksos conquest, the Egyptian imperial government did seem to have disintegrated into a number of petty parochial principalities. The second of the suggested ways out, however, could hardly be reconciled with Manetho's story of the Hyksos conquering Egypt at one blow; and Manetho's story, fantastic though it might sound, was not incredible on the hypothesis that the Hyksos had included in their ranks a contingent of Eurasian Nomad warriors who had swooped down upon South-Western Asia armed with new-fangled weapons which were irresistible to any adversaries who had not yet mastered the use of them. These archer-charioteers would have secured the full benefit of their armament in their assault upon Egypt because they would have descended on her suddenly, from the back of beyond, and so have taken her completely by surprise. This decisive element of surprise would, however, have been a wasting asset. As soon as military contact had been established, the victims of the horse-drawn chariot and the composite bow would have been bound to learn the tricks of their conquerors' trade sooner or later. In Egypt in the sequel to the Hyksos conquest, it did, in fact, take the Thebans rather more than a century—*circa* 1675 B.C.–1567 B.C.—to become sufficiently competent charioteers to be able to drive the Hyksos back into Asia. From this actual sequel we

[1] See p. 205, n. 1, above.
[2] This point is made by Drioton and Vandier, in op. cit., p. 283.

may infer that, if—contrary to the picture painted by Manetho—the original Hyksos conquest of Egypt had in truth been protracted over a period of about half a century, this 'staggered' challenge would have evoked on the Egyptian side an increasingly effective response; and indeed, if the conquest had really moved at that slow pace, it would have been unlikely ever to have been carried to completion.

On this showing, a layman might be inclined to abide by the testimony of Manetho in defiance of an interpretation of 'the Stele of the Year Four Hundred' which, after all, was not, and could not be, anything more than a tissue of conjectures. The inscription on the stele did not make it clear whether the four hundred years were to be reckoned back from the date of the erection of the stele by Ramses II or from the date of Seti's state visit. If the period was to be reckoned back from the date of erection, there was no statement of the year of Ramses II's reign in which the erection had taken place, and even the dating of Ramses II's reign in years B.C. was uncertain.[1] If, on the other hand, the period was to be reckoned back from the date of Seti's state visit, there was no indication of the year of Horemheb's reign in which this visit had taken place. Finally, whatever the initial date of the four-hundred-years-long period might be, there was no evidence that the event, commemorated by it, in the history of Tanis was the selection of Tanis by a Hyksos conqueror of Egypt to be his military headquarters and his summer residence.[2] Indeed, it was not certain that Tanis was identical with a Hyksos *place d'armes* which Manetho, in the sole piece of historical evidence concerning it, calls, not 'Tanis', but 'Avaris'.

If we were to renounce the manifestly hazardous endeavour to extract from 'the Stele of the Year Four Hundred' a dating for the Hyksos conquest of Egypt, a dating *circa* 1675 B.C. for this event would remain in

[1] Mr. M. B. Rowton had argued, in *The Journal of Egyptian Archaeology*, vol. xxxiv (1948), p. 72, that Ramses II's accession year should be dated, not 1301 B.C., but 1290 B.C.

[2] Alternatively the event taken as the inaugural date for an Era of Tanis might have been the selection of the city to be the local seat of government for one of the parochial principalities—some under native Egyptian princelings and others perhaps under Semitic-speaking alien war-lords from a no-man's-land beyond the eastern fringes of the Delta—into which Lower Egypt may have disintegrated during the last phase of the decline of 'the Middle Empire' before the Hyksos conquest. In a letter of the 20th November, 1951, to the writer of this Study, Professor Albright remarks that he would date the Hyksos Empire of the Fifteenth Dynasty about 1690–1580 B.C., 20–30 years below the initial date suggested for this by H. Stock in his *Studien zur Geschichte und Archäologie der 13. bis 17. Dynastie Ägyptens*. The Hyksos Empire, Professor Albright adds in this context, 'was clearly preceded by an anarchic period of Semitic domination lasting perhaps 30–40 years, during which the prestige of Egypt sank to zero'. Unlike a Eurasian Nomad Völkerwanderung from Central Asia to Egypt, an infiltration of local Semitic-speaking barbarians into Egypt from the Sinai Peninsula, or even from the Syrian Desert, was, as we have observed, evidently something that might have happened during Hammurabi's reign without having left any mark in contemporary Babylonian records.

The hypothesis that there may have been this infiltration of local Semitic-speaking barbarians into the Eastern Delta from *circa* 1730 B.C. onwards is, of course, quite compatible with the hypothesis that the Hyksos conquest of Egypt was a subsequent sudden catastrophic event, *circa* 1675 B.C., in which Nomads from Central Asia were participants. Säve-Söderbergh, who equates the Hyksos invasion with the local Semitic-speaking barbarians' infiltration, rejects Albright's dating of the Hyksos Fifteenth Dynasty *circa* 1690–1580 B.C., and proposes to date it *circa* 1720–1610 B.C., in order to leave time for his Hyksos Sixteenth Dynasty to follow on before the expulsion of the Hyksos by Amosis (see Säve-Söderbergh in loc. cit., p. 62, n. 4).

undisputed possession of the field; and our condition that Hammurabi's reign must have been over before the Hyksos conquest of Egypt took place would then fail to provide us with a criterion for judging between Dating (*c*) for Hammurabi's reign and Dating (*b*); for, if the Hyksos conquered Egypt *circa* 1675 B.C., Hammurabi was already dead by that date according to Dating (*c*) as well as Dating (*b*), and, indeed, this date for the Hyksos conquest fits in with Dating (*c*) very neatly. As Professor Albright points out,[1]

'According to my chronology [i.e. Dating (*c*)], the powerful Hyksos rulers of the Fifteenth Dynasty, who conquered Upper Egypt about 1675 B.C., reflect to a still unknown extent the irruption of the Hurrian and Indo-Aryan hordes who flooded Mesopotamia and nearly overwhelmed Babylonia after the death of Hammurabi, in the early years of his son, Samsu-iluna.'

In fact, the first appearance of the Hyksos' Kassite cousins in history, when, in the eighth year of Samsu-iluna's reign, they made an unsuccessful assault upon Babylonia,[2] would date, according to Dating (*c*), *circa* 1678 B.C.—that is, about three years before the Hyksos' successful assault on Egypt.

The Kassite Conquest of Babylonia and the Dating of the Reign of Hammurabi

If we hold that Hammurabi's reign must have been over before the conquest of Egypt by the Hyksos, *a fortiori* we are bound to hold that it must have been over before the conquest of Babylonia by the Kassites, and the chronology of the subsequent Kassite Rāj in Babylonia therefore gives us a sixth criterion for judging between the four rival datings for this epoch of South-West Asian history.

In A.D. 1952 this criterion, like the others, was not an instrument of precision; for in A.D. 1952 it was still uncertain exactly how long the Kassites had reigned, what was the exact year in the twelfth century B.C. with which the closing year of their reign was to be equated, and from what exact stage in their progressive conquest of the Land of Shinar they retrospectively dated the official inauguration of their régime. The closing year of the Kassite Dynasty's reign had been diversely dated *circa* 1172 B.C. by Eduard Meyer and *circa* 1150 B.C. by Albright.[3] On the lower of these two rival equations the official beginning of the dynasty's reign would fall *circa* 1727/1726 B.C. on the authority of 'King-List A', which assigns to the thirty-six Kassite Kings a total of 576 years and 9 months.[4] A discrepancy between this list and one of the synchro-

[1] In a letter of the 20th November, 1951, to the writer of this Study.

[2] See p. 186, above.

[3] See Smith, *Alalakh*, p. 20. The exact date was probably 1151 B.C. according to M. B. Rowton, in *Iraq*, vol. viii, p. 97; 1157–1155 B.C. according to Dr. Sidney Smith in a letter of the 13th October, 1951, to the writer of this Study; 1158 B.C. according to van der Meer, op. cit., p. 16; 1162 B.C. according to Cavaignac, E., in *Revue d'Assyriologie*, vol. xl (1945–6), p. 20.

[4] On Rowton's reckoning that, in the Ancient Near East, 16 years was the average length of a reign, a total of 576 years for the Kassite Rāj would exactly conform to the general average, supposing that none of the 36 reigns assigned to this epoch of 576 years

nous lists disinterred at Asshur indicated, however, that some of the reigns reckoned as successive in 'List A' might in truth have been at least partly contemporary with one another;[1] and this would mean that the date of the official inauguration of the dynasty might be appreciably lower than 1727/1726 B.C., even if the average length of all the thirty-six Kassite reigns was, not twelve years, but sixteen, while it could not be higher than 1749 B.C., even if, as now seemed improbable, 'King-List A' were correct and if, besides this, Eduard Meyer were, after all, not in error in dating its terminal year as early as 1172 B.C.

It will be seen that what was known in A.D. 1952 about the chronology of the Kassite Dynasty was almost certainly compatible with Dating (*b*), since the highest possible date for the inauguration of the Kassite Rāj was 1749 B.C., and, according to Dating (*b*), this was just later than the date of Hammurabi's death in 1750 B.C. and was only seven years earlier than the eighth year of Samsu-iluna's reign—reckoned as the year 1743 B.C. according to Dating (*b*)—in which the Kassites make their first recorded appearance. The probability that some of the Kassite reigns were contemporaneous and the possibility that the terminal date of the Kassite Rāj may have been *circa* 1151/1150 B.C., not *circa* 1172 B.C., make it highly probable that the inaugural date of the Kassite Rāj was later than 1743 B.C., even if the total duration of the Rāj was 576 years, as 'King-List A' states. At the same time, this Kassite criterion does not conclusively rule out Dating (*c*); for, as we have seen, the figure of 576 years for the total duration of the Rāj seems to be impugned by the figure for the average length of an individual reign that results from taking an average of the nineteen reigns of known lengths; and it is also significant that Dr. Sidney Smith, whose chronology (Dating (*b*)) would admit of a conquest by the Kassites of the whole of Babylonia up to the walls of Babylon itself at one blow at any time after 1743 B.C.—which, on this dating, was the date of the eighth year of Samsu-iluna's reign—marshals[2] an imposing array of evidence pointing to the probability that the Kassites made themselves masters of Babylonia by a gradual process of successive encroachments, beginning in Samsu-iluna's eighth year, which was not completed till the city of Babylon itself was occupied by Agum II Kakrime, the ninth king of the Kassite Dynasty, 148 years later, after the extinction of the First Dynasty of Babylon by the Hittite raider Muršiliš I. Agum II Kakrime was 'the first Kassite known to have undertaken restoration of buildings at Babylon. . . . There is no reliable evidence that any earlier king ruled the central provinces'.[3] Smith's inference is that the Kassites dated the inauguration of their rāj, not from

by 'King-List A' had overlapped with one another. On the other hand the average worked out at only 12 years apiece for 19 reigns of Kassite kings, out of the total of 36, for which the figures given in 'King-List A' had been preserved. Considering that this Kassite average, if applied to all 36 reigns, would produce a total duration of not more than 432 years for the Kassite Rāj, the figure of 576 years, given for this total in 'King-List A', looks as if it might be too high, even on the assumption that none of the reigns had overlapped with one another, notwithstanding its exact conformity with the general average.

[1] See Smith, *Alalakh*, p. 18.

[2] In *Alalakh*, pp. 21–25.

[3] Smith, *Alalakh*, p. 21.

the completion of their conquest of Babylonia,[1] but from their establishment of their first substantial foothold on Babylonian ground: perhaps from their acquisition of the eastern provinces as a consequence of their 'defeat' by Samsu-iluna, or perhaps from their subsequent extension of this first lodgement westwards over the Kingdom of Khana ('Anah) on the Middle Euphrates.[2]

Smith points out that two of Agum II Kakrime's (Kassite King No. 9's) successors, Kadashman-Harbe I (No. 16) and Burna-Buriash III (No. 20), were contemporaries of the Egyptian Emperor Amenhotep (Amenophis) III (*imperabat* 1413–1377 B.C., according to Wilson). The interval between Agum II's occupation of Babylon and the death of Amenhotep III would be 218 years (1595–1377 B.C.) according to Dating (*b*), 154 (1531–1377 B.C.) years according to Dating (*c*); and the possible duration of Kassite reigns Nos. 9–20 inclusive would be rather longer than this interval, whatever the length of the interval might be reckoned to be, since Agum II may have been on the throne some years before he occupied Babylon, while Burna-Buriash III may have outlived Amenhotep III. Since 12 reigns would run to about 192 years all told on an average of 16 years per reign, and to about 144 years all told on an average of 12 years per reign, it will be seen that Datings (*b*) and (*c*) were both alike compatible with the synchronism between the reigns of Kadashman-Harbe I and Burna-Buriash III and the reign of Amenhotep III.

On this showing, the chronology of the Kassite Rāj would not conclusively rule out Dating (*c*), though Dating (*d*) would hardly be compatible with the Kassite chronology on any interpretation of it.[3]

Some Provisional Conclusions from the Evidence as it stood in A.D. *1952*

We have now examined six criteria for judging between the four rival datings for a span of 210 years of South-West Asian history, extending from the date of the earliest of the letters in King Šamši-Adad I's diplomatic correspondence to the overthrow of the First Dynasty of Babylon by the Hittite war-lord Muršiliš I. We have found in all six cases that the evidence, up to date, was too fragmentary to allow of either exactness or certainty in our conclusions. Yet, inexact and provisional though these conclusions admittedly were, they did appear to throw some light at least on the relative merits of the four rival datings on the test of the evidence as this stood at the moment. The tentative findings of our inquiry may be tabulated conveniently in the form of an examiner's schedule of marks, if the distinguished scholars whose rival views are here in question will forgive a layman for this rather impertinent treatment of them.

[1] The ninth king, Agum II Kakrime, went a long way towards completing the conquest; for, according to Smith, ibid., this king annexed, not only the city of Babylon, but also 'the District of Nippur, previously held by the Sea-Land Dynasty.'

[2] The capital of Khana was Tirqa, the modern 'Asharah (Smith, op. cit., p. 22).

[3] This was pointed out by Professor W. F. Albright in a letter of the 5th January, 1952, to the writer of this Study.

Criterion	1	2	3	4	5	6
Dating	*The Khorsabad List of Kings of Assyria*	*The Twelfth Egyptian Dynasty in Syria*	*The Eighteenth Egyptian Dynasty in Syria*	*The Span of Hittite History between Muršiliš I and Tutkhaliya II*	*The Hyksos Conquest of Egypt*	*The Kassite Conquest of Babylonia*
(*a*)	$\gamma-$	$\gamma-$	α	β	α	γ
(*b*)	$\beta-$	$\beta-$	α	β	α	$\alpha+$
(*c*)	$\alpha+$	α	α	β	α	β
(*d*)	$\beta-$	α	β	γ	$\gamma-$	$\gamma-$

In this schedule, $\alpha+$ stands for 'probable almost to the point of certainty', α for 'probable', β for 'possible', $\beta-$ for 'just possible', γ for 'improbable', $\gamma-$ for 'improbable almost to the point of impossibility'. Any attempt to translate these symbols into precise numbers and then to add up each of the competitors' totals would be doubly misleading. It would suggest that it was possible to arrive at a much more definite assessment than was really practicable in A.D. 1952, and it would also suggest that all six criteria were of equal significance, whereas in truth No. 4 was, in its very nature, more subjective than the rest, while Nos. 3 and 5 were nets whose meshes were so loosely knit that they would let through gnats and camels indiscriminately. On this account the signal failure of Dating (*d*) to satisfy even Criterion No. 5 would have been a damagingly bad mark if there had not been grave doubts whether the date of the Hyksos invasion of Egypt was a valid criterion for our purpose of determining the chronology of South-West Asian history.

When we take into account all six columns of marks, we find that Datings (*a*) and (*d*) are both debited with two $\gamma-$, whereas neither Dating (*b*) nor Dating (*c*) has any gammas to its discredit. If we take account of Criteria Nos. 1, 2, and 6 only, we find that Dating (*a*)'s marks are $\gamma-$, $\gamma-$, γ, and Dating (*d*)'s marks $\beta-$, α, $\gamma-$, whereas Dating (*b*)'s marks are $\beta-$, $\beta-$, $\alpha+$, and Dating (*c*)'s marks $\alpha+$, α, β. We may perhaps fairly conclude that, though Dating (*d*) fares better than Dating (*a*), both (*d*) and (*a*) are practically out of the running, and that only (*b*) and (*c*) are left in the field. We may go on to conclude that, though (*b*)'s marks are appreciably lower than (*c*)'s, we should not be justified on that account in eliminating (*b*) and pronouncing (*c*) to be the winner; for, though (*c*) looks like the winner on Criterion No. 1, (*b*) looks no less like the winner on Criterion No. 6. As the evidence stood in A.D. 1952, Dating (*b*)'s strong point was its consonance with what was known so far about the chronology of the Kassite Rāj in Babylonia, and Dating (*c*)'s strong point its consonance with what was known so far about the Khorsabad List of Kings of Assyria. These two apparently winning cards could not be played against one another, because there was no means of assessing their relative value. Accordingly, in A.D. 1952 it seemed prudent simply to record Datings (*b*) and (*c*) side by side, without attempting to make any absolute appraisal of their respective merits. On the other hand the failure of Dating (*a*) to fit in with any possible interpretation of the Khorsabad List and its synchronization of Šamši-Adad's diplomatic correspondence with the apogee of the Twelfth Egyptian

Dynasty's ascendancy in Syria were marks which, between them, seemed to disqualify Dating (*a*); and Dating (*d*) seemed likewise to be disqualified by its placing of Hammurabi's death at a lower date than the lowest possible date for the Hyksos conquest of Egypt, together with its failure to allow sufficient time for the duration of the Kassite Rāj in Babylonia even on the shortest credible estimate of this.

The Chronology adopted in Volumes vii–x of this Study.

On the strength of the considerations set out above, the reigns of Hammurabi and of any other sovereigns belonging to the First Dynasty of Babylon have been dated, in passages where they are mentioned in volumes vii–x of this Study, by simply giving the figures according to Dating (*b*) and to Dating (*c*) side by side. Earlier events in Sumeric history have been given corresponding pairs of dates which have been calculated by reducing, to terms of Datings (*b*) and (*c*) respectively, the Time-intervals allowed, for the history of this age, in Eduard Meyer's chronology. The writer is aware that, for reasons given by Sidney Smith,[1] this procedure for dating the pre-Babylonian chapters of South-West Asian history is arbitrary and that the results can, at best, be no more than approximately correct. All the same, it seems better to hazard an approximate dating than to leave all earlier chapters of Sumeric history hanging in the air without even the vaguest chronological *point d'appui*.

In the field of Egyptiac history from the beginning of the Eleventh Dynasty to the end of the Twelfth Dynasty the writer has adopted Parker's chronology,[2] which, for the most part, is nine years lower than Eduard Meyer's. As for the earlier chapters of Egyptiac history, the writer has felt that here too, as in the Sumeric field, even the vaguest approximation is preferable to 'a perfect and absolute blank', and he has therefore reproduced, here, Wilson's datings,[3] which are commended not only by their authorship but by the reassuringly modest tentativeness of their author in his presentation of them. In following the lead of an eminent living Egyptologist in a course that seemed, here too, to be the lesser evil, the writer of this Study was aware that, in these earlier chapters of Egyptiac history, the probability of error—in the state of knowledge as it was in A.D. 1952—was considerable.[4] Wilson's datings have been followed likewise in the dates given in vols. vii–x of this Study for reigns of pharaohs in the age of 'the New Empire'.[5]

[1] See Sidney Smith's judgement cited on p. 171, above.

[2] As given in Parker, R. A.: *The Calendars of Ancient Egypt* (Chicago 1950, University of Chicago Press).

[3] As given in Wilson, J. A.: *The Burden of Egypt* (Chicago 1951, University of Chicago Press), p. vii. Dr. Sidney Smith, in a letter of the 13th October, 1951, to the writer of this Study, suggests, as minimum datings, the same dates as Wilson suggests for Dynasties III–V inclusive and for Dynasties VI–XI inclusive.

[4] See Sidney Smith's and W. F. Edgerton's judgements quoted on p. 182, above. Wilson himself notes, in loc. cit., that 'in general it may be said that dates proposed for the period around 3000 B.C. may have a margin of error of 100 years, those around 2500 B.C. of 75 years'.

[5] Wilson himself notes, ibid., that dates proposed by him for the period around 1500–1000 B.C. may have a margin of error of 10–15 years.

ACKNOWLEDGEMENTS AND THANKS

I

To Marcus, for teaching me to return Thanks to my Benefactors

Marcus Aurelius taught me by example how good and how pleasant it is for a writer to declare his gratitude to his pastors and masters. The first of the twelve books of Marcus's *Meditations* consists of a recital of his spiritual debts; and, when I read the *Meditations* for the first time in A.D. 1913, this one book moved me more than the eleven books containing Marcus's notes of his own philosophy. I was struck by the warmth of the human feeling that this first book displays, and by the sincerity and delicacy with which this feeling is expressed. The lesson that I then learnt from Marcus has been in my mind for the past thirty-nine years, and now the time has come for me to act on it.

II

To my Mother, for making me an Historian

My Mother awakened in me a life-long interest in History by communicating to me her own interest in it at a very early stage of my life. At the youngest age to which my memory can travel back, I was already possessed, thanks to what my Mother had by then already done for me, by a love for History which has never left me. If my Mother had not given my mind—and heart too—this early bent, I am sure that I should not ever have written this book; so she bears some responsibility for the undertaking.

III

To Edward Gibbon, for showing me, by Example, what an Historian could do

Edward Gibbon, in *The History of the Decline and Fall of the Roman Empire*, has always been my cynosure; and I have come to appreciate the greatness of his intellectual powers as I have come to realize that he did almost all that he did do by sheer intellectual prowess, in despite of the handicap imposed on his imagination by the narrowness of his sympathies with the human objects of his historical studies.

IV

To People, Institutions, Landscapes, Monuments, Pictures, Languages, and Books, for exciting my Curiosity

My great-uncle Captain Henry Toynbee (*vivebat* A.D. 1819–1909), who had commanded the East Indiamen *Ellenborough*, *Gloriana*, *Marlborough*, and *Hotspur* and had retired from the sea in A.D. 1866, to become Marine Superintendent of the Meteorological Office in London, without ever having served on a steamship, made me familiar with the build and life of the full-rigged sailing ship, which had been the master tool of the Western Civilization in its Modern Age, and which has vanished from the face of the seas within my own lifetime.

My great-uncle conjured up for me, as living realities, not only the Modern Western square-rigged sailing ship and the seas over which she sailed, but also the ports in India and China for which she was bound. I could picture the Hoogly pilot coming on board in all his glory, and the laskars chanting sonorous epic poetry as they laboured at the capstan. Every Sunday afternoon my uncle's old friend General Crofton, who lived in Westbourne Square and had sailed from England to India in my uncle's ship with reinforcements during the Indian Mutiny, used to come to tea at our house in London, No. 12 Upper Westbourne Terrace, and I was never tired of hearing the two old men exchanging reminiscences. (On one of these Sundays my uncle's nephew by marriage, Colonel Baden Powell, then just home from Mafeking and at the height of his fame, also came to call; and the two old men, after their usual talk about the Indian Mutiny, finally turned to their junior and asked him politely whether they were not right in thinking that he, too, had lately been on active service somewhere or other, and whether he would not tell them something about it. While my parents and I could hardly contain our laughter, the hero of the South African War had to tell us, as news, all that had been in the headlines months ago. He did what had been asked of him with a good humour that was vastly to his credit.)

The sea captain's and the sapper general's talk, the gigantic triple section of bamboo stem standing by the fireplace in the back part of the dining-room, the copper bonze riding the buffalo (then in the glass bookcase, and today on the mantlepiece in my study), the set of red and white Indian chessmen, Aunt Ellen's water-colour sketches of Indian scenes round the dining-room walls, and the fascinating legend of the duck-barge on the Yangtse, to which the ducks were summoned home at nightfall by a trumpet call—and came home quick, because they all knew that the last duck to return would be soundly thrashed—all this made India and China come alive for me. The evocation of these other worlds in my imagination was completed by my delight in the exotic trees in 'the Flower Walk' in Kensington Gardens, and by the models of Indian houses and villages (monkeys and all) and of Chinese rock-gardens in the Indian Museum. (These last, if I remember right, were gifts from the Manchu Imperial Court to Napoleon which had been intercepted by the British Navy.)

The Albert Memorial in Kensington Gardens peopled my world for me, while I was still in the perambulator, with continents, quadrupeds, poets, artists, sculptors, philosophers, and men of science.

The Indian Museum and the Victoria and Albert Museum in South Kensington, the United Services Museum in Whitehall, the British Museum, the Wallace Collection, the Tate Gallery, the National Gallery, and the Tower of London had put the visible works of Man on my mental map for me long before I had travelled as far as one day's journey from the Fountains at the head of the Serpentine in Kensington Gardens, which were and are the *omphalos* of my *Oikoumenê*.

Relfe Brothers' *Charterhouse Oxford and Cambridge Atlas*, which I acquired when I went to school in the autumn of A.D. 1896, put on the map for me New York, Vesuvius, and Palestine. A picture of Vesuvius smoking, and an equally exciting sketch-map of New York expanding, faced one another on the frontispiece, and the last map of all—'the World as Known to the Ancients'—excited me because it was centred on the Mediterranean Sea and not on the European peninsula of Asia. On this illuminating map I began to learn the names of the provinces of the Roman Empire; and I remember another boy putting his finger one day on the shore of the remotest corner of the land-locked sea and saying to me, 'That is Palestine'. I could hardly believe that a country which was already so familiar to me from the Bible could be marooned in such an out-of-the-way spot. It was not till long afterwards, when the Indic and the Sinic Civilization had risen above my horizon, that I realized how right our Medieval Western Christian forebears had been in locating the centre of the *Oikoumenê* at Jerusalem, and not at Rome, Paris, Greenwich, or any other point in their own eccentric Feringistan.

Karl von Spruner and Theodor Menke revealed to me the history of the civilizations in the bird's-eye view of cartography, in which, long before the days of flights at the altitude of the stratosphere, the human eye had found a means of taking in at a glance tracts of Space and Time so vast that it would have required innumerable volumes to describe them in the prolix medium of words. The first historical atlas that had come into my hands had been an English one, bought for me in a bookshop in Birmingham by my uncle, Percy Frankland, when I was staying with him and my Aunt Grace in the spring of A.D. 1903 during my convalescence from an illness, and this gift had already given me a new insight into History; but, as far back as I could remember, my Mother had been telling me that the best historical atlas in the World was the German masterpiece 'Spruner-Menke'; on my return to school at Winchester in the summer term of A.D. 1903, I came upon an early edition of this in Moberly Library; and, after that, my first purchase with my first prize money was a set of the latest editions of all three volumes of this supremely great work of German scholarship.[1] My Mother made me a brown holland cover for these folios, as a token that they were a κτῆμ' ἐς αἰεί; and, ever since, they have continued to be my constant companions and mentors.

The city of York lifted England for me out of an artificial insularity and put this would-be *alter orbis*[2] back into its proper place as an

[1] Spruner, K. von: *Atlas Antiquus*, 3rd ed., edited by Th. Menke (Gotha 1862, Perthes); idem: *Hand-Atlas für die Geschichte des Mittelalters und der Neueren Zeit*, 3rd ed., edited by Th. Menke (Gotha 1880, Perthes); idem: *Hand-Atlas zur Geschichte Asiens, Afrika's, Amerika's, und Australiens*, 2nd ed. (Gotha 1855, Perthes).

[2] See I. i. 17.

integral part of the *Oikoumenê.* In the names of the streets—Coney Street, Gudrumgate, and the rest—I rediscovered the Danish forefathers of my own family whose home was in the Lincolnshire fens, and I recollected that, in the reign of King Canute, England had been a province of a Scandinavian thalassocracy encircling the North Sea—as, in the days of Constantine the Great, who had been raised on the shield in York, and of Septimius Severus, who had died there, Britain had been a province of a Roman thalassocracy encircling the Mediterranean.

The glory of God, declared[1] in the beauty of *die unbegreiflich hohen Werke*[2] upon which the puny works of Man have been embroidered, was revealed to me when I saw Parnassus and Helicon and the Acrocorinthus from the Gulf of Corinth; the Acropolis of Athens from round the shoulder of Salamis; Olympus from Dhomokó (a white peak floating on air); Taÿgetus, stern-on, from Dhimitsána; the mountains of Crete from the crater-rim of Santorin, as they reared their heads out of the sea in the sudden visibility lent to them by nightfall; the Sun setting through the Golden Gate at San Francisco; the Via Appia Antica and the Inland Sea of Japan in the moonlight; Nara haunted by its holy deer; monasteries perched like eyries on the crags of Athos; cenotaphs of the heroes of Japan under the shadow of giant cryptomerias on Koya San; the Great Wall of China wriggling like a snake over billowy mountains; the Roman Wall crowning the crags at Howsteads; the Siebengebirge writhing down on to the Great North European Plain; the Great North Road running out of Seoul to seek Peking; the Rocky Mountains rushing, for an hour before we reached them, to meet our aeroplane at a speed of three hundred miles an hour; the skyline of New York from the eastern approaches; the battlements of the Kremlin at 2.30 a.m. on a winter's night; Lake Baikal with the Sun setting behind its engirdling mountains, as the train picked its way round the southern shore; the valley of the Connecticut River clad in its autumn scarlet and gold; the Mongol Valley of the Shilka and the Ottoman valley of the Hebrus; Boghazqal'eh offering a grander stage than Hisārlyq for the Second Book of *The Aeneid*; the apparition, between serried palm-groves and serried palm-groves, of *majnūn* wharves and refineries at Abadān; Cologne Cathedral looming up at the end of a transcontinental journey home to Western Christendom from Vladivostok; the purple citadel of Jodhpur and the blue sky piercing rose-red marble fretworks at Ahmadabad; the ruins of Rievaulx Abbey from the terrace above; the Sainte Chapelle; Chartres Cathedral; Durham Cathedral seen stern-on from across the river, and the overwhelming first impression of the giant round columns, weirdly carved in hypnotizing patterns; Waynflete's chantry in the cloisters of the College of St. Mary de Winton prope Winton; the ilex in the cloisters of the College of St. Mary de Winton ad Oxon; the Ayía Sophía, the Küchük Ayía Sophía, and the mosque of Mehmed Sököllü Pasha in Istanbul; the tiles in the mosque of Rüstem Pasha; the Qahrīyeh Jāmi'sy with its live

[1] Psalm xix. 1.

[2] Goethe: *Faust*, l. 249.

mosaics; the Green Mosque at Brusa; the masonry of Aleppo; the Altar and Temple of Heaven at Peking; the Pyramids of the Sun and Moon at Teotihuacán; the church-crowned pyramid at Cholula; Palenque defying the tropical forest; the thirsty cities of the Puuc; Monte Alban, at whose epiphany in his majesty the Acropolis of Sardis dwindles to the stature of a mole-hill; the cock-crows rising, faint but clear, from a sleepy city far below, as the dawn breaks upon the summit of the citadel of Afyūn Qāra Hisār; the blue wall of Taurus rising up sheer on either hand, as we sight it at the watershed *en route* from Nigdeh to the Cilician Gates; the bust of Antiochus the Great and the statue of Julian the Apostate in the Louvre; the bust of Nefertiti in the Reichsmuseum at Berlin.

As a present for my sixteenth birthday, my uncle William Toynbee gave me tickets for my Mother and me to see a performance of Gilbert Murray's translation of *The Trojan Women* of Euripides. As I write this, on the 11th May, 1951, I am taking out of the row of G. M.'s works in the bookcase, given me by my Mother, in my study at 45 Pembroke Square, the copy of the text that we bought at the theatre, with my name in it in my Mother's handwriting, dated '25th April, 1905'. That afternoon, I learnt that a Greek play could be conjured back to life.

My Mother introduced me to Robert Browning. In my fourth year at Winchester his poetry was one of the three special subjects set for our English Literature Prize, and, in the Christmas holidays of A.D. 1905–6, my Mother and I read Browning together. I can remember the evening, in the lamplight, when she opened a volume and said: 'I will begin with *My Star*; I wonder what you will think of it.' Her pleasure at the prospect of sharing her love of Browning's poetry with me had opened my heart to the poet before I had heard a line.

Cyril Bailey introduced me to Lucretius when I was finishing my education in the Hellenic literature by reading for the School of *Litterae Graecae et Latinae* at Oxford.

> Supremus veniet, clueat qui dignu' poeta—
> Hic deus, hic—fundens divinâ carmina voce.

I could never emulate my tutor's learning in the text of Lucretius's poem[1] or in the philosophy of Lucretius's master Epicurus,[2] or in the ideas of the atomic school of Hellenic scientists on whose system Epicurus drew for his own ethical purposes;[3] but I could and did catch from him his admiration for the Roman poet's work and his love for the nobly austere and sensitive personality that shines through an impersonal exposition of a drab theory about the nature of the Universe.

1 *Titi Lucreti Cari de Rerum Naturâ libri sex*, edited by Cyril Bailey (Oxford 1947, Clarendon Press, 3 vols.).
2 *Epicurus: The Extant Remains*, edited by Cyril Bailey (Oxford 1926, Clarendon Press).
3 Bailey, Cyril: *The Greek Atomists and Epicurus* (Oxford 1928, Clarendon Press).

Professor Sir Thomas Arnold and Professor H. A. R. Gibb gave me an invaluable start—not carried farther yet—towards learning Arabic, and 'Alī Rizā Bey towards learning Turkish.

Reynold A. Nicholson, in his *Translations of Eastern Poetry and Prose*,[1] gave me a glimpse of a Classical Islamic literature that I was unable to read in the original.

Arthur Waley, in his *A Hundred and Seventy Chinese Poems*,[2] gave me a glimpse of a Classical Sinic literature that I was unable to read in the original.

Moberly Library in the College of St. Mary de Winton prope Winton, the library of Balliol College, Oxford, the Finlay Library and the general library at the British Archaeological School at Athens, the library of the Societies for the Promotion of Hellenic and Roman Studies in London, the library of the School of Oriental Studies in the University of London, and the Long Gallery at Castle Howard opened up for me the vast universe of Modern Western printed books.

Thor Heyerdahl, in *Kon-Tiki*,[3] revealed to me 'the works of the Lord and His wonders in the deep,'[4] and this revelation taught me the secret of a latter-day Norwegian hero's Viking ancestors' achievements.

The genealogy of the descendants of Noah's three sons in the tenth chapter of the Book of Genesis gave me my first notion of the differentiation of the Human Race into divers groups and sub-groups, and of the historical problems raised by the question how these groups are related to one another. Coming across the chapter, as I did, in a lesson at school when I was seven years old, I was excited to find myself, as I supposed, being admitted to an inside view of the panorama of the unfolding of human history from the bud. It was not till I read E. Forrer's *Die Provinzeinteilung des Assyrischen Reiches*,[5] pp. 70–82, that I fully realized the lateness of the date and the shortness of the period represented by the catalogue, given in verses 2–5, of the sons and grandsons of Japheth. This catalogue proves, in the light of Assyriology, to be a mirror of the political map of the northern borderlands of the Assyrian Empire within the hundred years beginning *circa* 725 B.C. All the same, this late and ephemeral Israelitish *mappa mundi* did me the inestimable service of introducing me to the problem of Mankind's diversity-in-unity.

H. Drummond, in his *Tropical Africa*,[6] revealed to me, when I was a child, the life of Primitive Man in one of his last fastnesses, at a moment when this primitive way of life was being broken up by the Modern

[1] Cambridge 1922, University Press.
[2] London 1920, Constable.
[3] Chicago 1950, Rand McNally.
[4] Psalm cvii. 24.
[5] Leipzig 1920, Hinrichs.
[6] London 1888, Hodder & Stoughton.

Western Civilization's steam plough galloping in the tracks of the Islamic Civilization's harrow.

Sir Edward Creasy, in *The Fifteen Decisive Battles of the World*,[1] gave me my first notion of Universal History. In the Time-dimension the book carries the reader's mind backward as far as 490 B.C. and forward as far as A.D. 1815, while in the Space-dimension it carries him outwards, within that span of 2,305 years, from the Basin of the Aegean Sea across South-Western Asia to the Panjab, across the Black Sea to the Ukraine, and across the Atlantic Ocean to North America. Out of the fifteen battles in Creasy's canon of historical scripture, Arbela, Metaurus, Châlons, and Tours were the most fascinating for me. As I read, I saw Alexander, Hannibal, Attila, and 'Abd-ar-Rahmān rise in turn above my horizon; but, while my imagination was being stirred by these titanic figures, my mind was being educated by the intervening synopses of events in which the author had skilfully strung his fifteen great occasions along one continuous chronological thread.

The authors of four volumes of *The Story of the Nations*[2]—all four of them on my table on this twenty-first day of February, 1951, fifty-three years after they first came into my hands—suddenly revealed to me, when I was eight or nine years old, the histories of the Egyptiac, Babylonic, and Syriac civilizations simultaneously, and thereby initiated me into a synoptic view of History which has been illuminating my study of History since then. These four volumes had belonged to my grandmother Harriet Toynbee (her bookplate is in each of them), and, after her death in A.D. 1897, they were given to my Mother because she was the historian in the family. I remember, as if it were yesterday, catching sight, one morning after breakfast, of this batch of unfamiliar green and brown volumes on a familiar book-shelf. Curiosity moved me to pull them out, and, as soon as I opened them, I found them absorbing. They revealed to me a vista that has been widening and lengthening ever since. My first step towards enlarging it was to buy, with savings from my pocket money, Z. A. Ragozin's *Chaldea* (5th ed., 1896),[3] to which the same author's *Assyria* had been a sequel. 'Arnold J. Toynbee, March 1899', is inscribed in this volume in my Mother's handwriting.

1 The copy which my Father gave me in A.D. 1898 was of the forty-first edition, published in that year (London, Bentley).

2 The series was published in London by Fisher Unwin. The four volumes that were of momentous personal importance for me were George Rawlinson's *Ancient Egypt* (2nd edition, 1887); Z. A. Ragozin's *Assyria* (1888); Ragozin's *Media, Babylon, and Persia* (1889); Arthur Gilman's *The Saracens* (1887).

3 The first edition of *Chaldea* had been published in A.D. 1886. Notwithstanding the title of this book, the subject of it was not the wanderings of the Chaldaean Nomad barbarians who had filtered into the south-western fringes of the Land of Shinar out of the North Arabian Steppe in a Völkerwanderung *circa* 1425–1125 B.C.; it was the genesis and growth of a civilization that, in this Study, has been labelled 'the Sumeric' after the name of the Sumerian people who originated it. The Biblical terminology 'Ur of the Chaldees' (Genesis xi. 31) had led the pioneer Modern Western discoverers of this long buried and forgotten culture to jump to the mistaken conclusion that the Chaldaeans had been the earliest successors of the Sumerians, instead of realizing that they had been the latest comers before the Arabs.

A. J. Church's *Stories of the East from Herodotus*[1] introduced me to the vast and variegated landscape of Herodotus's *Oikoumenê*. The pictures opened my eyes to two distinctive styles of art that were the respective signatures of the Egyptiac and the Babylonic Civilization.

J. P. Mahaffy, in his volume[2] on *Alexander's Empire*[3] in the *Story of the Nations*, revealed to me the post-Alexandrine chapter of Hellenic history. I can remember my excitement when, as I opened the book in the foyer of a theatre to which my parents were taking me during one of my holidays from school, I came upon the map showing Hellenism pushing its way from European Greece into the Indus Valley across all the derelict satrapies of a shattered Achaemenian Empire. But it was not till I opened the book again, after an interval of many years, on the 17th April, 1951, that I noticed and appreciated the author's historical insight in reproducing on the cover the bust, not of Alexander, but of Epicurus.

Edwyn Bevan, in his *The House of Seleucus*,[4] carried me farther into the fascinating study of post-Alexandrine Hellenic history into which I had been initiated by J. P. Mahaffy in his *Alexander's Empire*. Afterwards, when I had the happiness of coming to know Edwyn Bevan personally, I learnt more from this great Christian historian than even he knew how to put into any book.

Emil Schürer, in his *A History of the Jewish People in the Time of Jesus Christ*,[5] revealed to me the illuminating historical truth that, in the time of Christ, the Coele Syria that had been conquered from the Ptolemies by the Seleucidae in 202–198 B.C. was a cultural arena in which the Jewish forlorn hope of a Syriac Society was engaged with an aggressive Hellenism *corps à corps*. I vividly remember a Sunday morning at Winchester in Cloister Time, A.D. 1907, when, as I was reading the Second Division, volume i, paragraphs 22 and 23, of Schürer's *History* in bed before breakfast, I made the exciting discovery of the Hellenic city-states—ranged in a pair of parallel tiers, one tier along the coast and another along the well-wooded and well-watered uplands of Transjordania—of which I had already taken a visual cognizance, without having grasped their full historical significance, on two maps[6] in Spruner's *Atlas Antiquus* on which they were coloured a conspicuous red and were labelled 'urbes Graecanicae'. This summer's morning, as I began to make myself better acquainted with this Coele-Syrian galaxy of Hellenic city-states in Schürer's industriously compiled gazetteer, I learnt for the first time that an Hellenic Gadara, which had been notorious to its Jewish neighbours in the time of Christ for nothing but

[1] London 1881 [1880], Seeley.
[2] Dedicated to the father of my two contemporaries and friends, Allen and Rex Leeper.
[3] Sixth edition: London 1895, Fisher Unwin.
[4] London 1902, Edward Arnold, 2 vols.
[5] English translation: two parts in five volumes, with a sixth volume containing an index: Edinburgh 1890–1, Clark.
[6] Nos. XIIII ('Mare Internum cum Populis Adiacentibus â Pompeii ex Asiâ Reditu usque ad Bellum Actiacum') and XXVI ('Judaea Maccabaeorum Tempore').

a Gentile disregard of the Mosaic tabu against breeding swine, had given birth, at the turn of the second and the last century B.C., to the Meleager who was the author of the famous garland poem in the *Anthologia Palatina*, and thereafter to a Theodorus who had made himself sufficiently eminent as a professor of Greek literature to obtain the post of tutor to the future Emperor Tiberius. As this fresh light on the scene of the stampede of the Gadarene Swine began to dawn on me, I felt as if the early morning sunlight, which at that moment was turning the walls of Chapel into glowing gold, were performing some equivalent alchemy in my mind.

Canon George Rawlinson, in *The Seventh Great Oriental Monarchy*,[1] which I read during my convalescence from an illness in the winter of A.D. 1902–3, revealed to me a Sasanian chapter of Iranian history in which Iran had held her own against a Rome that had commanded the united forces of the entire Hellenic World.

V. A. Smith, in *The Early History of India*,[2] revealed to me the histories of the rise and fall of the Indic Civilization and the rise of its Hindu successor. I stumbled on an early edition of it in the library of Balliol College, Oxford, in A.D. 1907. A later edition has been one of my constant companions since April, 1920.

Friedrich Hirth, in *The Ancient History of China*,[3] revealed to me the history of the Sinic Civilization down to a date thirty-five years short of the founding of a Sinic universal state by Ts'in She Hwang-ti. I stumbled on a copy in one of the book-shops on the south side of Broad Street, Oxford, while I was an undergraduate. A copy of the second reprint, bought in Boston, Mass., in October 1925, has been one of my constant companions.

Sir William Tarn, in *The Greeks in Bactria and India*,[4] revealed to me the crucible of the Mahāyāna.

Sir Aurel Stein, in a lantern lecture on his Central Asian expedition of A.D. 1907–8 which he gave in the great hall of the Examination Schools at Oxford while I was an undergraduate (*studia Oxoniae exercebam* A.D. 1907–11), revealed to me the Central Asian corridor in which the Indic and the Judaic religions had once run into one another and had afterwards travelled forward abreast on their eastward journey into a Sinic World. I followed up the vista that had been opened for me in this lecture by reading the archaeologist-explorer's *Sand-Buried Ruins of Khotan*.[5]

Sir Charles Eliot, in his *Hinduism and Buddhism*,[6] gave me the sensation of being shown the other side of the Moon by revealing to me the

[1] London 1876, Longmans, Green.
[2] Published at Oxford by the Clarendon Press (1st ed., 1904; 3rd ed., 1914).
[3] Published in New York in A.D. 1908 by the Columbia University Press.
[4] Cambridge 1938, University Press.
[5] M. A. Stein: *Sand-Buried Ruins of Khotan* (London 1904, Hurst & Blackett).
[6] London 1921, Edward Arnold, 3 vols.

history and êthos of that half of the *Oikoumenê* that has received its higher religious illumination from an Indic, and not from a Judaic, source. My geographical horizon, historical vista, and gamut of spiritual experience had all been doubled before I had finished reading this great book.

Michael Rostovtzeff, in his *Iranians and Greeks in South Russia*,[1] revealed to me the Nomad Civilization of the Great Eurasian Steppe.

Sir Henry Yule, in his edition of Marco Polo's book,[2] and Sir Henry Howorth, in his history of the Mongols,[3] revealed to me the heart of the Eurasian Steppe, with an *alter orbis* in Eastern Asia, on the far side of it, which Herodotus leaves still tantalizingly veiled when he lifts one corner of the curtain of ignorance to uncover the waterless ocean's western bay. I shall never forget my sensations when, one evening in June 1908, as the night-train for Aberdeen slid out of King's Cross Station, I opened the first volume of Howorth's pioneer work and saw a vast unknown landscape spread itself before my eyes: Kin and Sung and Tangut; Qāra Qitāy and Khwārizm; Naiman and Karāyit. When the train slid into Edinburgh early on the following morning, I was still busily taking on board a cargo of exciting new knowledge that has been a key part of my mental furniture ever since. Propped up with a pillow in my third-class corner-seat, I was sleepy but unsated. Thanks to Howorth's infectious enthusiasm for his subject, I had, I believe, that night, at second hand, some inkling of 'Messer Millione's' excitement when he saw his first sight of China with the eyes of the flesh.

W. H. Prescott, in his *History of the Conquest of Mexico*, which was read aloud to us at my preparatory school, put the civilizations of the New World on my mental map for me.

The Maudslay Collection revealed to me the history of the Mayan Civilization. As I was wandering round the British Museum one day in A.D. 1923, I stumbled on a room in which the central object on exhibition was a cast of a stone of a tortoise-like shape, but far larger than the largest giant tortoise that I had ever seen at the Zoological Gardens in Regent's Park; and I found that this object and its companions were covered with reliefs in a style, new to me, which was reminiscent of the Egyptiac, the Sumeric, and the Sinic, and yet was distinctively different from each and all of these. These casts and originals—the fruits of A. P. Maudslay's field work in Mayan lands since A.D. 1881—had then just been brought up from the basement of the South Kensington Museum and placed on view in Bloomsbury. I did not leave the British Museum that afternoon without having bought the *Guide to the Mauds-*

1 Oxford 1922, Clarendon Press.

2 *The Book of Ser Marco Polo*, translated into English by Sir H. Yule, 3rd ed., revised by H. Cordier (London 1903, John Murray, 2 vols.); Notes and Addenda by H. Cordier (London 1920, John Murray).

3 Howorth, H. H.: *History of the Mongols*, Parts I–III in 4 volumes (London 1876–1888, Longmans Green); Part IV, Supplement and Indexes (London 1928, Longmans).

lay Collection of Maya Sculptures from Central America, published in A.D. 1923 by order of the Trustees. The exhibits and the guide-book, between them, introduced me to a culture which had previously been beyond my historical horizon. I ascertained that the object which had first caught my eye was a cast of 'Monolithic Animal P' from Quiriguá. From that day onwards, the Mayan Civilization had a place on my mental map.

When, in July 1908, I was staying with my Mother's former pupil and life-long bosom friend Urith Perrot in her house at Blellach, near Dinnet, on Donside, I found there in the library Lactantius's *De Mortibus Persecutorum* and the Nuremberg Chronicle, and sat up reading them into the small hours of those twilight midsummer Scottish nights.

Thomas Hodgkin, in *Italy and her Invaders*,[1] awakened my interest in the post-Hellenic interregnum when I found and read the book in Moberly Library at Winchester.

The Benedictine Abbey at Ampleforth has made me aware of the spiritual impetus of the Western Christian monastic life, and has shown me that the secret of the historical continuity of the Benedictine Order is the whole-heartedness of the faith of Saint Benedict's spiritual sons. Listening to the singing of the Office in the church, and reminding myself that this *opus Dei* had been carried on without a break throughout the fourteen hundred years that had passed since the Founder's generation, I came to realize that this Western religious community, which was the matrix of Western Christendom, possessed a greater vitality than any of the secular institutions that had hived off from it. Driven from Westminster on to the Continent by the outbreak of the Reformation, this particular Benedictine community had struck root again at Dieulouard in Lorraine, where, for the next quarter of a millennium, it had been kept alive by a constant supply of English postulants who could follow the monastic calling only at the price of expatriation. Driven from Dieulouard back to England by the outbreak of the French Revolution, the community had struck fresh root in the vale of Ampleforth in Yorkshire. How had it managed to survive these successive uprootings? This question has been answered for me by my experience of the friendships that I have had the happiness of making with some of this community's living members.

My Mother made me aware that there had been a Byzantine, as well as a Carolingian, Empire, and that the Normans had conquered Sicily as well as England.

E. A. Freeman's *Historical Essays*[2] opened up for me vistas of Western and Hellenic history that led me out into the great open spaces beyond.

[1] Oxford 1892–9, Clarendon Press, 8 vols. in 9 parts.
[2] London: First Series 1871; Second Series 1873; Third Series 1879; Fourth Series 1892: all published by Macmillan.

Charles Oman, in *A History of the Art of War from the Fourth to the Fourteenth Century*,[1] introduced me to the Cataphract[2] and made it clear to me that an age which had witnessed so great a revolution in military technique as the Late Roman reversion to cavalry from infantry could not be a mere epilogue, but must mark the opening of a new chapter of history. The Psalter of Theodore of Caesarea, from which Oman had reproduced some of the pictures of Byzantine fighting men, was shown to me by a friend of my Mother's in the British Museum.

Geoffroi de Villehardouin, as I sat reading his *Conquête de Constantinople* in de Wailly's attractive edition[3] by the fireside in my Uncle Paget Toynbee's library at Fiveways, Burnham, Bucks, in December 1906, made me repeat to myself Lewis Carroll's satirical poem the *Walrus and the Carpenter* when I came to the gifted Champenois adventurer's unctuous account of the pious tears which the Frenchmen and the Venetians shed together over their cold-blooded bargains at Zara's and Byzantium's expense. I remembered that evening when, on the 21st February, 1912, I first set eyes on the Villehardouins' castle at Kalamáta.

Under Campbell Dodgson's auspices, my Mother and I spent many hours in the Print Room of the British Museum looking at Albrecht Dürer's drawings and sketches.

George Finlay, in *A History of Greece from its Conquest by the Romans to the Present Time, B.C. 146 to A.D. 1864*,[4] revealed to me the disintegration of the Ottoman Empire and the cultural reorientation of the Millet-i-Rūm from an Ottoman to a Western *qiblah*.

Colonel G. F. R. Henderson's *Stonewall Jackson*,[5] which my father gave me to read in the summer holidays one year while I was at school at Winchester, revealed to me both the tragedy and the romance of the American Civil War.

Beech Point, near Danville, Kentucky, where I stayed with my dear friend Robert Shelby Darbishire for the first time in the summer of A.D. 1925, gave me a glimpse, from inside, of a post-Bellum rural South that was then still as remote in spirit from Cincinnati, across the Ohio, as I found Lithuania to be from East Prussia when I crossed another cultural frontier there in the spring of A.D. 1928.

[1] London 1898, Methuen.

[2] This early introduction to a type of military accoutrement which has never ceased to fascinate me once got me into trouble when, at my preparatory school, I was given, for translation into Latin, an account in English of Crassus's march eastward in 53 B.C. When I came to a sentence recording the King of Armenia's advice to the Roman commander to hug the Armenian foothills and give a wide berth to the Mesopotamian plains for fear of the Parthian cavalry, I translated the English word 'cavalry' by the Latin word 'cataphracti'. 'Where on earth did you run across that outlandish word?' asked the master, as he crossed it out in red ink and substituted a banal 'equites'. I dared not protest or even explain; yet I knew that no stroke of a magisterial pen could really avail to divest those Parthian centaurs of their iron carapaces.

[3] Paris 1882, Firmin-Didot.

[4] New edition, revised by H. F. Tozer: Oxford 1877, Clarendon Press, 7 vols.

[5] London 1898, Longmans, Green, 2 vols.

Sir Herbert Maxwell, in his *Sixty Years a Queen*, 'The Story of Her Majesty's Reign, Illustrated Chiefly from the Royal Collections',[1] revealed to me, in his panorama, the achievements of Victorian England.

My Mother's account of her conversation with the disgruntled custodian of the deserted royal palace at Hanover, when she visited it during her stay in Germany in A.D. 1885, made me realize, even as a child, that all was not well under the surface in Prussia-Germany.

Sir Lewis Namier, when he made his memorable first appearance at Balliol College, Oxford, as an undergraduate, in A.D. 1908, put on my mental map for me the Danubian Hapsburg Monarchy and the Jewish Pale, which were then still quite unknown worlds for English undergraduates of our generation, though, within seven or eight years from then, half of us were to lose their lives in a general war fought to prevent Germany from establishing an ascendancy over Eastern Europe which, at the next stage, would have enabled her to make a bid for world dominion.

R. W. Seton-Watson ('Scotus Viator'), in his *Racial Problems in Hungary*,[2] lent to me by A. E. Zimmern in the summer term of A.D. 1909, illuminated for me a plague-spot in the East European landscape that Sir Lewis Namier had brought within my horizon.

Though 'historical novels' are apt to set my teeth on edge by offering me a stone instead of bread, I should be ungrateful indeed if I failed to acknowledge my debt to Herodotus for his tales of Mycerinus and Rhampsinîtus and Nitocris, to Leo Tolstoy for his *War and Peace*, to Naomi Mitchison for her *The Corn King and the Spring Queen*,[3] to L. S. Woolf for his *The Village in the Jungle*,[4] to O. E. Rölvaag for his *Giants in the Earth*,[5] to Georg Moritz Ebers for his *Uarda*,[6] to Victor Hugo for his *Quatre-Vingt Treize* and *Les Misérables*, and to Émile Erckmann and Alexandre Chatrian for their *Le Blocus*. When I looked in at Phalsbourg on the 26th July, 1929, *en route* from Calais to Constantinople, its bastions and casemates were already so familiar to me that I could hardly believe that I was now setting eyes on them for the first time. I had found *Le Blocus* in a row of discarded books on a shelf in the pantry at No. 12 Upper Westbourne Terrace, and *Quatre-Vingt Treize* on a shelf in my Aunt Gertrude Toynbee's flat.

C. G. Jung, in his *Psychological Types*,[7] opened up for me a new dimension in the realm of Life. The admirable catholicity with which Jung draws upon materials of the most diverse kinds for the illustration of his themes enabled me to find my way into the *terra incognita* of the

[1] London 1897, arranged and printed by Eyre & Spottiswoode, published by Harmsworth Bros.
[2] London 1908, Constable.
[3] London 1931, Cape.
[4] London 1913, Edward Arnold.
[5] New York 1927, Harper.
[6] English translation by C. Bull, Leipzig 1877, Low, 2 vols.
[7] English translation: London 1923, Kegan Paul.

Psyche's subconscious abyss by proceeding from the known to the unknown. I was fascinated to watch, under Jung's analysis, the same primordial image coming to light in a familiar myth and in some *rebarbatif* clinical case in Jung's own professional practice which might have repelled my mind if my interest in the analysis of the myth had not drawn me on to take a consequent interest in the myth's clinical counterpart.

After Jung had thus given me the freedom of the New World of Psychology, I found here the equivalents, in the experience of the Soul, of a number of phenomena that I had already observed for myself in the experience of Society. The polarization of the *libido* (psychic energy) when it strikes an obstacle was the equivalent of the schism in the Body Social (mirror of the Soul) after a failure to respond to a challenge. The depression of subordinated functions into the Subconscious was the equivalent of the estrangement of a proletariat from a dominant minority. The explosive discharge of obstructed *libido* was the equivalent of a Völkerwanderung of barbarian war-bands when the *limes* behind which they have been pent up at last gives way in a collapse that had been symbolized for me in the bursting of the Dam of Ma'rib. A salvation proceeding from the Subconscious was the equivalent of a salvation proceeding from the Internal Proletariat. The re-emergence, after a submarine voyage, of splinters of conscious psychic life that have been submerged in the Subconscious was the equivalent of the re-emergence in the myth of Jesus, after a submarine voyage along the underground river of Folk-Memory, of a history of Agis and Cleomenes which had descended into the folk-lore of an Internal Proletariat. The projection of elements of the Subconscious upon external objects was the equivalent of the radiation of elements of the life of a disintegrating civilization into its external proletariat.

V

To People and Books, for teaching me Methods of Intellectual Work

H. J. Haselfoot, who initiated me at Wootton Court School, Kent, into the art of coping with unseen translations from Ancient Greek authors in preparation for the Winchester College scholarship elections of A.D. 1901 and A.D. 1902, taught me the sovereign intellectual art of deliberately taking time—even when time is short—to let the mind play round a problem and try to grasp it as a whole before plunging into any attempt to solve it in detail. This is the most valuable single lesson in intellectual method that I have ever been given. It made so deep an impression on me at the time that I was able to take it to heart, and I have used it, ever since, in every piece of intellectual work that I have ever undertaken.

I remember that my master and I started operations together on a description of a naval battle in Thucydides' *History of the Atheno-Peloponnesian War*. My master used this text (I think it must have been Book II, chapter 91) to show me how to arrive at the meaning of the Greek word μετέωρος by bringing my scanty acquaintance with the Greek vocabulary into relation with the context of the word in this passage.

This was a masterly piece of educational work for which I am abidingly grateful.

J. A. Smith allowed me to educate myself by listening in to a spacious and fertile mind thinking aloud.

The experience of working in H.B.M. Foreign Office in Whitehall during the First and then again during the Second World War taught me, as a temporary civil servant, two lessons that I have found invaluable for an historian.

The first lesson is that the acquisition of information is, not an end in itself, but only a means to the end of taking action. In the service of a government or any other institution, the action which is the purpose of the acquisition of information is, of course, action of the 'practical' kind; but the golden rule which I had learnt in the Foreign Office from the business of acquiring information for use in such 'practical' action proved to apply with equal force to an historian's work. Action taken on any plane will be in danger of going wrong if it is not taken in the light of the truth and of nothing but the truth; but it will be in equal danger of getting nowhere if it is not also taken in the light of no more of the truth than the minimum that is relevant to the particular piece of action that is on the current agenda.

This golden rule which the Intellect has to learn for itself by 'practical' experience has been made fool-proof on the subconscious level by being made there to work automatically; for the human Memory, as Bergson has pointed out, is a psychic mechanism which gives the Will a chance of taking action by withholding from the Consciousness every record in the vast and ever growing complete collection of past impressions that lies stored in a subconscious psychic depository, unless and until a particular record is required by the Consciousness for the practical purpose of enabling the Will to put some design into effect. If the mechanism of the Memory did not thus implacably withhold from the Consciousness all registered information that was not pertinent to the action in hand, the Consciousness would be paralysed, and perhaps even be driven mad, by an overwhelming flood of irrelevant recollections.

This first lesson that is to be learnt from working in a department of state has a second as its corollary. The information that is to be found in an official document will have been put there—if we may assume that the document has been drafted competently—in order to serve some official purpose which, whatever it may have been, will certainly not have been the irrelevant purpose of informing a future historian. The relevancy of documents to their 'practical' purposes increases their potential value as pieces of historical evidence, but the historian will not be able to profit by them for his own intellectual purpose unless and until he succeeds in rediscovering, or reconstructing, those quite different purposes for which they were made.

John Stuart Mill, in his *Autobiography*, taught me to keep my mind fresh by alternating, on some regular rhythm, between different kinds of intellectual work. Between the wars I used to write the Chatham House Survey of International Affairs in the winter and spring in London and *A Study of History* in the summer and autumn in Yorkshire. In writing Parts VI–XIII of *A Study of History* since the 1st July, 1947, I have been able—thanks to the generosity of the Rockefeller Foundation of New York in making it possible for Chatham House to release my time to the necessary extent—to follow a daily cycle in London, working at home in the mornings and at Chatham House in the afternoons. The shorter the wave of this alternating rhythm of intellectual work, the longer, in my experience, is the time for which it is possible to go on working continuously on a long task without the mental engine's 'seizing'.

From seeing the mighty remains of Venetian fortresses in the Levant, I learnt to know something of Venice herself without having set eyes on her. From observing the impacts made by the Western Civilization upon other societies, I came to know something of the êthos of the West without having studied Western history.

Plato taught me, by example, not to be ashamed of using my imagination as well as my intellect. He taught me, when, in a mental voyage, I found myself at the upper limit of the atmosphere accessible to the Reason, not to hesitate to let my imagination carry me on up into the stratosphere on the wings of a myth. In never being either too proud or too timid to take to a myth for the sake of reconnoitring regions of the Spiritual Universe beyond the Reason's range, Plato was showing both the humility and the audacity of a great mind, and this Hellenic philosopher's example fortified me in an adverse Western mental environment in which I did not find any outstanding contemporary good example to follow. I have now lived to see the subconscious well-spring of Poetry and Prophecy restored to honour in the Western World by the genius of C. G. Jung; but, before Jung's star at last rose above my horizon, Plato's example, brought within my ken by an Hellenic classical education, had given me courage to part company with an early-twentieth-century Western Zeitgeist whose oracles were scales and dividers because, in this Geist's self-blinkered eyes, the only realities were those that could be weighed and measured.

Lionel Curtis taught me, by example, a method of production and an attitude of mind which I have found, by experience, to be a sovereign help in dealing with difficult and, above all, with controversial subjects. He taught me that, in the writing of a book, as in every other human activity, the worst of all vices is the hybris that is the nemesis of self-conceit. An author is convicting himself of being past praying for if ever he allows the Old Adam in him to close his mind to a suggestion for some modification of his first draft by answering 'What I have written I have written.'[1] An author had better retire from business if he has not the humility to conceive of the possibility that, after all, he may be mistaken,

[1] John xix. 22.

and if he has not also the common sense to see, in the living authorities on his subject, not critics to be combated after publication, but mentors to be consulted before it, at a stage when it is still not too late to profit by their fruitfully chastening strictures. Taking my cue from Lionel Curtis, I have learnt to put my work through two stages when a controversial subject is on my agenda. The first stage is to produce as good a draft as I can manage out of my own resources. The second stage is to circulate this draft to a number of authorities who have divers experience, knowledge, standpoints, and feelings, and then to rewrite the passage in the light of their comments on the first draft. The first stage is indispensable because a draft is apt to draw comment—in contrast to a questionnaire, which is apt to find its way into a pigeonhole, if not into the waste-paper basket. But this first stage is merely a prelude to the second, which is the fruitful one. The process of rewriting in the light of comments is fruitful because a synoptic view of comments from different angles gives an author a stereoscopic vision of his subject which is not attainable by a single pair of eyes. This method of taking counsel's opinion does not, of course, dispense the author from the responsibility of eventually taking a line of his own and staking his head on this. But it does put it in his power to give himself the best chance open to him of being of some service to his readers.

VI

To People and Books, for teaching me Methods of Literary Presentation

Theodor Mommsen, in *The History of the Roman Republic*, which I read, in my Aunt Gertrude Toynbee's copy of the English translation,[1] during the summer of A.D. 1907, between leaving school and going up to the University, taught me that an historical work was a better presentation of history for being also a work of art.

Pindar, the Attic playwrights, and Herodotus, interpreted for me by Sir John Myres,[2] taught me the use of the symmetrical rhythm of strophe and antistrophe. Herodotus also taught me his art of lightening the load on the main thread of a narrative by stowing away into annexes any matter remote enough from the central theme to be detachable from it, but not so remote that it could be simply left out of the book.

Aristotle taught me his method, of which he makes a masterly use in the *Politics*, of illustrating general propositions about human affairs by recounting apposite historical anecdotes.

Lucretius, in his *De Rerum Naturâ*, Book I, lines 58–61, taught me the literary value of ringing changes on synonyms for conveying the key terms in a system of ideas, as a device for avoiding the monotony of the effect that would be produced by invariably employing the same word

[1] English translation by W. P. Dickson: London 1887–8, Bentley, 4 vols. My Aunt Gertrude's copy, with my name written in it in her handwriting, dated 'September 1906', is here on my desk in May 1951.

[2] See Myres, J. L.: *Herodotus: Outline Analysis of Books I–VI* (Oxford 1912); *Herodotus, Father of History* (Oxford, 1953, Clarendon Press).

to denote the same inevitably oft-recurring term of art. His adroitness in manœuvring his cohort of interchangeable synonyms signifying atomic particles of matter—primordia, principia, prima elementa, corpora prima, semina rerum, genitalia corpora rebus[1]—moved me to follow his example by ringing changes of my own on such approximately synonymous words as 'civilization', 'society', 'culture', and 'world' and approximately synonymous compound terms as 'universal state' and 'oecumenical empire'.

Clarendon, in *The History of the Rebellion and Civil Wars in England begun in the Year 1641*, taught me always to give a reference in a footnote to chapter and verse for every quotation that I made from the Bible. If this was good practice in England in Clarendon's day, when the Authorized Version of the Bible was a household book, it ought not to be abandoned in our time, when the Bible is rapidly passing into oblivion in the English-speaking countries. On this principle, I have given references for my quotations, not only from the Bible, but also from the Greek and Latin Classics.

I am thankful for the personal good fortune of having been born just not too late in the day to receive an old-fashioned English humane education in the Classics and in the Bible. Enough of the language of the Authorized Version of the Bible has lodged itself in my memory, through having repeatedly come to my ears in the lessons read in church, to bring into my mind, when I am writing, a flow of phrases, or reminiscences of phrases, from the Scriptures.[2] But I was born too late to become a *hāfiz*, even in the sacred book of my own ancestral religion; I know by heart only a word or two of the Qur'ān; and I have no acquaintance at all with the Pālī Scriptures of the Hinayanian sect of Buddhism or with the Confucian Classics. If I had managed to possess myself of these spiritual riches, I might have been able to do greater justice to the subject of this Study.

F. M. Cornford, in his *Thucydides Mythistoricus*,[3] taught me to indicate, by the use of an abstract noun with its initial letter printed as a capital, the presence of one of those psychic principalities and powers—'The Tragic Passions', as Cornford calls them—for which there are no proper names in the sterilized vocabulary of a rationalist latter-day Western Society. Hilm and Aidôs, Civilization and Democracy and Industrialism, Archaism and Futurism, Time and Space, Law and

[1] See Cyril Bailey's edition of the *De Rerum Naturâ* (Oxford 1947, Clarendon Press, 3 vols.), vol. i, p. 140.

[2] An English-speaking writer who has been brought up on the Authorized Version of the Bible is apt to take the use of its language for granted. Sir Lewis Namier, who had grown up in a Catholic country where the living Polish vernacular was impervious to influences emanating from the Latin of the Vulgate and the Liturgy, once passed on to me his own exciting discovery, made by him in England, that an archaic translation of the Bible and the Liturgy into a living vernacular enhances this fortunate language's powers of expression, not only by doubling its vocabulary, but also by giving a speaker or a writer an effective means of evoking emotion, in any degree that he may desire, by drawing on the Bible for reinforcements, ranging from faint allusions to explicit quotations, in support of the pedestrian language of every-day life.

[3] London 1907, Edward Arnold.

Fortune, are a few examples, taken at random. This usage has, of course, its own drawback. On the analogy of personal names, it might be misinterpreted as conveying the false, and unintended, suggestion that these presences are personalities, when the truth is that they are non-personal emanations from a subconscious abyss of the Psyche that is the matrix of personalities as well. Yet a usage suggesting personification is at any rate less misleading than one suggesting that these entities are abstractions—as would be implied by printing the initial letters of the corresponding English words in lower-case type—for, though they are not personalities, they are charges of psychic energy that have power to work weal and woe in human affairs, and the lack of proper names for them in a latter-day Western vocabulary betrays a tell-tale lacuna in Modern Western thought and imagination and feeling. There are more things in Heaven and Earth than are dreamed of in Horatio's Western philosophy. *τὸ πᾶν δαιμόνων πλῆρες*;[1] and, if I had been writing in either Greek or Latin, I should never have been troubled with this problem of semantics. The Greek word *δαίμονες* and the Latin word *numina* bear joint witness to an awareness in Hellenic souls that these non-personal psychic presences are potent live realities.

In looking on at a Japanese puppet show at Osaka one afternoon in November 1929, I duly found, as I had been assured beforehand that I should find, it possible to entertain the illusion that the puppets were animated by an autonomous life of their own, although the human artists manipulating them were in full view of the spectators. An artistic effect which, in the West, would have been produced by the artifice of keeping the manipulators out of sight, was produced in Japan by their artistry in keeping themselves out of mind notwithstanding their visibility. The Japanese manipulators achieved this *tour de force* of managing to deflect the spectators' attention away from themselves and on to their puppets by making their own movements appear lifeless and their own countenances impassive. They succeeded, in fact, in subjectively effacing their objectively visible living human forms; and this *chef-d'œuvre* of Japanese art taught me a trick for serving my readers' convenience by signalling to them the careers and dates of persons mentioned in my text without distracting their attention from the narrative. I learnt to make these useful insertions unobtrusive by putting them into Latin and printing them in italics between brackets.

VII

To People, Monuments, Apparatus, Pictures, Books, and Events, for giving me Intuitions and Ideas

Robert Browning presented me with the phrase 'Challenge and Response'. I had flattered myself that this phrase was of my own coinage

[1] *νοῦν τοῦ κόσμου τὸν Θεόν, τὸ δὲ πᾶν ἔμψυχον ἅμα καὶ δαιμόνων πλῆρες* (Thales, fragment 23); *πάντα πλήρη θεῶν εἶναι* (Thales, fragment 22).—Diels, H.: *Die Fragmente der Vorsokratiker*, 5th ed., vol. i (Berlin 1934, Weidmann), p. 79.

till, more than ten years after I had first put it on paper, I came upon it in the fourth stanza of Browning's *Master Hugues of Saxe Gotha*:

> —O you may challenge them, not a response
> Get the church-saints on their rounds!

The collocation of the two words must have lain submerged on some subconscious level of my mind for about a quarter of a century since the Christmas holidays of A.D. 1905–6, when I had first read the poem with my Mother. When I fancied that I was inventing it, I was only hauling it up from the hold of my memory.

Professor F. J. Teggart, in his *Theory of History*,[1] chapter 14, showed me where to find the entry into my subject after I had been groping for it without succeeding in discovering it by my own native lights.[2] The baffling obscurities in my initial problem of method and procedure were illuminated for me by Teggart's dicta[3] that 'in the study of Man . . . the first step must be a return to the Present'; that 'the point of departure must necessarily be observation of the differences which particularize the condition of Humanity in different parts of the World'; and that 'the observation of the cultural differences which distinguish human groups leads at once to a recognition of the major problem of the Science of Man', namely: ' "How are these differences to be accounted for?"; "How have the differences which we observe in the cultural activities of men come to be as we find them at the present time?"' I took these directives to heart, and have followed them from beginning to end of the present work. They have proved to be a sovereign clue which has not only initiated me into my subject but has piloted me through it.

Alfred Zimmern taught me, eight years before the publication of Benedetto Croce's *Teoria e Storia della Storiografia* in A.D. 1917, that 'all true history is contemporary history'.[4] I learnt this from the intellectual ferment raised in my mind in New College hall in the summer term of A.D. 1909 as I listened to A. E. Z. delivering a course of introductory lectures on Hellenic history, for undergraduates starting to read *Litterae Humaniores*, which was the matrix of *The Greek Commonwealth*.[5] As I sat listening to those catalytic words, the conventional partitions between 'Past' and 'Present' and between 'Ancient' and 'Modern' dissolved out of my mind and have never since returned to hamper it. I had learnt that life, thought, and feeling in the Hellenic World in the fifth

[1] New Haven, Conn. 1925, Yale University Press.

[2] In my first attempt, made in the summer vacation of A.D. 1920, I had tried to cast my ideas into the form of a commentary on the second chorus in Sophocles' *Antigone* (ll. 332–75). The theme of this poem—'The Mystery of Man'—was apposite and the poetry was magnificent, but the approach was unpromising; for this expedient of referring a question to some classical oracle was the Medieval and Early Modern Western approach into which I had been initiated at school, whereas the intellectual enterprise on which I had now embarked was an attempt to take bearings in the uncharted seas of a post-Modern chapter of Western history. My appeal to Sophocles had, in fact, been a false move, and it was therefore neither surprising nor regrettable that it had been a failure.

[3] In op. cit., p. 171.

[4] 'Ogni vera storia è storia contemporanea'—Croce, B., op. cit., 2nd ed. (Bari 1920, Laterza), p. 4.

[5] Published by the Oxford University Press (1st ed., 1911; 2nd ed., revised, 1915).

century B.C. were living presences working upon me in a fourteenth-century Western Christian hall in which a crowd of twentieth-century Western undergraduates was sitting at that moment at the feet of a master.

Eduard Meyer, in his essay 'Der Gang der Alten Geschichte: Hellas und Rom',[1] helped me to break away from the conventional nineteenth-century Western presentation of History as a play in three acts—'Ancient, Medieval, and Modern'—by showing me that the history of 'Greece and Rome' was a unity, and that this unity was a whole that was complete in itself with its own Dark Age, Middle Age, and Modern Age. This unitary view of Greek and Roman history, which Eduard Meyer had given me, led me to look for a unitary name to describe the society whose history this was. I labelled it 'the Hellenic Civilization', and, when once I had identified one civilization, twenty other societies of the same species came into focus, one after another, in my field of historical vision.

Polybius, in his *Oecumenical History*, Book I, chapter 4, gave me my marching orders in his dicta that 'the coincidence by which all the transactions of the World have been oriented in a single direction and guided towards a single goal is the extraordinary characteristic of the present age'; 'the unity of events imposes upon the historian a similar unity of composition'; 'the study of general contacts and relations and of general resemblances and differences is the only avenue to a general perspective, without which neither profit nor pleasure can be extracted from historical research'.

The Western general war of A.D. 1914–18 ('World War One') opened my eyes to the historical and at the same time philosophic truth that my world in my generation was entering upon experiences which Thucydides, in his world in his generation, had already registered and recorded.

When, as a child, I used to come home from Kensington Gardens on winter evenings, after dark, across the bridge leading from Westbourne Terrace to Upper Westbourne Terrace over the Great Western Railway, a palaeotechnic arc light was mounted on a tall standard, overlooking the bridge, to illuminate the marshalling yard below; and, as I passed by, I used to be fascinated by the blue flame flickering between the two black carbon points. Long afterwards, when I was ruminating on the mysterious process through which spiritual illumination arises out of schism in the Soul and in Society, a vivid memory of my early visual impression of the arc light came to the aid of my imagination.

Eduard Meyer, in his masterly picture of the Achaemenian Empire,[2] revealed to me the specific historical function of a universal state. By

[1] In his *Kleine Schriften* (Halle 1910, Niemeyer), pp. 231–2.

[2] Meyer, E.: *Geschichte des Altertums*, vol. iii (Stuttgart 1901, Cotta), Erstes Buch: 'Der Orient unter der Herrschaft der Perser', pp. 1–233.

liquidating a host of idolized parochial states without succeeding in inspiring the same degree of devotion to itself, a universal state liberates, for conversion to the worship of God, psychic energy that has previously been concentrated on mutually conflicting idolatrous worships of Man's Collective Self.

Alfred von Kremer, by revealing to me in his *Culturgeschichte des Orients unter den Chalifen*[1] the morphological resemblance of the Caliphate to the Achaemenian Empire, led me to see in the Caliphate a 'reintegration' or 'resumption' or 'avatar' of the original Syriac universal state after a millennium during which the normal course of the disintegration-process in the life of a broken-down civilization had been interrupted in the Syriac World by the forcible intrusion of Hellenism into the Syriac Society's domain.

J. B. Bury, in *A History of the Later Roman Empire from Arcadius to Irene*,[2] which I found and read in Moberly Library at Winchester, not only revealed to me the existence of the Orthodox Christian Civilization, but showed me the spectacle of one civilization changing into another under the lens of the historian's magnifying glass. In the autumn of A.D. 1912 I had the happiness of coming to know the great historian personally.

Lord Bryce, in *The Holy Roman Empire*, not only revealed to me the Dark Ages and the Middle Ages of Western history, but also gave me my first insight into the process by which time-honoured institutions can acquire a new purpose and new significance without any ostensible breach in the continuity of their history. In A.D. 1915 I had the happiness of coming to know personally this great scholar-traveller-statesman—a patriarch whose perennial zest had made him immune against the doom of Tithonus—thanks to my good fortune in having been given a piece of work to do under his direction.

A. H. Lybyer, in *The Government of the Ottoman Empire in the Time of Suleiman the Magnificent*,[3] revealed to me the blue-print of Plato's ideal commonwealth translated into real life in the Ottoman Pādishāh's Slave-Household, and this revelation taught me what could and could not be achieved by handling human beings as if they were domesticated animals. I first heard of Lybyer's work from D. G. Hogarth, before meeting Lybyer himself, and working with him, in Paris during the Peace Conference of A.D. 1919–20.

General J. C. Smuts, in his *Holism and Evolution*,[4] communicated to me his insight into the cosmic movement in which Reality passes through different orders of being without losing its continuity or its identity.

[1] Vienna 1875–7, Braumüller, 2 vols. [2] London 1889, Macmillan, 2 vols.
[3] Cambridge, Mass. 1913, Harvard University Press.
[4] Second edition: London 1927, Macmillan.

The orders differ, but the genius of Creation and the goal towards which its course is set are the same at each and every level of the rising hierarchy of successive creatures.

The more southerly of the two round barrows on Slingsby Moor, on which I used often to lie on summer afternoons in the nineteen-thirties while I was writing Parts I–V of this Study, served as a physical receiving station for catching still unspent reverberations of waves of psychic events that had been breaking upon this fringe of the *Oikoumenê* since the unrecorded time at which this barrow had been heaped over the ashes of the unknown man whose presence was still brooding here in my day. When my dog Tilda and I were lying side by side on the barrow's pelt of heather, she used to prick up her woolly ears as she heard the rabbits stirring beneath us in their burrows, while my own sixth sense used to tingle with the inaudible music of 'the horns of elfland faintly blowing'.

Heine's *Reisebilder* and Goethe's *Faust*, which I read at Winchester, opened up two new worlds to me. The *Reisebilder* gave me an inside view of Napoleon's Empire; *Faust* gave me an insight into the good of Evil. I have been perpetually grateful to E. J. Turner ('the Hopper') for introducing me to these German works of Western literary art with an enthusiasm for them that was infectious because it was the offspring of understanding.

The Gospels and Herodotus made me aware of the divine irony in human affairs: the most tremendous of all the lessons of History.

Aeschylus anticipated my experience of Life in teaching me, while I was still at school, that learning comes through suffering, and that this is a law that has been ordained for us by God. Though I had not yet tasted the cup for myself, the truth of his words—

τὸν πάθει μάθος
θέντα κυρίως ἔχειν[1]

—was warranted for me by their beauty.

The Authorized Version of the Bible, made in the reign of King James I, gives me, whenever I read it or hear it being read, an intimation of the divine presence informing our fragment of a mysterious Universe. The effect of a diction that is archaic yet at the same time familiar is more like that of music than like that of ordinary speech. It pierces through the Intellect and plays directly upon the Heart.

Paradise Lost, when I discovered it and devoured it in three days before I was eight years old, instilled into my mind, without my understanding it, my first idea of a theodicy.

[1] Aeschylus: *Agamemnon*, ll. 177–8.

Ibn Khaldūn, in his *Muqqadamāt* (the Introduction to his *Universal History*), gave me a vision of a study of History bursting the bounds of This World and breaking through into an Other World.

Saint Augustine, in his *De Civitate Dei*, gave me a vision of the relation in which those two worlds stand to one another.

Henri Bergson, in *Les Deux Sources de la Morale et de la Religion*,[1] taught me that the ideal of the brotherhood of Mankind presupposes a belief in the fatherhood of God.

Fra Angelico's picture[2] of the angels and the souls of the elect, marshalled *πρασιαὶ πρασιαὶ* and adoring Christ in His glory, gave me a visual image of the Communion of Saints.

VIII

To People and Institutions, for showing Kindness to me

'Let us now praise famous men, and our fathers that begat us'.[3] William of Wykeham gave me my education; and he had made this provision for me 507 years before I was elected a scholar of his College of Saint Mary de Winton prope Winton. Here was a man who had served God by making himself a minister of God's providence. *Fui et ego puer Wiccami*, and, like other sons of his, I feel towards our Founder a direct personal gratitude and affection which could not, I believe, have been warmer if I had known him in the flesh, instead of being born, as I was, 485 years after his death. 'The souls of the righteous are in the hand of God',[4] and Time has no power to put distance between them and their adopted children.

M. J. Rendall revealed to me the beauty of the English poetry that he used to set to us for translation into Greek and Latin verse, and the beauty of the Italian pictures that he used to show to us in magic lantern lectures out of school. 'By strenuous intellectual communion and intimate personal intercourse' he communicated his love of beauty to us 'like a light caught from a leaping flame'.[5] But his greatest revelation of beauty was one that was unintentional and unconscious. As we sat at his feet, we learnt what it meant to find ourselves in the presence of an *ἀνὴρ μεγαλόψυχος*.

'And some there be that have no memorial'[6] in any of those pedestrian achievements that are the slow work of Time and are therefore at the mercy of all the chances and changes of this mortal life. The play of Chance that, by the 23rd September, 1952, had prolonged the life of the writer of this Study into its sixty-fourth year[7] had cut short the

[1] Paris 1932, Alcan.
[2] Now in the National Gallery in London.
[3] Ecclus. xliv. 1.
[4] The Wisdom of Solomon iii. 1.
[5] Plato's Letters, No. 7, 341 B–E.
[6] Ecclus. xliv. 9.
[7] By leading him on the 26th April, 1912—on faith in a sheet (lying at his elbow at this moment) of the Austro-Hungarian staff map of Greece which showed a carriage-

lives of contemporaries and friends of his who had been killed in battle some thirty-eight years earlier; and, at the moment of completing a work of his own that had taken more than thirty years to carry out, he could not be unmindful of the unwritten works lost to the World through the heroic untimely deaths in action of Guy Leonard Cheesman, Leslie Whitaker Hunter, Alexander Douglas Gillespie, Robert Hamilton Hutchison, Arthur Innes Adam, Wilfrid Max Langdon, Philip Anthony Brown, Arthur George Heath, Robert Gibson, and John Brown—ten representatives of the innumerable brave and self-sacrificing young men—of whom the World was not worthy[1]—whose lives had been cut short in the wars that had been waged since the beginning of the Age of the Civilizations. These scholars who gave their lives as soldiers in their early manhood in the First World War lived on in the hearts and minds of their surviving friends, and the life and work of one of these survivors owed more than he could say to his perpetual memory of these prematurely dead companions.

The Council on Foreign Relations in New York held in safe keeping for me, from before Munich week until after VJ-Day, my notes for Parts VI–XIII of this book and the notebooks in which I had put down the gist of my reading during the previous twenty years. This act of kindness gave me many times over during the Second World War the consolation of feeling *non omnis moriar*.[2]

Dr. Sylvia Payne helped me, in a time of great personal trouble, to find a way through the dark wood which I could not have found by myself—

> E quanto a dir qual era è cosa dura
> Questa selva selvaggia ed aspra e forte,
> che nel pensier rinnuova la paura.

The Rockefeller Foundation of New York made it possible for me, after an eight-years-long interruption, to write the first draft of Parts VI–XIII of this book within the four years beginning on the 1st July, 1947, and to send these four volumes to press in the second half of the year 1952, by providing the Royal Institute of International Affairs in London with the financial means for releasing a substantial part of my time by reinforcing the staff of the department producing their *Survey of International Affairs*, which had had to be taken up again, after the war, with eight years (and these no ordinary years) of arrears to make good. More than this, the Foundation made it financially possible for my wife and me to accept invitations from the Institute for Advanced Study at Princeton to pay periodical visits there which have been invaluable to us for making progress in our work.

road along a stretch where there proved not even to be a goat-track—to miscalculate the number of hours' walking distance between Káto Vezáni and Ýýthion, and consequently to exhaust the contents of his water-bottle and replenish it from a stream which proved to be infected with germs of dysentery. ('That is very bad water', as a cottager correctly said, after he had silently watched the unwarned traveller drink his fill of it.) This accident incapacitated the writer for military service in the War of A.D. 1914–18.

[1] Hebrews xi. 38.

[2] Horace: *Carmina*, Book III, Ode xxx, l. 6.

If the Rockefeller Foundation, the Royal Institute of International Affairs, and the Institute for Advanced Study at Princeton had not all co-operated with one another to help me in these most imaginative, considerate, and effective ways, I should not have been able to finish the book by this time, and I might never have managed even to make a fresh start with the writing of it.

Sidney Marsh showed himself a friend in need by helping me on my way when I was passing through a time of troubles. His kindness was touching, because it came from the heart; but it was hardly surprising, because it was characteristic. The loggia at Ardens, opening southwards over Ashdown Forest towards the Downs, was a place where I found myself able, after an eight-years-long interruption in the writing of this book, to recover my resolution and to recollect my thoughts when I was setting myself to take my half-finished enterprise up again and to carry it through to its conclusion.

Professor Roland G. Kent and Professor George G. Cameron generously spent much time and trouble on helping me to correct some of the more glaring faults—ranging from errors of judgement, through mis-statements of fact, to mistakes in spelling—in an amateur essay on the administrative geography of the Achaemenian Empire.[1] These two eminent scholars are not, of course, implicated, by my declaration of my gratitude for their help, in any of those faults that have not been eliminated. Professor Kent's invaluable comments on the first draft of my essay must have been one of the last of the many such characteristic acts of kindness that he was able to do before his death on the 27th June, 1952.

Mr. Martin Wight gave up the best part of a much-needed summer holiday to working through the first draft of Part VII of this Study and writing out for me his considered comments and criticisms. I have shown my high appreciation of these by incorporating them *in extenso* in footnotes and appendixes. The effect has been to turn my original monologue into a dialogue which should be decidedly more interesting and valuable to the reader. Mr. Wight has made it clear, apropos of my references to Christianity, what the unabrogated traditional Christian positions are, and the points in which my personal standpoint differs from them. He has drawn attention to the abiding Judaic vein of exclusiveness and intolerance in Christianity, and he has correctly convicted me, on this crucial issue, of holding with Symmachus as against Saint Ambrose, with Mangū as against William of Rubruck,[2] and with Radhakrishnan as against Karl Adam, Jean Daniélou, and Hendrik Kraemer.

[1] VI. vii. 580–689.

[2] 'Even as God has given several fingers to the hand, so has He given Man several ways.'—The Mongol Khāqān Mangū in his conversation, on Whitsunday A.D. 1254, with the Franciscan Friar William of Rubruck, as reported by Friar William in *Itinerarium Fratris Willielmi de Rubruquis, de Ordine Fratrum Minorum, Galli, Anno Gratie 1253 ad Partes Orientales*, chap. 51 (see V. v. 114–15 and VI. vii. 106).

Mr. Thomas Wallas, of the London and Lancashire Insurance Company, has most kindly communicated to me authoritative information about the statistical material that was accessible to the earliest insurance companies in Great Britain at the time when they first went into business.

Mr. James Laver, Keeper of the Departments of Engraving, Illustration and Design and of Paintings, at the Victoria and Albert Museum in London; the Rev. Father P. Benedetto Renzi, Rector of the Church of San Francesco at Arezzo; and Signor Pietro Zampetti, Soprintendente alle Gallerie delle Marche, have all given me most kind help in my inquiries into the affinities of certain forms of headgear.

Dr. Sidney Smith, Professor Albrecht Goetze, Professor F. W. Albright, Mr. M. B. Rowton, and Mr. D. J. Wiseman have most kindly come to my aid over my amateur essay on the chronology of South-West Asian history during the first half of the second millennium B.C.[1] It might be no disgrace for an amateur to come to grief in a field in which the professionals agree only in frankly declaring that their own divers reconstructions can be no more than tentative in the present inconclusive state of the evidence. Our knowledge of early South-West Asian history through the progress of archaeological excavation is increasing so fast that this present chronological puzzle may be solved any day—perhaps before this volume is published—by some decisive new discovery. Meanwhile, the essay which the five scholars to whom I am now declaring my gratitude have helped me to revise may serve the reader as an interim report on the main alternative possible reconstructions of this passage of history in the light of the evidence as it stands today (the 24th September, 1952).

I am particularly grateful to Mr. Rowton for the great trouble that he has taken to pilot me through the maze with his steady hand.

My sisters, Professor J. M. C. Toynbee and Miss M. R. Toynbee, have shown their kindness by tolerating my queries, and their learning by never failing to tell me the answers to them.

The librarian of the Royal Institute of International Affairs in London, Miss Barbara Kyle, and the librarian of the Institute for Advanced Study at Princeton, Miss Judith Sachs, with all their colleagues, have helped me on my way at every stage of a long literary journey by their inexhaustible obligingness and resourcefulness in meeting a formidable flow of queries, besides requests to procure for me the loan of books dealing with a great variety of subjects.

Miss Elizabeth Horton of the Institute for Advanced Study at Princeton has made it possible for me, by her kindness to me on repeated visits, to enjoy the full benefit of the rare facilities that the Institute offers to scholars. In January 1951, when the international situation looked so

[1] Printed in this volume on pp. 167–212, above.

grave that it seemed folly to carry the unique text of a still untyped manuscript back with me to Europe, Miss Horton and her colleague Miss Farr generously gave me ease of mind by undertaking to type for me the manuscript that I had written at Princeton during the preceding three months.

Miss J. K. Galbraith has checked, with Miss Reddin, the whole of the typescript against the manuscript. Her generous help has made it possible to do something that could not have been done without the co-operation of two minds and two pairs of eyes. The process has been as exacting and laborious as it has been indispensable for securing the accurate reproduction of the text. To cope with such outlandish pieces as, for example, the Annex on the Administrative organization of the Achaemenian Empire has been not merely a kind act but an angelic one.

Miss Bridget Reddin has done the typing, from beginning to end, of a complicated manuscript in crabbed handwriting, infested with footnotes and festooned with annexes. Her patience, care, accuracy, perseverance, and friendship have carried all ten volumes of this book on their passage from the writer's hands to the printer's across a gulf as broad as the Atlantic.

One of the red-letter days in my life is a day in 1933 on which, after I had ventured, with my heart in my mouth, to submit the typescript of volumes i–iii of this Study to Sir Humphrey Milford, I received from him a characteristically laconic note saying: 'I will take your big book'. Since that date, I have been continuing to receive the kind and skilled help of all concerned at Amen House, at 114 Fifth Avenue, and at Oxford in the heavy and exacting task of printing and publishing a work on this scale. Five times within twenty years, I have unloaded on them a suitcase full of copy; and the aggregate weight of these five loads must have been large. At every stage in the long process of production, these friends and collaborators on the technical side of the undertaking have given me innumerable occasions for looking back with gratitude to a decision of Sir Humphrey Milford's which has meant so much to me, first under his auspices and then under Mr. Geoffrey Cumberlege's at Warwick Square and under Mr. H. Z. Walck's on the other side of the Atlantic.

Mr. John Lodge—Headmaster *emeritus* of Nantwich and Acton Grammar School—has read the proofs of volumes vii–x in galley and, besides making a number of suggestions which have been gratefully adopted by the author, and detecting a number of errors that had escaped both the author's and the printer's eye, he has generously taken off the author's shoulders the laborious but indispensable task of verifying cross-references between passages in this Study and references to the Bible, to the Greek and Latin Classics, to works of Western literature in English and other vernaculars, and to other books that are on the shelves of Mr. Lodge's library. Help so kind, disinterested, timely, and effective as this is a gift that touches the heart. I lament my friend's sudden death on the 1st April, 1954.

Professor E. D. Myers, the head of the Department of Philosophy in Washington and Lee University, Lexington, Virginia, has compiled the gazetteer of geographical names, covering all ten volumes of this book, which will be issued as a supplementary volume, and has planned and drawn—in a form in which Mrs. Gomme could put them into shape for the Oxford University Press—many of the maps, illustrating all ten volumes, which will also appear in volume xi. The gazetteer illuminates passages in the book in which the geographical setting of the narrative may be unfamiliar to some Western readers, while the maps make it possible for a reader to acquaint himself at a glance with geographical facts which would have required many pages of uninviting letterpress if the author had tried to describe the same facts in words. In thus coming to the reader's rescue, Professor Myers has given a pleasure to the author as well; for it has been pleasant indeed for him to have the chance of working in partnership with an old friend who knows the contents and structure of his book, understands its purpose, and has had the skill and kindness to interpret the book to the public—as, for instance, in the chart reproduced in vol. xi.

The Royal Institute of International Affairs—on whose staff I have had the happiness of serving for almost thirty years (and my wife for still longer)—has given me a profession that has been an education and a fellowship that has been a stimulus. In the course of producing, for the Institute, a *Survey of International Affairs* from the morrow of the peace-settlement of 1919–21 to the morrow of the Second World War, I have been continually educated in the study and the writing of History; and, in doing this work at Chatham House, I have had the immense advantage of finding myself in the society of men and women—on the Council, among the members, and among my colleagues on the staff—who have had a varied experience of practical affairs in responsible positions in many walks of life. I am grateful, above all, for the particularly favourable conditions under which the authorities of Chatham House have always allowed me to do my work. While the production of the *Survey* has been a valuable discipline, because it has been an exacting task (even with the wonderful assistance that I have had), I have been left free to be my own master in the use of my time, and have been given a generous margin of leisure for the writing of the present *Study* under Chatham House's auspices. Both works have, I believe, benefited greatly by being carried on simultaneously for a quarter of a century.

Chatham House means, for me, a host of friends. I cannot name them all, but I cannot leave unnamed my colleagues Ivison Macadam and Margaret Cleeve or my master and mentor Sir James Headlam-Morley, who taught me how to launch our *Survey*. I never forget the generosity with which he gave his time and thought and encouragement in helping a younger historian; and I also never forget the great history of the antecedents of the First World War which Headlam-Morley would have given to the World if his life had not been cut short.

My wife, for the third time, has made the magnificent index without which no batch of volumes of this Study would be complete. These three indexes, which are the keys to vols. i–iii, iv–vi, and vii–x, are labours that have been none the less strenuous for having been labours of love. These indexes have been hard to make because they are no mere catalogues of names and facts, but are masterly analyses of the ideas propounded in the book; and this analytical exposition, which has been such an exacting intellectual task for the indexer, will have been found proportionately valuable by the reader. As for the author, each time that he has read, in draft, one of these indexes to a batch of his volumes, he has been given a fortifying sense of assurance that, after all, his book cannot be altogether nonsense, since some sense seems to have been made of it bona fide by a mind whose critical power is as well known to him as its charity. Yet this is only one of the innumerable things that his wife has done for him.

There are people—some of them mentioned already—to whom I owe so much and with whom I have been so intimate that I cannot put into words the full measure of what they have given to me and can only express my feelings for them by here inscribing their initials—*tot pignora amoris*—in the alphabetical order of their first names, *videlicet:* B.H., B.H.S., C.C.-E., D.D., E.P.F., E.R.M., G.M., H.T.W.-G., J.A.S., J.D.D., J.L.H., M.F., R.M.Y.G., R.S.D., R.T., S.E.T., V.M.T.

INDEX[1]

In the cross references in this index, references in small capitals (e.g. ARAB CALIPHATE at end of the heading 'Abbasid Caliphate) are to other main headings, while references in ordinary type are to subdivisions of the same main heading.

[1] This index includes only those place-names that are of importance as subject-headings. A full list of all place-names mentioned in volumes i–x is being published in vol. xi (Maps and Gazetteer). Many of the battles entered in this index have been given their dates, but the dates of the lives or reigns of individuals and of the durations of states have not been entered. Notices, in the text, of the dates of reigns have, however, been indexed, and the durations of universal states, with their antecedent Times of Troubles, though not the durations of other states, will be found in vii. 769, Table I. If ever a consolidated index of vols. i–x is made, a systematic insertion of dates might be an addition that would be useful to the reader.

The compilation of an index draws attention to variations in the spelling of names. Some of these variations have been deliberate. For instance, while Greek names of people living in 'the Hellenic Age' (*circa* 1125 B.C. – A.D. 675) have been spelled in these volumes in the Latin travesty of them which is familiar, because conventional, in English and other Western languages, Greek names of people living in 'the Orthodox Christian Age' (i.e. since *circa* A.D. 675) have been spelled in a romanization of the original Greek spelling as this has been pronounced and accented by speakers of the Greek language in this age. This has been done in order to make the reader's eye constantly remind him that the Byzantines are neither belated Hellenes nor eccentric Franks, but are members of a distinct society of the same species as both the Western and the Hellenic. Again, the vowels in Turkish names have been differentiated from those in Arabic names in order to take account of the vowel harmonies that are a characteristic feature of the Turkish family of languages; and, in Ottoman Turkish names that include the equivalent of the Arabic name Muhammad, account has been taken of the Ottoman Turkish pronunciation by spelling the name as Mehmed. On the other hand, variations in the spelling of Teutonic barbarian names are due to the vagaries of Modern Western scholars, and variations in the spelling of Chinese names to the writer's own ignorance. If he and his wife live to produce a consolidated index for a standardized new edition of vols. i–x, he will ask authorities on the Chinese language to come to his help by standardizing the spelling of all Chinese names consistently in one or other of the current competing systems of romanization.

Even so, in a book in which the names mentioned are taken from a considerable number of different languages, originally conveyed in different scripts, complete consistency could hardly be attained without abandoning the Latin Alphabet and substituting for it some system of phonetic symbols, and few readers would welcome consistency at this price.